Victorian Maps
of the
British Isles
David Smith

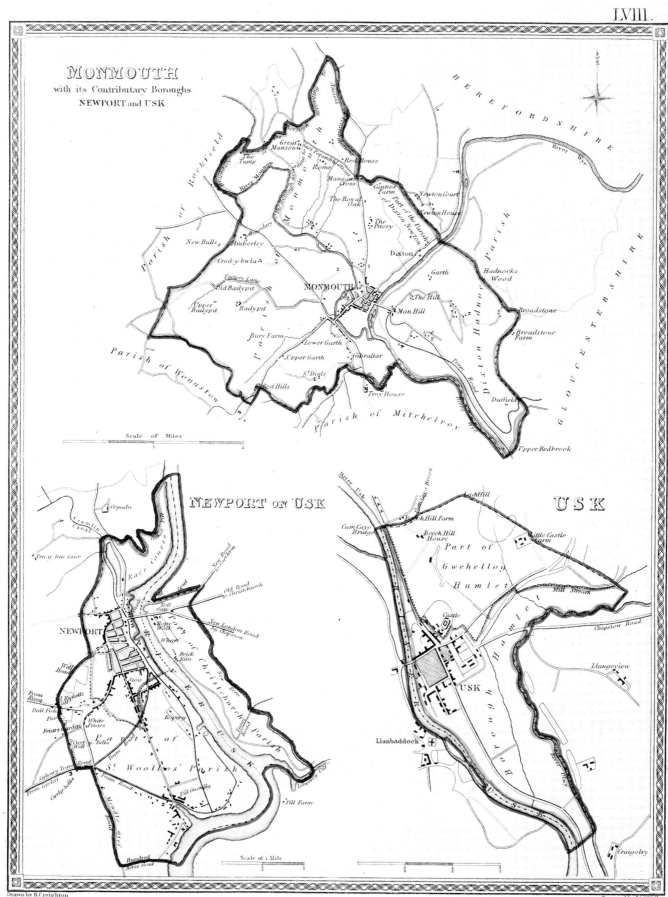

LVIII.

MONMOUTH
with its Contributary Boroughs
NEWPORT and USK

HEREFORDSHIRE

River Wye

GLOUCESTERSHIRE

Parish of Rockfield

The Tump
Great Manson
Red House
Rome
Manson's Cross
Gannes Farm
The Royal Oak
Newton Court
The Priory
Newton House
Part of the Parish or Dixton Newton
River Monnow
Boundary
New Bulls
Amberley
Croft-y-bwla
Dixton
Garth
Hadnocks Wood
Factory Lane
Old Bailypit
Broadstone
Upper Bailypit
Bailypit
MONMOUTH
The Hill
Man Hill
Broadstone Farm
Bury Farm
Lower Garth
Tram Road
Upper Garth
Gibraltar
Dixton Hadnor Parish
Parish of Wonastow
St Dials
Duffield
Red Hills
Troy House
River Wye
Upper Redbrook
Parish of Mitchelroy

Scale of Miles

NEWPORT on USK

Crindu
Cramlin Canal
Pen y lan tawr
Race Course Hill
New Road to Christchurch
Old Road to Christchurch
Toll Gate
Stone Walk
New London Road by Chepstow
NEWPORT
Wharf
Brick Kiln
Well Heads
Parish of Christchurch Parish
Stone
From Risca
J. Ricketts
Bull Field
Pool
White Friars
Ropery
Friars Garden
River y Bella
River USK
River y Well
Part of
Sirhowy Tram Road
St Woollos' Parish
From Cardiff
Curly bella
Tram Road
Tram Road
Till Gwenlly
Laswern Pill
Meads Gwt
Till Farm
Hundred Acres Goul

Scale of ¼ Mile

USK

River Usk
Lach Hill
Cam Cayo Bridge
Beech Hill Farm
Little Castle Farm
Beech Hill House
Cam Dowlais Brook
Part of Gwehellog Hamlet
Mill Stream
Castle
Chepstow Road
Llangeview
USK
Borough Hamlet
Llanbaddock
River Olwy
Craigolry

Scale of ¼ Mile

Drawn by R. Creighton.

Engraved by J & C Walker.

Explanation
Boundary of the old Borough
New
Parishes or Townships

Victorian Maps
of the
British Isles

David Smith

BT Batsford Ltd · London

To Mo

FRONTISPIECE
'*MONMOUTH with its Contributary Boroughs NEWPORT and USK*', *published by Samuel Lewis in his* View of the Representative History of England, *1835.*

© David Smith 1985

First published 1985

ISBN 0 7134 4178 X

Typeset and printed in Great Britain by
Butler & Tanner Ltd, Frome and London
for the Publisher
B.T. Batsford Ltd
4 Fitzhardinge Street
London W1H 0AH

Contents

List of Illustrations

77 (i) Leeds, Benjamin Rees Davies, 1863
(ii) Derbyshire, John Dower, 1884
78 (i) Isle of Man, John Bartholomew, 1883
(ii) Snowdon and vicinity, John Bartholomew, 1881
(iii) Galway, John Bartholomew, 1883
79 Exeter, Robert Kearsley Dawson, 1837
80 Wigtonshire, Archibald Fullarton, *c.*1856
81 Post Office Map of North Wales, Benjamin Rees Davies, *c.*1861
82 Meath, John Kirkwood, 1848
83 Longford, Samuel Lewis, 1837
84 Linlithgowshire, W.H. Lizars, 1862
85 Boston, W. Schmollinger, 1837
86 Cambridgeshire, Pigot & Co., *c.*1841
87 Shropshire, Edward Stanford, *c.*1904
88 York, John Tallis, *c.*1850
89 (i) Oxfordshire, J. & C. Walker, *c.*1839
(ii) Wiltshire, J. & C. Walker, 1836

Author's note

Throughout the text reference is made to the Heads of the Ordnance Survey and the Geological Survey by name only, without explanation of status. No military rank is noted since the incumbent was sometimes promoted during his period of tenure. Similarly no title is noted.

Directorship/Superintendency/Director-Generalship of the Ordnance Survey

		Controlling Department	
1791–8	Edward Williams		
1798–1820	William Mudge		
1820–46	Thomas Colby	1791–1855	Board of Ordnance
1847–54	Lewis Alexander Hall		
1854–75	Henry James	1855–70	War Office
1875–8	John Cameron		
1878–83	A.C. Cooke	1870–90	H.M. Office of Works
1883–6	Richard Hugh Stotherd		
1886–94	Charles Wilson	1890–	Board of Agriculture
1894–9	John Farquharson		
1899–1905	D.A. Johnston		

Directorship of the Geological Survey of Great Britain and Ireland

1835–55	Henry Thomas De la Beche
1855–72	Roderick Impey Murchison
1872–81	Andrew Crombie Ramsay
1882–1901	Archibald Geikie

MAP SCALES

Representative Fraction	*Inches to the mile* / *Miles to the inch*	*Centimetres to metres* / *Centimetres to Kilometres*
1:2500	25 in. to 1 m.	1 cm: 25 m
1:10 000	$6\frac{1}{4}$ in. to 1 m.	1 cm: 100 m
1:10 560	6 in. to 1 m.	1 cm: 105.6 m
1:25 000	$2\frac{1}{2}$ in. to 1 m.	1 cm: 250 m
1:50 000	$1\frac{1}{4}$ in. to 1 m.	1 cm: 500 m
1:63 360	1 in. to 1 m.	1 cm: 633.6 m
1:100 000	$1\frac{1}{2}$ m. to 1 in.	1 cm: 1 km
1:126 720	2 m. to 1 in.	1 cm: 1.26 km
1:150 000	$2\frac{1}{4}$ m. to 1 in.	1 cm: 1.5 km
1:175 000	$2\frac{3}{4}$ m. to 1 in.	1 cm: 1.75 km
1:200 000	$3\frac{1}{4}$ m. to 1 in.	1 cm: 2 km
1:250 000	4 m. to 1 in.	1 cm: 2.5 km
1:253 440	4 m. to 1 in.	1 cm: 2.53 km
1:500 000	8 m. to 1 in.	1 cm: 5 km
1:633 600	10 m. to 1 in.	1 cm: 6.33 km
1:750 000	$11\frac{3}{4}$ m. to 1 in.	1 cm: 7.5 km
1:1 000 000	$15\frac{3}{4}$ m. to 1 in.	1 cm: 10 km

'... I look with pleasure on my book, however defective, and deliver it to the world with the spirit of a man that has endeavoured well. That it will immediately become popular I have not promised to myself: a few wild blunders, and risible absurdities, from which no work of such multiplicity was ever free, may for a time furnish folly with laughter, and harden ignorance in contempt; but useful diligence will at best prevail, and there never can be wanting some who distinguish defect.

'... In this work, when it shall be found that much is omitted, let it not be forgotten that much likewise is performed; and though no book was ever spared out of tenderness to the authour, and the world is little solicitous to know whence proceeded the faults of that which it condemns; yet it may gratify curiosity to inform it, that .... was written with little assistance of the learned, and without patronage of the great; not in the soft obscurities of retirement, or under the shelter of academick bowers, but amidst inconvenience and distraction, in sickness and in sorrow ....'

Samuel Johnson, Preface to *A Dictionary of the English Language* (1755)

Preface

Although it is almost inevitable that the map collector will find the earliest maps of the British Isles the most seductive, it is clear that rapidly rising prices have put them beyond the financial reach of the average enthusiast whose budget generally precludes such extravagances. Maps sold in the reign of Victoria have much to commend them as an alternative, for they are not only as fascinating in their own right, but are also both readily available and relatively cheap. In recent years sundry fine, detailed studies on the cartographic development of this period have been researched and often published, but the collector has been little served because, quite rightly, academic work has concentrated on the history of method, organization and technique. Whilst of obvious interest to the collector, such studies do not give him specific information about the maps which he can add to his collection, nor do they provide a background related directly to those maps—rather these studies provide highly detailed insights into narrow topics which may divert him but which are not central to the building of his collection. The collector's primary concern is the maps themselves—what they show, how they show it, and how they changed during publication—and other facets of their history are peripheral to this core interest which must, therefore, be the essential thrust of this work.

Victorian maps of the British Isles should not be dismissed by the collector for their relative youth, for they were born in an age when those Isles led the map-making world with the most prolific output and the most innovatory technology ever known in cartographic history. Victorian maps will become increasingly collectable as knowledge of them increases; and as demand grows they will become scarcer and more expensive. This work is a step towards increasing the collector's knowledge of those maps available to him; the detailed history of methods, concepts, organizations, and techniques is left to others, as is the detailed study of little-collected specialized map forms, such as sea charts, enclosure and tithe maps, transport proposals, and maps produced on material other than paper. Although only maps which first appeared from the year of Victoria's accession are subjected to detailed carto-bibliographical analysis, they were not the only maps on sale during her reign. It is clear that most of the material published from about the turn of the century was also available and, indeed, sold extensively whilst she was on the throne and that, too, must,

therefore, be considered as 'Victorian' in its broad sense. Thus, for the purpose of the general narrative, 'Victorian' is interpreted as 'being characteristic of Victoria's reign' in order to avoid that blinkered view afforded by restricting the work solely to her years on the throne.

Carto-bibliography builds on foundations laid by others. It is an edifice that can never be completed, for previously-unknown maps and atlases are continually coming to light through new research and exchanged information. Each new publication generates its own response of revelations, rendering it obsolete at the outset. Thus, the subject can never be truly definitive, although, of course, it approaches that ultimate state with every step forward. Any work on the subject is inevitably, therefore, only a statement of current knowledge and will be liable to future change through re-interpretation and research. That carto-bibliographic works are subject to later correction is in no way a criticism of their quality or achievement and the highest praise must be given to those unhappy few who have had the courage to take on this tortuous work. The pioneering studies of Sir H.G. Fordham, Harold Whitaker, Thomas Chubb, and the other writers of the early twentieth century, were carried forward by such as R.A. Skelton and Geoffrey Cowling, and in recent years have culminated in the sophisticated and detailed works of Paul Harvey, Donald Hodson, and David Kingsley. This tradition of scholarship must be continued by new enthusiasts in the future and it is hoped that this book will provide a reference framework to guide more detailed studies of Victorian topographical maps. Copious footnotes and attributions are inappropriate in a book designed for collectors, but, in time, it is hoped to prepare an annotated reference copy, detailing evidence and sources, which will be made available to researchers. Like A.L. Rowse 'My aim has been to reduce references to a minimum. Those acquainted with the subject will know how to interpret them; those who are not will not need them. I dislike books that make a parade of apparatus. . . . I regret that I have not simplified my references even a little more.'[1] The book's more immediate purpose is to provide the collector of Victorian maps of the British Isles with a means of identifying and dating any map generally available to him, and to offer a picture of map development during the period which will place that map in a contextual relationship with others.

Acknowledgements

Innumerable individuals and institutions have been generous in their support and help, and in supplying information and research facilities. The happy memory of so much kind and unselfish assistance almost expunges the sour taste left by those few who refuse to accept that they have a responsibility, as guardians of the whole community's heritage, to make material accessible and provide information, rather than guarding it jealously for the benefit of a privileged minority. I must say a special thank-you to the following who have gone beyond the call of duty.

For providing information and research facilities: Birmingham Reference Library; Bodleian Library, University of Oxford; British Library Map Library, with thanks for its infinite, good-humoured patience; British Library Newspaper Library; Brotherton Library, University of Leeds; Cambridge University Library, with special thanks to Roger Fairclough; Holborn Public Library; Guildhall Library; Kensington Public Library; Lancashire Record Office; Linen Hall Library, Belfast; Manchester Central Library; National Library of Ireland; National Library of Scotland, with particular thanks to Margaret Wilkes; National Library of Wales; Queen's University Library, Belfast; Royal Geographical Society, with thanks to the late George Dugdale and Francis Herbert; Royal Irish Academy; Trinity College Library, Dublin; and Warwickshire County Record Office.

For information on and access to privately owned material: Adam & Charles Black (Publishers) Ltd for the free-run of their 'historic library'; Clive Burden; Donald Hodson; S.H. Jollye; Richard Miller; Jason Musgrave; Dr Iain C. Taylor; and all the numerous map dealers who have brought maps and atlases to my attention.

For permission to quote without credit and draw material and inspiration from their written works: Dr John Andrews of the University of Dublin; John Bartholomew & Son for *Bartholomew 150 years*; Clive Birch of Barracuda Books for *Maps of Bucks*; John Booth; David & Charles for *The Early Years of the Ordnance Survey*; Eason & Son for *Irish Maps*; Ebury Press for *London in Maps*; Essex Record Office, particularly Victor Gray, the County Archivist; Dr Brian Harley of Exeter University; Elizabeth Harris of the National Museum of American History; Professor Paul D.A. Harvey of Durham University; Dawson Publishing for *A History of the Ordnance Survey*; Donald Hodson; Ralph Hyde of the Guildhall Library; David Kingsley; Cornelius Koeman, late professor of Utrecht University; Harry Margary for the *Old Series Ordnance Survey*; Donald Moir of the Royal Scottish Geographical Society; Ian Mumford of the Mapping and Charting Establishment; Richard R. Oliver; Walter W. Ristow, late of the Library of Congress; Professor Arthur H. Robinson of the University of Wisconsin; Oxford University Press for *Lark Rise to Candleford* by F. Thompson; Surveyors Publications for F.M.L. Thompson's *Chartered Surveyors*; and the late Professor Coolie Verner through his associates Roger Bosher and Basil Stuart-Stubbs, both of the University of British Columbia.

I have mercilessly quoted from innumerable works and writers, both ancient and modern, with minimal credit or attribution, in the belief and knowledge, respectively, that extensive footnotes of acknowledgement are more appropriate to academic works, and would merely irk the average collector and force the exclusion of other material in the cause of economy. To the small number of living authors whose phrases I have briefly quoted, my thanks and apologies for the scant attribution—I trust that the spreading of your words to a wider audience is sufficient reward and that the noting of your works in the bibliography is adequate acknowledgement. To the far-greater number of long-dead writers whose works I have plundered, my thanks and hope that it is sufficient recompense that your words live on. To all who have inspired ideas, my thanks.

For the generous loan of illustrations: Ivan Deverall; Richard Miller; and Jason Musgrave. Thanks are due to Sidney Ferris for his photographic printing. B.T. Batsford in general, and Samuel Carr in particular, have supported the project throughout with much encouragement. Mo not only doubled the expense of many research trips but made them fun as well!

The Author 'is not less obliged to the kindness of a host of friends, whose zeal to serve him is evinced in their several valuable contributions distributed throughout the work, and to whom he regrets that limitation of space precludes the possibility of individually returning his thanks'.[2]

Needless to say all errors and omissions are entirely my own responsibility, and I shall be pleased to receive details of amendments and additions. 'A painful work, I'll assure you; wherein what toyle hath been taken, as no man thinketh, so no man believeth, but he that hath made the trial.'[3]

DAVID SMITH
December 1984

Introduction

The second half of the eighteenth century had been a period of extraordinary cartographic activity in England, and to a lesser extent in Wales, Scotland, and Ireland, presaged by fundamental advances in mathematics, trigonometry and astronomy, initiated by Newton's work, and vital innovations in instrument design by Hadley, Harrison, and Ramsden. Initially these technical advances were translated into the improvement of hydrographic charts; but the impetus was later transmitted to map production, and, combined with the mass of new information generated by exploration and fast-growing trade, it placed London at the head of the cartographic world and stimulated the consolidation and reinforcement of this position during the following century. This developing ascendancy was reinforced by a great increase in demand at home from a growing number of land-owners and both civil and military authorities, for this was a period of hyperactive economic development with accelerating enclosure, industrial growth, and the first signs of a national communication infrastructure in the form of the turnpike trusts.

The most obvious internal cartographic sign was the first virtual re-mapping of the country since the sixteenth century. Between 1765 and 1780 alone, 65 per cent of England was re-mapped at scales of 1″: 1 mile or larger on 25 published maps covering 32,900 square miles; and overall from 1759 to 1809 virtually all English (and many Scottish, but relatively few Irish and Welsh) counties were mapped at these large scales by a mixed band of itinerant independent map-makers competing with each other in the private sector. Obviously there were often specific local factors encouraging new survey work, but the greatest overall national stimulant was the Society of Arts' decision to offer premiums, from 1759 to 1809, 'not exceeding one hundred Pounds, as a Gratuity to any Person or Persons, who shall make an accurate Survey of any County upon the Scale of one Inch to a Mile'.[1] Despite their inevitable technical limitations, surveyed as they were often only by the traditional road-traverse with topographical in-filling, and caused not least by the age-old habits of copying earlier maps and incorporating estate plans of dubious reliability, these large-scale maps provided a more detailed and accurate delineation of the landscape than ever before, clearly showing land- and resource-use, settlement, communication, and industrial and social development. This comprehensive coverage was to provide a unique source of topographical data for makers of small-scale maps in the early nineteenth century, just as the Ordnance Survey was to do in the century's later years. The Society of Arts' offer reinforced two specific trends in British cartography, thus ensuring that they continued strongly on into the nineteenth century. By offering awards to county maps it confirmed the county as the most suitable unit of regional mapping, and by adopting the 1″ scale it ensured its popularity and later adoption by the Ordnance Survey.

Scotland experienced a similar upsurge of large-scale mapping but confined to the wealthier and more densely populated areas. This expansion was made possible perhaps by the spur of the Military Survey, but certainly by the growth of the land-surveying profession in response to the need for accurate land surveys for agricultural improvement. In contrast, Ireland was to a large extent by-passed by this development, with production dominated, on the one hand, by the 'French'[2] school of estate surveyors with its elegant marginal decoration, and, on the other, by the heirs of the seventeenth-century 'plantation' surveys with their stiff, geometrical decoration and out-dated conventional signs. Irish map-making was very much estate-based apart from the county maps prepared for the grand juries (the local-government authorities, many of whom refused to publish their large-scale map), who partially funded them, and the influential Government-authorized survey of the principal peat bogs of 1809 to 1814 by such engineers and surveyors as Thomas Townshend, Richard Griffith, Thomas Colbourne, and Alexander Nimmo, engraved in 66 sheets by James Basire. However, it was also clear in Ireland that a comprehensive large-scale mapping was urgently needed as the gross inequalities in the burden of the cess (tax) became more apparent.

Despite the remarkable advance which this large-scale movement represented, widespread doubts were being expressed, by the turn of the century, on the quality of British maps, for they were proving inadequate for military, civil, and commercial use. Much blame was put on copying from outdated sources. In particular, the portrayal of relief was criticized. As William Roy wrote to George III in 1766: 'THESE County Maps are sufficiently exact, in what regards their geometrical measurement, for common purposes, but are extremely defective with respect to the topographical representation of the ground, giving scarcely any Idea, or at least but a very imperfect one, of what is remarkably strong or weak in the nature of the Country.'[3] Since, more often than not, smaller-scale maps of counties and plans of towns, estates, enclosures, and communications were derived from the large-scale maps, they too were defective and open to criticism. In 1791, the President of the Royal Society bemoaned the fact that Bengal was better mapped than Britain—'I should rejoice could I say that Britons, fond as they are of being considered by surrounding nations as taking the lead in scientific improvements, could boast a general map of their island as well executed as Major Rennell's delineation of Bengal and Bakar'.[4] The lack of any more advanced alternative ensured continued life for eighteenth-century large-scale maps and their simple inset town plans after the turn of the century. New editions were published—for example, Prior's 1779 map of Leicestershire, reappeared in 1804 and 1819, and Burdett's map of Cheshire of 1777 was finally re-issued by William Faden as late as 1818, probably in an effort to intercept the potential demand for Greenwood's map due to be published in the following year. The continued life of eighteenth-century handiwork was inevitable since official mapping in Britain lagged behind other European countries, notably Austria, Denmark, and France, and, more alarmingly, behind parts of India and eastern North America. Fear of the French Revolution and of invasion emphasized the need for reliable maps, particularly of southern England, for military purposes and, consequently, the position of the Ordnance Survey had been regularized in 1791 as the official solution to the problem. For the first time, an official body, financed by Government, was to be responsible for the production of the nation's maps, and no longer would cartography depend entirely on the patronage of the nobility and gentry.

Fortunately the birth of the nineteenth century marked the beginning of a period ripe for the development of a new age of cartography in which both official and private sectors would flourish in a close symbiotic rather than parasitic relationship. In 1800 Britain was in the midst of an Industrial Revolution which changed it from a thinly populated, rural, agricultural afterthought on the edge of Europe into the densely populated, urban, industrial hub of world progress and commerce. The keynotes of the Victorian age were energy, self-confidence, hope, and a belief in progress and the future (there was no major war after 1815)—no problem was insoluble! Population growth and productivity increase contributed to the creation of a national, rather than regional, consciousness, fostered by the development of the telegraph, the penny post, new-style popular newspapers, near-universal literacy (by the end of the century) and, in particular, the growth of the railway network, the archetypal achievement of Victorian faith and energy. The rate of progress was actually far faster than often assumed on the basis of legislation alone—for example, although the fundamental Education Act was passed only in 1870, there was already then an 80 per cent literacy rate in England and Wales, and the Public Health Act of 1875 was preceded by half-a-century of local-authority action on health and municipal improvement. The emergence of conditions favourable to an explosive growth of map-making was not confined to England alone. The same economic and social forces were at work in Scotland, Wales and, to a lesser extent, Ireland; and Edinburgh was already at the centre of Scottish map printing and publishing, with its established 'school of geographical engravers',[5] and was on the verge of achieving international recognition and importance.

The conception of a uniform national map to be constructed by an official body was a natural adjunct to the development of a national identity, but it did not mean that there was no place for private map production, nor that rivals would be driven out of business. In its early years the Ordnance Survey was reluctant to compete with the commercial sector by publishing on small scales, and, indeed, followed a policy of publishing its scientific data for the benefit of private enterprise. Independent map-makers began constructing their maps on the Ordnance's basic ready-made triangulation, thus injecting a new element of uniformity and revolutionizing the mathematical accuracy of privately produced maps. The slow and fitful early progress of the Survey over the southern and Midland counties offered a commercial opportunity for the use of its triangulation data to satisfy the growing demand for large-scale maps which the Ordnance could not yet meet. Two major schemes to map the country at large scales were embarked upon in the 1820s and '30s by the last of the great *laisser-faire* practitioners in this medium, the Greenwoods and Andrew Bryant. Between them they produced a second re-survey of Britain. Although the Greenwoods were commercially far more successful than Bryant, and almost completed their project, neither scheme could reach fruition as the Ordnance Survey established an unassailable competitive position at these large scales. By 1850 the Survey monopolized the production of the basic maps of Britain, but the large-scale county map-makers had been allowed a slow and relatively painless death with most of the successful exponents of the previous century, such as Cary and Faden, able to continue their enterprises mainly unaffected by Ordnance competition.

As the Ordnance tightened its grip on large-scale mapping, so private map-makers turned to the production of smaller-scale and specialized maps which they could largely construct from Survey topographical data (following the official utilitarian style and standardization of content and appearance), but which would not compete with its sheets. The Ordnance Survey captured 'the middle ground of cartography'[6] but there was still a demand for a wide range of less costly and more remunerative maps which could be satisfied by the private sector. Independent map-makers, in the true individualist spirit of the age, copied, enlarged, and reduced Ordnance maps; but they also made their own contribution by adapting this material to the needs of guide-books, gazetteers, small-scale county atlases, road and thematic atlases, commercial directories, and a host of other popular publications. Although the re-use of out-dated existing plates was so often too commercially attractive to resist, many new maps were engraved based on Survey material, destined for a long life through the lithographic transfers which were so easily taken from them. These derived maps, edited and standardized by commercial map-makers, flourished into the twentieth century by satisfying the insistent demand for map forms which the Ordnance would not or could not produce. As the Ordnance Survey came to dominate 'the middle ground' in the second half of the century, so the private sector became increasingly controlled by fewer firms publishing material of increasing authority and similarity under the influence of the Survey.

SELECT BIBLIOGRAPHY

ANDREWS, J.H. 'The French school of Dublin land surveyors'. (*Irish Geography*, 5; 1967)

HARLEY, J.B. *Christopher Greenwood County Map-Maker, and his Worcestershire map of 1822*. (1962)

HARLEY, J.B. 'The Society of Arts and the Surveys of English Counties, 1759-1809'. (*Journ. of the Royal Soc. of Arts*, 112; 1963-4)

HARLEY, J.B. 'The re-mapping of England 1750-1800'. (*Imago Mundi*, 19; 1965)

JONES, I.E. 'The mapping of Radnorshire before the Ordnance Survey'. (*Trans. Rad. Soc.*, 47; 1977)

LAXTON, P. 'The geodetic and topographical evaluation of English county maps 1740-1840'. (*Cart. Journ.*, 13; 1976)

PARRY, M.L. 'County maps as historical sources: a sequence of surveys in southeast Scotland'. (*Scottish Studies*, 19; 1975)

SKELTON, R.A. 'The Military Survey of Scotland, 1747-55'. (*Scottish Geog. Mag.*, 83; 1967)

SKELTON, R.A. 'The origins of the Ordnance Survey of Great Britain'. (*Geog. Journ.*, 128; 1962)

TAYLOR, E.G.R. *The mathematical practitioners of Hanoverian England 1714-1840*. (1966)

WALTERS, G. 'Themes in the large scale mapping of Wales in the eighteenth century'. (*Cart. Journ.*, 5; 1968)

WHITE, T. PILKINGTON. 'The romance of State mapping'. (*Blackwood's Edinburgh Magazine*, 144; 1888)

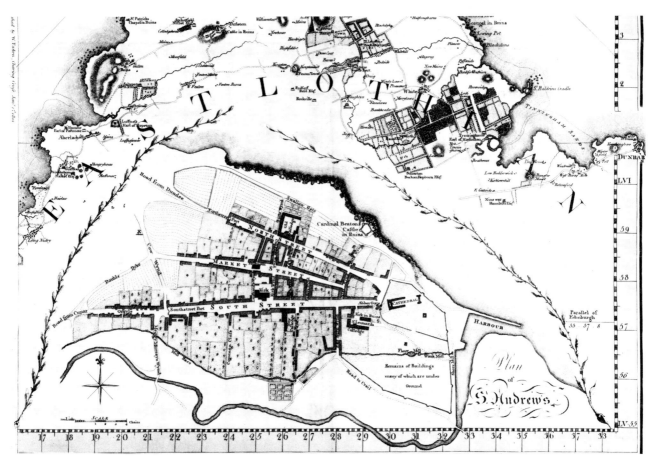

1: *Although the large-scale county maps with their elegant inset town plans, produced in the chase for the Royal Society of Arts' award, represented a remarkable advance in their own time, by the early years of the nineteenth century it was plain that their shortcomings made replacement urgently necessary in order to meet the needs of post-Industrial Revolution Britain.*
Detail: 'THE COUNTIES OF FIFE AND KINROSS WITH THE RIVERS FORTH AND TAY Survey'd & Engraved BY JOHN AINSLIE. LONDON Published by W. Faden, Geographer to the King and to his Royal Highness the Prince of Wales, Charing Cross, Jan.y 1.st 1801. Second Edition'. By permission of the British Library (Maps 8895 (2)).

I

Production

Although the study of production methods was considered by Farquharson to be a very dry subject which, 'however interesting to specialists or those who have taken part in it, can hardly be made interesting to a general audience',[1] an elementary understanding, at least, of this complex subject is central to any appreciation of Victorian maps, for the nineteenth century was 'a period of intense experimentation and innovation in ... printing methods which had profound effects on cartography'.[2] At the turn of the century the established and only practicable means of map reproduction was by intaglio printing from the copper plate, and, indeed, this method was destined to remain in use throughout the century despite the increased shortage of skilled engravers and the introduction of mechanical methods better suited to the faster production of longer printing runs. Most persuasively, perhaps, copper engraving was judged to be the best means of obtaining clarity in both outline- and hill-features 'whether the printing is done from the copper direct or by transfer to stone or zinc'.[3] Increasing pressure to pack the maximum detail into an already overcrowded landscape encouraged the search for clearer methods of reproduction, but, in the event, copper engraving continued to be thought of as the most effective means of obtaining maximum detail for most of the century.

The growing cartographic demands of post-Industrial Revolution Britain emphasized the inherent limitations of the highly skilled, laborious, and costly engraving process, and the unfitness of this archaic manual method, capable of producing only about 200 impressions an hour, for the new machine age. The Industrial Revolution created a new sense of time and infused an unfamiliar urgency into commercial affairs; thus map-makers were increasingly frustrated by the duration of plate preparation. Engraving took a remarkably long time, inevitably often rendering the topographical information obsolete even before the map appeared—Cary, for instance, advertised his large map of England and Wales which appeared eventually in 1794 as 'now engraving'[4] as early as 1787 and Edward Stanford complained of the Ordnance Survey that their 'maps have been renowned for beauty and accuracy, as they ought to be, considering the money spent upon them; but practical considerations are too often ignored, and a map, however beautiful and accurate, loses much of its value if it be published some years after the survey was made. Important changes may have occurred in the interval, and the map is merely a record of the state of things some years back.'[5] Obviously engraving time was determined by the size of the map and the complexity of the detail, but studies suggest that the average working day produced generally an engraved area of between 15 sq. cm. and 50 sq. cm, averaging only about 32 sq. cm. Scarce, expensive atlases, produced by hand for the wealthy classes over an extended period, could not satisfy the requirements of a society of spreading literacy and limited but slowly swelling affluence, and of a market fundamentally expanded by the mass-production made possible by the paper-making machine and the steam press. Nor could the presentation of out-dated topographical data meet the demands of the quickened pace of economic, civil, military and social activity.

Inevitably, the unprecedented innovation in production technique which emerged in response to these changed circumstances influenced the graphic design of the map, not least because the development particularly of the transfer technique allowed the cartographer himself to reproduce his own map's draft, at last releasing him from another's interpretative skills. This was something of a mixed blessing for, although it ensured the correct elucidation of the cartographer's intent, it frequently caused the loss of the engraver's conventions of cartographic design, lettering, and graphic representation. The importance of the engraver's influence, skill, knowledge, and cartographic tradition, in his close working relationship with the cartographer, was, perhaps, only appreciated when they had disappeared from map design.

By 1837 the engraving of the fair drawing on the copper plate had become a highly sophisticated, skilled and expensive stage of production, which was crucial since the cartographer's work was committed to the delicacy and precision of the engraver who would determine its ultimate accuracy and artistic quality. At best, as in the large county series of John Cary, Charles Smith, and J. & C. Walker first produced in the early years of the century, private-sector engraving standards could rival all but the finest of the Ordnance Survey's later work. Apprentices or semi-skilled journeymen prepared the copper plates by planishing and polishing to a perfectly smooth finish and then covering evenly with a white wax on to which the map design was drawn in reverse and cut into the plate using the traditional range of tools. The copper was engraved by pushing a steel graver along its surface to incise the groove and the resulting burr along the groove edge was scraped away leaving a line which could range in width from the very fine to the broad. Furthermore, copper engraving could execute precise lettering and also, by this time, effective shading which was used particularly to delineate landforms. Corrections could be made by hammering the back of the metal plate to fill-in the groove and then reburnishing the surface. This facility for alteration was widely used when stocks of engraved plates changed hands in business take-overs in order to alter or remove imprints and, indeed, to give the maps a changed appearance to suggest a completely new work—for example, when Henry Teesdale reissued Robert Rowe's county maps in 1829, he completely erased Rowe's title panel, replacing it simply with the county name in plain lettering.

Once the image had been cut into the copper surface, the plate was inked and wiped clean so that the ink remained only in the incised grooves and was then printed under pressure in a rolling press onto paper dampened to increase ink absorbency. Since the ink would thus be wiped out of wide grooves, it was consequently impossible to produce areas of solid colour with coloured inks in engraving. Generally, repetitive detail would be engraved by apprentices and journeymen, and only the most artistic and complex work would be undertaken by the master craftsmen, who, in a large workshop, might have the opportunity to specialize, as, for instance, with the engraving of lettering by Ebenezer Bourne and hills by Richard Tovey for the Ordnance Survey at the Tower of London. Proof copies, 'pulled' from plates at intermediate stages of preparation, were often sent out for comment and correction, particularly of place-names, to local 'experts' and were sometimes also used as advance copies for the military.

Despite being the traditional mode of map reproduction, intaglio printing was neither technologically stagnant, nor static in methods, which were continually improved through mechanization and more effective division of labour. Manual, mechanical and chemical techniques were developed from the turn of the century to improve the effects of both shading and tone and the printing of conventional signs. Although condemned as heavy, printing badly, and lacking tonal variation, standardized punched conventional signs and patterns of shading were considerably developed. For

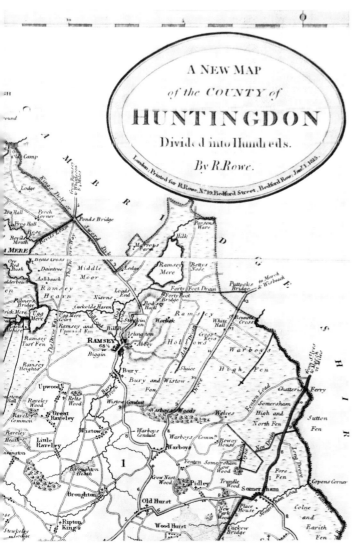

example: 'The difference between cultivated and barren ground was expressed by a rolling machine instead of by hand, the numerous figures of altitude, and trees of particular classes were inserted by punches, instead of being separately engraved. The like application of machinery produced a very beautiful mode of representing the sand, beach, and water, which before were the work of separate and highly paid artists.'[6] Much of this innovation emerged from the Ordnance Survey's energetic and inventive Irish branch. One example was 'a water-lining device invented by civil assistant John Oldham to cope with the tortuous pattern of lakes and islands in county Fermanagh';[7] others included a roller for impressing the signs for bogs, and hand-punches and spring-punches for hedgerow trees and altitude figures, devised by the engraver William Dalgleish. The ruling-machine which could produce both solid and broken lines was also invented by Dalgleish. Remarkable effects were achieved by both manual and mechanical roulettes, rockers and rollers, which created shading patterns of indentations in the plate varying in tone according to depth and density, and by mechanical ruling which produced tonal variety by engraving patterns of line or stipple. The versatile ruling-machine, which provided the engraver with a series of uniform, closely spaced, parallel lines, could modify shading tones both by the use of cross-hatching and by the alteration of line spacing and thickness, and the shading patterns so produced could then either be engraved directly into the plate or alternatively be cut through the wax ground covering the plate as a preliminary to etching. As the 'Official Catalogue' of the Great Exhibition noted for the Ordnance Survey's exhibited 6″ map of Lancashire, just completed using Becker's 'Omnigraph': 'A large proportion of the ornament (woods and hedgerows) and the whole of the altitude figures, are engraved on the copper-plates by the aid of stamps.'[8] The ultimate mechanical application of this development was undoubtedly Francis Paul Becker's 'Omnigraph', invented in the early 1840s as a means of speeding-up engraving. The copper plate was passed through a machine comprising a series of punches for each character—buildings, lettering, towns, hills, and even hill-shading units—which could be impressed into the plate surface using an automatic hammer. Becker sold his 'Omnigraph' to the Ordnance Survey, claiming that it would save it £5000 a year on a staff of 45 engravers. It was used until 1875 when the Survey decided that it was actually more costly than hand production because of the great amount of manual retouching required by 'Omnigraph'-produced signs.

The increasing demand for subtler variations in tone led to the introduction of a variety of chemical processes into map engraving. The Ordnance Survey found that the most effective hachuring was achieved by surfacing the plate with an 'etching ground' of 'asphaltum, Burgundy pitch and virgin wax', marking the hill features through the ground onto the copper with a needle and then biting-in the features with 'aqua fortis'. Tonal variation was produced by controlling the depth of etching using a varnish mask, which could be removed for printing, to protect the metal from further acid action once the desired strength of shade had

2: Detail: 'A NEW MAP of the COUNTY of HUNTINGDON Divided into Hundreds.' By Robert Rowe, 1815. When Henry Teesdale re-issued Rowe's county maps in 1829, he completely erased the original title panel, replacing it simply with the county name, but made only minor other revisions, thus creating the impression that the maps were a new production.

been achieved. 'The processes of stopping out and biting in are repeated until all the required tints from the lightest to the darkest are sufficiently corroded.'[9] Alternatively, the process could be reversed by covering the whole plate with 'stopping varnish'[9] and progressively removing it as shallower etching was required to produce lighter tones. Subsequently continuous tonal changes with no obvious divisions could be achieved by the skilful burnishing of the plate so that the varying depths of etching ran into each other smoothly.

Other chemical processes of shading were less effective. Henry Harness's use of aquatint shading, for example, in 1837 to represent Ireland's population density was relatively unsuccessful because the categories of 'shade'[10] tended to merge due to the lack of control over the process. By the 1850s the Irish Survey was experimenting with alternatives to the line engraving of relief, in the hope that a solider style of hill shading would interfere less with outline detail, using stipple, relief shaded by ruling-machine, and, in particular, James Duncan's triotint process. This latter combination of mezzotint, aquatint, and stippling was remarkably effective, much praised, and cheaper than hachures, but although actually used after 1885 to produce the hill version of the Irish 1/4″ map, was discontinued possibly for a variety of technical reasons, possibly for its dissimilarity from established style, but probably mainly because only the Duncans mastered the technique.

The established mode of plate preparation by 'pencilling the plan and rubbing it on the wax ground' delayed preparation until the engraver was ready to cut the copper since 'the sulphur, with which, in all pencils, the plumbago is mixed' interacted rapidly with the metal producing a 'thick and indefinite line'[11] if there was any delay in engraving. However, the Irish Survey's improved method of transferring the cartographer's fair-drawings to the plate 'by tracing them with a peculiar ink on transparent paper' not only increased the accuracy of its engraved maps, but also solved the problem of advance preparation because 'the charcoal of the ink remained sharp and definite for any length of time'.[11]

Despite these improvements in intaglio printing, it still suffered from the same problems that had bedevilled it from its inception—the problems of inking, wear, and revision. It was almost impossible to obtain consistent inking, and multi-sheet maps were often difficult to match together because of the differences in inking between sheets. The very process of inking, in which the whole plate was inked and then cleaned, leaving the ink only in the incised lines, was inefficient in that it caused wear by 'rubbing the plate with whiting by the bare hand, the tendency of which was rapidly to wear out the plate itself'.[11] As a result, uneven wear caused contrasting 'blackness' both on different parts of a sheet and between sheets 'pulled' off the press at different times and in small batches—William Faden, for example, reported that a customer was dissatisfied with the variations in ink shades between sheets of the Hampshire 6″ Ordnance Survey because his assistant had not been 'perfectly attentive in matching the colour of the sheets, consequently the Gent has returned it'.[12] Whilst most private-sector map-makers were content to face the declining quality of maps produced from deteriorating plates with commercial equanimity, the Ordnance Survey was obliged to maintain the highest standards and sought energetically to solve the problem by adopting 'a process practised in Paris', which not only minimized friction by combining an alkaline solution with the ink to produce 'a soapy matter

which is readily wiped away' by 'fine muslin' thus reducing plate wear and facilitating longer print runs, but also speeded production since instead of the 'tedious' process of removing 'the stiff and clammy ink' from the plate, 'the delicate action of the rag meets with no resistance and a workman is enabled to take off about 150 impressions in a period of time in which he would not produce twenty-five by the ordinary method'.[13]

Notwithstanding improvements in inking technique to reduce wear, copper was a soft metal and, therefore, the quality of the engraving still deteriorated quickly. The Ordnance Survey estimated that 'A copper-plate with fine work upon it will generally give about 500 good impressions'[14] but another contemporary estimate put the figure at 2400 and yet another quoted a maximum of 5000. Beyond the good impressions, wear became more and more apparent, producing blurred, heavily inked lines which Cary complained of in 1819: 'The unnecessary degree of blackness which prevails in our best maps, confounds the objects and makes it extremely difficult to read the names or distinguish the features.'[15] In such circumstances it was necessary for the engraver to 'repair' 'plates worn out by printing'[16] by retouching when lines began to appear faint or broken. Reworking of plates was also necessary in order to keep them up-to-date, particularly in relation to transport developments. The constant revision of railway information became a crippling financial burden for the Ordnance Survey, and the up-dating of roads proved completely beyond its resources. In the private sector, amendment frequently became an economic proposition only when a sufficient demand for revised maps had built up. The London School Board's bulk order for Stanford's 6″ map, for example, made possible an overdue full-scale revision of his 'Library Map of London', which in turn brought about the up-dating of other maps by plagiarizing rivals who harvested the fruits of Stanford's review at no survey cost to themselves.

One response to the problem of wear in the 1820s was the introduction of steel plates which were much harder and, therefore, lasted much longer, making extended printing runs without retouching possible. The hard metal, which was softened by heat so that it could be worked with engraving tools and afterwards re-hardened, allowed a more refined engraving style in which lines could be laid more closely, and subtler and more delicate effects of light and shade could be achieved. Although widely adopted for the printing of small items such as bank notes, stamps, and book illustrations, steel plates were less suited to map production because their very hardness made them difficult to engrave, revise, and keep up-to-date. A further disadvantage was that steel plates were difficult to store because of their tendency to rust! Nevertheless steel engraving was popular for half a century and maps were frequently produced from steel plates, especially where long runs and multiple issues were expected, and where, therefore, the advantages of reduced wear would be fully realized. In particular, maps, such as Tombleson's magnificent Thames and Medway, were produced on steel specifically to accompany the collections of topographical prints which were so remarkably popular during the age of steel engraving.

A more effective response to the problem of wear was the cartographical development of electrotyping by William Dalgleish, for the Ordnance Survey, between 1837 and 1840, in order to produce duplicate printing plates without the expense of new engraving. A layer of copper, known as the matrix, was deposited electrolytically onto the existing engraved plate so that the incised detail of the original stood out in relief on the matrix. Old errors or obsolete features could be scraped away from this matrix, thus leaving blank space which could be re-engraved on the new plate. The electrolytic process was then repeated to produce a layer of deposited copper on the matrix itself; this would again convert the raised lines to depressions producing a plate which could be used for intaglio printing after the addition of new information or features—such as railways, prices, or border frames—by engraving in the normal manner. This new method was a lifeline to copper-plate printing for a plate which would have cost up to £100 to re-engrave, could now be electrotyped for £5, and, thus, intaglio printing remained competitive, for a time at least, with new cheaper processes. In contrast to time-consuming engraving, the slowest part of the process was depositing a copper layer thick enough to withstand the rigours of printing under pressure; reports of backing the plates with steel to increase strength and speed plate production, however, seem doubtful. The process of scraping away detail and re-engraving made possible the correction of complex material which could not have been corrected by the old 'hammering out' method; as, for example, in the Ordnance Survey's addition of administrative boundaries to its Dublin 6″ plan. Similarly, since new detail was added to the duplicate plate not the original, it became possible to derive a mass of analytical, correlational, thematic, and variant maps from a common base map; as, for instance, when the Survey produced a special version of the Donegal 6″ map with the Inishowen contours. As long as the original plate was in good un-worn condition, all duplicates from it would produce good, clear, black impressions and there would be no need for re-engraving; from the 1850s it became standard practice to take electrotypes of plates in demand, at regular intervals, as a matter of routine.

Variants of the electrotyping process, known variously as cerography, cerotyping, electrographic printing, glyphography, typographic etching, wax engraving, and wax process, involving relief printing from a metal-backed matrix, became popular for map production in some countries but not in Britain, although such processes were certainly used by Henry George Collins, Chapman & Hall, and W. A. Blackie.

During the early development of lithography, intaglio printing remained in a strong competitive position against the cumbersome lithographic stones (laboriously prepared, difficult to handle, and easily broken) and the slow hand-operated lithographic presses. Its position weakened with every improvement in lithographic technology—the development of transfer technique, grained paper, and machine ruling; the substitution of metal plates for stone; and the introduction of the rotary steam-power press, colour printing, and photolithography. The need for speed of production and flexibility of medium, which had stimulated the

3: *Topographical prints engraved on steel plates were popular from c.1820 to c.1870 for their subtle treatment of light and shade. Maps were also engraved on steel plates where a large demand was anticipated, particularly to accompany the collections of topographical prints which were published in large numbers. Detail: 'TOMBLESON's Panoramic Map of the THAMES AND MEDWAY. LONDON PUBLISHED BY J. REYNOLDS, 174, STRAND.', 1846, from William Tombleson's* Eighty Picturesque Views on the Thames and Medway. *By permission of the British Library (Maps 1240 (37)).*

development of the electrotype, heralded the slow demise of copper engraving for maps. Nevertheless, almost until the end of the century, copper engraving was considered to be superior to lithography in graphic quality and purity of line, and, indeed, lithographers often attempted to make their maps actually look like engravings. The heights of cartographic engraving were reached by the Irish Survey whose 6″ maps achieved 'great clearness and beauty' proving that 'even an outline map might be made a work of great artistic beauty and merit'.[17]

Yet it was this very quality that brought about the final downfall of copper engraving in its last great stronghold, the Ordnance Survey. In 1897, long after the Survey's abandonment of engraving at its Southampton headquarters, the Irish branch finally accepted that its engraving-room could not cope with demand and switched its little remaining engraved production to heliozincography. Copper had been abandoned slowly and step-by-step, but, in the final analysis, it was too extravagant in every sense. By the late 1870s, for long printing runs, intaglio printing from copper was about four times as expensive and 50 times slower than mechanized lithographic printing. Bartholomews estimated that it took only 45 minutes for a girl to feed a ream of paper into the mechanized printing press—she 'could then get on with her knitting for fifteen minutes while a printer washed and gummed-up the stone for another ream. This went on all day, the eight hours producing a steady 4000 impressions'.[18] For shorter runs, hand-printing costs only slightly favoured lithography, but for a run of any length the cost of materials was lower, and the lithographic-draughtsman's fee was less than a quarter of the engraver's, making the cost of engraving about seven times greater than that of preparing a stone. Henry James, in comparing the likely costs of intaglio and lithographic printing for the English 25″ scale, estimated that only lithography could be economic because so many sheets had so few potential purchasers, and that lithography would give the Survey a break-even sales level of only 30 copies per sheet. Additionally, the final change-over was forced 'by considerations not only of time and cost, but also by the limits imposed by the number of available copper-plate engravers and by the extent of the publication establishments at Southampton and Dublin'.[19]

Commercial map publishers accepted the inevitability of the change more realistically, for they were faced with the additional problem of the acute shortage of engravers caused by this declining craft's preference for employment with the Ordnance Survey. Both John Bartholomew and James Wyld III complained indignantly that the Ordnance poached their engravers after they had served their apprenticeship and learned the trade: '... the Government snap them up as soon as they have got anything like well trained'[20]. Transfer was encouraged apparently by the illusion of better pay and less supervision. The development of new processes combined with this shortage of engravers, and the resultant tendency to advance the semi-skilled on to skilled work too quickly, was seen as the reason for a general decline in engraving standards. 'Modern engraving is nothing like so perfect as was engraving in the days of our grandfathers ... there is not so much attention given to engraving nowadays by reason of these new processes that have come into operation ... in some of the sheets the engravers have been, I will not say apprentices, but men who have been somewhat young at the business. They have not got the firmness of hand of the old engravers, men who have been in the trade for twenty, thirty, or forty years.'[20] It was Wyld who

4: 'No one who has seen the six-inch Ordnance Survey maps of Ireland, more especially those of the southern counties can fail to be struck with their great clearness and beauty. They, for the first time, showed that by properly proportioning the relative strengths and sizes of the outline, writing and ornament, even an outline map might be made a work of great artistic beauty and merit....'
Detail: Ordnance Survey: 6″: 1m.: County Wicklow, 1839.
Reproduced from the 6″ Ordnance Survey map and by courtesy of Eason & Son.

threw perhaps the ultimate insult at the quality of some of the Ordnance's engraving—'the public do not want to have to put their glasses on to look at a map'![20]

Lithography was invented by the Bavarian Aloys Senefelder about 1798 as a means of printing his plays. Inevitably knowledge of the new process diffused slowly, particularly as it was kept 'in perfect seclusion from society'[21] pending the granting of Senefelder's English patent in 1801. It was really only from the publication of the English and French translations of his book in 1819 that lithography experienced growth and development in Britain, becoming fairly well established by about 1825. Despite its slow start, in time lithography represented a profound revolution in map production because it eventually allowed a map to be drawn right-reading on paper in flexible line so that it was directly reproducible. It also introduced a new influence into map design—that of the lithographic draughtsman and printer whose impact, however, declined as advancing technology allowed cartographers to transfer and, later, photograph their own drafts. Lithography allowed anything that could be drawn to be reproduced. Senefelder viewed his invention, his 'chemical printing'[21] as he called it, as a chemical process which could be applied in several ways, and, indeed, was already experimenting with improvements, modifications, and alternative uses in the early years of the century, many of which would come into use for map production long before the century's end.

Lithography was the first planographic printing process; that is, the image was transferred from a smooth, or nearly smooth, surface on which the areas which printed and those which did not were at the same level. The fundamental chemical principle of the process was very simple—that all 'fattish or resinous matters'[21] attract similar substances but repel water, especially water 'which hold a vegetable gum or any acid in solution',[21] and that both grease and water are attracted to the same porous material. In the early days of the process, the sedimentary limestone quarried at Solenhofen, near Munich, was considered to be the most suitable ground material. This stone was 'polished' with 'soap-water',[21] and dried well, to ensure that it was chemically clean and, therefore, highly sensitive to grease. The image was then drawn on it, in reverse, using greasy water-repelling lithographic chalk or ink made of wax, soap, and lamp-black. This greasy mirror-image adhered to the limestone and was partially absorbed. The stone was moistened with weak solutions of nitric acid and gum arabic which repelled grease, further desensitized non-greasy areas, and increased the porosity and water-absorbency of the unchalked/un-inked area. Greasy printing ink was then rolled over the stone's surface, being attracted to the drawn image but repelled by the moistened non-greasy area, and the image could then be printed onto dampened paper under pressure in a press.

This basic lithographic production process emerged from a number of imitative techniques, all founded on the lithographic stone, as the dominant method of reproduction, but it then underwent important modifications which often increased its suitability for map production. In the early days it shared the field with processes in which the stone was 'etched or incised to imitate a wood engraving, and sometimes it was etched or engraved as on copper'.[21] The procedure of covering the stone with a protective ground and then opening the covering with a needle for the stone to receive the ink could produce detail and fineness of line almost as good as copper engraving. Similarly, the actual cutting of the image into the stone with a needle or etching into it with acid—the 'engraved manner of lithography'[21]—and forcing of the ink into the incised lines with a 'dabber'[22] could also produce equivalent quality. Senefelder thought this latter method to be particularly suited to map production—'[it] is nearly equal to the best copper-plate printing ... the stone can be wrought rather more expeditiously and easily than copper; for fine writing and maps, it is peculiarly well adapted, as the number of lithographic maps published sufficiently prove'.[23] However, this method, although adopted widely 'by foreign map-makers as being less costly than that of engraving on copper'[24] was little used in Britain, often because commercial map-makers were content to publish poorly designed and poorly produced lithographic maps to 'cash-in' on their easy and cheap duplication. The engraving technique of shading with line patterns created by a ruling-machine was successfully adapted to lithography. Shading could also be obtained by the action of wax crayon on a slightly roughened stone surface or a grained transfer paper which produced a shaded pattern corresponding with the specks of crayon adhering to the tiny projections. The method was particularly useful in thematic mapping for producing continuous tone variations which might reveal the structure of a distribution as in Petermann's 1851 population density maps of England and Wales and of Scotland.

Of greater significance was the spread of the transfer technique, which had been in use since 1804 (although it was only after the mid-century that the use of high-quality materials and techniques became widespread) and which Senefelder believed to be 'the principal and most important part of my discovery'.[25] This technique allowed the transfer of the greasy image, both line and shaded, from specially prepared paper to the stone—'there is another manner in Lithography where the drawing or writing with the same unctuous composition is made on paper, and is transferred from thence by artificial dissolution to the stone'.[25] The greatest advantage of the use of transfer paper was that it eliminated the need to draw in reverse. The right-facing image was now reversed ready for printing when transferred to the stone—'it is no longer necessary to learn to write in an inverted sense; but every person who with common ink can write on paper may do the same with chemical ink, and by the transfer of his writing to the stone, it can be multiplied *ad infinitum*'[25]—thus, for the first time, the cartographer could prepare his own drawing for printing. The technique had the additional advantages of being quick, allowing rapid revision of the image on the transfer paper (thus avoiding the problem of correcting the stone itself with its accompanying risk of damage or destruction), and requiring very few materials. The conservative Ordnance Survey, however, considered that although 'for these reasons it is the method which is sometimes used for the reproduction of maps or sketches in the field',[26] and that 'it is useful for adding small corrections',[26] it was 'not a satisfactory method of reproducing a topographical map'.[26] The most refined use of transfer was to take the image from an engraved copper plate and transfer it to the lithographic stone by means of the transfer paper, thus combining the precision of the former (particularly as the copper plates could be kept in pristine original condition, free from wear and alteration) with the economy of the latter. It was also, incidentally, the practice to take transfers from the originally prepared lithographic stone to other stones, so that the condition of the original would not deteriorate and to reduce its chances of damage or breakage. The development of transfer technique contributed to the decline of the county as the standard

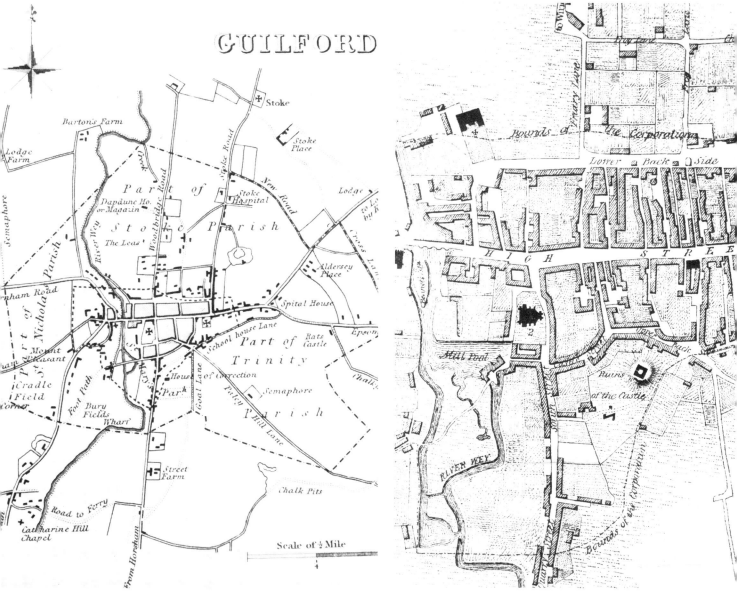

5: *Production by lithography was very much cheaper than from engraved plates. However, in comparison with the clarity of intaglio printing, particularly from steel plates, lithographed maps not transferred from existing engraved plates tended to be heavy and crude.*
i *Detail:* 'GUILFORD', *engraved by J. & C. Walker, published by Samuel Lewis, 1835, in* View of the Representative History of England. *By courtesy of Jason Musgrave.*
ii *Detail:* 'GUILDFORD', *lithographed by* 'J. Greig, Lithog.ʳ Islington.' 'Published February 1.ˢᵗ 1822 by Mess.ʳˢ Longman & Co. Paternoster Row.'

unit of British cartographic representation for it became possible and increasingly common to 'pull' portions from the plates of larger general maps and have a 'patcher' add 'borders, scales and notes'[27] to the transfer to create a regional map. It also did much to encourage the development of thematic mapping since transfer made it a simple matter to prepare overlays of specific information, often using patterns and shadings, both monochrome and variously coloured, which could be printed onto existing maps.

The slabs of limestone used for lithography had several major inherent disadvantages which encouraged the search

for an alternative, and as early as 1819 zinc plates had been substituted. Stones were expensive, easily broken, cumbersome, bulky, and space-consuming if stored 'in order to be able to take off copies as they are wanted ... from their unevenness, weight, and fragility, often prove troublesome; and, besides, take up a great deal of room, and thus require extensive space for even a moderate establishment'.[28] Since 'the Solenhofen stone' was so fragile, it was essential to have sufficient thickness to 'prevent its breaking in the press'; for 'a common folio sheet', a thickness of 'at least one inch and a half' was necessary, and if it was intended to re-use the stone, necessitating re-grinding and re-polishing, then 'its thickness must be at least two inches, and then it may be re-polished nearly 100 times'.[28] Such a stone would weigh 'between twenty and thirty pounds, sometimes more', but the 'biggest weighed nearly a ton apiece and all had to be moved about on trolleys and manoeuvred painfully into position in the bed of the printing machine'.[29] Further problems were caused by variable stone quality and 'from mismanagement, from warming them, and from sudden frost, especially when they have been previously wet'.[30]

Zinc plates, mentioned by Senefelder as a possible alternative but apparently 'invented'[31] by Chapman & Co. of London, began to be substituted in Britain from about 1830. Day & Haghe apparently printed a plan of West-

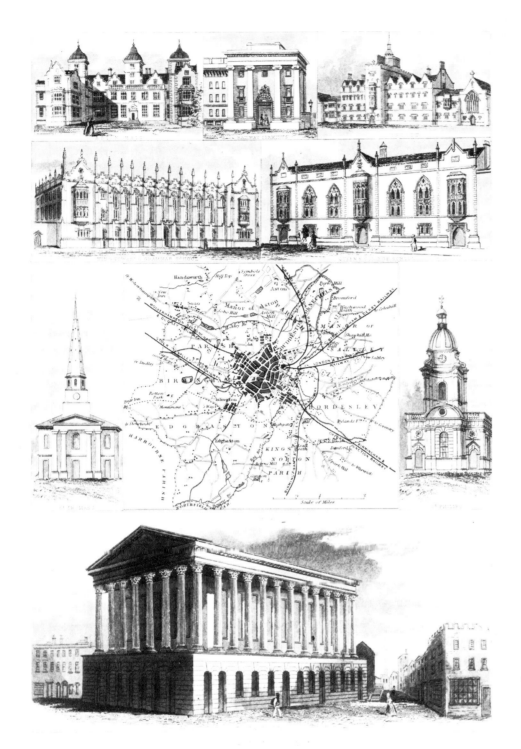

6: *Lithographic transfer allowed portions of maps to be 'pulled' from the original engraved plate for use in guide-books, gazetteers, etc., often with new information or decoration added to adapt the transfer to its new use. Charles Knight, c.1850, 'pulled' the inset map of Birmingham and its environs from the Society for the Diffusion of Useful Knowledge's map of Birmingham, and added attractive vignettes of Birmingham's important and prestigious buildings around its frame.*

minster by zinc lithography in 1835; C.F. Cheffins and J.R. Jobbins published railway maps by the method in 1838; and J. Grieve, 'Zincographer', used it in 1841 for plans of proposed Thames embankments. Although requiring a slightly different preparation for printing, zinc had the major advantages of 'lightness, portability, and non-liability to fracture, and in the large sizes you may obtain the plates'.[32] It was apparently rare to find a lithographic stone as large as five feet by three, but zinc plates up to nine feet long were common; the largest lithographic stone offered, for example, in a catalogue in 1867 was only three feet six inches by three feet. Zinc, of course, had its drawbacks: 'corrections are easier on stone';[33] 'great care is necessary to prevent zinc work from thickening and deteriorating when drawing

or correcting a plate';[33] 'its great susceptibility for imbibing grease makes it very difficult to keep clean in printing';[34] 'when laid by it is apt to corrode; and this other fact is conclusive in favour of stone, that with all its risks we never knew an artist or printer that did not infinitely prefer it to zinc'.[34] Interest in zinc, however, was furthered by the brief popularity of the commercially unsuccessful anastatic printing process which produced high-quality facsimiles of maps previously printed in a greasy ink 'of a saponaceous or fatty nature'.[35] Despite the death of anastatic printing about 1862 and stone's 'conclusive' advantage, zinc plates inevitably won the day through their greater practicability; the Ordnance Survey, for example, by 1882 used the 'so much more easily handled' zinc plates because it would need so many

London William Darton 58 Holborn Hill.

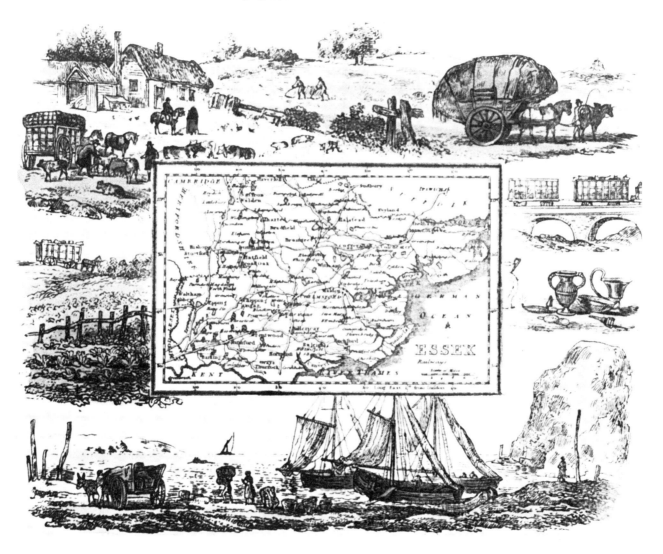

stones that their 'weight and bulk ... would render their employment impossible'.[36]

Although the Bavarian Survey decided to use lithography as early as 1809 and by 1820 the process was in use in 15–20 European cities, particularly for military purposes to illustrate a period of international tension and hostility, lithography was relatively slow to establish itself for cartographic printing in Britain. Senefelder's original press was operated in London firstly by Philipp André and then by J.G. Vollweiler, but was concerned with printing only artistic works. It was Vollweiler's failure in 1807 and the consequent sale of the press and licence for £100 to the Quarter-Master General's Office in Whitehall that marked the birth of cartographic lithography in Britain, for henceforth it was used to produce a wide variety of official maps and plans, notably relating to the Peninsular War—'this mode of printing ... was found very serviceable in giving immediate circulation to military plans of battles and other surveys, amongst the Staff-officers of the Army, the Ministers, and those connected with the Department of the Commander in Chief....'[37] Despite this early successful cartographic application—starting in May 1808 with a plan of Bantry Bay—it was only several decades later that the process was generally adopted either by the Ordnance Survey or by commercial map-makers. By 1826 the Quarter-Master General's press was reported to be printing nearly 170,000 maps, plans, and circulars per annum, with improvements in quality year by year. In 1819 Ackermann published an English edition of Senefelder's *Complete Course of Lithography* and in 1824 Hullmandel published *The Art of Drawing on Stone*. Nevertheless, map-makers took up lithographic production only slowly, perhaps because the 'British were not so well versed in chemistry or skilled in drawing'[38] or perhaps deterred by the poor products of non-cartographic draughtsmen—'this art ... has fallen into the hands of an ignorant class of person, viz., the picture-copiers and lithographic printers. It were impossible to detail the mischief annually done by persons being intrusted with this class of business, who are totally ignorant of the construction or use of maps ...'.[39] Lithography was used by Brown & Nelson from *c.*1831, by James Pigot from *c.*1835, by Samuel Arrowsmith in 1836 for the Church Commission, for route maps by Madeley in 1837, for some of the maps which accompanied the 1837 reports of the Irish Railway Commissioners, and about 1854 for reprinting some of the large-scale skeleton Ordnance Survey of London; but George Philip & Son partially changed to lithographic production only in 1846, W. & A.K. Johnston only in 1855, and John Bartholomew & Son only in 1880. However, inevitably as the century progressed the demand for cheap maps increased at such a rate that only lithography could cope. There was an explosive increase in the market for quick-response maps and plans to illustrate parliamentary and other official reports (Samuel Arrowsmith lithographed maps for the 1831 Census Report; lithography was used for maps of franchise reform in 1832; and Hansard was using lithographed maps by 1840), military developments, tithe awards, property taxation, estate sales, transportation proposals and developments, improvement proposals, town development, and social change, as well as the obvious growth in demand for topographical maps and nautical charts. By the end of the century lithography was catering for enormous printing runs; Bartholomews, for example, provided the London & North-Western Railway with 225,000 timetable maps and George Newnes with half-a-million London plans for the Jubilee (an order which was, in fact, repeated!).

Experiment and innovation in printing technology during the century threw up ephemeral processes and variations of method which were used for a short period, often with much acclaim, before falling into disuse as their limitations became clear. The complexity of the map always made it an effective demonstrator of a new process's prowess, but, in aggregate, production was minimal in comparison with intaglio and lithographic output. Although used in the past, white line engraving, which cut or punched the image into the surface of a wood or metal block so that it appeared in white on the inked ground when printed, enjoyed greater but limited popularity in the nineteenth century, particularly for astronomical maps, town plans, and a few county series, such as that produced by Joshua Archer and Sidney Hall for William Pinnock's *Guide to Knowledge*. However, the method suffered from technical difficulties in obtaining a good print from the inevitably variable inking of a wide unbroken relief surface, and from limitations in the amount of information which could be expressed. The resulting crude prints did not prove popular, and in some cases projected full county series were abandoned at an early stage and in others later issue of the image reverted to the usual representation of black on a white ground as the Pinnock maps did when published by Thomas Johnson in 1847 (however, they returned to white line on a red or brown ground when issued by R. Groombridge and Shepherd & Sutton in their doomed atlas project of about 1844).

Typographic or typometric maps were printed from movable type specially constructed to reproduce signs and line work as well as lettering. Although it was occasionally used abroad, its obvious limitations deterred even experiments in Britain. The mechanical tracing of the contours of a relief surface onto a flat surface—medal engraving or anaglyptography—was obviously of little importance for commercial map production since a relief model of an area had to be constructed before the process could produce a means of printing a map of it. (The Irish Survey, however, experimented with contouring from such a relief model of Kilkenny and actually sold duplicates at 5s. a model.)

Undoubtedly the culminating technological triumph of map-printing development in the nineteenth century was the marriage of photography and lithography to create photolithography, although this was not the only way of applying photography to printing. Inevitably the supporters of copper engraving dismissed photolithography as 'too coarse and mechanical in its nature',[40] but by the last quarter of the century the process was growing in dominance, not least because the cartographer was at last totally released from the interpretation of his material exercised by the craftsman in committing his map to the printing medium and by the design constraints imposed on him by the various transfer processes—at long last the printer was able to print anything given to him.

7: *Children's maps were produced by 'Reuben Ramble' by adding entertaining and educational scenes around county maps which had been lithographically transferred from the plates engraved for Robert Miller's* New Miniature Atlas, c.1821, *subsequently issued by William Darton* c.1822 *and* c.1825.
i *Essex, published by William Darton*, c.1822, *in* Darton's New Miniature Atlas.
ii *Essex, published by 'Reuben Ramble'*, c.1845, *in* Reuben Ramble's Travels through the Counties of England. *By courtesy of Ivan Deverall.*

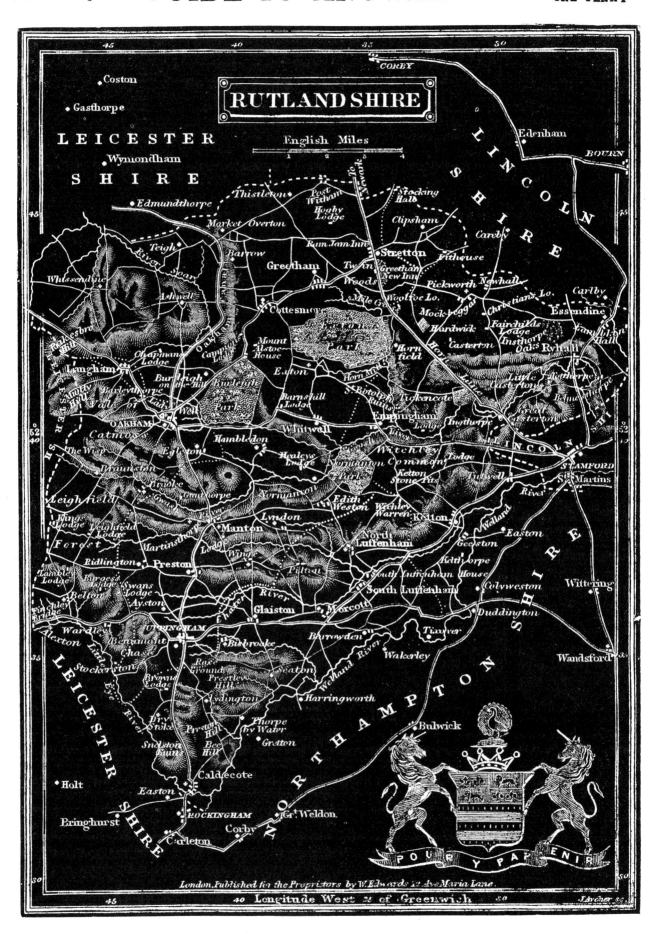

RUTLANDSHIRE

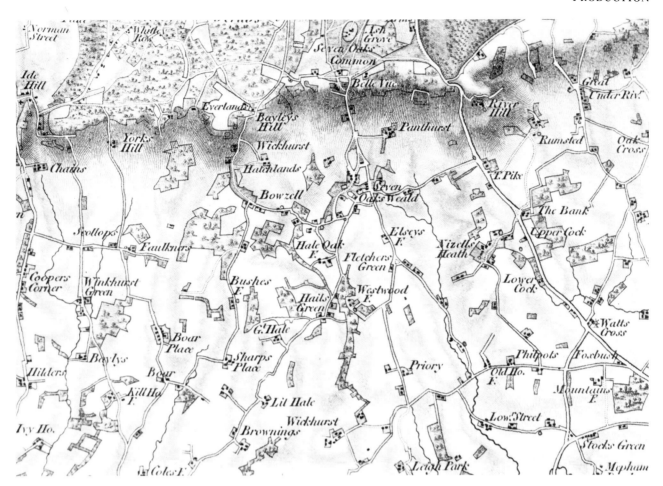

9: i *Detail: Ordnance Survey, Old Series*
Sheet No. VI Kent, 'Engraved at the Drawing
Room in the Tower under the Direction of Col!
Mudge, by Benj". Duke¹ & Assistants The
Writing by Eben'. Bourne,' 1819. Reproduced
from the 1" Ordnance Survey map.
ii *Detail: Ordnance Survey, 6": 1m.: Kent,*
'Surveyed in 1868-9 by Captain Palmer, R.E.
Contoured in 1870 by Captain James, R.E.
Engraved in 1870 under the direction of
Colonel Cameron, C.B. R.E. at the
ORDNANCE SURVEY OFFICE,
SOUTHAMPTON, and Published by Major
General Sir Henry James, R.E., F.R.S. &c.
Superintendent. 31ˢᵗ, October 1871. Outline
engraved by E. May, the Writing by W.
Cooper, the Ornament by J. Muir.' Sheet XL:
The village of Seven Oaks Weald as shown on
(i) of the 1":1m. Old Series sheet of the same
area. By courtesy of Richard Miller.

OPPOSITE

8 *Rutlandshire, engraved by J. Archer,*
published by W. Edwards in William Pinnock's
The Guide to Knowledge, *c.1835. Maps*
produced by white line engraving proved
unpopular and the method was little used.

The first successful photomechanical printing plate had been produced in France by Joseph Nicéphore Niepce by 1826, but it was not until the 1850s that it became possible to overcome the problem that his process produced too few impressions for commercial viability. Printing plates could be produced by photography in two ways—firstly, by printing the photographic image on to the light-sensitive coating of a stone or zinc plate and then working over it in lithographic ink, or, secondly, by tracing the positive photographic print on to transfer paper for transfer to the stone or plate. This latter method was first used in Britain by the Ordnance Survey to reduce its 25″ scale to the 6″ so that the reduced maps could be traced and transferred to the waxed surface of the copper plate as a guide for the engravers.

It was this urgent need to reduce the Survey's 25″ plans that drove Colonel Henry James to search for an effective method of mass reduction, since the existing and traditional method of reduction by the rather unstable hand pantograph could cope with the increased demand only with enormously enlarged costs of staff and accommodation. Clearly photography could produce satisfactory results if an effective process could be devised, but as late as 1882 James was reporting that the reduction of the 6″ to the 1″, with 'only as much of the detail being reduced as can be shown on the one-inch without impairing its distinctness',[41] was by pantograph because attempts to reduce by photograph had been temporarily unsuccessful. It had long been realized that a quick, effective, mechanical method of reduction would represent an enormous contribution to cartographic technology: 'It is generally the case that the scale on which a map is drawn by the surveyor of a district is very much larger than that which would be wisely selected for publishing his map; inasmuch as the details become too minute and tedious, and would take him more time than should be expended upon one copy, if he were to draw upon the usual publishing size; the consequence is that his plan must be reduced before it is engraved or drawn upon stone.'[42] The most novel solution to the problem was Henry Collins's cartographic application of the process of printing on an elastic surface for transfer to ceramics. This inappropriately named 'electro-printing block process' made a transfer print onto a sheet of rubber stretched on a frame; the sheet could then be stretched further or relaxed and at the desired size the image could be transferred onto stone and printed.

Neither the pantograph nor any other method was satisfactory for the mass reduction required to derive the Ordnance Survey's 6″ maps from its 25″ plans. What was required was '... some system by which the reduction of the plans from the 1/500 scale to the 1/2500 scale, and from the 1/2500 scale to the scale of 6-inches to 1 mile, and again from the 6-inch to the scale of 1-inch to a mile, could be effected much more rapidly than by the pentograph or any then known method',[43] otherwise 'the progress of the work of the Survey would be much too slow and too expensive to be satisfactory to the country'.[44] The process of tracing a photographic reduction on transfer paper with 'a composition of lamp-black and gum and water'[44] and transferring it to a copper plate for engraving was costly and slow, to the extent that the 6″ production programme fell increasingly behind schedule. Criticisms of the accuracy of photographic reduction led to official investigation which concluded 'that the greatest deviation in any part of the plans from the perfect accuracy does not amount to one four hundredth part of an inch in the angle of the rectangle, and even this minute error is not cumulative'.[45] Evidence that

photographic reduction was currently saving the Survey £1615 per annum and would save an estimated £31,952 for the whole survey was, perhaps, even more persuasive in encouraging the pursuit of improved methods. As early as 1859 the Survey was experimenting with a method 'by which the reduced print is in a state to be at once transferred to stone or zinc, from which any number of copies can be taken, as in ordinary lithographic printing, or for transfer to the waxed surface of the copper plates'.[46]

Experiments using Pouncey's chromocarbon printing process and the subsequent development of the process of photolithography by the Ordnance's Scott and Rider led to a method by which photographic prints could be ready-made in lithographic ink for transfer directly to the stone or zinc plate. Thus, the intermediate step of preparing a separate transfer paper by tracing, with its risk of draughtsman error, was eliminated. 'The chief value ... consists in the facility with which the photograph of the drawing, which it is desired to copy, can be transferred to a zinc plate and printed therefrom with great rapidity and at a very trifling cost, in permanent ink.'[47] The new process, christened 'photozincography' by James, came into regular service in 1881, although it had been used experimentally to transfer part of the Northumberland survey as early as 1859. Now cartographic draughtsmen had to adapt in order to produce, for the camera, a fair-drawing which would photograph as a finished map rather than as a draft for the engraver or lithographic draughtsman.

Photographic reduction required some change in the traditional style of Ordnance maps since 'names and ornament when so reduced were often illegible'.[48] In order to ensure satisfactory reduction without illegibility, Survey sheets at the larger scale had to be bolder and coarser, with heavier lines which could be photographed in poor light, and with some of the ornament and names at an 'exaggerated scale, so that when reduced they shall be of a suitable size'.[48] The need for heavy lines which could be photographed in poor light was partially solved by the introduction of electric light in 1886 which enabled much-improved photographic prints to be produced in gloomy weather. A further problem was that reduction often caused topographical detail to 'crowd ... too much on the reduced scale'.[48] Attempts to block out unwanted detail by photographing a carmine version of the 6″ map 'on which such parts of the detail as it was desired to retain were penned in'[48] proved unsuccessful, causing the reversion to reduction to the 1″ by pantograph in 1882; but the use of cobalt, which was not reproduced by photography, did prove successful since detail which was not wanted at the reduced scale could be drawn in cobalt on the manuscript plan but would not appear on the photograph of it. This process was quickly further developed so that the 25″ plan was printed in blue and on it the 6″ was redrawn in black over the blue detail 'in a style suitable for reduction',[49] following only those features which were to appear on the 6″ map. When photographed through a blue filter only the black drawing would appear on the photographic print, thus eliminating all unwanted detail and generally re-styling the map to suit the smaller scale.

Although 'The sheets have not, of course, the finish of the old engraved sheets', they were 'perfectly legible, and form an excellent map'.[50] The new production process had several important advantages. 'Any possibility of error in reduction is eliminated'[50] because there could be no tracing or engraving errors. 'The operation is much quicker; a sheet, the engraving of which took months, can now be

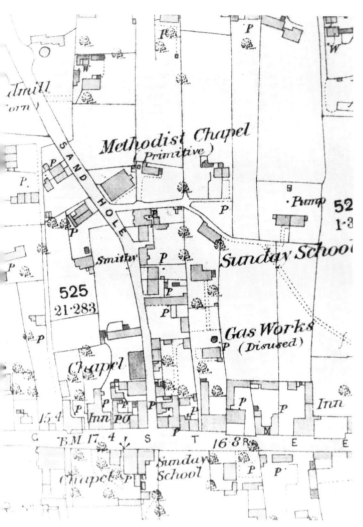

10 *Detail: Ordnance Survey, 25″:1 m: Lincolnshire (Parts of Lindsey) Sheet XLI.9. North Somercotes, 'Zincographed and Published at the Ordnance Survey Office, Southampton, 1889.' Reproduced from the 25″ Ordnance Survey map.*

tion except the hardened image.... For all practical purposes there is a printing plate consisting of a reproduction of the original drawing in greasy ink on a clean zinc plate.'[51] Heliozincography had the particular advantages that an indefinite number of plates could be produced from the same negative and that 'the negatives can be easily corrected or altered by hand. It is, in fact, just as easy to draw or write names on the negative as on paper, and any office for reproducing maps by this process should always have a staff for touching up and correcting negatives'.[51]

Conductor Vandyke of the India Survey developed the process, reversing its action; he eliminated photography altogether by the 'Vandyke process', introduced to the Ordnance Survey in 1900. 'The drawing is laid face downwards on a sensitized zinc plate and exposed to light through the back of the paper in a printing frame. The light hardens the sensitive coat except where it is protected by the lines of the drawing.... An image of the drawing is thus left in clean zinc....'[51] Its great advantages were that it was cheap, simple, and required little apparatus; but it was 'not suited for the reproduction of any except very simple topographical maps, but for sketches, diagrams and large-scale cadastral maps it is invaluable'.[51]

Thus, military requirements, technical virtuosity, cartographic demand, and sheer enthusiasm had combined to change map reproduction beyond recognition during the nineteenth century. Of necessity, this technological revolution was led by the Ordnance Survey, particularly its imaginative and innovatory Irish branch, by virtue of its greater resources and higher standards. No longer did maps have to be engraved on copper and printed in one colour only from an engraving made at the scale of reproduction. Inevitably rapid and diffused innovation created many processes which were short-lived due to commercial impracticality, but transient as these processes were, they all contributed to the technological advance of map reproduction and provided means of satisfying specialized requirements of limited significance. The mainstream of development, however, is clear, and, indeed, the turn of the century represented the threshold of another period of rapid technical progress with Dr Strecker's invention of the chromium-gum copying process on zinc in 1901 and the appearance of the offset press in 1904.

SELECT BIBLIOGRAPHY
MUMFORD, I. 'Lithography, photography and photozincography in English map production before 1870'. (*Cart. Journ.*, 9; 1972)
ORDNANCE SURVEY *Account of the Methods and Processes Adopted for the Production of the Maps of the Ordnance Survey.* (1875)
ORDNANCE SURVEY *Account of the Methods and Processes adopted for the Production of the Maps of the Ordnance Survey.* (2nd. edition; 1902)
RISTOW, W.W. 'The anastatic process in map reproduction'. (*Cart. Journ.*, 9; 1972)
TWYMAN, M. *Lithography 1800–1850, the techniques of drawing on stone in England and France and their application in works of topography.* (1970)
WAKEMAN, G. 'Lithography, photography and map printing', in *Aspects of Victorian Lithography.* (1970)
WOODWARD, D. (ed.) *Five Centuries of Map Printing.* (1975)

produced in a few hours'[50] making it possible to publish the 6″ map concurrently with the 25″; and 'There is a great saving in cost; it is estimated that the total saving will exceed 100,000l.'[50]

Of the numerous techniques applying photography to cartographic printing, the most generally useful photomechanical process was heliozincography, introduced to the Ordnance Survey in 1893, by which it was possible to transfer the image to the printing plate, at any required scale, without using transfer paper. The negative produced by the camera was simply reversed and exposed to light in contact with a sensitized zinc printing plate. 'The light hardens the image, leaving the remainder of the composition soft. The whole plate is now covered with greasy ink before the plate is washed, and the washing then removes all the composi-

II

Paper

The advancing technology of paper manufacture had an obvious effect on the form of maps, for the nature of paper changed as the nineteenth century progressed. In 1800, paper manufacture was a scattered, small-scale, handicraft industry able to produce white paper only from white rags because there was no means of bleaching pulp. The inability to bleach was a mixed blessing—on the one hand it avoided the deterioration produced in paper by bleaching, but on the other it increased the problem of the shortage of rags of the required quality. However, change was at hand through the spread of mechanized rag-pulping, through the use of bleaching processes (following the discovery of chlorine by Scheele in 1774 and the invention of bleaching powder by Tennant in 1779) which allowed the production of white paper from coloured rags, and through the addition of china clay to clean and add bulk. The drawback of the new bleaching processes was that they attacked the paper, weakening it and thus increasing the number of complaints about quality.

Growing demand created pressure for a new type of paper suited to lithography and for a faster mechanical alternative to the slow output of high-quality hand-made paper. The first effective machine emerged from the collaboration between the engineer Bryan Donkin and the London stationers Henry and Sealy Fourdrinier who provided the 'know-how' and capital respectively to create a machine capable of producing 600 lbs of paper in 24 hours. Although the vast expense of developing the Fourdrinier machine caused the collapse of the firm, the machine itself was an undoubted success. Other similar processes followed, including the development of the calendered and filled papers necessary for lithography and chromolithography. Consequently, by 1830 half Britain's paper was machine-made and by 1860 machines produced 96 per cent of an output which had increased sevenfold since 1800 accompanied by a halving of price. In quantitative terms, tonnage of hand-made paper was roughly halved in the first half of the century and halved again by 1900.

The potential scale of mechanized production emphasized the shortage of raw materials, and various rag substitutes came into use, particularly esparto grass which had been introduced by Routledge in 1860. This grass fibre was especially suited to the making of high-class paper. Scottish mills excelled at this quality production and the Edinburgh area developed a specialist output of fine, white paper to feed, amongst others, the city's growing number of internationally important map publishing houses. 'The Scotch have during the century especially cultivated the trade of printing and bookselling. In the former branch alone, ten thousand persons are employed in Scotland, five thousand of whom are engaged in the capital. In 1860 there were in Edinburgh no less than thirty firms, who combine the united business of publishing and bookselling.... The advantage of cheap labour, which includes, of course, cheap paper, are here so great, especially in the issue of large editions, as to more than counteract the drawback in the shape of transit cost to, and agents' commission in, London.'[1]

A similar demand from London publishers created a similar form of specialization. The last 20 years or so of the century saw the development of paper manufactured from timber and other types of pulp, thus solving the raw-material shortage and keeping costs low, and allowing production to keep pace with a rapidly growing demand stimulated by increasing population and expanding industry, trade, and education.

The sweeping away of the last vestiges of protectionism on the road to total free trade provided an important stimulus to the demand for maps, since it cheapened the paper on which they were printed and also cheapened the publications which carried them. The stamp duty 'originally imposed with the object of checking the growth of seditious newspapers'[2] stood, in the early part of the century, at fourpence on each copy of a newspaper issued. It was reduced in 1836 to a penny, represented by a red stamp on every paper, and abolished in 1855 leading directly to the appearance of many new cheap newspapers and journals. Similarly, the abolition of the duty on advertisements did much to enhance circulation. Most significantly, the duty on paper itself, enormously heavy at threepence per pound, was halved in 1836 and finally abolished in 1860 despite the spirited opposition of a minority who believed that its cheapening would mean 'the establishment of a daily propaganda of socialism, communism, red republicanism, blasphemy, bad spelling, and general immorality'.[2] The stunting influence of the paper duty on the map trade is indicated by the vigour with which map publishers campaigned for its removal in the mid-century, with such as Chambers, Knight, Orr and Wyld serving on the committee of the Association for the Abolition of the Duty on Paper.

The cheapening of paper and newspapers, combined with the economies of mechanized methods, made possible the mass-production which brought cheap maps within the financial reach of the vast majority of a population hungry for them. Maps printed on high-quality hand-made paper for a limited wealthy clientèle had largely been replaced by a mass-production of maps on cheap machine-made paper for a mass market (despite the fact that it was possible mechanically to manufacture laid paper which looked and worked like hand-made paper). Inevitably this change often meant some deterioration of quality, for mass-production techniques were not yet sufficiently sophisticated to ensure uniformity. James Wyld III was particularly vociferous in denouncing the inadequate quality control of paper used by the Ordnance Survey: '... for the purpose of mounting the sheets have to be damped, often wetted, but certainly damped, because paste has to be put on the back of them for the purpose of making them adhere to the calico, and much depends on the quality of the paper, its texture and thickness—by texture I mean whether there is more rags in it and it is of a better quality or whether it has more straw in it. As to thickness you will find a great diversity of thickness when you come to put a thick and thin sheet together.'[3] And: 'One of the greatest difficulties we experience is that the paper is not of uniform thickness, of uniform quality, nor of uniform colour. The consequence is that in joining several sheets together you get a diversity of colour; you can never get them to join, and you get maps with main roads half an inch out in the centre, for instance, although the sheets are properly done.'[3] Similarly, Edward Stanford complained in 1891 that the Ordnance Survey's use of different makes and colours of paper was 'an endless source of trouble and annoyance .... The Survey seems to forget that many of the sheets are wanted for mounting purposes, and the trouble caused by the several kinds of paper and the differences in the colour of the paper, are most injurious. We find two sorts of paper, hard and soft, and two colours, white and creamy brown, used for the 6-inch maps alone. The sheets of soft paper will stretch a quarter of an inch when pasted for mounting, while the sheets on hard paper scarcely stretch at all, so that the proper joining of a number of sheets is practically a frequent impossibility. It is the best and most influential customers who require such made-up maps, and the effect produced is frequently that of a patchwork quilt. I have even had to stain certain sheets of a map, because the customer declined to have it in its natural colours.'[4]

SELECT BIBLIOGRAPHY
LABARRE, E. J. *Dictionary and Encyclopaedia of Paper-Making.* (2nd edn.; 1952)

III

Presentation and Content

By 1837 the depiction of topographical features generally followed an accepted system of conventional signs, both semi-pictorial and geometrical, to indicate function and character; only the lack of an accepted sign allowed the map-maker scope for improvisation. The most noticeable format changes of the Victorian age were the proliferation of signs used and the in-filling of the remoter areas as they were more fully mapped. The Victorian map-maker had at his disposal an array of administrative, commercial, industrial, demographic and sociological information not available to his earlier counterpart. Despite this plethora of reliable information, however, the age-old practice of simply copying existing maps undoubtedly continued. It is impossible to estimate the extent of such plagiarism but it must have been extremely common for even Robert Kearsley Dawson, who had access to the Ordnance Survey's official data, continued the existence of the mythical 'Unnear' on his outline map of Radnor produced to accompany the 1832 Reform Act. Nevertheless, new information was increasingly translated into cartographic form. It emanated not only from the Ordnance Survey but from other sources such as the Board of Agriculture, the Boundary Commissions, the Census, myriad official and private investigations, and a multitude of guide-books, commercial directories, gazetteers, county and road atlases, and other topographical works. Naturally, it was the Ordnance Survey which exerted the greatest influence through its representation of the earth's surface in the greatest detail that a scale would allow—in so doing it determined those features which should appear on contemporary maps either through its rejection of survey material on the grounds of questionable accuracy, as in the case of many archaeological sites, or through its deliberate suppression of data, as, for example, in its strategic discontinuation of the marking of forts, magazines, and martello towers in the late 1870s or its omission of Irish inns because of their inhospitality! Undoubtedly, despite the Survey's increasing unwillingness to publish its survey data, its high standards persuaded some commercial publishers to attempt equivalent quality, delineating an increasingly complex countryside in ever-greater detail. Widespread reference to the 'Ordnance' in map titles underlines the value placed on such an authoritative source by the map-purchasing public despite the obvious fact that generally little use had been made of official material beyond the straightforward perfunctory copying of the Ordnance maps—such typical opportunism caused Edward Stanford, for example, to quarrel with Bartholomew and resign his agency over the latter's unwarranted claims concerning the Ordnance.

However, in fairness to Bartholomew, his 'Reduced Ordnance' maps were the most ambitious and technically advanced popular maps of the age, produced over several decades and imposing a severe financial burden on the firm—the 1/2" 'Reduced Ordnance Survey Maps of Scotland' in 30 'District' sheets appeared between 1875 and 1886, being replaced by a new series in 29 sheets in 1890; the 1/4" map of Ireland in seven sheets appeared between 1896 and 1904; the 1/4" map of England and Wales in 12 sheets was published in 1897, and the 1/2" map in 37 sheets between 1897 and 1903. ('These Maps are all reduced by permission from the Ordnance Survey, and Specially Revised to date before going to press. The Land is coloured according to Contours of Altitude. Counties are named and their boundaries defined. Roadside Inns and Hotels are indicated. Also all Fishing Streams, Locks, Woods and Forests, Antiquities, etc. The Roads are coloured Red to distinguish First-Class, Secondary, and Indifferent Roads for Motoring and Cycling purposes. Footpaths and Bridlepaths are also shown. OPINIONS OF THE PRESS. THE TIMES—"Nothing better in the way of Maps. They are beautifully clear and with every detail for all practical purposes." GLASGOW HERALD—"These are admirable specimens of Tourist Maps".'[1])

Pilferage of Ordnance material, and indeed that of any other source, was a simple matter in an age when copyright protection was rarely enforced with any strength. By 1800 maps, like other engravings, had copyright protection for 28 years and there were remedies for piracy which had been considerably enlarged in the previous half-century. In 1836 the provisions of the Engravings Acts were extended to Ireland, and in 1852 copyright protection was extended to material printed by lithography or other mechanical processes. Some publishers felt the legal protection insufficient and further covered themselves by obtaining a Royal Patent which gave sole rights to printing and publication, forbidding other subjects to reprint, abridge, or import copies without the patent-holder's consent. John Wilkes, noted for his own piracy of others' works, published his *Encyclopaedia Londinensis* under such a patent. Archibald Fullarton was accused of reprinting not only the maps but also the text of James Bell's *New and Comprehensive Gazetteer of England and Wales* in his *Parliamentary Gazetteer*. Although admitting that material (which included the maps) 'still possessed of value' had been taken from Bell and 'digested into and incorporated with the present Work', he dismissed this 'extremely disingenuous attempt ... to underrate the value and importance of their laborious and accurate Compilation' on the grounds that 'these materials do not constitute one-third part of the present Publication'[2]—a proportion of plagiarism which he clearly considered to be both acceptable and commonplace. The most celebrated case of copyright action occurred when John Cary sued Francis Newbery, the then publisher of Daniel Paterson's *Roads*, for breach of copyright. This acrimonious case of charge and counter-charge was won by Cary, with the judge, Lord Kenyon, clearly favouring him: 'I thought the Twelfth Edition of Paterson was a most impudent Plagiarism. They had used a Pair of Scissors, and only inserted a little of their own here and there.'[3] However, the case reveals the complexities involved in such legal action, for Paterson's publishers insisted that Cary was the marauder, having stolen their material: '... not only the scheme and design of Paterson's Book had been seized upon, but that the greatest part of the matter or substance which it contained, where the partial survey of the Post-Office did not extend, had been transplanted with as little scruple into this publication;—and that often in a manner so servile, as not to disguise the plagiarisms by a change of words. It was manifestly a Copy at the beginning, the middle, and the end.'[4] This was a view which enjoyed some contemporary support, not least from Lord Lough-borough, the Lord Chancellor, who considered that 'Paterson's was the original production, and had received improvements and alterations from time to time' and 'That Mr. Cary might think himself well off, if Mr. Newbery, the Proprietor of Paterson, did not file a Bill against him'.[4] The action was fought from 1799 to 1801 through the Courts of Chancery and King's Bench with the latter finally awarding Cary damages of one shilling! Such protracted and expensive proceedings, with so little compensation, clearly deterred most publishers from action, even where the case was watertight, and it is indicative of the ineffectiveness of the law that the verdict seems to have had little effect on the sales of Paterson's work which enjoyed a continuously healthy life, being issued another eight times and simply succumbing to old age, dying only c.1832 with a senile re-issue of its eighteenth edition.

No great hindsight is needed to appreciate the inevitability of the plagiarism that the Ordnance would suffer throughout the century, nor to understand the Survey's ambivalent and fluctuating attitude towards the question of copyright. In its early days the Survey seemed to imply that it was deliberate policy to make its triangulation data available to the private sector so that it could produce 'more correct maps of the counties over which the triangles have been carried'.[5] Hence, it was to be left to 'individual speculation' to survey the topographical detail required to 'fill up the triangles'[6] and in order to facilitate this, triangulation stations were marked by 'small stakes placed over the stones sunk in the ground, having their tops projecting a little above it'.[7] Thus, commercial map-makers utilized published Survey data without any question of the infringement of copyright laws, without any dissent from the Board of Ordnance, and without any secret. Yeakell & Gardner's large-scale map of Sussex was the first to use official data and it subsequently became common practice to refer to the use of the Survey's material. Greenwood, for example, proposed that his maps of Lancashire and Yorkshire would be '... laid down on the Basis of Col. Mudge's Trigonometrical Survey of the Principal, and such other of the Secondary Triangles, as are published in the 3rd Vol. of the Trigonometrical Survey of England'[8] and Archer's 'New Plan of London' of 1840 was taken 'from Actual Survey, The Trigonometrical Points being accurately laid down from Government Documents'. It was also readily admitted that the Survey's topographical data was utilized; for instance, in giving evidence to the Select Committee on Railway Bills in 1845, witnesses agreed that virtually all Irish railways were planned and their parliamentary maps were prepared from Ordnance Survey maps.[9]

Perhaps it was John Cary who finally brought-home to the Survey the extent to which private map-makers could

use its material: 'ORDNANCE SURVEY OF DEVON-SHIRE. J. CARY respectfully acquaints the Public, that he is now engraving by Subscription, a Map of the county of Devon, from the above Work: to be printed on two sheets of large Atlas paper, comprehending, with a very few exceptions, all the places which are given in the Ordnance Map. The most minute exactness has been observed in the reduction of this Work from the Survey....'[10] The myopic Ordnance had not foreseen that publication of its own maps would offer a source of topographical information to the commercial map-maker, in addition to its published trigonometrical information, which would place the Survey maps in direct competition with commercial maps derived from them. Whilst Mudge saw a scientific obligation to publish the angles of triangulation, distances between trigonometrical stations, and tables of the latitudes and longitudes of the 218 principal triangulation stations, he had, by 1816, started to complain of the commercial drawbacks of unfettered plagiarism—'an Idea has gone abroad among the Mapsellers of London that as a portion of the Public, at whose expence the Ordnance Survey is carried on, they have a right to reduce from and publish, Copies of the Ordnance Survey on Scales suited to their own convenience; a circumstance, whether they have that right or not that seems likely in a greater or less degree to affect the Sale of the original Work. Under this Idea, ... Essex and Devonshire were so reduced and sold; the great Body of the latter County had been incorporated in the general Map of England lately published by Mr Arrowsmith; and I know for certain that the Map of Cornwall which has not been published more than a Fortnight, is now reduced to the Scale of half an Inch to a Mile, and is about to be put into the hands of an Engraver for publication.'[11] The Board chose conciliation as the best policy, simply advertising to the trade '... cautioning them against copying, reducing or incorporating into other Works, and publishing all or any part of the said 'Trigonometrical Survey' or of the Ordnance Maps which have been or may be engraven therefrom ...'[12] Despite giving Cary permission to produce a reduced version of the Ordnance map of Cornwall in 1817, the Survey was again in dispute with him over the use of their material in 1820, but Colby believed that it would not be possible to determine the degree of piracy sufficiently for legal purposes and the copyright question was simply kept 'in view'.[13] In fairness to private map-makers, it is impossible to judge the extent to which they copied from the Ordnance and certainly in the case of the Greenwoods, commonly accused of the most systematic pillage of Survey material, a close comparison suggests that their topographical material was very frequently derived from non-Ordnance sources.

Apparently a tacit truce was assumed in which Ordnance maps could be used as the topographical source, free of hindrance, as long as the derived maps were not published on the same scale and, therefore, did not compete directly with the Survey's publications. However, the problem was still causing difficulties in the late 1880s when Stanford complained bitterly of the misappropriation of Ordnance material and his resulting loss of revenue as Ordnance agent: 'In 1886 I brought a very flagrant case of piracy before the controller of H.M. Stationery Office. The new 1-inch map of Sussex had been reproduced on the same scale by photo-lithography, and was being sold, in Brighton and elsewhere, at about half the price of the real Ordnance Map. Such was the effrontery of the producer that on the title it actually professed to be the "Ordnance" map, and probably only an expert would have recognised the fraud at a glance. *No steps were taken by Government, pour encourager les autres.* This means that one individual is to be allowed to appropriate the results of money raised from the whole body of the taxpayers to his own use, and to supply the public with an inferior article on false pretences';[14] and 'Many country booksellers now publish maps of their own neighbourhoods which are direct photo-lithographic reproductions of the Ordnance map, with a few additions, and of course, such booksellers sell their own improved versions rather than the official publications.'[14] In 1887 a Treasury minute noted that for Ordnance maps 'it seems desirable that the Copyright should be enforced in the interests of the taxpayer. Notice of the intention to enforce the copyright in any work should be given to the public. In the case of future works this notice can be given by prefixing to the work a notice to the effect that the rights of copyright are reserved.'[15] Consequently, from the following year, all Ordnance maps bore the note 'All Rights of Reproduction Reserved'.

However, such a threat was no more practical in the 1880s than it had been found in the early decades of the century, and the realistic attitude adopted by the Survey was summed up by Sir Charles Wilson: '... the principle on which, rightly or wrongly, the Ordnance Survey has always been conducted. The Department is directed to make maps on certain scales, which were settled after many years of controversy, for state purposes. The construction of special maps for popular use was designedly left to private enterprise and any attempt to compete with private firms in "catering for the public" has been discouraged.... guide book maps ... are all based on the Ordnance Survey and could not have been produced and sold at such slight cost without it. The public thus and in many other ways indirectly derive benefit from the great national survey.'[16] This attitude was made explicit in 1892 by the influential Dorington Committee which recommended that reproductions of Survey maps should be sanctioned officially if they had a genuine difference of form or matter and if a nominal payment had been made for copyright permission. Certainly, the glut of maps published 'By Permission of the Ordnance Survey' in the later years of the century indicates the willingness with which the Survey allowed private map-makers, both large and small, to copy its maps or even transfer directly from its sheets. Admittedly 'people did buy the 1″ and smaller-scale Ordnance Survey maps when they might have bought a commercial map, but there was not much positive encouragement to do so, and for the whole of the nineteenth century, the official view was that the Ordnance Survey was primarily an information-gathering rather than an information-publishing agency.'[17]

CONVENTIONAL SIGNS
Nineteenth-century map-makers followed the well-established precedent of emphasizing certain features at the expense of others; the emphasis was frequently determined by economic pressures, rather than cartographic considerations, and by the resulting need to flatter potential buyers. Thus, maps concentrated on features likely to attract subscribers and consequently they reflect most strongly what was of interest to the wealthy minority of landowners and the growing group of prosperous merchants and industrial capitalists that constituted the market for maps in the early part of the century. Maps gave exaggerated prominence to parks, estates, and country houses, frequently naming the owner, and often showing the layout (the work, perhaps, of a fashionable eighteenth-century *dessinateur de jardins* such

as 'Capability' Brown) in great detail. Clearly country houses were considered to be sights of considerable interest—'pleased with the numberless Villas which so often attract ... attention, ... enquiry is naturally directed to whom do they belong'[18]—and consequently cartographers added to their travelling maps 'that kind of information which will give pleasure to ... peregrinations.'[19] The interests and pastimes of the gentry were also emphasized, and the maps generally were designed to appeal to their tastes, as, for example, in Greenwood's addition of 'appropriate Embellishments ... got up and introduced in the most tasteful and masterly style'.[20] Even such 'modern' works as Bartholomew's *Atlas of Scotland*, which managed to throw off the shackles of nineteenth-century autocracy by reducing emphasis on the church and the country estate, could not resist the temptation to map deer forests and salmon rivers! The exception to this sycophantic approach was the Ordnance Survey, for it did not need overly to please the landed gentry in order to obtain funding and, therefore, had no need to distinguish gentlemen's seats with their owners' names in such obsequious fashion.

Otherwise, the Survey's recruitment of staff from the established private sector ensured the continued use of accepted conventional signs, and, indeed, the extension of their use particularly at the expense of explanatory notes which largely disappeared. Thus the traditional personality of British topographic representation was retained. Larger-scale maps tended to concentrate attention on land-use, since their potential market was principally agricultural, reflecting the final disappearance of the great ancient woodlands and the erosion of heath, common, and waste by enclosure. The developing industrial nature of the landscape, initially spread widely and thinly due to the scattered nature of raw materials and water power, but increasingly concentrated on the coalfields and in their rapidly growing industrial towns, was represented by the marking of mills, glassworks, brickworks, ironworks, collieries, lime kilns, tanneries, saltings, forges, furnaces and mines; there were clay, chalk, sand, stone, marl and gravel pits, and all the other burgeoning elements of rapid industrialization. However, the very unfamiliarity of many of these new industrial processes frequently caused surveyors to record them incorrectly and, thus, they were often marked wrongly on the map. Similarly, the rapidly evolving social environment was delineated by a proliferation of signs representing courts, workhouses, public baths, board schools, pleasure parks, exhibition halls, hospitals, asylums, and the whole panoply of a new industrial society which the Victorians vigorously investigated, criticized, and reformed, so creating yet more conventional signs. The end result, encouraged by the ease and cheapness of developing lithographic technique, was vastly to increase the number of generally accepted standardized signs and to add a veneer of other signs and representational techniques, often simply added to an Ordnance Survey sheet or similar base map, devised by cartographers for their own particular purposes of thematic illustration—'almost every technique now known for representing population numbers, distribution, density and movements'[21] seems to have been born during the period 1835-55. Much of this thematic representation was pioneered by Henry Drury Harness, the English engineer officer who drafted the maps for the 1837 Irish Railway Commission. He not only used levels of aquatint shading and different-sized signs to represent population densities, but also introduced flow lines for the first time with his 'streams of shade' relating movement densities to line thickness.

11: *In order to secure a guaranteed market for their maps, cartographers pandered to potential customers by emphasizing country houses and estates, naming their owners, and generally designing their maps to appeal to the aestheticism of the established gentry and the pretensions of a newly wealthy class of successful entrepreneurs.* 'MAP OF the County of BEDFORD, From an Actual Survey made in the Year 1825, By C. & J. GREENWOOD', 1826. By permission of the British Library (Maps 1,335(27)).

Clearly, communications were a vital factor in this process of industrial growth and social evolution. Victorian maps display a mass of signs for roads, lanes, droveways, bridleways, tracks, toll-bars, canals, fords, ferries, railways, tunnels, bridges, stations, and so on. The traditional dependence on the improved navigable river for inland commercial transport had long since given way under the pressure of increased trade to reliance on canals, made possible in part by the development of new levelling instruments in

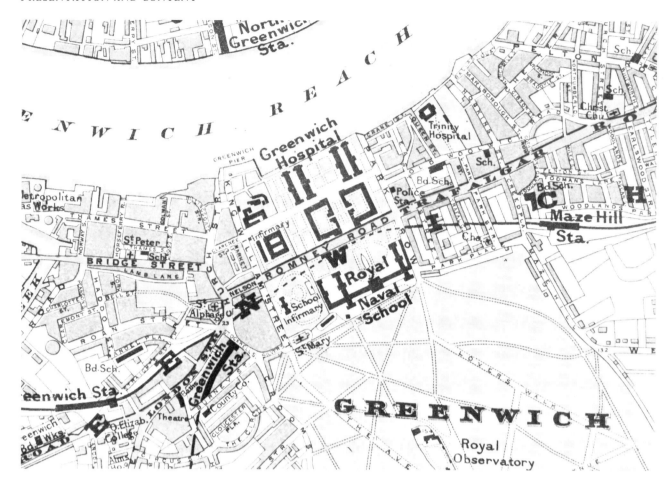

the previous century. The Victorian age saw the emergence of the railway as the dominant transport form and the spread of the turnpike system of road improvement. Map-makers emphasized changing transport facilities and route-finding by concentrating on road, water and rail informa-tion, often at the expense of other features. Maps were produced specifically to cater for different types of trans-port, providing specialist information for the users of turn-pikes, canals and rivers, for railway and steamship travellers, and later for cyclists and motorists. The Ordnance Survey attempted to engrave new railways as soon as they were opened but the task of up-dating roads on the same basis was too great. In contrast, commercial map-makers rarely waited for a canal or railway to be opened—mere projection was sufficient for them to add it to their maps and fre-quently schemes destined never to be built appeared as fact on maps.

BOUNDARIES
In contrast to the general agreement which characterized most aspects of the content of Victorian maps, the choice of boundaries to be shown proved troublesome, reflecting different views of their relative importance. There evolved during the age a profusion of boundaries with justifiable claims to representation—county, city, barony, town, par-ish, ward, field, parliamentary borough, Poor Law union, county-court district, rural deanery, postal district, registra-tion district, metropolitan local-management district, sani-tary district, and so on. Although a few eighteenth-century large-scale maps, such as Thomas Martyn's Cornwall (1748) and John Rocque's Middlesex (1754) and Berkshire (1761), had included parish boundaries, it was only when the Greenwoods produced their large-scale county series and the Ordnance Survey issued the 'Index to the Tithe Survey'

that these boundaries were mapped for most of the country (however, then only with great difficulty for the location of many boundaries was vague and not recorded on any local maps). Likewise, a few large-scale eighteenth-century maps and the 'Mudge' map of Kent had marked field boundaries, but the whole of England was not covered until the com-pletion of the 6″ Ordnance series. Only gradually did some order emerge from this confusion, led, of course, by the Ordnance Survey. Legislation in 1841 placed the responsi-bility for ascertaining and recording public boundaries in Great Britain and the Isle of Man on the Board of Ord-nance; the county index maps to the 25″ Ordnance series marked parish boundaries throughout; in 1879 the boun-daries of ecclesiastical parishes, hundreds, and wapentakes were replaced by civil parishes on Survey maps; and in 1887 the Ordnance introduced urban districts, in 1888 Poor Law unions, and in 1899 rural districts. In Ireland, parliamentary borough boundaries had been mapped in 1831–2, as they had been for the rest of Britain, and in the late 1830s and '40s there followed the delineation of the municipal boundaries, the petty-session districts, the elec-toral divisions, and the Poor Law unions following the Irish Poor Relief Act of 1838. (The decision to introduce the Poor Law and poor rates to Ireland in 1824 had been car-tographically far-reaching because it required a survey on a sufficient scale to satisfy cadastral and valuation re-quirements. Consequently, since there was no local supply of competent land surveyors, the Ordnance Survey had been given the task of conducting a general survey of the country at the minimum satisfactory scale of 6″ to provide the basis for a general and uniform valuation.) Map-pub-lishers, in a competitive situation, realized the commercial necessity of incorporating the latest administrative changes into their maps as quickly as possible and, just as the Ord-

OPPOSITE

12: *Map-makers laid special emphasis on Victorian economic and social development by marking such novel features as railway stations, gas works, sewage pump stations, fire-brigade stations, police stations, theatres, board schools, infirmaries, hospitals, baths, and so on, in addition to the traditional concentration on churches and public buildings.*
Detail: 'STANFORD'S NEW MAP OF THE COUNTY OF LONDON'. '20 Sheets, On the Scale of Four Inches to a Mile. London: EDWARD STANFORD, 26 & 27, Cockspur Street, Charing Cross S.W. Geographer to Her Majesty the Queen'. 'London: Published by Edward Stanford ... Oct 1, 1894'. By courtesy of Richard Miller.

13: *Nineteenth-century change, in particular transport development and social legislation, created a proliferation of new conventional signs and up-dated information which could be added to existing maps quickly and cheaply during lithographic transfer and photolithography as Henry Collins did when transferring from Robert Rowe's original copper plates. Similarly, Stanfords added signs to the Ordnance Survey 1" map representing 'earthworks; megalithic remains; coins and miscellaneous; villas, buildings &c; camps; walled towns; Roman roads; possible Roman roads; and Offa's Dyke' to create an 'Archaeological Map'.*
i *Detail: 'EXPLANATION' from Nottinghamshire, published by Henry George Collins, 1852.*
ii *Detail: 'ARCHAEOLOGICAL MAP OF HEREFORDSHIRE',* from An Archaeological Survey of Herefordshire, *by Rev. J.O. Bevan, James Davies, and F. Haverfield, 1896.*

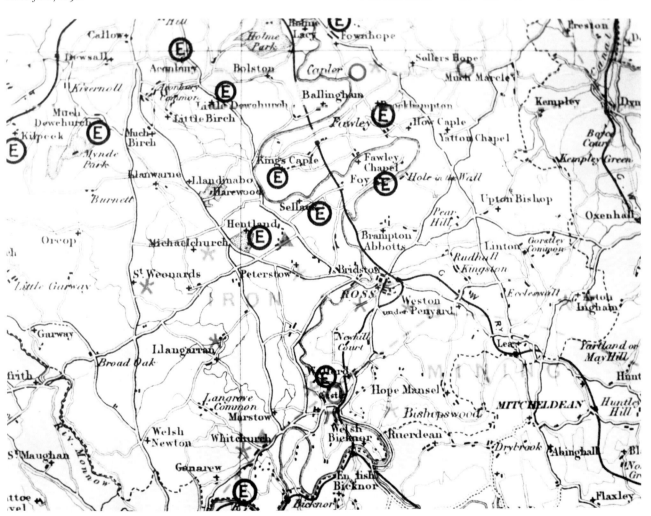

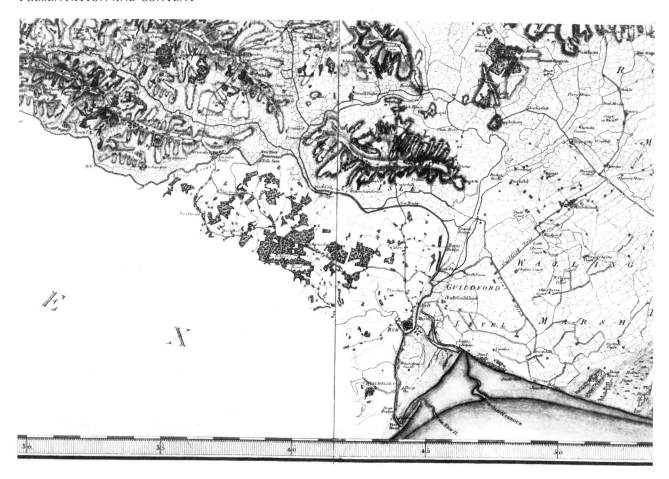

14: *The prototype Ordnance Survey map was printed from four copper plates designed to be mounted as a single map. The marking of field boundaries was abandoned by the Ordnance Survey at the 1″ scale after the publication of this 'Mudge' map of Kent.*
Detail: 'General Survey of ENGLAND and WALES. An entirely new & accurate Survey OF THE COUNTY of KENT WITH PART of the COUNTY of ESSEX, Done by the Surveying Draftsmen of his Majesty's honourable Board of Ordnance, on the basis of the Trigonometrical Survey carried on by their Orders under the direction of CAPTᴺ. W. MUDGE of the ROYAL ARTILLERY. F.R.S. London. Published by W. Faden, Geographer to His Majesty and to His Royal Highness the Prince of Wales. Charing Cross, January, 1ˢᵗ 1801.' By permission of the British Library (Maps 8c38).

nance Survey might produce special printings of its 25″ sheets to incorporate changes in local-government boundaries, so the commercial map-maker might issue simplified explanatory series spawned by such new legislation.

Although the census, first taken in 1801, only gradually evolved into a useful source of sociological data, it did in time develop into a prolific and fundamental source of information, the decennial appearance of which often stimulated the up-dating and re-issue of atlases. Map-makers added these population statistics to their maps and atlases in order to satisfy the widespread interest in population growth, internal redistribution and urbanization. In addition to this general use of census data and derived maps of population density and distribution, four sets of maps were produced specifically to accompany the Censuses of 1831, 1851, 1871, and 1891 respectively, which proved a ready-made source of cartographically analysed Census findings for map-makers.

The 1831 lithographed maps of grouped counties were divided into 'Parish-Register Limits', gave tables of population statistics around the map for each county, and on the map face, for each area, listed population figures for 1801, 1811, 1821, and 1831, and baptism, burial and marriage figures for 1800, 1810, 1820, and 1830.

The 1851 divisional maps bore the signatures 'W Bone Del' and 'Day & Son, Lithʳˢ to the Queen', and denoted only registration counties and registration districts, with the districts listed with their 'Area in Acres' and the 1851 population.

The 1871 divisional maps of registration districts covering the 11 registration divisions were 'LITHOGRAPHED BY W. & A.K. JOHNSTON, 74 STRAND.' 'The population of each town (in 1871) is shewn in round numbers by the character of the lettering of its name, as well as by the symbol which indicates its position. In the case of towns which have a population of between 10,000 and 250,000 each black dot (●) represents 10,000 inhabitants.'

The 1891 Census maps were adapted from the 1871 maps by the deletion of the lithographers' signature and the addition of a 'Reference to Boundaries & Symbols' defining registration divisions, registration counties, registration districts, registration district symbols, and registration county symbols. A note describing 'Detached portions' was also added.

The persistence of a Poor Law expenditure of around seven million pounds a year combined with the pessimistic preaching of Malthus, the new economics of Smith and Ricardo, and the utilitarianism of Bentham, persuaded the government of the need for Poor Law reform. Parishes were consequently combined into unions in 1834 'for the purpose of workhouse management, and for providing new workhouses where necessary',[22] and, thus, a new set of bound-

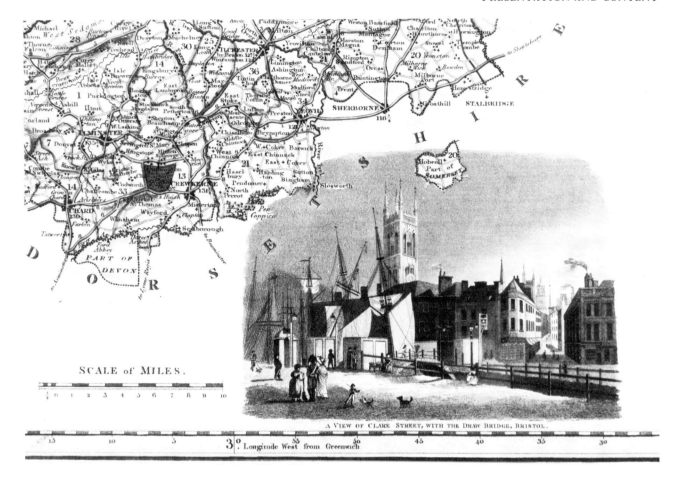

SCALE of MILES.

A VIEW OF CLARE STREET, WITH THE DRAW BRIDGE, BRISTOL.

Longitude West from Greenwich

15: *'Insulated parcels' of one county located within the boundaries of another were a tiresome complication which interfered with a map's overall design.*
Details Somerset, by Thomas Dix, published by William Darton, 1822, in A Complete Atlas of the English Counties.

aries was added to maps—'the most convenient limit of unions ... a circle, taking a market town as centre and comprehending those surrounding parishes whose inhabitants are accustomed to resort to the same market'.[23] In addition to their incorporation on contemporary maps, these new union boundaries had a more significant long-term effect, for the Commissioners 'proceeded without much regard either to ... ancient divisions or to the county boundaries' and, consequently, cut across the boundaries of the traditional hundred and county, so helping to undermine the divisions commonly accepted by map-makers and contributing to the decline of the county as the standard unit of cartographic representation. In time the Poor Law unions became the basis for the formation of rural districts, generating, in turn, maps 'adapted to display the rural districts'[25] as in *Philips' Handy Administrative Atlas* of *c*.1908.

'Insulated parcels'[26] of one county located within the boundaries of another were an annoying complication for the map-maker, particularly when producing a county map. Some, such as Andrew Bryant, reacted simply by ignoring the most troublesome detached areas, whilst others, like Thomas Dix, refused to allow the offending detachments to interfere with the overall design and balance of their maps. In contrast, map-makers such as the Greenwoods took pains to represent such areas accurately in their true positions. The question was investigated in 1825, and some aspects of administration were transferred before 1844 when the

County Boundaries Act rationalized the administration of separated sections. This and other related legislation 'merged liberties and the detached parts of counties for administrative purposes in the counties in which they were entirely surrounded, with the exception of a few specially exempted cases ...'[27] Nevertheless, in 1882 the Ordnance Survey was still complaining that the 'difficulty of dealing with the boundaries is greatly increased by the large number of detached portions of counties and parishes which exist and which give rise to great complications'.[28] Consequently the Boundary Commissioners of 1888 'recommended the merger of all those parts of counties which are wholly or nearly detached from the county, in the county in which they are situate for union purposes, or by which they are entirely surrounded'.[29] However, responsibility for a few parcels was still being transferred at the end of the century. Similarly, 'Parishes and Townships which extend into two or more counties'[30] were investigated in 1826 and the Divided Parishes Acts of 1876, 1879, and 1882 provided for the alteration of county boundaries to correspond with changes in parish boundaries made under those acts.

Undoubtedly, the most cartographically significant legislative changes were the series of reforms extending the franchise which required extensive alteration of existing material and the publication of special explanatory maps. The First Reform Act of 1832 was the best-mapped legislation of the century with each proposed change and the final reforms fully illustrated not only officially by Robert Kearsley Dawson on both county maps and town plans, but also by such unofficial plagiarists as Samuel Lewis. The Boundary Commissioners appointed 'to inquire into the temporary Boundaries of every Borough constituted by' Disraeli's Reform Act of 1867 and 'also ... into the Boundaries of every other Borough in England and Wales ...' placed heavy demands

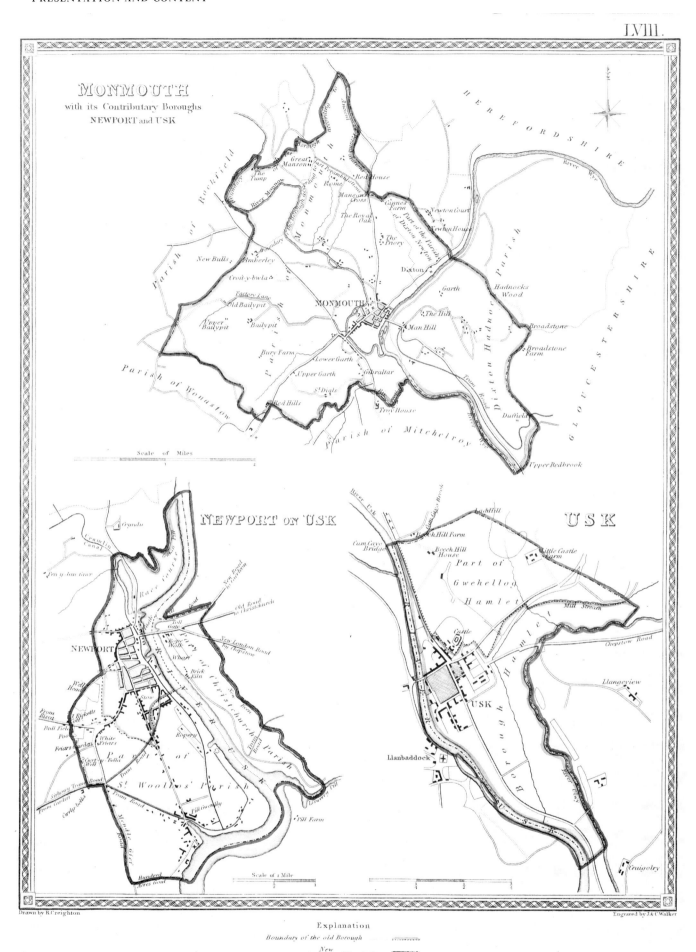

on the Ordnance Survey; the Survey was required to prepare specially for the Commissioners 13 county sets, showing boundaries of parliamentary divisions, hundreds, wapentakes, and parish and petty-sessional divisions, and 207 borough sets showing the parliamentary, parish, and municipal boundaries. The final report was accompanied by 530,352 hand-coloured plans, printed by the Stationery Office because the Ordnance could not cope with the volume, showing the extensions or alterations to boundaries which were being recommended to Parliament. The Redistribution of Seats Act of 1885, which followed the Reform Act of the previous year, also proved onerous for the Ordnance which was again charged with producing the accompanying maps.

The desire to simplify and codify this profusion of often conflicting boundary legislation and to rationalize '... irregularity of their outline, the spreading of towns, especially where a river was the line of separation, the growth of fresh centres of business and administration common to portions of more than one county, and the difficulties thereby placed in the way of the solution of urgent questions of administration'[32] led to the Local Government (Boundaries) Act of 1887 which established Boundary Commissioners to consider the adjustment of the 'boundaries of the county and of other areas of local government as to arrange that no union, borough, sanitary district, or parish shall be situate in more than one county ...'[32] Once again the requirements of the Commissioners imposed a heavy burden on the Ordnance Survey, requiring specially prepared maps of English and Welsh counties and plans of 47 towns.

ANTIQUITIES

The Ordnance Survey led the development of two other aspects of the Victorian map—the representation of archaeological remains and the use of lettering and writing styles as a means of representation—establishing conventions which were inevitably adopted by private-sector map makers. In the previous century the market for county maps was mostly classically educated and it was, therefore, commercially sensible to pander to antiquarian pretensions by the marking of archaeological features. The Romantic Movement provided a further stimulus to the presentation of such information and, consequently, although there was no positive policy in the early days, antiquities were marked on Ordnance maps with varying emphasis depending on the individual surveyor's interest and access to local antiquarian information. However, from about 1816 the Survey adopted a more positive attitude towards the marking of antiquities and, henceforth, they were portrayed with increasing frequency and care, although there was always a lack of specialist guidance for a surveying force without special skills in archaeology. Similarly, although lettering and writing styles had been used on earlier maps to differentiate representation, the Ordnance Survey carried this technique

forward, particularly through the work of its specialist writing-master Ebenezer Bourne—employed 'at 3 guineas per week'[33]—who introduced a refined use of elegant lettering, particularly for the definition of antiquities.

It is perhaps surprising that pioneering as the Ordnance Survey was in its use of signs and lettering, it should be so apparently unhelpful in its explanation of them. The profusion of signs and writing styles could not easily be read without reference to a characteristic sheet, but the Ordnance was decidedly slow in recognizing this need and its early maps bore no key to signs or lettering styles. In contrast, commercial map-makers, particularly the Greenwoods and their rival Bryant, took pains to explain their sign-use clearly even on smaller-scale maps.

ORTHOGRAPHY

The Ordnance Survey also takes credit for settling another long-standing cause of confusion and disagreement—the regularization of the spelling of place-names—which had troubled map-makers for many years. John Cary, for example, in advertising 'a large MAP of ENGLAND and WALES, which he is now engraving' in 1787, promised to pay 'a particular attention ... to the Orthography of this Map, a circumstance so frequently complained of, (owing to the difference of pronunciation from the locality of situation) ...'.[34] The traditional practice of establishing place-names by local enquiry and verifying spellings with local 'experts' was adopted by the Survey in its early years, but inevitably it led often to several alternative versions, determined not least by varying pronunciation and phonetic representation. This established technique was justified by Cary in 1823. 'I cannot hope to render my map correct without the aid of gentlemen possessed of local information—any errors which may be observed in the spelling of the names corrected.'[35] Other map-makers, however, were content to be more slap-dash; the Greenwoods, for example, surprisingly excused their orthography by appealing 'to the liberality of the reader' because 'from the nature of the compilation, error is unavoidable'.[36] The Survey Act of 1841 allowed names to be collected more effectively by the Ordnance, not least because it provided a legal authority for name collection which could overcome the obstruction of suspicious residents. However, the crucial advance was the introduction of the practice of keeping parish namebooks, recording historical and agreed modern spellings, initially to the Irish Survey about 1830, and to England and Wales when the 6″ survey started in 1840. Increasingly the Survey reduced its dependence on unreliable local sources. Instead: 'The greatest care is taken to obtain the correct orthography of the names to appear upon the Ordnance Plans and that no names of importance are omitted. The detail examiner obtaining the names with the residential authorities, these are further verified by the superintendent of the party or other competent person who finally examines the whole of the work and then compares the names locally collected with the extracts supplied to him.'[37] Predictably the standardization of Irish and Welsh place-names posed particular problems, but the Survey was generally sympathetic to national language forms and preferred not to anglicize local names; these Welsh and Gaelic names were, however, to be a source of continuing argument long after English names had achieved widespread acceptance. The fact that a name, once established, would only be altered with the support of 'at least two good authorities'[38] meant that in most cases the Ordnance's chosen name was here to stay since 'names which have already appeared on the Ordnance Survey maps

16: *Boundary legislation and franchise reform generated the production of maps, both official and unofficial, explaining the changes and new provisions. Samuel Lewis produced unofficial versions of both borough plans and county maps, in 1835, in his* View of the Representative History of England. *'MONMOUTH with its Contributary Boroughs NEWPORT and USK', engraved by J. & C. Walker, drawn by R. Creighton, published by Samuel Lewis in* View of the Representative History of England, *1835.*

should not be altered, or new names inserted, except on the best authority'.[38] Generally, once an Ordnance spelling had been engraved, it became acceptable to most authorities and it seems that only obvious omissions and inaccuracies were pointed out by landowners and local 'experts' who were otherwise content to adopt the official version.

RELIEF

As in previous centuries, the map-maker's most trouble-some problem was the representation of relief; a subject which caused much controversy in the early years of the century. The relatively crude hachuring of the eighteenth century was gradually refined into a more effective tech-nique as engravers developed their skill and experience, but inevitably features were either over- or under-emphasized and it was felt that the 'system fails ... in representing long slopes and gentle undulations'.[39] In Europe cartographers, particularly Lehmann, who suggested varying hachure width according to angle of slope, sought to develop the hachuring technique into a precise mathematical form using a minutely graded system of hachures—the 'scale of shade'[40]—to depict slope. In Britain, commercial map-mak-ers were content to rely on imprecise cheaper techniques. However, there was evidence of improvement; William Smith, for example, boasted that his geological discoveries improved the '... Art of Mapmaking ... Mr. Cary and Mr. Arrowsmith, in their new Maps having evidently attended to the courses of the Strata in their shading of the Hills'.[41] Such imprecision was not tolerable for the military whose general manoeuvres depended totally on angle of slope and whose artillery needed an accurate representation of both relative height and slope angle. Consequently, the Ordnance Survey developed a highly sophisticated form of hachuring, based on the skills of the field sketcher and the engraver, which presented an almost three-dimensional view of the landscape.

Although the system was picturesque and effective, pro-ducing beautiful, elegant relief representation, it was never very accurate and always uneconomic in its use of labour, since both sketching and engraving were lengthy, skilled, and expensive processes. Such a system, based, as it was said, on 'taste, imagination and fancy',[42] was inappropriate to an increasingly precise age, particularly to the demands of mapping fortifications. Despite spirited defence by its proponents, it became increasingly clear as the century pro-gressed that it was not sufficient to combine the artist's skilful use of light and perspective with only a generalized knowledge of land forms and geological structure to produce drawings 'from nature'[43] from which the engraver would hachure the landscape. The compulsory drawing classes teaching Dawson's hill-sketching methods at all military schools were an anachronism in an age when the increasing complexity of settlement and development demanded a clearer topographical representation—not one cluttered with elegant, imprecise, unstandardized hachures. Equally, a more extensive use of the spot height, used on some larger scales, could not solve the problem of accurate delineation.

In an effort to attain greater precision, hill sketching was brought under the control of contouring which was to pro-vide guidelines to the sketcher, firstly in Ireland about 1840 and in Great Britain from about 1843, so that all hachuring became based on contours. Lines of equal depth, first used in 1584 by Pieter Bruinsz to map the River Spaarne and developed from 1697 by Ancellin, Blackmore, Cruquius, and Buache, had been adapted by Continental military to-pographers to represent land elevations towards the end of the eighteenth century, and this 'French mode'[44] of repre-sentation was taught to English engineer cadets, possibly as early as 1803, and was certainly familiar and widely used by the 1840s. However, although the contours controlled the hill sketching, they did not appear on the finished map. An alternative, but unadopted, suggestion was that the Survey should employ Van Gorkum's method of contouring at equal intervals and joining them with equally spaced per-pendicular lines to indicate slope, giving a visual impression of the ground. Carmichael-Smyth, the advocate of Van Gorkum's method, presented the case against hachures: '... the draftsman was deceived by the seemingly great appearance of ... small objects when seen by him on the ground entire and close above his eye, and particularly as he cannot at the same time see—as a whole—the mountains of which they form part so as to be able to form a just estimate of their relative importance. The contours on the contrary exhibit the mountains with their proper impor-tance on the scale.... A drawing based on contours at once clearly defines the mountain on the map with all its subor-dinate prominences, but a drawing founded merely on sketches will imperfectly define these objects except by re-ference to the ground, particularly when the representation is made by hachures, as they increase the isolation of small parts and therefore considerably add to the difficulty of defining an entire feature. The effects will be that when the natural features are based on contours the map itself will explain the ground but when they are founded merely on sketches a reference to the ground will frequently be neces-sary to explain the map.'[45]

Not surprisingly, the introduction of contours to the Survey's maps experienced teething-troubles. The first ex-periments were carried out in Ireland and contouring pro-per began in the Inishowen peninsula of County Donegal in 1839-40, followed closely by its introduction to the 6" series of England and Wales. In comparison with the rest of the British Isles, Ireland suffered fluctuations of contour policy which eventually resulted in the publication of its Survey's maps without contours—instead of finishing Do-negal, Colby transferred his contourers to County Louth, but the first county to have contours published was Kil-kenny, for which they were engraved between 1846 and 1849 because the Louth contours were decidedly suspect and there was a ready-made excuse for not using them in that the county was not due for revision. Donegal, Derry, and Tyrone followed in the next decade, but the realization that the costs of contouring, instead of being 25 per cent cheaper than hachuring as predicted, were running at $12\frac{1}{2}$ per cent more expensive brought an abrupt halt to Irish contouring in 1857. Henceforth, contouring was confined to Britain and, with a few local exceptions, there was no further contouring in Ireland until 1890 when it was started again, being finished only in 1914. Consequently the Irish 6" maps lack contours (although some plates had them added later) whereas the British 6" have them.

An important result of these policy changes was to ge-nerate discussion and make contours more familiar as a means of representing the configuration of the landscape. By the late nineteenth century, contours had won the day and their introduction to all Survey and commercially pro-duced maps became merely a question of time and money, since they were clearly seen as superior to hachuring.

By the late nineteenth century the Ordnance Survey had developed a remarkable representation of the landscape with a contoured 6" series and a stunningly detailed 25" scale which introduced many features never previously recorded

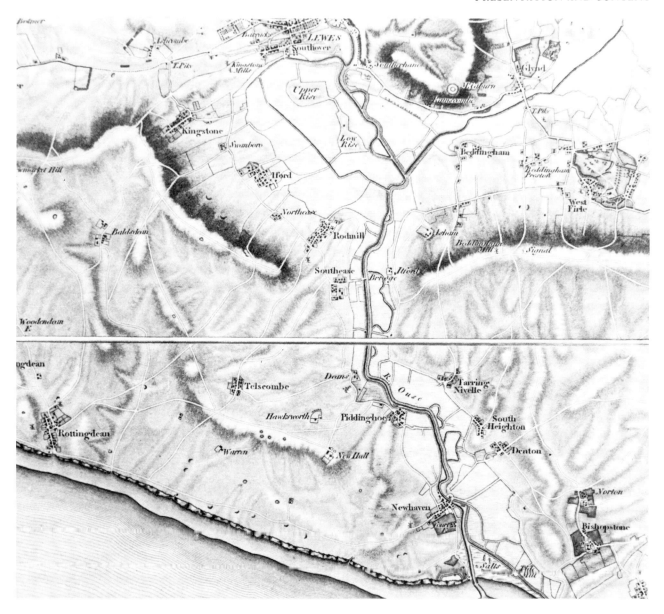

17: *The Ordnance Survey developed a highly sophisticated and effective style of hachuring which presented an almost three-dimensional view of the landscape. Detail: Ordnance Survey, 1″:1m.: Sheet V, Sussex, 1813. 'Engraved at the Drawing Room in the Tower of Benjm. Baker & Assistants ... The writing by Eben: Bourne. Published 1st Feb. 1813. by Lt Col! Mudge. Tower.' Reproduced from the 1″:1m. Ordnance Survey map.*

on maps. The latter series, which discontinued the representation of individual trees in hedgerows, flower beds, and bay windows only in 1892, provided all the source material any commercial map-maker could want with its detailed definition of natural and man-made features in exact plan. Such detail and accuracy had never been known before and would, henceforth, prove an endless source of information for the construction of smaller-scale maps. The Survey eventually realized that it too must exploit its data for a more general commercial market. George Washington Bacon's evidence to the Committee on Sale of Ordnance Survey Maps in 1896 clearly highlighted the Survey's uncompetitiveness in comparison with commercial rivals who produced maps aimed at the popular market. He was asked if the reason for the private sector's dominance in the field of travelling maps was 'Because they are better adapted for the purposes for which the public buys maps? ... Yes,

certainly, the general travelling public.... Following that up, I assume it is not merely a question of scale with the travelling public, but also of how the map is mounted and got up; so that, for instance, it can be put conveniently into the pocket? ... Yes, printed on thin paper, but strong paper, for folding up in the pocket.'[46] Consequently, during the 1890s, the Survey made a deliberate effort to make its 1″ maps more attractive to the public in general by tinting hachures light brown so that they did not obscure other features, by colouring water, roads, woods, and contours, by adding a list of conventional signs, and generally by making the maps clearer for route-finding. The Ordnance Survey's acceptance of the need to print its maps in colour was symptomatic of the increasing awareness of the commercial importance and potential of the use of colour.

COLOUR
With the exception of a few isolated experiments, maps were still being coloured entirely by hand at the start of the Victorian age, since metal engraving could not print areas of solid colour except through simulation by covering the area with closely spaced ruled patterns or a dense spread of small indentations. Hand colouring followed well-established and accepted conventions, initially determined by eighteenth-century military draughtsmen but by this time

internationally recognized despite the claim that it was Keith Johnston who introduced the practice of colouring water areas blue. Generally, blue represented water features; red settlements; ochre main roads; buff post roads; green open spaces, parkland, or pasture; brown upland or arable land, and so on. The complexity and sophistication of the best hand colouring can be judged from this description of the Military Survey of Scotland of *c*.1764: '... blue-green for water features, green for woodland, yellow for land under cultivation, buff for moors, grey washes of various tones for relief, solid red for houses, red outline for formal grounds, brown (a single line) for roads ...'[47] Clearly the colouring of maps was considered an important aspect of their production not only for the obvious reason that it distinguished physical features and political divisions more distinctly, but also because it was commercially desirable to render maps more saleable. James Wyld III commented: '... the public like pictures there is no doubt, and if a map is produced—I am speaking now purely commercially—if a map is produced artistically in the way of a pretty coloured picture, its chances of sale are very much better than if it is printed in black'.[48]

Colour, however, was not always seen as an advantage— the *Athenaeum*, for instance, in commenting on the map illustrating W.R. Wilde's sanitary report on Dublin in the 1841 Census report, criticized its use of 'different tints of blue, crimson, yellow, red, purple, and brown' to classify streets on the grounds that it 'would produce infinite discord and endless confusion. Those who live in a blue (or first-class) street, will turn up their noses at those who dwell in a crimson (or second-class) street; the inhabitants of crimson streets will look down on the inhabitants of yellow streets ..., we may confidently anticipate a rupture of all social relations. The influence of colours is prodigious ... We have no doubt that this egregious blunder in map-making will set ten thousand families, in Dublin, at loggerheads ...'[49] Similarly, in *Bacon's "Excelsior" Memory-Map Atlas*, Percy W. Ryde, F.R.G.S., 'Lecturer on Geography, at the Day Training College, Moorfield's, counselled students that 'Extensive colouring of an examination Map is a mistake, and it is useless to endeavour to hide defects by a liberal use of coloured pencils. A blue pencilled line can be allowed round the coast, but no shading of the seas should be attempted.'[50]

To suit all tastes, maps were usually offered for sale both plain and coloured at an appropriate price differential. George Bradshaw, for example, charged a 50 per cent premium for the colouring of some of his maps 'by careful and skilful artists';[57] the Greenwoods had a complex price-list distinguishing between various combinations of mounting and colouring and, in particular, having different prices for outline and full colour; and George Washington Bacon advertised his maps as '... coloured to suit any particular requirement'.[52] Always, map colouring was made as attractive as possible with soft and gentle tones deliberately used to appeal aesthetically when stronger colouring might well have proved more effective in differentiating features.

The best hand colouring was highly skilled. For example, water areas 'should be coloured blue. This may be done either by a wash or by water lining or by tints of blue, graduated to show the various depths of water. ... A wash may be either uniform or shaded'.[53] It required talented and therefore expensive exponents and it is not surprising that such quality increased a map's basic price greatly. Obviously, these exclusive items were aimed at a narrow 'luxury' market, but, despite their affluence, customers may

well have flinched at some of the more frighteningly exorbitant colouring and mounting prices and cast around for cheaper substitutes. In contrast, most map-makers saw colouring as one area of production where they could keep costs down despite the need for a large staff if most maps were to be sold coloured. Commercial map-makers frequently maintained extensive colouring departments; Philips, for example, employed as many as 80 'girl tinters', but it was also common for the work to be carried out by pauper 'apprentices' or other children (George Washington Bacon ingeniously offered £20 in prizes in order to recruit the pupils with the best map-drawing ability from the top classes of the London Board schools). It was also sub-contracted: 'In Edinburgh it was a popular occupation for decayed gentlewomen and spinsters with time on their hands.'[54] Later, in the period of lithographic-colour printing, Bartholomews always employed girls in its 'Tint Stones' department to prepare transfers and stones for colour reproduction. The employment of females in colouring was an unusual feature of map production; perhaps feminine intuition added an extra dimension to their colouring work! Paradoxically the most ardent economizer was the Ordnance Survey, perhaps because its 'extravagant' expenditure was continually under attack, with its insistent employment of 13- and 14-year-old lads to colour maps at between 6d. and 1s. a day—'... coloured by boys, who are supplied with approved specimens for their guidance. All surfaces of water are tinted with cyanine blue, ... buildings are tinted with liquid carmine, and roads with raw sienna. After being colored the impressions are subjected to hydraulic pressure between glazed boards for about 18 hours to improve their appearance ...'[55] Since it was calculated that the average cost of colouring the Survey's sheets was a penny-farthing each, but the extra charge for the colour was sixpence, the employment of youths should have proved highly profitable. However, the Survey was criticized for not giving value-for-money on the grounds that commercial map-makers could employ skilled, experienced, higher-paid colourists to colour Ordnance maps and could still sell these better-coloured maps profitably at the published prices.

The chief thorn in the flesh of the Ordnance and other official map-making organizations was James Wyld who, as M.P. for Bodmin, castigated their unrealistic estimates, their expenditure, and their use of military personnel instead of private surveyors: 'MR. WYLD thought the survey for the Sanitary Commission was entirely unnecessary. It was calculated that it would cost 25,000 l. But he was satisfied it would cost at least 200,000 l.';[56] 'MR WYLD said ... much money had been wasted in this survey.... It had already cost something like £2,000,000; an amount enormously exceeding what the French paid for their survey, which was as good or better ... the surveying, the engraving, and the commercial parts of the business were all ill-managed, while the Director General also had the most unlimited and uncontrolled power';[57] and 'MR WYLD said ... Metropolitan Sewers Commission ... calculated that the survey and plan would cost 61,000 l. It would cost more than five times that sum.'[58] Wyld, of course, was attempting to 'feather his own nest' by shifting cartographic work from the public to the private sector; his opposition, for example, to the 5′ survey of London was merely a means to promote his own large-scale map which he hoped the Metropolitan Commissioners of Sewers would pay for.

The summit of the hand-colourist's art came not on topographical maps but with the development of a nineteenth-century phenomenon which required the effective use of cartographic colour more than any maps before. The development of the thematic map, representing geographical relationships of physical and social data, required a sophisticated use of colour and tone in order to achieve its desired impact and to present its complex information by means of coloured overlays on a topographical base. Often such complexity could be distinguished only by colour; often only by a sophisticated use of colour tones, as Kombst, for example, did in using 'mixed colour, in such a manner that the colour predominant in the mixture points out the predominant national element' to identify the 'crossing of.... varieties or subvarieties' of the 'three great varieties of the Caucasian species' on his ethnographic map of Europe in Johnston's *National Atlas*.[59] Augustus Petermann used coloured signs to portray city population densities. Thomas Milne's magnificent land-utilization map of the London area used the technique of combining colours, engraving and letters to differentiate 17 types of land use; and the Board of Agriculture used colours to show soil texture and fertility. However, it was probably in the representation of geological features that hand colouring reached its apogee and that simultaneously its drawbacks became most pronounced, stimulating a more energetic search for a mechanical alternative.

Colour was first used on a geological map in 1775 by Gottlieb Gläser of Leipzig, and, following this lead, high standards of geological hand colouring were subsequently developed in England in the first half of the nineteenth century. The greatest work of all was undoubtedly William Smith's 'Map of the Strata' of 1815 for which the Royal Society of Arts awarded him a premium of £50. In general, prior to Smith's work, geological information had been represented only by signs showing where various rocks and minerals occurred. He rightly identified that this system's weakness was the problem of interpreting the signs and generalizing from them—'for want of some method of generalizing the information, which could only be supplied by a map that gives, in one view, the locality of thousands of specimens'.[60] His solution was to represent the strata by colours—'by strong lines of colour, the principal ranges of strata are rendered conspicuous, and naturally formed into classes, which may be seen and understood at a distance from the map, without distressing the eye to search for small characters. This is the advantage of colours over any other mode of representation'.[60] It is no surprise that it took his 'artist' from 14 to 22 May 1815 to produce the required tonal variations in the 20 different colours used and to achieve the fading-away of the colour from the basal edge of each outcrop to emphasize the dip of the strata. Smith adopted a system of associative colouring, the chosen colour being as close as possible to the natural colour of the rock. 'The colours, though brighter than those they represent, are in some degree assimilated to the colour of each stratum, except the chalk, which being colourless, seemed best represented by green, strong colours being necessary and no stratum of equal extent requiring that colour.'[60] The wise choice of colouring was fortunate, for the system was followed by other contemporary geological map-makers and adopted by the Geological Survey, thus establishing an on-going colouring tradition; it was defied only by cheap, hideously coloured geological maps compiled by the private sector from official sources for the popular market later in the century. The Geological Survey recorded a fitting tribute to Smith's most influential map in 1840: 'In the distribution of pigments he endeavoured to accommodate the colour of the pigment to that of the substance represented;

to apply to substances mineralogically similar, similar tints; to place in juxta-position those colours only which would either harmonize or contrast, as the occasion might require; to confine the opake colours to those parts of the map which are least charged with engraving; to reserve the most forcible colours for the smaller spaces; to denot marked differences in adjoining rocks by strong opposition of hue; and lastly, to apply the brightest colours to the centre, carrying them off by gradation towards the extremities. All these objects ... can rarely be attained in any case, but all were taken into consideration before the colouring of any portion was finally decided upon.'[61]

In one sense, Smith's map spelt doom for hand colouring for it set standards so high that few others could reach them and there was a growing dissatisfaction with the limitations of lesser hand colouring. Such quality colouring could be achieved only by the most skilled and therefore the most expensive artists, but, in general, results rarely justified the expenditure. It is recorded, for example, that Cary 'paid liberally for the labour, it was not always at first properly performed'.[62] Complaints increased over the incorrect colour copying of the 1″ Geological Survey maps which, in any case, could not be sold at a price which covered hand-colouring costs. The Survey was forced to create its own hand-colouring department, much against its will, because sub-contractors could not cope with the demand for coloured revised geological sheets. Thus, the pressure for cheap colour-printed maps became more insistent, inducing greater effort in the search for new and improved mechanical colour representation.

Colouring costs were becoming a major headache and it is understandable, for example, that many of the Ordnance Survey's customers preferred plain plans at 2s. rather than coloured at 5s., a differential of 150 per cent just for the colouring. However, customers often experienced difficulty in obtaining uncoloured maps because retailers earned extra profit by selling the coloured—'... for a town plan costing 10s to colour the public paid 15s.'.[63] Further problems concerned multi-sheet maps, particularly Ordnance sheets, which often had to be recoloured by retailers in order to match the colours on adjoining sheets 'to make the map look anything like passable',[64] and the time taken to meet specific orders—'it is a comparatively quick business printing one ... uncoloured. It is done with comparative promptness, but it takes sometimes two or three weeks to colour one of them'.[65]

Despite the introduction of mechanical colouring, manual colouring, both freehand and using stencils, continued throughout the century until the early 1900s. Although increasingly common after the 1840s and familiar by the 1860s, it was not until the 1880s that coloured maps were generally printed by power-driven lithographic machines, but even then hand colouring lingered on; the first colour-printed Geological Survey map appeared only in 1902, hand colouring of the Ordnance 1″ map ceased in the same year, and the 25″ Ordnance plans were hand-coloured until 1909. However, inevitably hand colouring had to give-way to new technologies which might keep pace with the mass production of maps. Immense labour was involved in a large-scale hand-colouring operation with the ever-present danger of human error (although in the early days of printed colour correct hand colouring was generally more accurate since it proved difficult to print colours exactly in position). It was essential to check the accuracy of each hand-coloured copy in order to ensure uniformity. Hence, costs were pushed up, again providing a growing incentive to find an alternative mechanical means of colouring—elevated eventually to a level at which mechanical costs, reduced by advancing technology, were more attractive than manual despite the expense of the additional stones or plates required and the extra run needed to print each colour. In some cases the Ordnance Survey simply abandoned hand colouring altogether, as, for example, when in the 1870s it replaced grey (indicating thatch) and carmine (stone or slate roof) on its town plans by a uniform shading of ruled lines, and later, after 1893, by stipple. Similarly, on Irish Survey maps a 'ruling machine' was used to shade 'houses, demesnes & foreshores'.[66] This substitution was forced by the pressure of customer opinion—'... it was hard that they should have to pay 18s. or 20s. for a coloured map when they only wanted an uncoloured one at 3s.';[67] consequently, for the 25″ series the Survey 'introduced a system by which all new maps are shaded and stippled instead of coloured ... at 3s.'.[67] A more persuasive influence even than cost was the increasingly-loud demands of the military for a map that was easier to read, for the Survey was obviously particularly sensitive to the requirements of its powerful erstwhile masters.

The growing pressure for a mechanical means of uniform colour reproduction had been translated into experimental activity, and numerous examples of coloured lithographic printing are known from the beginning of the century. However, these were usually isolated experiments often involving the impractical use of several stones, and no satisfactory system was developed in the early decades. It appears that Charles Knight produced the first colour-printed atlas in England in 1840 using his relief process, patented in 1838, which printed colours in simple shapes, but it was lithography which was destined to provide the truly commercial means of colour reproduction through the development of chromolithography. The new era began about 1840. However, despite such early colour-printed examples as Captain John Washington's 1848 map of lighthouses in south-eastern Ireland, colour printing in Britain only came of age at the Great Exhibition of 1851 where the exhibits convinced publishers of its commercial potential.

As early as 1837 in England blue and yellow were overprinted to produce green, and in France in 1843 the Kaeppelin firm produced 11 colours on a geological map from four superimposed ink printings. By 1845 there were some 80 lithographic firms in Paris alone printing in colour. The work of Engelmann (who patented 'chromolithographie' in Paris in 1837), Hullmandel, Day and Haghe had created chromolithography and, henceforth, as techniques developed into a commercially viable form, it was possible to ensure uniformity throughout the printing of an issue; it became possible also to eliminate the often baleful influence of the hand-colourist who could easily corrupt topographical information when laying the colour design directly onto the lithographic stone. A technical revolution had been induced bearing a process which reproduced flat colour and, although knowledge and use of the technique spread slowly, inevitably hand colouring was dead. Now the map-maker had to hand a more flexible and expressive device of representation than ever before; a tool which allowed him to use colour independently to present a variety of information with greater clarity. In time, as technique developed, it became possible to print up to 40 different colours and shades from just three stones of the primary colours red, yellow, and blue; and to ensure perfect register (the printing of the colours in the right place—an essential much simplified by the introduction of heliozincography in the last years

of the century) by frames with pins attached to the printing press and the use of punched printing paper. Thus was overcome a long-standing problem of all experiments with non-manual colouring which had helped as much as anything to maintain colouring by hand. However, since each colour was printed onto the map from a separate stone or plate bearing a matching image, register was frequently inaccurate because it was extremely difficult to draw an exact replica of the original. Furthermore, the coloured image did not necessarily correspond with each printed map due to the fractional size variations induced by the pressure exerted by the printing press on dampened paper of varying moisture content.

Despite the use of chromolithography to print coloured maps for official reports from the 1840s, it was commercial publishers who were rather faster in recognizing the potential of the new technique than their official fellows. Philips replaced their staff of 'girl-tinters' by 'Senefelder's Lithographic Process'[68] to produce coloured maps on power-driven lithographic machines, and the first series of county maps with printed colour appear to be as early as c.1862-63, produced by George Philip for 'Philips' New Series of County Maps' and by William Hughes for his National Gazetteer. Perhaps the reason for the Ordnance Survey's slow attachment to chromolithography (experiments in colour were first mentioned only in 1886) was Colby's lack of enthusiasm for colour. In any case, the Survey's initial flirtation with colour was bedevilled by silly setbacks as, for example, when the experimental colour printing of hills on the Irish maps was abandoned due to a poor response from agents in Dublin, and when the Irish colour work was transferred to England because Dublin seemed able only to print expensive and poor-quality 'fully coloured'[69] maps at a very slow pace. However, by the early 1890s it was agreed, not least by the Dorington Committee, that both military and public required a 1″ map printed in five or six colours so that it would be easier to read. Despite Treasury opposition to such a 'spendthrift' scheme, a pilot project was approved which led to the publication of the experimental 1″ map in colour, with detail in black, water in blue, hachures in brown, first and second class roads in 'burnt sienna', and contours in red. This combination gave the map an overall brown tinge which was reduced only by adding green for woods in 1904. The result was disappointing and generally considered to be inferior to commercial equivalents. The coloured 1″ map was not completed for England and Wales until 1903, by which time Scotland had not been started at all and Ireland was only half-covered. Despite its drawbacks, the new coloured map was more legible than its predecessors and, although technically inferior to commercial competition, was much favoured by the public.

The first English colour-printed geological map (of Yorkshire), by John Phillips, the orphaned nephew of William Smith, appeared in 1853 during a period in which chromolithography was rapidly adapted to geological use. Other early colour-printed geological maps were produced by Vincent Brooks of Covent Garden for the Geological Society. Between 1889 and 1896 the Geological Survey published colour-printed 1/4″ maps at a cost which compared very favourably with the production of the hand-coloured 1″ maps. In 1902 the Survey finally began production of a colour-printed 1″ series which was notably successful both being better-coloured than the earlier hand-coloured series and having lower production costs. Experiments in more effective colour printing of geological features led to the development of the printing of colours using prefabricated

18: *The calligraphic exuberance of the Ordnance Survey ensured that decorative lettering continued to ornament Victorian maps when most other embellishment had disappeared.*
Detail: 'MAP of the County of SOMERSET from an Actual Survey, made in the Years 1820 & 1821. BY C. & I. GREENWOOD, Published by the Proprietors C. GREENWOOD & C⁰ 13, Regent Street Pall Mall, LONDON. CORRECTED TO THE PRESENT PERIOD AND PUBLISHED JULY 4.ᵀ·ᴴ 1829'.

19: *The vignette became such a refined art-form that draughtsmen and engravers sometimes specialized in this popular decoration and were credited for their vignette work whilst the actual map was prepared by other specialists.*
Detail: Vignette of Dublin, drawn by John Salmon and engraved by Robert Wallis, from Ireland, published c.1851 by John Tallis in The Illustrated Atlas and Modern History of the World.

paper sheets. These produced textures or patterns in the flat colour when transferred to the stone.

Printed colour was, likewise, adapted to the representation of sociological data; for example, Booth's great survey of poverty in London, published from 1889, based on a massive house-to-house enquiry, was illustrated by the overprinting of the central portion of Stanford's 'Library Map of London' with a colour categorization of social class ranging from black (representing the poor and semi-criminal) to gold (for the wealthiest). The choice and application of Booth's colours created not only a detailed picture of social conditions in each street but also a more significant overall impact by exposing the unexpected extent of London poverty. However, despite technical advance it was still impossible to vary colour sufficiently to account for all the shades of poverty and comfort as Booth admitted, recognizing the failure of his limited system of colour combinations to represent a mixture of living standards—'at best the graphic expression of almost infinate complication and endless variety of circumstance cannot but be imperfect, and a rainbow of colour could not accomplish it completely.'[70]

The most effective innovation in the use of printed colour was John Bartholomew's development of layer colouring which, combined with contours, achieved the most successful means of showing map relief—a method destined to become universally accepted.

Experiments from about the turn of the century gradually made layer colouring familiar not only for altitudes but also for other themes delineated by lines of equal value, and through the influence of Berghaus it became established amongst German cartographers. Despite Larcom's use of the technique in 1845 on a map of Ireland accompanying a report on land occupation, it was effectively Bartholomew who introduced the method to Britain in M.J.B. Baddeley's 'Thorough Guide' to the *English Lake District* ('With 15 Maps, General and Sectional (Corrected up to date from the Ordnance Survey)'[71]) in 1880 despite the generally unfavourable reaction to his display of the method at the Paris Exhibition of 1878. However, it was his use of layer colouring on his 1/2″ maps from 1888 that popularized the method to such an extent that it was adopted by the Ordnance Survey in 1902. '... John Bartholomew's contour layer colouring, each step of 100 feet or so (the intervals varied in the series he first made famous with it) having its own colour. There were delicate tints of green and brown for the plains and foothills, shading to deep brown and purple for the highlands and touches of white for the Matterhorns and Jungfraus. He extended the system to cover the seas: pale blue denoted shallow water, the darkest ultramarine the profound depths of ocean trenches.'[72] At last the map-maker had a means of representing relief in an easily and quickly intelligible manner; the public's enthusiasm for the system was sufficient to overcome the cartographer's conservatism and layer colouring came into widespread use.

DECORATION

The influence of the Ordnance Survey was all-powerful in driving most of the irrelevant decoration and calculated symbolism, so prominent in earlier periods, from the maps produced by commercial publishers during the Victorian age. Admittedly some map-makers carried on earlier traditions at the beginning of the century, but they were a dying breed; the Survey allowed itself only the concessions of ornamental lettering in its early titles and overall calligraphy, and the attractive 'piano-key' style frame; both widely adopted by such as Greenwood, Reynolds, Ebden, and

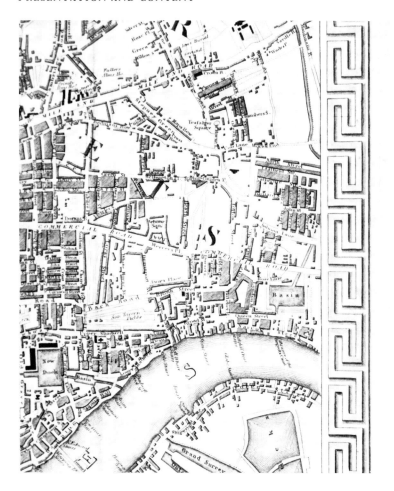

20: *Frames were constructed of vignettes to surround plans of towns. Detail: 'PLAN OF LONDON FROM ACTUAL SURVEY. 1833.', by John Shury.*

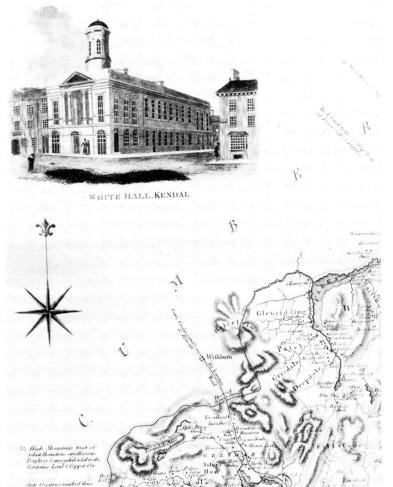

· WHITE HALL, KENDAL.

21: *In later life some of John Cary's large county-map series, first published together in 1809 in* Cary's New English Atlas, *were revamped with added vignettes and most were adapted to display the geological findings of William Smith for his incomplete geological atlas.*
Detail: Westmorland, by John Cary, 1829.

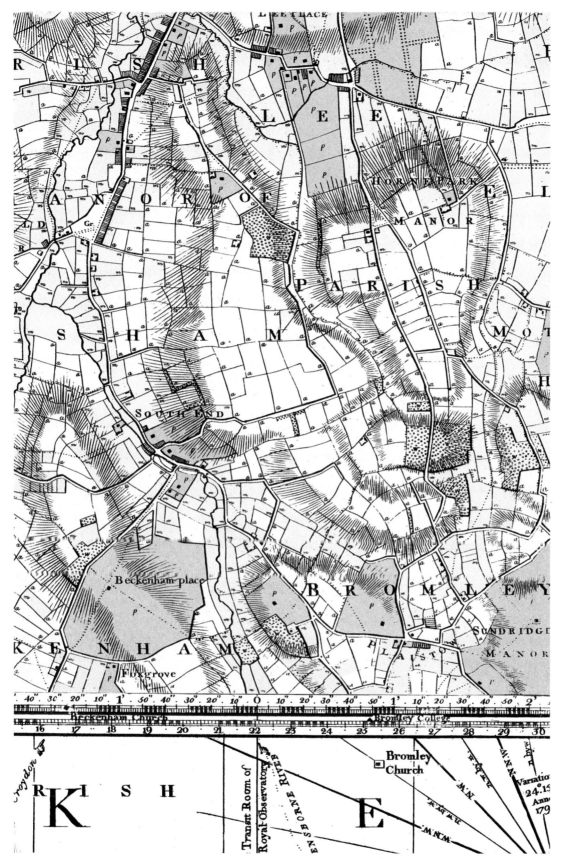

I: Thomas Milne used hand-painted colour to represent the use of fields, with pale brown for arable land, light green for enclosed meadow and pasture, dark green for woodland, light blue for enclosed market gardens, orange for nurseries, blue for orchards and osier beds, pink for 'Paddocks or Little Park,' grey-green for drained marshland pasture, brown for arable common fields, brown and green stripes for mixed arable and grass-strip common fields, solid green or green and brown bands for common meadow, and blue or blue and brown bands for common market-garden fields.

Detail: 'MILNE'S PLAN of the CITIES of LONDON and WESTMINSTER, circumadjacent TOWNS and PARISHES, &c, laid down from a TRIGONOMETRICAL SURVEY taken in the YEARS 1795-1799', 'Survey'd & Engrav'd by Thos Milne', 1800. By permission of the British Library (K Top VI 95).

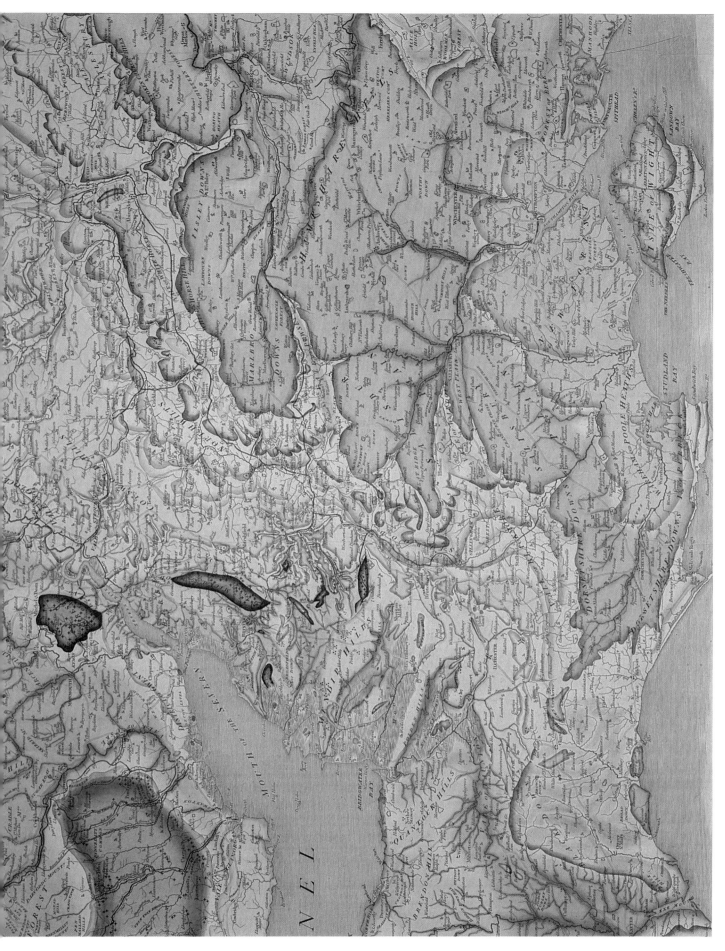

II: Detail: 'A DELINEATION OF THE STRATA OF ENGLAND AND WALES, WITH PART OF SCOTLAND; EXHIBITING THE COLLIERIES AND MINES, THE MARSHES AND FEN LANDS ORIGINALLY OVERFLOWED BY THE SEA, AND THE VARIETIES OF SOIL ACCORDING TO THE VARIATIONS IN THE SUBSTRATA, ILLUSTRATED by the MOST DESCRIPTIVE NAMES BY W. SMITH Augst 1. 1815.' By permission of the British Library (Maps 1180(20)).

III: The manual colouring of Geological Survey sheets was so time-consuming that production costs were pushed up to an unacceptable level. Such was the complexity of the colouring on most of the 1″ sheets that they could not be sold at a price which covered hand-colouring costs.

'Geological Survey of Great Britain. No LXXVIII S.E. (Bangor). Engraved in the Tower of London, at the ORDNANCE MAP OFFICE. The Outline & Writing by J. W. Froggett, the Hills & Water by J. Peake & Published by Colonel Colby, R.E. F.R.S. L.&E. M.R.I.A. &c. – Septr 30th 1841.' By courtesy of Jason Musgrave.

XIX

Engraved by J.& C.Walker

Drawn by R.Creighton

IV: Manual colouring was often surprisingly sophisticated in its combination of styles and its use of colour to differentiate the growing number of conventional signs. The map of Devonshire which appeared in Samuel Lewis's parliamentary atlas is coloured in outline to mark boundaries of county (pink), hundreds (yellow, blue, light green) and electoral divisions (dark green). Roads are marked in brown and the county boundary is edged with a subtle pink wash to make the county stand out from surrounding areas. Blue and red are used to pick out the parliamentary signs. The harmony of the colouring is enhanced by using pink and yellow to colour the outline title, the frame, the north point, and the scale bar; an attractive overall appearance is created, despite careless application, from colouring which is highly functional.

'Devonshire. Engraved by J. & C. Walker. Drawn by R. Creighton.' Published by Samuel Lewis, 1835.

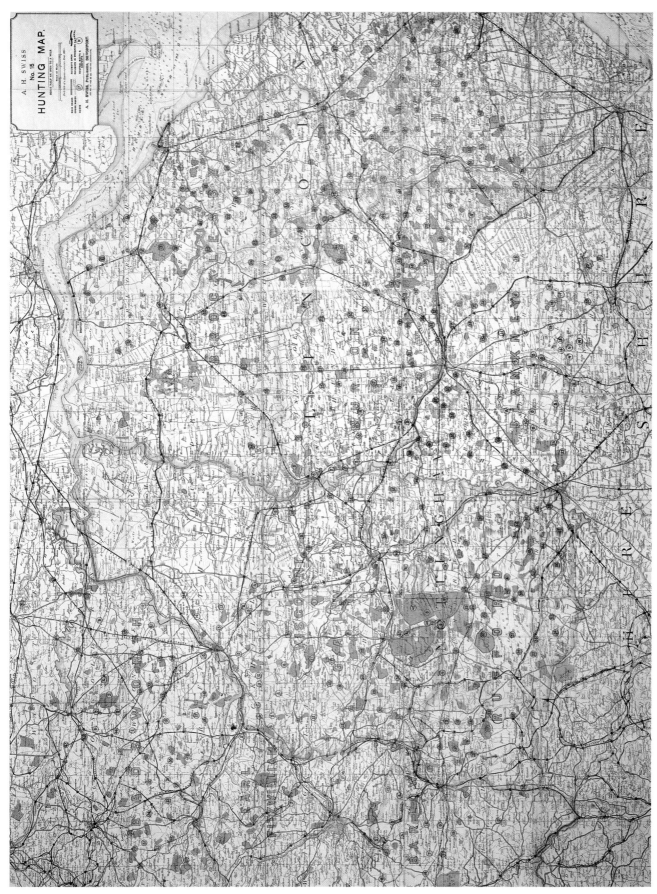

V: Lithographed colour offered greater opportunities for the use of colour for thematic representation. For his hunting maps, A. H. Swiss coloured 'each Hunt . . . as a "county," thus showing at a glance its boundary; which, it is hoped, will meet with the approval of those interested in the Hunts displayed thereon'. In addition to the colouring of roads, railways, woodland and water, each hunt is represented by a 'Distinguishing Color' of red, yellow, brown or green, with brighter colour to emphasize the boundaries and the name of the hunt picked out in bright blue. Numbered circles, brightly coloured to echo the hunt boundary, mark the hunt meeting places, and meets in areas shared 'by arrangement' are picked out in green, yellow and purple. 'Neutral meets & coverts' are marked with brown circles.

Detail: 'A H. SWISS' No. 15 Hunting Map. THE NOTTINGHAMSHIRE, LINCOLNSHIRE AND SOUTH YORKSHIRE DISTRICT'. Lithographed in blue by Gall & Inglis, c. 1888.

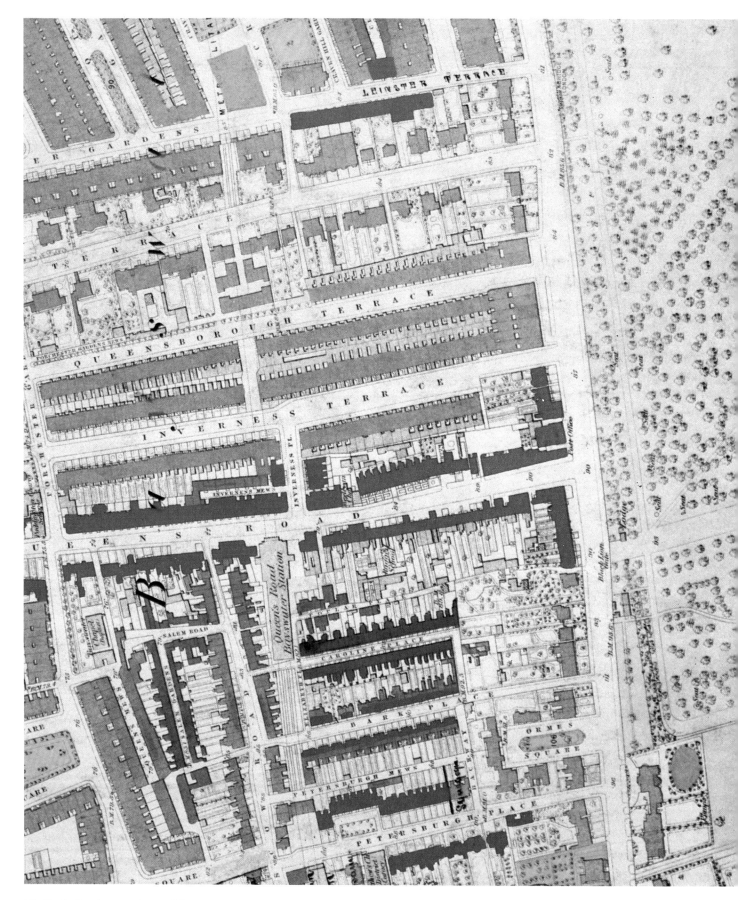

VI: Charles Booth used colour to differentiate the 'social condition of inhabitants', with yellow for 'wealthy' streets inhabited by families with three or more servants, red for 'well-to-do' streets inhabited mainly by middle-class families with one or two servants, pink for 'fairly comfortable', purple for 'poverty & comfort (mixed)', light blue for 'moderate poverty' streets inhabited mainly by low-income families, dark blue for 'very poor' streets inhabited mainly by casual labourers and suchlike, and black for the 'honest class' streets inhabited mainly by occasional labourers, vagrants, and petty criminals.

Detail: Bayswater from Booth's poverty map of London, 1899, produced to accompany his *Life and Labour of the People in London*. By permission of the Museum of London.

VII: Detail: Layer colouring. 'SECTION MAP No IX,' by John
Bartholomew, from the 'Thorough Guide' to the *English Lake District*,
by M. J. B. Baddeley, published by Dulau & Co., *c*. 1895.

SCOTLAND.

A gallant piper, struggling through the bogs,
His wind bag broken, wearing his clay clogs;

Yet, strong of heart, a fitting emblem makes
For Scotland—land of heroes and of cakes.

VIII: Printed colour offered an opportunity to make novelty maps more enticing and entertaining by colouring them brightly at nominal cost.

Scotland, from *Geographical Fun: being Humorous Outlines from Various Countries* by 'Aleph,' *c.* 1869. 'Chromolithographed by Vincent Brooks, Day & Son of London.' By courtesy of the Trustees of the National Library of Scotland.

A South View of **QUEEN ELIZABETH'S FREE GRAMMAR SCHOOL** in Tooley Street in the Parish of S. Olave. Southwark: *with a Plan of the adjacent Neighbourhood.*

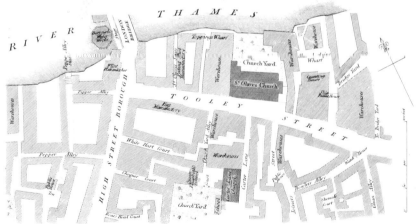

London. *Published 1. Dec.1813, by Rob. Wilkinson, N.º 58 Cornhill.*

22: *In some cases, the map was subsidiary to the illustration, merely locating the subject of the print within its neighbourhood or area, or delineating the plan of the buildings shown.*
'*A South View of QUEEN ELIZABETH'S FREE GRAMMAR SCHOOL in Tooley Street in the Parish of S. Olave. Southwark:* with a Plan of the adjacent Neighbourhood', *published by Robert Wilkinson, 1813.*

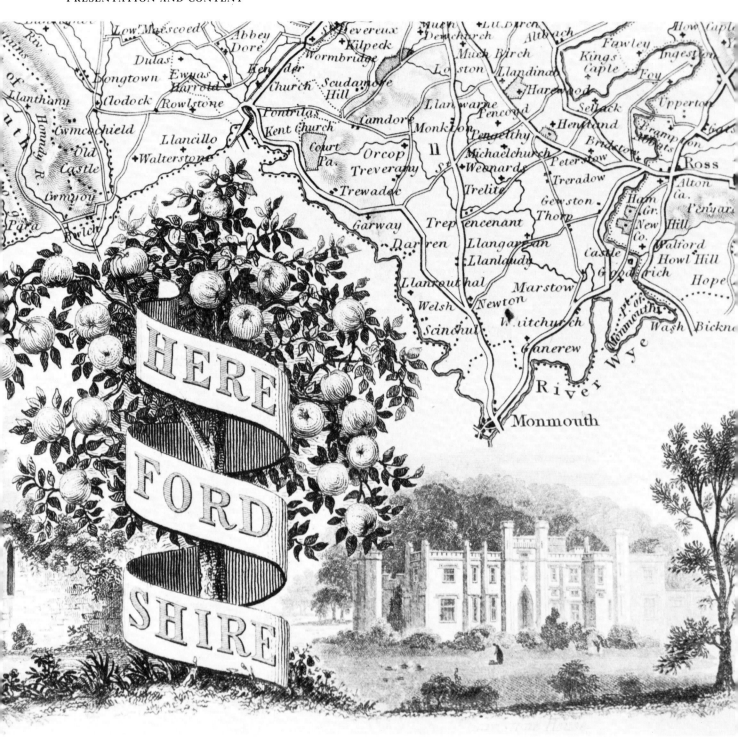

Teesdale. Only the influence of the Romantic Movement and the popularity of the topographical engraving and its attendant grand voluminous works could withstand this new austere utilitarian force. Engraved views were particularly popular from the early 1820s to the 1850s due to the delicate lighting effects attained by engraving on steel. This popularity was cartographically translated into a widespread use of the vignette to decorate either the map face, as in the works of Greenwood, Langley, Fullarton, Dix, Pigot, and others, or as elaborate frames of architectural views bordering, particularly, the town plans of Shury, Tallis and Wyld. An unusual use of the vignette, reminiscent of the practical coastal profiles of hydrographic charts, was to illustrate views of the coast as seen from a distance out at sea, although this was simply decoration rather than for serious position-fixing—B.R. Davies's Sussex, published by J. Baxter

23: *Thomas Moule's exuberant Gothic-revivalist decoration was unusual in an age of restrained ornamentation dictated by the austere Ordnance Survey.*
Detail: Hereford, engraved by J. Bingley, published by G. Virtue, 1837, in Thomas Moule's English Counties Delineated. *By courtesy of Jason Musgrave.*

24: *Profiles of buildings were less popular and less utilized in Victorian days than in earlier times. The map was accompanied by* 'THE STRAW HAT AND BONNET DEALERS GUIDE, OR A REFERENCE TO THE PICTORIAL MAP OF LUTON, For 1853, WITH THE PRINCIPAL BUSINESS ADDRESSES. BY R. TODD.'
Detail: 'A Pictorial MAP OF LUTON, THE GREAT STRAW BONNET EMPORIUM. With Elevations of the Principal Buildings WAREHOUSES, &c', by R. Todd, 1853. By permission of the British Library (Maps 1380 (1)).

of Lewes in 1834, was particularly spectacular. The impact of the vignette on potential sales was considered sufficient for map-making houses to employ talented artists and specialist art engravers to create delicate images of wide appeal. The addition of vignettes to a long-established map was sometimes an attempt to revive flagging demand; John Cary, for example, added vignettes to a few of his large county series from c.1834 after they had been on the market for some 30 years. On occasion, the map actually became subsidiary to the topographical or architectural print itself, being used merely to locate the subject of the print within its neighbourhood or area, or alternatively to delineate the plan of the buildings shown, particularly in historical representations of important demolished buildings. Occasionally Victorian romanticism overwhelmed this restraint with unexpected exuberance, and limited decoration gave way to a riot of foliage, figures, and flowers, traditionally uncoloured even when the map itself was, as in the Gothic revivalism of Moule's county maps and Tallis's foliated frames. Although some map-makers continued to incorporate perspective or profile views of important or new buildings, particularly on town and street plans as R. Todd did with the 'Elevations of the Principle Buildings WAREHOUSES, &c.' on his 1853 plan of Luton, 'The Great Straw Bonnet Emporium', generally, nineteenth-century mapmakers were content to indulge themselves only with the occasional frippery as in Cary's use of the cross of Lorraine to decorate his north-points or the *Dispatch*'s logo of the flying Mercury. The one obvious exception was the production of lithographed maps for children which could easily be decorated with rough, supposedly educational, sketches, as, for instance, Robert Miller's county maps were by 'Reuben Ramble'.

SELECT BIBLIOGRAPHY

JONES, I.E. 'Unnear—A Radnorshire example of plagiarism on 18th and 19th century maps'. (*Trans. Rad. Soc.*, 46; 1976)
WINTERBOTHAM, H. ST. J.L. *A Key to Maps.* (1936)

Antiquities
PHILLIPS, C.W. 'The Ordnance Survey and archaeology, 1791–1960'. (*Geog. Journ.*, 127; 1961)

Orthography
HARLEY, J.B. 'Place-names on the early Ordnance Survey maps of England and Wales'. (*Cart. Journ.*, 8; 1971)
HARLEY, J.B. and WALTERS, G. 'Welsh orthography and Ordnance Survey mapping 1820-1905'. (*Archaeologia Cambrensis*, 131; 1982)

Relief
CARMICHAEL-SMYTH, SIR J. *Memoir upon the Topographical System of Col. Van Gorkum.* (1828)
COLLIER, H. 'A short history of Ordnance Survey contouring with particular reference to Scotland'. (*Cart. Journ.*, 9; 1972)
JONES, Y. 'Aspects of relief portrayal on 19th century British military maps'. (*Cart. Journ.*, 11; 1974)
LYONS, H.G. 'Relief in cartography'. (*Geog. Journ.*, 43; 1914)

Colour
BURCH, R. M. *Colour Printing and Colour Printers.* (1910)
CAYLEY, H. 'On the colouring of maps'. (*Proc. of the Roy. Geog. Soc.*, I; 1879)
JAMESON, R. 'On colouring geognostical maps'. (*Memoirs of the Wernerian Natural History Society*, I; 1810)
PEARSON, K.S. 'The nineteenth-century colour revolution: maps in geographical journals'. (*Imago Mundi*, 32; 1980)

25: '*Reuben Ramble*' *decorated his children's atlas with rough, supposedly educational, lithographed sketches.*
Detail: England & Wales, by '*Reuben Ramble*', c.1845, in Reuben Ramble's Travels through the Counties of England.

IV

Purpose

The average collector of Victorian maps of the British Isles will naturally concentrate on medium-scale topographical maps. The major Victorian series of such topographical maps are detailed in a later part of this book. However, in addition to this familiar and widely available output, the period brought forth a vast array not only of other topographical material at very large and very small scales, but also of maps designed for specific thematic purposes. Such nineteenth-century products are to be found and offer an excitingly unusual alternative to the standard collection. Whilst it is clearly either impossible or impractical to define the publication history of each map or even series in the way that medium-scale topographical atlases are analysed later, nevertheless it is useful to indicate potential 'collectables' in the hope that this will encourage a wider view.

As in previous centuries, the mainstream of Victorian British cartographic production was the topographical map, usually of the standard county unit. The development of lithography, and, in particular, of the lithographic transfer technique, enabled sub-divisions to be 'pulled' cheaply and easily from larger general maps, and, thus, the region increasingly replaced the county as the standard unit of representation as the century progressed. These regional sections, often at such small scales that a whole country was covered by only a handful of maps, were ideal for illustrating the abundance of guide-books, history texts, regional geographies, and other works that appeared in ever-increasing numbers, for they allowed the area covered by the map to be directly related to the subject of the text rather than requiring the abstraction of regional information by inference from a series of county maps.

ESTATE PLANS
The long-standing tradition of mapping small parcels of land in detail was reinforced and extended during the Victorian age by the increased demand for estate plans stimulated by expanding land-use and by the growing demand for plans to accompany ownership and taxation changes. Particularly, there was a process of fragmentation afoot; long-established estates were being broken-up and new estates formed by a *nouveau riche* class whose land-owning ambitions were supported by wealth created by success in industry and commerce. Predictably these new landowners wanted maps of their estates. As increased agricultural demand fostered the enclosure of the waste, so previously marginal land was mapped in detail for the first time, and local land surveyors were busily employed in extending rural estate mapping into new areas, particularly in Ireland, Scotland, and Wales which experienced a delayed agricultural revolution as the impact of new techniques and equipment was at last felt. In Scotland, for example, 'the bulk of manuscript plans were produced in the century 1750-

1850.'[1] In these Celtic fringes the majority of rural estate maps date only from the nineteenth century. Similarly, the growth of towns, urban improvement, and the Victorian rebuilding of decaying medieval city centres, created an increasing demand for urban estate plans defining property boundaries and ownership. Urban expansion consumed the rural fringes of the towns and the process of land sale from estates for building and commercial development created a further demand for plans of small land parcels.

An estate plan, commissioned by the individual private landowner rather than required by governmental or parliamentary action, covered the land, both rural and urban, owned by one landowner, and, consequently, could range from a single small farm to an extensive area sometimes spanning several parishes and requiring multiple sheets for adequate coverage. In some cases, coverage extended to include the land in or around a village or town, sometimes detailing settlement layout. The plan gave 'detailed information on farm and field patterns and names, agricultural usages, houses, roads and paths and many other topics ... frequently of outstanding artistic merit',[2] mirroring the decorative style of the day. Although these large-scale plans were in manuscript, intermediate drafts were often prepared. Similarly, a number of copies of the final plans were also usually produced not only for the landowner and his estate manager but also as reference copies for the surveyor himself. Such copies were generally prepared by an apprentice surveyor who laboriously hand-copied the plan, frequently inadvertently introducing transcription errors. (Apprentices often developed and practised their drawing skills by copying examples of earlier plans in different styles, thus creating another form of Victorian manuscript plan.) Such experience gained in estate mapping was invaluable for those with pretensions to a grander cartographic career; John Cary, for example, built up his business in its early years not only by map- and print-selling but also through estate work—'ESTATES surveyed and planned with Accuracy and Dispatch'.[3] Improvements in instrument precision and greater skill in technique and care in procedure (despite uneven diffusion and variable local practice) created plans of ever-greater accuracy and the private local land surveyor enjoyed a profitable existence until the large-scale work of the Ordnance Survey, after the third quarter of the century, became sufficiently extensive to undermine his monopoly of large-scale estate mapping. Once a large-scale Ordnance map, or its enlargement, was available, a private survey was no longer necessary, for specific details of the estate could be plotted onto an accurate topographical base plan. In fact, the Ordnance was actually willing to adapt its 25″ parish plans to manufacture maps of specific estates—'Estate Maps can be arranged on this scale, and coloured and mounted to order'.[4] The resultant estate map, whether

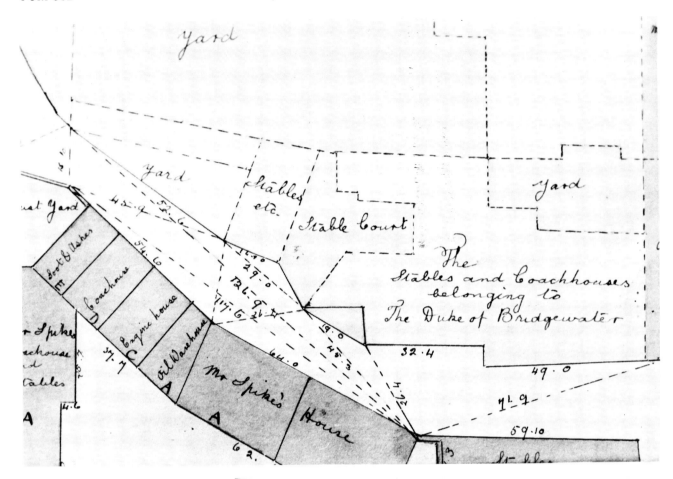

The plan contains various handwritten labels including: "Yard", "Stables etc.", "Stable Court", "The Stables and Coachhouses belonging to The Duke of Bridgewater", "Mr Spikes House", "Coachhouse", "Engine house", "Oil Warehouse".

26: *Apprentice surveyors and draughtsmen frequently developed their skills by copying earlier plans in different styles.*
Detail: A plan of Lincolns Inn Fields, drawn February 20 1796, copied 29 October 1895 by 'RS'.

POPE'S VILLA.

THE LODGE.

TWICKENHAM.

27: *Many estate plans were prepared to accompany property sale. Attractive vignettes were very much part of the sales drive of estate agents, offering an enticing view of available up-market property.*
Detail: Vignette from 'Plan of THE LODGE, TWICKENHAM, for Sale by Auction by MESS.ʳˢ E. & H. LUMLEY, LONDON 1876'. (Although the original home of Alexander Pope, the poet, had been demolished in 1807 by Baroness Howe, the replacement building continued to be known as 'Pope's Villa'.) By permission of the British Library (Maps 137a11(14)).

the product of private or Ordnance survey, could be produced cheaply *en masse* by lithography to satisfy not only the landowner's demands but also those of official bodies requiring detailed plans; the estate agent and property developer could distribute it in numbers to advertise land sale, lease, and auction as did 'LUMLEYS, Surveyors & Land Agents' with their enticingly decorated plan when auctioning 'The Lodge', Twickenham, in 1876.

ENCLOSURE PLANS

The enclosure of land which attended the agrarian revolution was necessarily accompanied by the mapping of the area concerned, whether it was required by legislation as in England and Wales, or as a by-product of independent initiative as in Scotland. (However, since Scottish plans resulted from private enterprise rather then legislative requirement, there is considerable variation in design and content; and since they generally cover a particular estate, often before and after enclosure, they are, perhaps, better thought-of as estate plans. In Ireland, local surveyors rarely had the opportunity to map open-field strip patterns such as delineated in English enclosure awards.) Statutory requirements stipulated that copies of the written record of the enclosure award and its complementary large-scale plan identifying the enclosed land should be deposited, usually with the parish and the Clerk of the Peace, but this ensured uniformity of neither scale nor style. As with the maps accompanying independent enclosure, there was variation in both scale and design ranging from a bare sketch of a featureless waste area of forest, heath, marsh, or moor, to a highly detailed parish plan of common-land enclosure in a well-populated rural area; the latter might delineate not only the enclosure information itself but also much subsidiary data relating to local legal rights and responsibilities. Following its early-century acceleration, the enclosure movement slowed and halted about the middle of the century; with the consequent reduced production of enclosure maps, variation tended to diminish and a more uniform approach was adopted.

TITHE MAPS

Tithe maps, produced mainly in a concentrated period of about five years following the Tithe Commutation Act of 1836, tend to complement enclosure maps by covering some 11,800 parishes or townships in England and Wales (approximately 79 per cent of the area) which had not had their tithes already commuted and replaced by corn rents on the occasion of an enclosure award. Three copies of the large-scale plans and accompanying written apportionments were prepared for deposit with the Tithe Redemption Commission, the diocese, and the parish respectively, but, inevitably, as with estate and enclosure plans, there were additional proof, intermediate, duplicate, and reference copies also made at the time. These very large scale manuscript plans—'which shall indicate such properties with sufficient accuracy to enable parties to identify the lands which are respectively subject to the several amounts of the rent-charge'[5]—were of variable quality, accuracy, and scale since the Tithe Commissioners shied away from their intended high standards and an estimated cost of £1½ million (in the event the Tithe Survey cost between two and three million!), and, in the cause of economy, accepted sub-standard maps covering voluntary commutation agreements. Maps accepted by the Commissioners as 'first class'—some 1900, about 17 per cent of the total, including those prepared by the Ordnance Survey—are a unique cadastral record of both

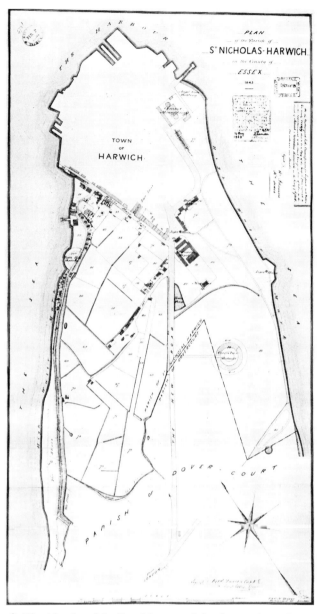

28: *The tithe plan of the Harwich area excludes the actual town but includes details of the harbour and fortifications.*
'PLAN of the Parish of S^T. NICHOLAS-HARWICH in the County of ESSEX 1843', by Capt. Rob. K. Dawson, Assistant Tithe Commissioner. By permission of the Essex Record Office.

rural and industrial areas, often being the first reliable delineation of parish boundaries. In contrast, however, all too often tithe maps were produced from poorly executed, unskilled surveys, or, worse still, were notoriously inaccurate copies of earlier estate, enclosure, or parish plans or else were some composite of older maps, produced at different dates, with a few modern details added by guesswork.

Since size was proportional to that of the parish and scale varied from one to 12 chains per inch (usually the scale was 13.3″ or 26.7″ to the mile and towns were sometimes inset at a larger scale, although alternatively urban areas on other maps were simply left blank), the tithe maps varied in size from one square foot to over 100. Each map showed each individual titheable plot—often elaborately coloured to distinguish ownership, land-use, and freedom from tithes—numbered to correspond with the written details of ownership, land-use, tithe payable, and recipient. Additionally the Ordnance Survey produced a special printing of the 1″, the 'Index to the Tithe Survey', with the limits of titheable

29: 'Map OF THE PARISH OF HALIFAX In the West Riding OF THE County of York, Shewing the Township Borough & Manorial BOUNDARIES From an Actual Survey MADE IN THE YEARS, 1834 & 1835. BY J. F. Myers, Surveyor. HALIFAX.' By permission of the British Library (Maps 32b25).

lands engraved on a set of 1" plates to show the names and boundaries of parishes covered by the tithe surveys.

PARISH PLANS

Parallel, perhaps, with this development of large-scale estate, enclosure, and tithe maps, was the continued production of parish and ward plans which in the past had satisfied a narrow local market through publication in the numerous Georgian antiquarian and topographical local studies. In the Victorian age, demand for local detailed plans, in fact, grew; this was not so much because of the growth of such leisurely intellectual interests, but rather a response to the quickened pace of local economic and social development which required an accurate delineation of parish boundaries, land and property ownership, and field and site acreages. In particular, detailed large-scale plans were required by the parish vestry for rate assessment and effective administra-

tion of services such as street cleaning and lighting. These plans, usually produced specifically for the vestry or with the support of the church or local gentry, often relapsed into eighteenth-century decorative style with fancy dedications to local landowners.

Most of these parish maps were produced as single copies in manuscript to be hung in the vestry room and used for local government. However, in some cases they were printed and one London parish went as far as presenting a lithographed copy to every parishioner. In other cases map-makers produced reduced versions of the large-scale surveys for popular consumption, often flattering their local areas with attractively decorated plans. The publisher J.K. Starling of Upper Street, for example, complimented his home Islington with a fine plan of the parish produced with the church's blessing, and the engraver Thomas Starling of Lower Street decorated his trade card with a miniaturized version ('T. Starling, Map, Chart & Plan ENGRAVER. 13 Norfolk S! Lower S! Islington, Cards, Drafts, Bills, Notes &c. Fac Similes accurately made'). Most parish plans were produced by local land surveyors, as in the case of Myers's magnificent map of Halifax, but the richest parishes were

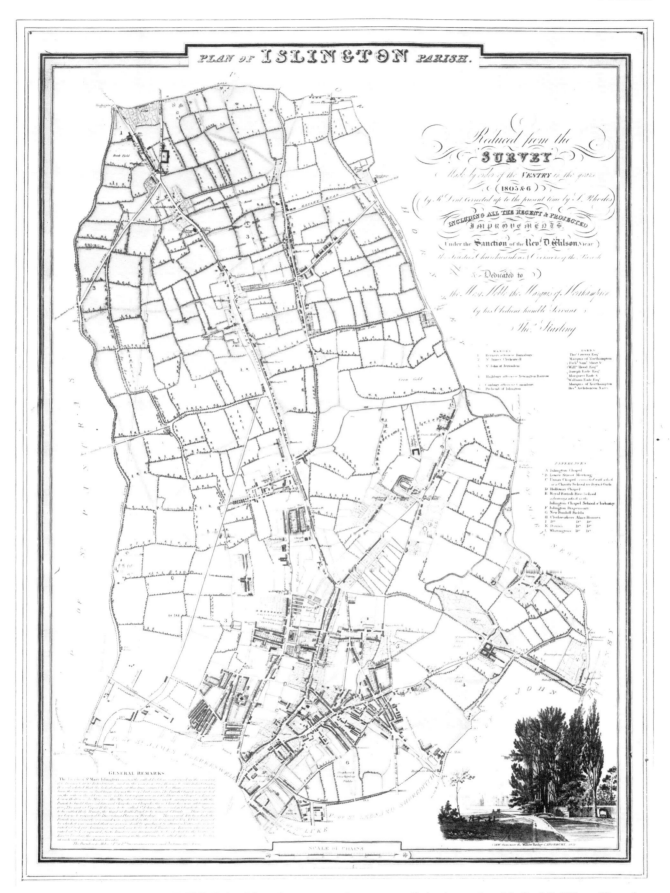

30: '*PLAN OF ISLINGTON PARISH. Reduced from the SURVEY Made by order of the VESTRY in the years 1805 & 6 by R. Dent, corrected up to the present time by J. Rhodes INCLUDING ALL THE RECENT & PROJECTED* Improvements Under the sanction of the Rev.d D. Wilson, Vicar, the Trustees, Churchwardens & Overseers of the Parish. Published by J. K. Starling Upper Street Islington August 1.st 1831.' By permission of the British Library (Crace 15/50).

prepared to meet the considerable expense of hiring better-known map-makers such as James Wyld to survey and map their areas. Unfortunately, since so many of the fastest-growing and wealthiest of these local administrative units were concentrated in London, the capital's parishes and wards were more extensively mapped than those of other areas. The most comprehensive mapping of parishes was undertaken for the Poor Law Commissioners, under the provisions of the Parochial Assessments Act, when some 4000 parishes in England and Wales were surveyed and revalued between 1836 and 1843, and by the Ordnance Survey which produced its early 25″ sheets as parish plans— '... being nearly one square inch to an acre. This Scale is sufficiently large to give block Plans of Houses, and Plans of the Gardens and Grounds in which they stand ... Indexes to each Parish, 3d.; or per post Four Penny Stamps'.[6]

SCIENTIFIC MAPS

In the early years of the century Continental cartographers began to develop thematic uses for the map, other than the straightforward representation of landscape, by conveying specific limited information overlaid on a topographical base. The growth of concepts of geographical causality and interrelationship induced Alexander von Humboldt and Carl Ritter to adapt cartography to show this geographical interdependence. Ritter and Humboldt published the first systematic thematic maps in 1806 and 1812 respectively, introducing such concepts as the isotherm and area- and altitude-limits of vegetation. This lead was enthusiastically followed by such innovating Continental geographers as Justus and Wilhelm Perthes, Heinrich Berghaus, and Gustaf Kombst. Similarly, the representation of statistical material was developed during the same period, somewhat crudely, by Dupin, Balbi and Guerry, and Quetelet. Not surprisingly, these new techniques appealed to the progressive Victorians and their ingenuity helped develop wider uses for the thematic map, extending its range to the representation not only of proven scientific relationships but also of pastimes, politics, and prejudices.

Keith Johnston was much influenced by Berghaus when travelling in Europe and turned his attention to the production of thematic work, based partly on Berghaus's material, with *The National Atlas of Historical, Commercial and Political Geography* in 1843 and the influential *Physical Atlas of Natural Phenomena*, covering meteorology, hydrology, geology, phytology, and zoology. In turn, Johnston influenced Augustus Petermann who drew on the experience gained in working on Johnston's *Physical Atlas* to produce his own *Atlas of Physical Geography* in 1850 and other thematic works which earned him the title 'Physical Geographer and Engraver on Stone in Ordinary to the Queen'. Johnston's enthusiasm clearly rubbed off on other Edinburgh publishers, for Blackwood published an apparently popular reduction of the *Physical Atlas* in 1850, 1854, and 1856, and by the late 1880s John Bartholomew considered that the standard topographical atlas should be accompanied by 'special maps'[7] representing geographical relationships and physical and political features. It was, in fact, John Bartholomew who embarked on the most ambitious scheme to sum up the state of knowledge at the end of the nineteenth century with his projected *Physical Atlas* in which 'You could read ... of Storm Tracks and Frequency, Distribution of Medicinal Plants, Distribution of Domestic Animals and Parasites, Distribution of Christian Missions, the Clothing of Man, the Population of the Seas, the Comets and Meteors and many another strange topic'.[8]

However, the economics of such a grand project, involving seven volumes covering physiography, geology, hydrography, orography, oceanography, botany, zoology, ethnography, and cosmography, were impractical and the only volumes to appear were *Meteorology* in 1899, with over 400 maps dealing with all aspects of climate and weather, and *Zoogeography* in 1911 dealing with the animal kingdom: 'A series of 36 Plates, illustrating the Distribution of over 700 Families, Genera, and Species of existing Animals.'[9]

More realistically, individual thematic maps were created; for example, in 1849 William Orr published Augustus Petermann's 'Hydrographical Map of the British Isles, Exhibiting the Geographical Distribution of the Inland Waters', dedicated to Queen Victoria, which divided the country into drainage basins and gave information on, amongst other things, the length and fall of the rivers; and in 1851 Trelawney Saunders 'produced a weather chart of the British Isles and the neighbouring coasts, and posted it daily at the Great Exhibition in Hyde Park; it is believed that it was this map that inspired the lad G.J. Symons to start a register of British rainfall.'

Thematic atlases were produced on a smaller, more specialized scale, such as the Meteorological Council's *Meteorological Atlas of the British Isles*, published in 1883, with its weather maps lithographed by Dangerfield, or the maps showing botanical divisions which frequently accompanied works on local flora. Gradually the new data being generated by the developing earth sciences—geology, hydrology, meteorology—and the geography of soil, plant, animal, and man, was translated into cartographic form. Such thematic material was even produced specifically for schoolchildren as in *Gleig's School Series* which included Walter M'Leod's *Physical Atlas of Great Britain and Ireland*, published in 1861, '... specifically illustrating the Physical Features of Great Britain and Ireland ... invaluable to those who are directly engaged in the education of youth, whether they are Teachers in Public or in Private Schools'[10], with its small, uniform-scale, lithographed maps of both individual and grouped counties with relief cross-sections by Edward Weller, and its more general thematic maps of the nations. Similarly, the National Society for Promoting the Education of the Poor published a thematic atlas (*c.*1852) covering population density, mineral production, temperature, rainfall, occupations, and ecclesiastical geography 'For the use of Schoolmasters, Pupils, Teachers, and the Upper Classes of Schools'.[11] Additionally, there was clearly a wider market for such scientific maps; Charles William Deacon, for example, included in his 'court guides' transfers 'pulled' from W. & A.K. Johnston's 'Modern Map of England and Wales' which had been overprinted to create hydrographical, geological and climatological maps.

Eighteenth-century agrarian improvement, stemming from technical advance and the introduction of new crops and improved livestock breeds, demanded a more accurate physiographic representation than offered by existing maps. Cartographers, thus, showed increasing interest in the mapping of land cover, surface soil, and underlying rock. The makers of eighteenth-century large-scale maps, such as John Rocque, experimented with the representation of land-use by semi-pictorial signs and colour. New scientific studies produced maps of the land surface, such as the soil maps of Scottish counties, engraved by Neele, Ainslie, and others, commissioned by the Board of Agriculture and published between 1794 and 1814. Soil improvement and drainage also generated explanatory maps, as, for example, with the engravings of Irish bogs by James Basire, published in the second decade of the nineteenth century, 'on which are laid down the Lines of the proposed Drains for the improvement of the Bogs'.[12] The most imposing of the early land-use maps, setting new standards of analysis and portrayal, was undoubtedly Thomas Milne's breakdown, published in 1800, of some 260 square miles around London into 17 categories of field-usage by means of letters, colour, and engraving. However, the most important branch of such physical representation was geological mapping which had been first attempted, somewhat unsuccessfully, by French cartographers dating from the Abbé Coulon's map of 1664 and most notably by Jean Etienne Guettard who produced primitive geological maps, drawn by Philippe Buache, in the mid-eighteenth century.

Although as early as 1683 Martin Lister had suggested to the Royal Society that a '*Soil* or *Mineral Map*'[13] should be produced, and in 1743 Christopher Packe had actually published a chart of East Kent distinguishing chalk districts, stone hills, clay hills, and so on, it was only in the later years of the eighteenth century and the early years of the nineteenth that the fundamental importance of accurate geological maps was recognized for agriculture, building, drainage, economics, engineering, land-use, mining, sanitation, transport, water supply, and, later, particularly, for the estimation of mineral reserves. The late eighteenth century witnessed a quickening of interest in geological science through the formation of scholarly associations such as the Askesian Society and the British Mineralogical Society, and in 1807 the most influential body, the Geological Society, was formed in London with the stated intention of laying 'the foundation of a general geological map of the British territory'.[14] The demand for better maps was fostered by advances in British geology, petrology, and palaeontology, and by an expansion of these subjects in the universities following the pioneering work of Cuvier, Hutton, Lamarck, and Werner. As early as 1802, this demand was translated into the offer of a premium of 50 guineas for mineralogical maps of not less than 15m.:1″ by the Society for the Encouragement of Arts, Manufactures, and Commerce—an offer which remained unclaimed for 13 years until William Smith submitted his great map of the strata in 1815. Naturally, early maps, produced to accompany the publication of memoirs and the description and illustration of fossil remains, were relatively sketchy and unsophisticated, being really only geognostical maps showing just the distribution of rock types by area without establishing any sequence of formations. The 'Transactions' of learned societies and the scientists' specialist tracts became important vehicles for the publication of geological maps, establishing a tradition of small-scale illustrative mapping which continued throughout the century in such series as the geologically-coloured Scottish county maps (some, engraved by W.H. Lizars, also appearing in Blackwood's county atlas) published between 1837 and 1847 in the *Prize-Essays and Transactions of the Highland and Agricultural Society of Scotland* and the sketchy county geological maps accompanying monographs, published by J. Murray between 1843 and 1870, for the Agricultural Society of England.

Early geological maps were distinctly variable in quality, often depending for their effectiveness on the quality and reliability of the chosen topographical base map. The cost of engraving a completely new geological map was obviously high, and, therefore, newly engraved maps tended to delineate topographical detail only in outline. It made better commercial sense to superimpose geological data from a separate plate onto an existing topographical base map.

Thus, geological map-makers established links with such commercial publishers as Arrowsmith and Cary, creating a collaborative relationship in which each influenced the other so that the scientist persuaded the responsive cartographer to contrive maps suited to the addition of geological information. The liaison between William Smith and John Cary was especially fruitful in creating effective geological maps by reducing emphasis on political divisions and increasing it on drainage; Cary was even able to adapt some of his large county maps to produce Smith's incomplete geological atlas. After the creation of the Geological Survey, official geological maps were simply constructed from existing Ordnance Survey sheets, although this was sometimes found to be unsatisfactory because the density of hachuring could obscure geological detail.

One particular form of geological mapping was only slowly developed during the course of the century as its importance was realized. In the early days of geological mapping—in fact, until the century's middle decades—little attention was paid to the 'drift' deposits laid down over the 'solid' base rocks by glacial action. During the Glacial Period rock debris was scoured away by the movement of ice over the rock surface, transported within the glacier, and then this 'extraneous rubbish' (as some geologists called it!) was finally deposited elsewhere when the ice melted. Consequently, by the late third and the final quarters of the century it was common for the Geological Survey to produce both 'solid' and 'drift' maps—the former showing the area as it would appear with all 'drift' deposits stripped-away, and the latter showing the nature of the surface rock whether 'drift' or exposed 'solid' base—with Ireland, generally, being more satisfactorily mapped than most other areas because of its particularly effective combination of 'solid' in colour and 'drift' in engraved stipple on the same map.

Sir Joseph Banks, President of the Royal Society for 42 years, did much to encourage early geological mapping through his support of such pioneers as William Maton who published his 'Mineralogical Map of the Western Counties of England' in 1797, compiled from his own observations and other sources 'though it has rarely happened that I had occasion to apply to other quarters, as the gaps in my observations were few'.[15] It was Banks also who advised the Board of Agriculture to appoint William Smith's pupil John Farey to survey Derbyshire. Farey produced the earliest-known geological section across the country, from Derbyshire to the Lincolnshire coast, in 1808, and his *General View of the Agriculture and Minerals of Derbyshire*, the first official geological memoir published in Britain (in three volumes between 1811 and 1817), contained the earliest-known geological map to show faults. Although the Swiss Louis Albert Necker presented the first geological map of Scotland in 1808 to the Geological Society (showing seven rock types coloured in manuscript, superimposed on a map of Scotland by Thomas Kitchin), it was really John Macculloch who made the initial Scottish breakthrough with his *Description of the Western Isles of Scotland* of 1819, which contained geological maps of several islands, and with his various verbose contributions to the Geological Society. Subsequently, the indefatigable '... Dr M'Culloch, by the desire of the Government, commenced a Geological Survey of Scotland ...'[16] on a scale of 4m.:1″. Despite his death in 1835 at the age of 62, as a result of a carriage accident on his honeymoon, his map was published in 1836, but was little thought of officially for the survey 'was never completed and is very inaccurate'.[16] In Ireland the pioneering work was undertaken by Richard John Griffith through his early investigations into the nature and possibilities of peat bogs, his 1814 and 1818 maps of the Leinster and Connaught coalfields respectively, his work as an H.M. Inspector of Mines, his teaching of geology and mining engineering, and, particularly, through his supplement to the 1837 *Second Report of the Commissioners appointed to consider and recommend a General System of Railways for Ireland*. This latter *Outline of the Geology of Ireland* contained the first geological map of the country, on the scale of 10m.:1″. On its improved form, published in 1839 on four sheets at 4m.:1″, Sir Archibald Geikie commented, 'This work must be admitted to be the most remarkable map of a whole country ever constructed by a single individual.'[17] In addition to these embryonic but fundamental works, the 1820s and '30s saw the appearance of many other rudimentary geological maps of local districts in the *Transactions* of the Geological Society and in other papers and books by such as Buckland, De la Beche, Lyell, Murchison, Phillips, and Sedgwick.

Without doubt the most important and influential of the pathfinding geological cartographers was William Smith, 'Land-Surveyor and Drainer, and Member of the Bath Agricultural Society',[18] who achieved the most dramatic and far-reaching advance ever to occur in the history of geology by establishing the system of strata identification through their contained fossils—'that wonderful order & regularity with which Nature has disposed of these singular productions and assigned to each class its peculiar stratum'.[19] His early work included a geological map of the Bath area (1799) and a coloured geological map of England and Wales (1801), but his masterpiece was his map, published in 1815 with an explanatory memoir, at a scale of 5m.:1″ on 15 sheets (plus an index map on a separate sheet), dedicated to Sir Joseph Banks: 'the production, after the labour of more than 20 years, of a most ingenious man, who has been singularly deficient in the art of introducing himself to public notice.'[20] This 'was the first published geological map of England and Wales and was to provide the foundation for modern geological cartography'.[21] Although the work was projected as early as 1801 and despite prodigious energy (his biographer records an aggregate annual travel distance of 10,000 miles in an age of poor communications!), Smith's perfectionism delayed publication until 1815. 'A Delineation of the Strata of England and Wales, with part of Scotland' won for Smith the 50 guinea premium, the first Wollaston Medal ever awarded by the Geological Society, and the accolade 'Father of English Geology'.[22] Credit should also be given to the publisher John Cary for his courage in undertaking an obviously risky commercial venture and his undoubted contribution to the production of a very fine map which was offered in a variety of forms—'in Sheets, with the Memoir', 'Mounted on Canvass and Rollers' with optional varnishing, 'fitted in a Case for Travelling', and 'on Spring Rollers'.[23] A reduced copy of the map, 'A New Geological Map of England and Wales, with the Inland Navigations', on a scale of 15m.:1″, with some additional information, was published by Cary in 1820, and Smith's data was part source for the advanced map produced by George Greenough for the Geological Society published in 1819, with a second edition in 1839. Apparently the plates for the 1815 map were finally owned by Edward Stanford but were simply sold off for scrap since the Geological Society was not prepared to purchase them for posterity (this was a typical fate for obsolete copper plates—the Royal Geographical Society, for example, in

1894 sold off all but 50 of its plates at 4½d. per pound because of its lack of storage space). The effective collaboration between Smith and Cary continued with geological sections of southern England, published by Cary in 1817-19, and the adaptation of Cary's large county maps to convey Smith's data for his unfinished *New Geological Atlas of England and Wales* published 1819-24—'calculated to elucidate the Agriculture of each County, & to show the situation of the best Materials for Building, Making of Roads, the Construction of Canals, & pointing out those Places where Coal & other valuable Materials are likely to be found'.[24]

Thomas Colby always saw the Ordnance Survey not only as a topographical survey but also as a foundation for antiquarian, geological, natural-history, and statistical studies. Consequently, although the Survey initially eschewed geological maps, officers were encouraged to acquire geological knowledge and to map geological boundaries in areas surveyed. In 1832 Henry Thomas De la Beche was authorized to add geological information to Ordnance 1″ maps of the South-West and the results were so impressive that the Geological Society enthusiastically campaigned for the establishment of an official, national geological survey: 'Mr. De la Beche, one of our Vice-Presidents, acting under the Direction of the Board of Ordnance, has produced a geological map of the county of Devon, which, for extent and minuteness of information and beauty of execution, has a very high claim to regard. Let us rejoice in the complete success which has attended this first attempt of that honourable Board to exalt the character of English topography by rendering it at once more scientific and very much more useful to the country at large.'[25] Inevitably, in 1835 the Ordnance Geological Survey was established as a branch of the Trigonometrical Survey with De la Beche as its first Director destined to the 'successful completion of a great National Establishment'.[26] Henceforth, the Ordnance's topographical sheets were adapted to convey geological information.

This is no more the place to write a history of the Geological Survey than it is of the Ordnance Survey; suffice it to say that map production, as in the case of the Ordnance, suffered from vacillating policy with publication at various scales subjected to expansion, contraction, and suspension according to current thought. Initially publication was at the 1″ scale, based on the middle or late printings of the Old Series Ordnance Survey, much loved by the early geologists. However, concentration on coalfield surveys in the 1860s and '70s emphasized the claims of the 6″ scale which was far more useful and important for mineral areas, as the Coal Commission of 1866-71 continually stressed, and which could be used to obtain the 1″ map by a simple reduction. Despite the advantages of 6″ publication there is little doubt that some of it was not justified in areas lacking mining possibilities. At smaller scales the Survey was generally content to leave production to commercial publishers such as Reynolds, Stanford, and the Walkers, who synthesized its work for the benefit of the general public. Its principal small-scale publication was that at 4m.:1″ which was expected to be particularly valued by tourists and teachers, and which, in the event, proved popular and sold well. Additionally, however, there were many other small-scale publications, including:

1859, 1866, 1879	England and Wales	11m.:1″
1861, 1862	Scotland	25m.:1″
1864, 1896	British Isles	14m.:1″

1867, 1870	Ireland	8m.:1″
1876, 1892, 1910	Scotland	10m.:1″
1878	Ireland	8m.:1″
1897	England and Wales	10m.:1″
1907	Ireland	10m.:1″

Revision of Survey sheets was obviously a piecemeal affair for attention was naturally concentrated on completion of the primary survey rather than revision; but as early as 1839 De la Beche's own maps of Cornwall and Devon, published in 1834 and 1835, had been amended and many of the first Survey sheets published had undergone more or less complete revision before 1867. It seems that there was never an extensive programme of revision, but small modifications were made and errors corrected when judged necessary. The Survey's attitude to revision was summed up by Geikie in 1885: 'It is gratifying to be able to state that the published maps of the Geological Survey are on the whole so correct that during the re-examination of the ground for the completion of the mapping of the surface deposits, it has been chiefly in matters of detail that amendments have had to be made upon them.'[27]

By 1901 the coalfields of Northumberland, Durham, Cumberland, Yorkshire, Lancashire, and Scotland had all been mapped on the 6″ scale and nearly all published. Although the earliest had been mapped in 1860, most sheets had appeared in the 1870s and all, therefore, required revision urgently by the end of the century. Revision on the 6″ scale had been in progress in South Wales for several years and had been started in North Staffordshire and Leicestershire, but the revised data was not published because 6″ engraving had been suspended since 1881 and, in any case, only a small part of the fields had been covered. No 6″ maps existed of the coalfields of South Staffordshire, Nottingham, Derby, Warwick, Denbigh or the West Midlands. England north of the Humber and the Mersey had been surveyed with drifts on the 6″ scale, and very considerable areas in the Thames valley, Hampshire basin, London area, Oxfordshire, Bedford, and the south-east Midlands had been 'revised for Drift' on the 6″ scale. Some revision had also been carried out in Devon, Dorset, Somerset, and Wiltshire, but for nearly half the country there were no 6″ maps and no drift maps. About two-thirds of Scotland had been surveyed, almost all at the 6″ scale, and 6″ maps had been published of nearly all the coalfields, but as these maps had appeared between 1861 and 1878 they, too, were, to a large extent, out-of-date. Vast areas of the Highlands had not yet been surveyed and coverage of the Southern Uplands was accepted as being unsatisfactory. In Ireland the situation was more favourable with 6″ maps being published from the beginnings of the Survey, with coverage completed in 1887, and with a process of revision operative in some areas.

Thus, by the end of the century, much had been accomplished; the Wharton Committee, when recommending the completion of the primary geological survey on the 6″ scale as the first duty of the institution, summed up its achievement: 'With regard to the practical uses of the Survey ... there is no doubt that, apart from the scientific and educational aspects, it has been of great practical service to the country. It has been shown to us that great benefit has been found to be obtainable from the results of the Survey in the matter of mining, agriculture, water-supply and sanitation; and we believe that the cost of the Survey has been more than justified by the practical services rendered to the country at large.'[28]

STATISTICAL MAPS

As in many other aspects of contemporary cartography, Britain was particularly blessed at this time by conditions suited to the rapid development of new modes of representation. The remarkable progress of agriculture, industry, transport, and communications, combined with new techniques and standards in investigatory science, both physical and social, the birth of many scientific and statistical societies, and the emergence of accurate topographic mapping—all these influences created a climate in which thematic cartography flourished. Indeed, in the short space of 20 years from about 1835 most modern techniques of non-topographic cartographic representation came into being. The most surprising innovatory package, although probably of little contemporary influence except perhaps on Augustus Petermann, was the 1837 atlas produced to accompany the *Second Report* of the Irish Railway Commissioners which set a new standard of sophistication for the representation of statistical relationships. Not only did the atlas contain the first geological map of Ireland and did Lieutenant Thomas Larcom of the Irish Survey introduce 'the continental system of delimiting contours on maps ... into the survey of the United Kingdom for the first time';[29] but also Henry Drury Harness (probably at Larcom's instigation) revolutionized statistical geography by the use of shaded bands proportional in width to quantity to show traffic movements of passengers and freight. The latter further re-shaped the cartographic representation of statistical data by the variation of shading strengths to indicate population density, and by the representation of towns by 'dark spots of which the areas are regulated by the number of their inhabitants'.[30] This is apparently the first use of proportional point symbols. By the 1841 Irish Census report, Larcom was creating original shaded statistical maps depicting literacy rates, population density, standards of house-accommodation, and livestock values, although his scheme to illustrate the agricultural enumeration of 1847 with land-use maps came to nought. In 1849 the statistician Joseph Fletcher, who must surely have studied the Irish Census, produced a population map of England and Wales for his *Moral and Educational Statistics of England and Wales* on which he represented density by a 'Scale of Tints'. After moving from Edinburgh to London in 1847, Petermann was probably persuaded by the maps of Larcom and Harness to produce his shaded population density maps of the British Isles in 1849 and of Scotland and of England and Wales published in 1852. ('THE SHADING exhibits the various degrees of density of the population in every part of England and Wales. The very darkest shading represents a density of 600 persons and upwards to a square mile; the tints gradually becoming lighter as the density decreases—the perfectly white ground indicating a comparative absence of population'.[31]) He (or rather Samuel Clark—the designer of the map) also used Harness's system of representing urban population by graduated circles ('the size of each spot being proportioned, approximately to the population and the average extent of ground covered by the town'[31]) on his 1851 map of the British Isles drawn for the National Society for Promoting the Education of the Poor and on his 1851 Census map, thus spreading knowledge of these new techniques and popularizing their use so that population maps became increasingly common after the 1850s. The only full statistical atlas of the British Isles, covering agricultural, criminal, demographic, educational, geological, hydrographical, legal, marine, military, naval, pauper, political, railway, religious, and sanitation statistics, produced by George Phillips

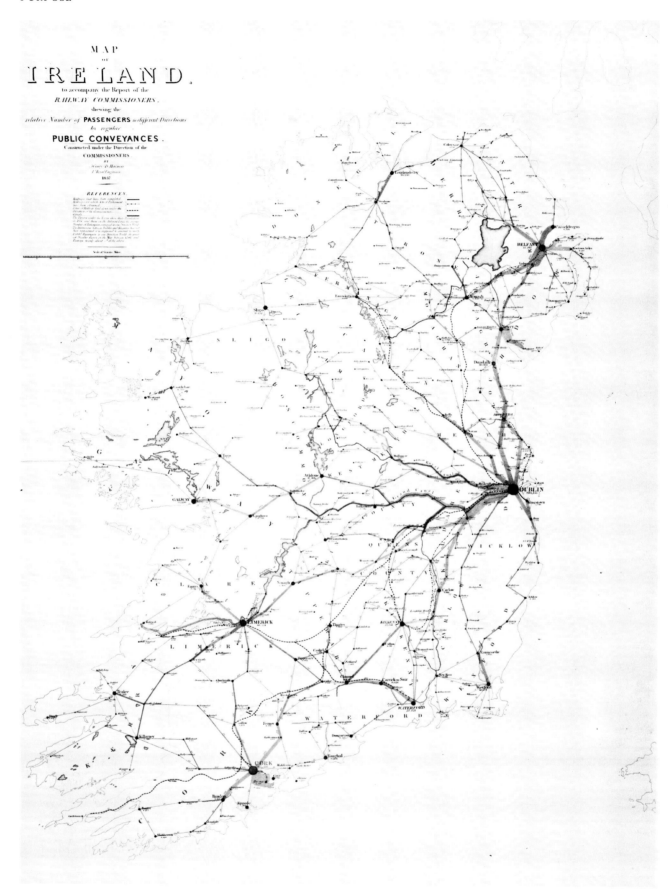

31: i 'MAP OF IRELAND, to accompany the Report of the
RAILWAY COMMISSIONERS, shewing the relative Number of
PASSENGERS in different Directions by regular PUBLIC
CONVEYANCES. Constructed under the Direction of the
COMMISSIONERS, By Henry D. Harness Lt. Royal Engineers.
1837'.

OPPOSITE
ii Detail: Harness's map 'Showing the relative Quantities of
TRAFFIC in different Directions', as (i).
By permission of the British Library (Maps 145e29).

example, mapped electoral divisions in Bristol, delineating 'the qualifying residences of the constituencies ... both parliamentary and municipal'[33]. James Wyld mapped England and Wales 'SHEWING THE STATE OF THE REPRESENTATION BEFORE THE REFORM BILL OF 1832. As amended by the Reform Bill of 1832 AND THE GOVERNMENT REFORM BILL as Proposed by LORD JOHN RUSSELL. 1860.'[34]. The most popular electoral analysis was *Stanford's Handy Atlas and Poll Book of the Electoral Divisions* which represented the political parties by colours altered in accordance with the election results for each issue.

Particularly, there was a greater curiosity than ever before in social conditions and problems; evidence was collected and analysed enthusiastically as social investigators became increasingly aware that the richest nation in the world contained great pockets of extreme poverty, and that over one-third of the population lived a life of chronic shortage in overcrowded slums. The Irish Census of 1841 was accompanied by a colour-shaded map 'giving a general graphic representation of the relative prevalence of the worst class of lodging',[35] classifying streets as either first (high class residences) or second (more unhealthy nature, some shops) class private; first, second or third (lowest class of traders, artisans, huxters) class shop; and third (small shops, middle-class private residences) class mixed. On Merseyside Rev. Abraham Hume, the antiquarian, naturalist and social investigator, 'Incumbent of the New Parish of Vauxhall, Liverpool', differentiated between 'Pauper Streets', 'Semi Pauper Streets', and 'Streets of Crime & Immorality' on the 'ecclesiastical and social' map of Liverpool, 'First exhibited before the National Association for the Promotion of Social Science: October 1858'[36], which illustrated his *Condition of Liverpool, Religious and Social.* It was perhaps Hume's work that sowed the seeds of the greatest of all cartographic studies of poverty by influencing Charles Booth during his youth in Liverpool, for Booth went on to publish the monumental *Life and Labour of the People in London* from 1889 illustrating in a remarkably detailed series of coloured plans that 35 per cent of London's population lived in perpetual poverty.

Likewise, the correlation between slum accommodation and disease was being exposed by the cartographic analysis of medical statistics which undermined the general acceptance of dirt as a natural accompaniment to industrialization and urbanization, and led to the sanitary revolution represented by the spread of the water closet and proper drainage.

Despite the protest of *The Times* that 'we prefer to take our chance of cholera and the rest than be bullied into health. There is nothing a man hates so much as being cleaned against his will'[37], it came to be accepted that 'the various forms of epidemic, endemic, and other disease' were 'caused, or aggravated, or propagated chiefly amongst the labouring classes by atmospheric impurities produced by decomposing animal and vegetable substances, by damp and filth, and close and overcrowded dwellings ...'[38]

Medical cartography was signally stimulated by the horrifying cholera outbreaks of the mid-century with the first 'cholera plan', surveyed by Charles Fowler to accompany Dr Robert Baker's 1833 report to the Leeds Board of Health, depicting 'the districts in which the cholera prevailed'. Likewise, Ormerod's 1848 study of Oxford delineated areas affected by cholera and fever, and Dr Thomas Shapter demonstrated cholera deaths in Exeter by a dot distribution distinguishing deaths in three consecutive

Bevan, appeared in parts from 1881. It offered 45 splendid, large chromolithographed maps, and was published, predictably, by W. & A.K. Johnston—'invaluable to libraries and public men', 'indispensable to a wide circle of students of contemporary affairs', and 'invaluable to those who desire, as every one should, to know the real condition of their own country'.[32]

The growing interest in urban population densities reflected a more general concern with conditions within the rapidly expanding towns and with social geography in general. Census findings, for example, sometimes generated explanatory maps giving details of population and registration as in the regional maps published for the House of Commons in 1833, the official map accompanying the 1841 Irish Census, W. Bone's reference maps to the 1851 Census, Petermann's sophisticated maps of England and Wales and of Scotland also illustrating the 1851 Census, and the divisional series accompanying the Censuses of 1871 and 1891. Similarly, franchise reform throughout the century produced its share of interpretive cartographic material, both official and unofficial, and, indeed, elections themselves were frequently followed by maps and atlases of voting patterns, election districts and seat distribution; William Lander, for

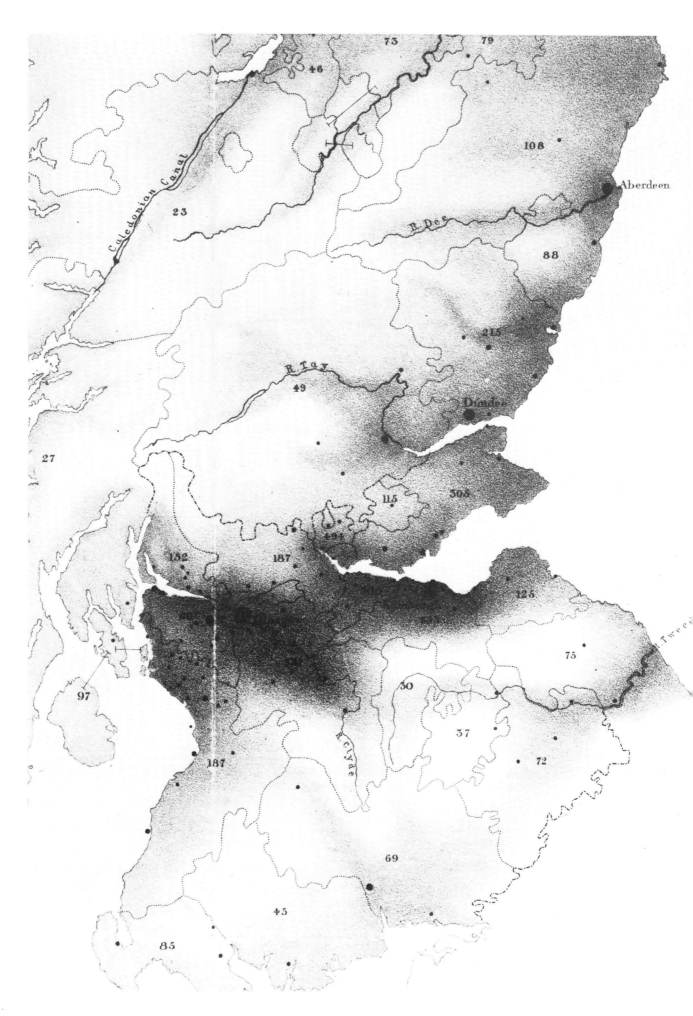

Caledonian Canal

23

27

97

152

187

187

73

79

46

108

Aberdeen

R. Dee

88

215

R. Tay

49

Dundee

305

115

121

125

R. Tweed

75

30

37

72

R. Clyde

69

45

85

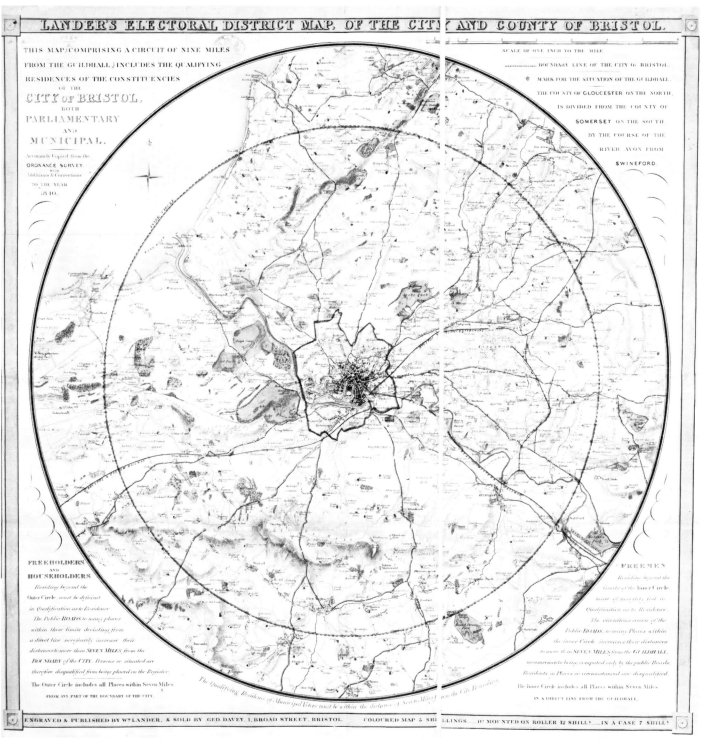

32: *Detail: 'SCOTLAND. DISTRIBUTION OF THE POPULATION. CENSUS OF 1851. Designed by Augustus Petermann, Phys! Geographer to the Queen. Lith. by A. Petermann 9, Charing Cross, London'. By permission of the British Library (Maps 7345(6)).*

33: *'LANDER'S ELECTORAL DISTRICT MAP, OF THE CITY AND COUNTY OF BRISTOL'. 'THIS MAP, (COMPRISING A CIRCUIT OF NINE MILES FROM THE GUILDHALL,) INCLUDES THE QUALIFYING RESIDENCES OF THE CONSTITUENCIES OF THE CITY OF BRISTOL, BOTH PARLIAMENTARY AND MUNICIPAL. Accurately Copied from the ORDNANCE SURVEY WITH Additions & Corrections TO THE YEAR 1840'. Engraved by William Lander. By permission of the British Library (Maps 5060(2)).*

years: 'The map ... has been constructed with great care and attention to particulars, and at the expense of much labour; for I have not only consulted the official returns, the registers of deaths, and the registers of burials, but personally and diligently sought information from those engaged in the burials themselves ... .'[39] In 1852 Petermann produced a map of the British Isles to show 'all districts visited by the cholera' by shading 'darker in proportion to the relative amount of mortality', and, in so doing, explained the advantage of cartographic representation: 'Geographical delineation is of the utmost value, and even indispensable; for while the symbols of the masses of statistical data in figures, however clearly they might be arranged in Systematic Tables, present but a uniform appearance, the same data, embodied in a Map, will convey at once, the

relative bearing and proportion of the single data together with their position, extent and distance, and thus, a Map will make visible to the eye the development and nature of any phenomenon in regard to its geographical distribution.'[40] The most influential cholera map was that of London, published in 1855 by Dr John Snow, for it clearly established the centre of the 'cholera field'[41] in Soho as the water pump in Broad Street and, thus, demonstrated that cholera was water-borne. Medical maps became increasingly common as the century progressed—Dr Robert Perry, for example, published in 1844 a map of Glasgow 'marking with a darker shade those parts where the epidemic was most particularly prevalent' showing that 'those places most densely inhabited, by the poorest of people have suffered

OPPOSITE

34: *The terrible ravages of the cholera epidemics in the mid-nineteenth century stimulated the use of cartographic techniques to investigate disease incidence.*
i *Detail: Map of the distribution of cholera deaths illustrating the second edition of Dr John Snow's* On the Mode of Communication of Cholera, *1855, showing clearly the concentration of deaths around the pump in Broad Street.*
ii *Detail: Distribution of 'Cases of choleraic diarrhoea' and 'Cases of Cholera' in Oxford in 1854 illustrating H. W. Acland's* Memoir on the Cholera at Oxford, *1856.*

35: *Urban improvement was a fertile field of employment for town surveyors, and textbooks catered specifically for the requirements of drainage and sanitation mapping.*
Detail: Textbook plan for improved house drainage using piped sewer. 'IMPROVED BACK DRAINAGE', Drawn by Edward Ryde, engraved by W. Beever, and published in London by John Weale, 1853. From Ryde's General Textbook for the constant use and reference of Architects, Engineers, Surveyors, Solicitors, Auctioneers, Land Agents, and Stewards. *By permission of the British Library (8529dd36).*

most severely'[42] from, probably, influenza; Dr Henry Wentworth Acland published detailed cholera plans of Oxford in 1856; the Metropolitan Board of Health began to publish annual surveys showing the outbreak-distribution of common epidemic diseases; Dr Alfred Haviland produced 'health-guide' maps of Brighton and Scarborough in the early 1880s; and medical officers began to illustrate their reports with disease-distribution maps.

IMPROVEMENT PLANS
Increasing understanding of the causes of disease was a natural concomitant of a growing concern with public health and preventive medicine. The sordid reality of 'streets ... generally unpaved, rough, dirty, filled with vegetable and animal refuse, without sewers or gutters, but supplied with foul stagnant pools instead' and of '... the bad, confused method of building'[43] persuaded progressive towns from the late seventeenth century to establish bodies of commissioners to seek power from Parliament to 'improve' by paving, cleaning, lighting, and other measures to raise the quality of the urban environment. In order to obtain the private Act of Parliament required for introduction of an improvement scheme it was necessary to submit details, including a large-scale plan, to Parliament of the commissioners' proposals for housing, slum clearance, lighting, paving, sewerage and drainage. Similarly, plans were drawn up for the establishment of gas- and water-company areas, police-court divisions and sanitary districts, and for the creation of highways, docks, public buildings, pleasure grounds, public baths, and all the other paraphernalia of municipal reform and improvement. The sudden and startling injection of the railways into long-established towns in particular presented a unique opportunity for re-development as swathes of old property were demolished. *The Times*, for example, in March 1861 welcomed a railway proposal because it would

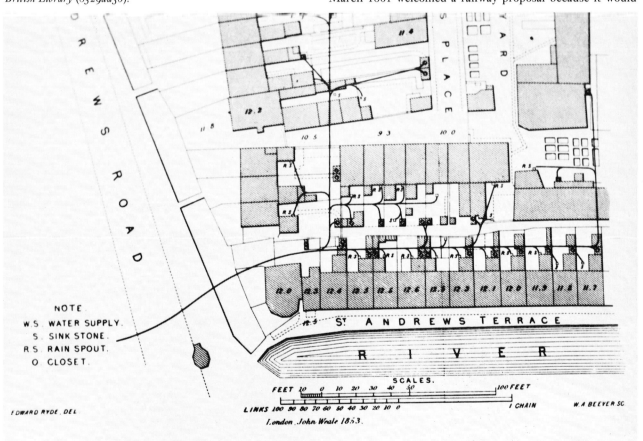

clear 'the ill-ventilated culs de sac and dens of wretchedness of Shoe Lane and Saffron Hill'[44] in London. After 1853, railway companies had to produce 'demolition statements', accompanied by large-scale plans, in order to obtain Parliamentary permission to demolish more than 30 houses in the same parish. The railways brought with them schemes for new property, bridges, sewers, roads, embankments, and so on, all requiring plans; and the railway companies commissioned large numbers of property plans as they energetically acquired estates in many towns.

The extent of re-development in most cities was quite staggering; in London, for example, approximately 80 per cent of the City was re-built, not only, of course, as a result of railway incision, in the half-century between 1855 and 1905. The growing pace of the Board of Works's programme demanded an increasingly rapid revision of London plans as the century progressed. Such schemes as Brunel's Thames Tunnel—exciting 'the admiration of all visitors, and, regarded as an exhibition, ... perhaps the most interesting of which the metropolis can boast'[45]—stimulated remarkable popular interest and curiosity, offering a tempting opportunity for adventurous map-makers. London civic pride and consequent improvement was undoubtedly the most extensive and widely documented in the British Isles. Perhaps the most acclaimed 'improvement' of all was John Nash's Regent Street, 'affording a broad and uninterrupted access from the Houses of Parliament and other Public Buildings in Westminster, to all the principal Streets in the West & North West part of the Town between Pall Mall and the New Road'[46]—such grandiose projects not only generated the detailed large-scale official plans required by Parliament, but also reduced versions for popular consumption. In the case of Regent Street the 'House of Commons' printers', J. Booth, and William Faden produced such popular small plans 'Abstracted from the Drawing presented to The Hon. House of Commons'[47] as, no doubt, did other private map-makers. Even comparatively new industrial towns were, by the 1870s, well-appointed with grand public buildings—a town hall, a free library, churches and schools—all necessitating the preparation of detailed plans in their creation and often generating small-scale reductions for the popular market. Additionally, completion of an improvement often encouraged the decoration of maps with vignettes of the new building or development which would glorify its elegance and style.

However, piecemeal control and improvement was obviously unsatisfactory because permissive, rather than mandatory, legislation left progress to the vagaries of changing local-authority moods. By the 1830s the Poor Law Commission, particularly its outspoken secretary Edwin Chadwick, was demanding better sanitation in order to improve disease prevention and raise the very variable national standards of public health. The permissive Public Health Act of 1848 allowed towns to set up a local board of health to enforce proper drainage, provide and maintain sewers, and force the installation of privies. One of the first required steps in the creation of these sanitary districts, which were formed throughout the period until the imposition of compulsory legislation, was the submission of a large-scale plan of the area to the Board of Health. For zones not covered by Ordnance Survey plans, particularly suburbs ignored by

the Survey, it was necessary to commission private surveys; for example, the Garston area on the outskirts of Liverpool was surveyed by Gotto who used colour to differentiate building-type on his 20-sheet manuscript map at the scale of 10':1m. of 1855. Similarly, Wallasey, in Cheshire, was mapped by Mills and Fletcher on 17 sheets, also in 1855; St Michael's Hamlet in Toxteth Park by C. Terbutt in 1856; Wavertree by A. F. Orridge in 1854; and West Derby also by Gotto in 1855 on 40 sheets.

The appalling cholera epidemics convinced town dwellers of the necessity of rates, by-laws, and municipal control, and the most energetic authorities, such as Joseph Chamberlain's Birmingham in the 1870s, enthusiastically 'parked, paved, assized, marketed, Gas-and-Watered, and *improved*'.[48] The most important change in the planning of improvements, and, consequently, in the mapping of the towns themselves, was brought about by Chadwick's condemnation of private surveyors—whether land, rating, municipal, or building—as inefficient, incompetent, and expensive in his *Report on the Sanitary Condition of the Labouring Population of Great Britain* of 1842 (which, incidently, was accompanied by maps of Bethnal Green and Leeds showing classes of housing and the distribution of disease-incidence). In contrast, Chadwick extolled the virtues of the military surveyors, thus shifting the onus of large-scale town-plan production onto the Ordnance Survey which embarked upon a programme of officially encouraged urban survey, destined to last for most of the century, with a 5':1m. plan of St Helens published in 1843–4 (Irish towns had actually been mapped at this scale for valuation purposes, but not for publication, from 1833). This programme, which was initially to cover all towns of over 4,000 population north of the Hull–Preston line, was largely completed by 1855, although not all plans were engraved and

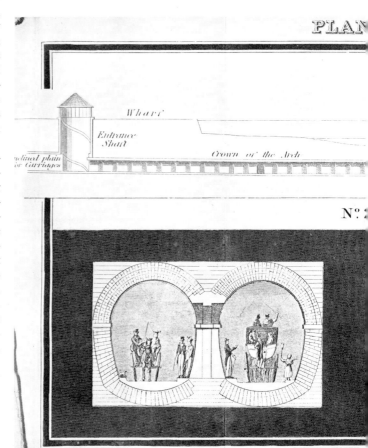

36: *'PLAN AND SECTION OF THE THAMES TUNNEL'*, *published by Edward Mogg, 1847, in* Mogg's New Picture of London; or, Strangers' Guide to the British Metropolis.

published. However, the Public Health Act of 1848, which was applied by some 180 British local authorities, and the equivalent Irish legislation of 1854, emphasized the need for even larger-scale plans to clarify improvement proposals by showing such sanitary and drainage features as cesspits, drains, and privies. Consequently a 10′ scale was introduced for towns prepared to contribute to project expenses. The closely related scale of 10.56′:1m. was widely adopted after 1855 following the Treasury's acceptance of the need for the extra expense involved (although, nevertheless, the Treasury seems subsequently to have subjected Ireland to a series of economy measures!). The new scale applied to British towns of over 4,000 population and Irish, initially of over 1,000, but from 1872 only of over 4,000. In all, over 500 towns in the British Isles were mapped at the 10.56′ scale before 1893/94 when the Ordnance Survey abandoned town plans at all these large scales. Clearly, because of the large scale, towns were covered by multiple sheets—Nottingham, for example, appeared on 352 and Liverpool on 304; consequently, indexes at the mainly 6″ scale had to be published showing the sheet divisions for each town. Generally, only a first edition of the plans was produced, although some English and Irish town plans were revised by the Ordnance between 1898 and 1908 for towns prepared to meet the expense, and others, including a few in Scotland, were revised by the towns themselves or used as base maps on which specialized detail was added. Possibly there was also a process of minor piecemeal revision at work throughout; at least four states of the 5′ plan of Liverpool have been identified and there was clearly a major revision in 1864 with about two-thirds of the 50 sheets being revised for railways, docks, major public buildings, street names, and so on, providing the basis for the revision of the 6″ sheets in the same year. These remarkable plans were so

Town Plans Published by the Ordnance Survey in the Nineteenth Century

	Scale		
	1:1056 5′:1m.	1:528 10′:1m.	1:500 10.56′:1m.
England	59	17	365
Wales	–	1	32
Scotland	15		56
Ireland	42 + Greater Dublin (covered on 10 separately titled sections)	–	66

detailed that individual buildings were named, commercial and industrial uses specified, and such detailed features as pillar boxes, fire hydrants, and the interior design of public buildings shown. Stanford, in particular, realized the value of the Ordnance Survey sheets prepared for the Commission of Sewers, using them to construct the 'Library Map' of 1862—'the most perfect map of London that has ever been issued'.[49]

The very distinction of the Ordnance's magnificent town plans disguises the fact that private map-makers were also involved, obviously to a much lesser extent, in large-scale provision for the use of municipal improvers and planners. James Wyld (who, for example, overprinted his large map of London with levels 'taken by order of the Commissioners of Sewers'[50]), George Frederick Cruchley, Charles Smith, Edward Stanford, and the like, produced special versions of their large-scale maps with improvement information, both suggested and sanctioned, superimposed on them.

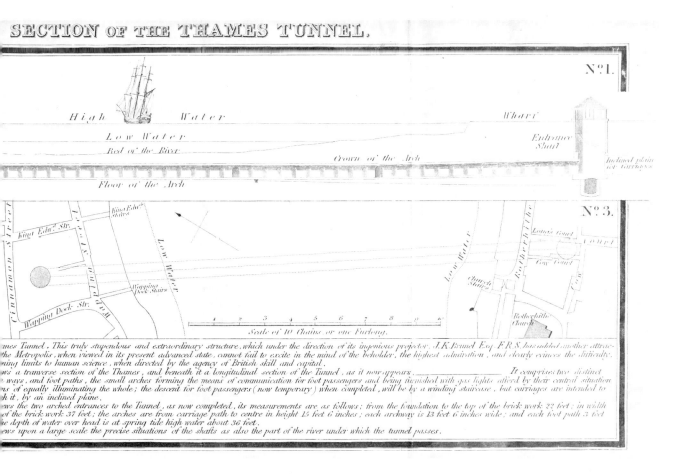

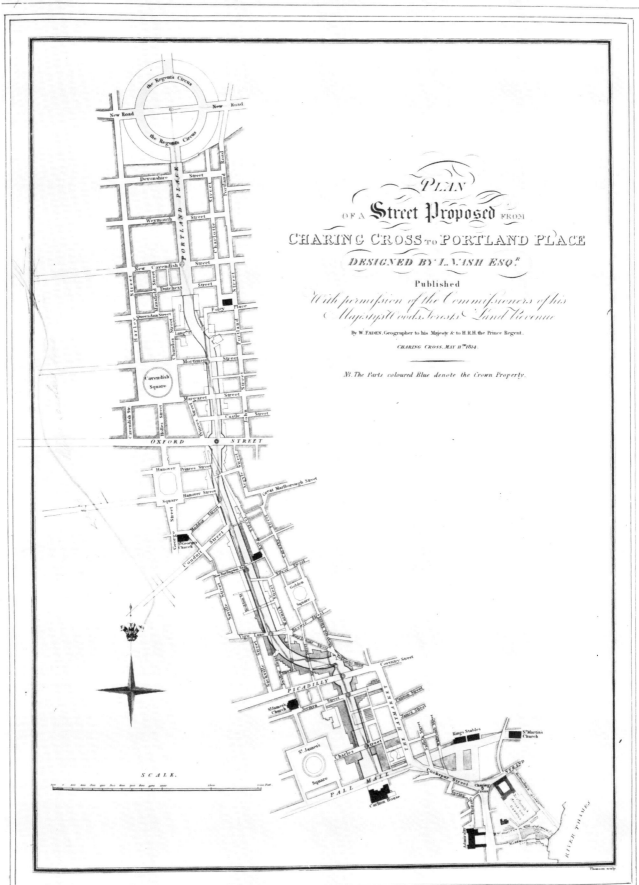

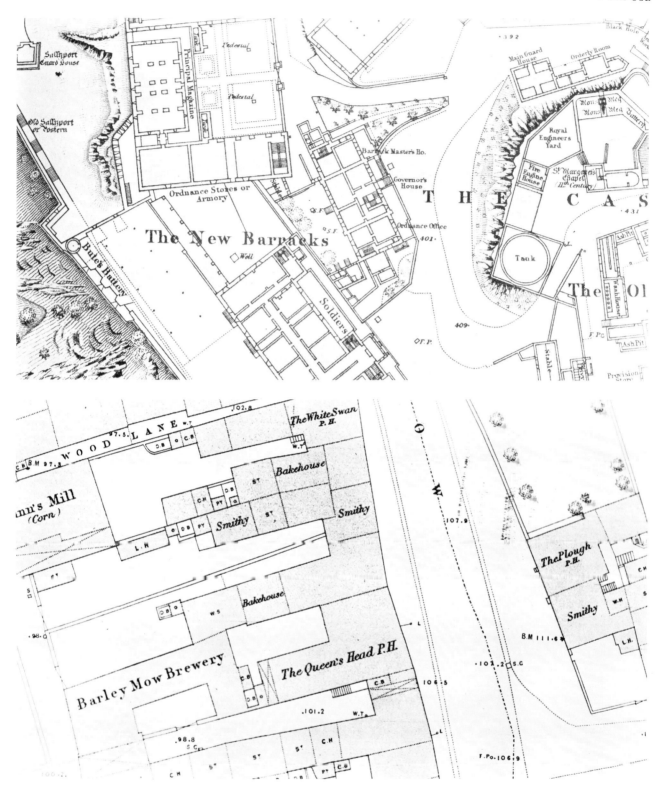

OPPOSITE
37: '*PLAN OF A Street Proposed FROM CHARING CROSS TO PORTLAND PLACE DESIGNED BY I. NASH ESQ^R. Published With permission of his Majesty's Woods, Forests & Land Revenue By W. FADEN, Geographer to his Majesty & to H.R.H. the Prince Regent. CHARING CROSS, May 11^T.H 1814*'. By permission of the British Library (Crace 12/17).*

38: *The Ordnance Survey's large-scale mapping of towns created the most detailed delineation of urban areas ever seen with scales of 5' and 10' to the mile.*
i *Detail: Ordnance Survey, 5': 1m. 'Edinburgh and its Environs', Sheet 35, 'Surveyed in 1852, by Captains H. James & W. Driscoll Gosset, R.E. Engraved in 1853, under the direction of Captain W. Driscoll Gosset, R.E. at the ORDNANCE MAP OFFICE, SOUTHAMPTON, and Published by L! Colonel Hall, R. E. Superintendent. 31^s!, March 1854.' By kind permission of the Ordnance Survey.*
ii *Detail: Ordnance Survey, 10':1m. plan of Sunderland, surveyed 1856. By kind permission of the Ordnance Survey. Reproduced also in* A History of the Ordnance Survey *edited by Col. W. A. Seymour, published by Dawson Publishing, Folkestone.*

TOWN PLANS

It was, however, the overall morphology of the whole town that was of the greatest interest to the greatest number, and was, therefore, most extensively mapped; and it was the private map-maker, rather than the official, who was usually responsible for the vast number of popular, generally small-scale, town plans produced in ever-increasing numbers as the century progressed. In the recent past, plans had been mainly plagiarized from the elegant but imprecise insets of eighteenth-century large-scale county maps or were the result of cursory survey concentrating on those fashionable features likely to appeal to a narrow affluent clientele; but their style and content no longer served the needs of a rapidly growing, increasingly urban, affluent, and literate population. Graceful plans such as Ainslie's inset of St Andrews with its emphasis on archaeological remains and Godwin's romantic edition of Donn's Bath survey with its time-worn concentration on churches and other stylish architecture could not survive long in the new purposeful age. Although a few privately produced large-scale town plans, such as the Greenwoods' magnificent 'Map of London' which remained in publication from 1827 to 1856, combined the quality of Ordnance Survey production with more commercial presentation and practical scale, most were less expensively designed to satisfy not only the obvious small-scale requirements of route-finding and commercial delivery, but also those of social study, municipal improvement, boundary alteration, and other particular purposes. Hence historical curiosity, for instance, was satisfied by copies of earlier plans—Knight's article on 'Norwich and Yarmouth', published in *The Graphic* of 25 August 1883, being, for example, illustrated with a woodcut version of Braun & Hogenberg's 1581 plan of Norwich. In contrast, insurance plans were prepared to facilitate fire insurance by indicating construction materials, street widths, building heights, window numbers, position of skylights, and even the names of occupying firms and the use of individual

rooms. This plethora of plans not only appeared in atlas series such as those of Cole & Roper, Robert Kearsley Dawson, Samuel Lewis, Thomas Moule, and John Wood, but also in more general geographical texts and a wide array of commercial and street directories, gazetteers, histories, guides, and other works, as well as being published individually or for issue with newspapers. Thus, obsolete reproduction, style and content gradually gave way to a more functional approach which, although still often attractively decorated and emphasizing religious institutions, was designed for specific practical uses or for a modern mass market through the inclusion of civil, commercial and social features previously largely ignored.

This burgeoning interest in urban topography, particularly from the man-in-the-street, is hardly surprising, for the century was one of spectacular town growth, obvious to all, as the pre-eminent eighteenth-century rural lowland zone gave way to the dominance of London and the new manufacturing and mining centres of the North and Midlands. Urbanization and industrialization epitomised Victorian Britain, creating new and greater demands on the town cartographer who faced increasing difficulties in revising his plans to keep pace with a phenomenal rate of urban expansion—Bradford, for example, grew by a staggering 700 per cent in the first half of the century. In 1891, the Director-General of the Ordnance Survey remarked that the area of London had nearly doubled since the time of the Ordnance's first survey and that some districts had al-

39: *Insurance plans were prepared to facilitate fire insurance by indicating construction materials, street widths, building heights, window numbers, position of sky-lights, and even the names of occupying firms and the use of individual rooms.*
Detail: Sowerby Bridge, by Charles E. Goad, Nov. 1896. By courtesy of Charles E. Goad Ltd.

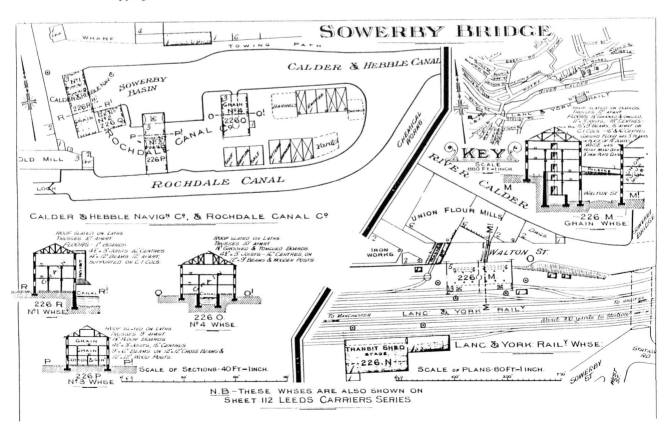

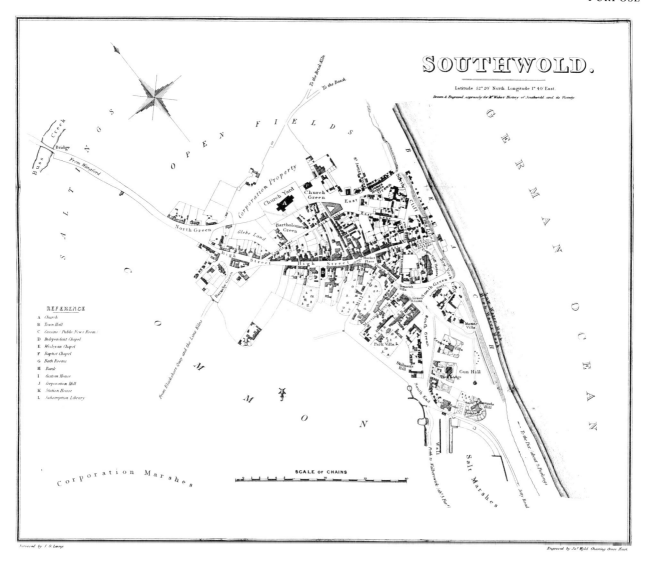

40: *Town plans were produced in great numbers to illustrate a wide array of commercial and street directories, gazetteers, histories, guides, and other works.*
Southwold, surveyed by J. G. Lenny, engraved by James Wyld, 'expressly for M". Wake's History of Southwold, and its Vicinity,' 1839.

tered so radically that re-survey had become urgently necessary. The century witnessed virtually a complete reversal in population distribution: in 1801 approximately 80 per cent of the population lived in rural areas, by 1901 the same percentage lived within boroughs or urban districts; and by 1851 already over half the population lived in towns of over 2000 population. This multiplicity of new, growing urban centres represented a unique cartographic opportunity, for not only did businessmen require maps for the commercial exploitation of these new markets, but also inhabitants and visitors needed them in order to find their way about in addition to feeding their healthy interest in development and improvement for its own prestigious sake. No longer were finely decorated, ingratiatingly dedicated town plans produced for the gentleman's library; rather, plain, heavily drawn, frequently revised, cheap maps were published in ever-increasing numbers to satisfy the growing demands of the ever more literate and mobile working and middle classes.

Categories of Nineteenth-Century Town Plans

Note that both count and categorization are necessarily very rough and are designed merely to offer a general picture of the types of plans produced and their relative importance for an established regional centre in relative decline during the century and a new industrial centre of rapidly increasing regional and national significance. Since base maps were frequently used as the foundation for maps on varying themes, or underwent revision between issue, or appeared in works of differing nature, all editions of a plan have been counted. No distinction between the town and its immediate environs has been made, but plans of specific districts are generally not counted; in particular, those concerning individual transport schemes and building projects are excluded.

	Norwich	Leeds
Historical street and boundary plans	24	3
Copies or reproductions of sixteenth- and seventeenth- century plans	9	–
Street plans in topographical works	18	21
Plans relating to sewerage, drainage, water supply and sanitary districts	5	8
Plans in commercial directories	5	17
Plans relating to boundary alterations	5	8
Ordnance Survey plans	3	13
Drink plans	4	–
Insurance plans	1	1
Transport and communications' plans	3	14
Religious plans	1	–
Medical plans	–	11
Other plans	19	33

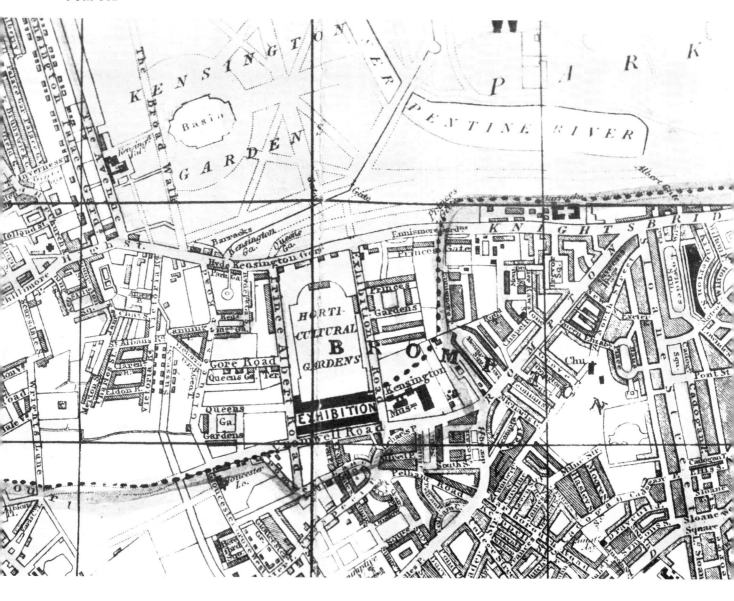

Transport developments, in particular, fostered a widening demand for maps which clarified the routes of tramways, omnibuses, and suburban railways, and the sites of cab stands, bus stops, and stations. The cheap availability of railway transport stimulated interest in the towns, and the excursion to local and national centres became an increasingly common feature of the leisure activity which accompanied the shorter working week. Private map-makers seized upon this potentially huge market by producing guide-plans and guide-books specifically aimed at the daytripper, tourist, and holiday-maker. Edward Mogg, one of the most skilful exploiters of this genre, for example, produced a variety of tempting works 'containing, in a small compass, a fund of information ... respectfully recommended to all Rural Visitors ...';[51] his *London in Miniature* delineated '... the Improvements, both present and in-

tended, ... actually reduced, *by permission*, from the Surveys of the several Proprietors ... on reference to the Plan, the smallest place will be immediately found.'[52] Similarly, *Cruchley's New Guide to London*, the work of another adept exponent of the art, available 'Price 2s.6d., in Illustrated Cover, or bound in Cloth, with a large Map of London, 3s.6d.', contained 'full information about ... every object or place of interest in the Metropolis.'[53] Clearly a good guide was considered essential for the visitor. 'To avoid the inconvenience of taxing his friend to an attendance upon him in his perigrinations, it is indispensable that he provide himself with a good plan ... like the clue of Ariadne, they will conduct him through the labyrinth, and occasionally consulted, will enable him unattended to thread with ease the mazes ... .'[54] Opportunist publishers vied to attract the custom of visitors with the 'latest' novel approach to street representation and route finding: 'The ordinary sheet Map has become, even to residents, nearly as difficult a problem to solve as it always has been to strangers.'[55] Thus, Sulman, for instance, resurrected the Tudor bird's-eye view to show buildings in perspective, for Herbert Fry's popular, frequently re-published, work on London in the 1880s and '90s 'ILLUSTRATED BY TWENTY BIRD'S-EYE VIEWS OF THE PRINCIPAL STREETS';[56] and Thomas Hodgson published 36 sectional maps, in his *London at a Glance* of 1859, decorated usually with vignettes

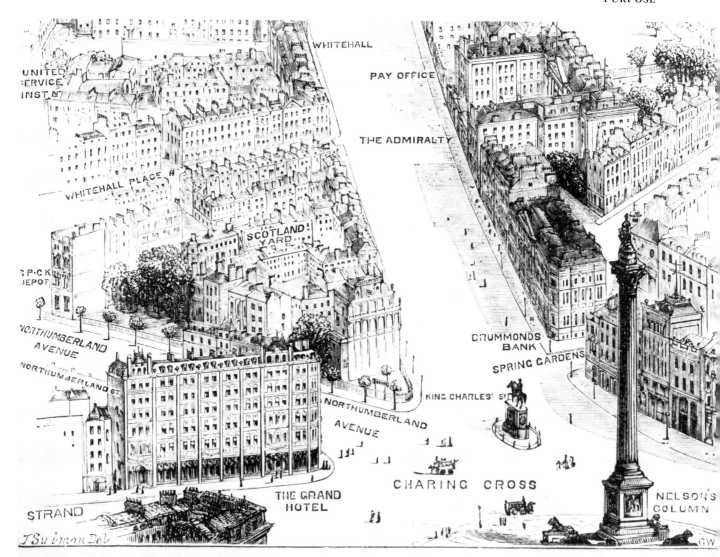

FROM CHARING CROSS THROUGH WHITEHALL TO WESTMINSTER.

42: *Publishers vied with each other to present their maps in a novel eye-catching way to attract a fickle public. T. Sulman, for instance, re-introduced the Tudor-style bird's-eye view for his street plan of the Whitehall area.*
Detail: 'FROM CHARING CROSS THROUGH WHITEHALL TO WESTMINSTER', by T. Sulman, c.1892.

and concentrating on places of interest, 'each embraces some principal route, from one well-known point to another ... the stranger can easily find his way from one part of London to the other'.[57] Like the rambler, the ambler was specifically provided-for with works like *Walks through London* which guided the sight-seeing stroller by means of route maps accompanied by illustrations and explanatory text.

Naturally London was the most powerful magnet to visitors, but provincial centres also had their attractions as did the increasingly accessible watering places and coastal resorts that came within the reach of, at least, the middle classes through rising prosperity and a rapidly sprawling rail network. The 1871 Census listed 56 seaside towns and inland watering places in England and Wales, including (in its own words!) Torquay and Torbay 'with the charms of an Italian lake' and Scarborough 'the fair mistress of that coast'.[58] Private local initiative catered for visitors to these resorts with directories, illustrated by maps and plans, of

merchants, hotels, lending libraries, doctors, banks, lodging houses, and the various 'attractions'. Likewise, guide-books and town plans exhibited, in the words of John Bruce's *History of Brighton* (which contained a delightful Brighton plan 'with the latest Improvements'), '... the several public buildings, churches, and other places of worship, most esteemed rides, remarkable characters, manners, fashion &c &c'.[59] Other more ambitious guides purported to cover a multitude of destinations, as, for example, did *A Guide to all the Watering and Sea-Bathing Places with a Description of the Lakes; a Sketch of a Tour in Wales; and Itineraries* published by Richard Phillips in 1804 with its 20 index, environs, regional, and town maps. Similarly, A. & C. Black produced 'Road and Railway Guides' to the nations containing 'plans of the principal cities' which were 'admirably 'got up'' and 'should find a corner in the portmanteau of every person about to undertake a journey of pleasure or business ...'.[60]

Private production for an unsophisticated and undiscerning market was frequently unreliable and out-of-date, with map-makers content simply to add areas of new urban growth to existing plates or stones around the edge of earlier development, without any revision of re-developed areas. However, the increasing availability of the large-scale accurate plans produced by the Tithe and Ordnance Surveys provided more reliable sources for plagiarist commercial

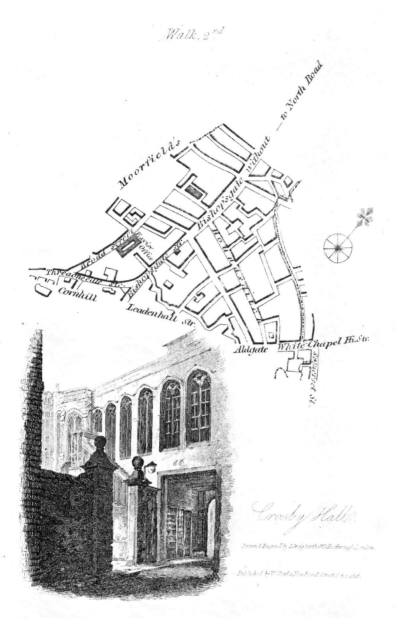

43: *Map-makers produced planned tours for the tripper. Walk 2 of Walks through London, drawn and engraved by L. Greig and published by W. Clarke in 1816, guided the ambler through the north of the City past Crosby Hall.*
'Walk, 2ⁿᵈ', by L. Greig, 1816.

44: *'A NEW MAP OF BRISTOL, CLIFTON, AND THE HOTWELLS. Engraved for Chilcott's Guide to Bristol, Clifton & the Hotwells'. 1826. Engraved by William Lander. By permission of the British Library (Maps 5045(22)).*

map-makers. It was no longer necessary to conduct a private survey or to copy unreliable earlier maps because relatively up-to-date plans could now be derived from the plans of the Surveys, and from the Ordnance's interim revisions and large-scale 25″ maps. This did not mean, however, that private map-makers had nothing to contribute. Charles Knight's 'Environs of Dublin', for instance, published about 1852 at a scale of only 1.33m.:1″ showed names and symbols of houses, institutions, roads, inns, factories and antiquities not found on either the 6″ or the 1″ sheets of the Ordnance Survey. Likewise, John Bartholomew's 1891 'really perfect Plan of the City of Edinburgh, engraved in minute and exact detail', reduced from the Ordnance 5′ plan to a scale of 15″ to the mile, showed: 'Every tree and

bush in Greyfriars churchyard ... delineated with absolute clarity. Every lamp-post dotted in on every pavement. So are the flower-beds in the gardens, the garden sheds, the stairways and steps of the courts and closes.'[61] 'There is scarcely a bracket on the wall of a wynd which has not been frozen for posterity on that plan, and the reproduction does not stop, as most reproductions do, at the outsides of the buildings. You may trace the seating arrangements in the Surgeons' Hall, count the stalls in the Court of Session, measure the curves of the benches in University lecture-rooms and study the layout of the display cases in the Science Museum.'[61] In addition to these wonders, purchase of a copy mounted on cloth for 45s. qualified one's house or place of business for personalized colouring free of charge!

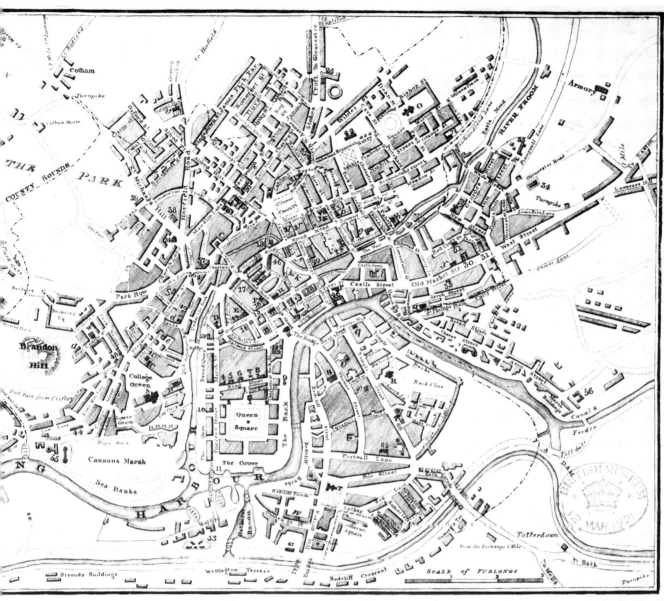

Engraved for Chilcott's Guide to Bristol, Clifton & the Hotwells.

ENVIRONS' MAPS

Town mapping was not limited to official boundaries. Town environs became increasingly important and increasingly mapped throughout the century because town dwellers used surrounding rural areas for leisure with growing frequency with the development of the railway, the omnibus, the bicycle, and, later, the motor car. There was also a steady population movement away from the decaying city centres to pleasanter outlying suburbs and villages, 'almost entirely in the possession of the cow-keepers'.[62] The increased mapping of environs, often producing circular maps by delineating the area within the radius of some central point, was another nail in the coffin of the county map for the compass of such environs' maps totally disregarded county boundaries. Inner-city depopulation was already apparent at the start of the century and it was predictable that the 'well-to-do', those with the option offered by affluence, preferred to abandon the squalid towns to live in 'their little colonies outside'.[63] With foreseeable business acumen, map-makers flattered this lucrative market by concentrating on the representation of gentlemen's seats, the naming of landowners, and sometimes the delineation of their sophisticated intellectual and sporting pursuits. In time outlying

areas became accessible not only by the private post-chaise and carriage, but also by the public horse-bus, tram, and suburban railway. Thus came the opportunity for pleasant excursions and for the lower-middle class at least to invade such high-class rural villages as Islington and Tottenham outside London and still travel to work cheaply on the workmen's tickets which were introduced from 1861 on many lines. With each new development of suburban transport, the limits of the day-trip and the commuter-belt, and, thus, the limits of profitable town cartography, were extended, with town workers able to make excursions and to live further and further from their place of employment.

The rapid spread of the towns added significance to the mapping of the environs, for already the development of conurbations was apparent as the urban area extended beyond its official boundaries to swallow outlying villages and form suburbs. In many cases the map of the environs became a more realistic representation of the town than the town plan itself—London, for example, could well be considered a conurbation at the start of the century; by the mid-century the West Yorkshire conurbation was almost half its mid-1970s size; and by the end of the century central Clydeside had a population of one-and-a-half million. By

77

1847, for instance, Edward Mogg was complaining that existing maps of London misrepresented its extent for by that time it not only included 'the City and Liberties' and 'the City and Liberties of Westminster' but also 'nearly thirty of the surrounding villages of Middlesex and Surrey'.[64] This explosion of urban Britain was reflected in a host of fine, fascinating maps 'Compiled' not only 'specially to exhibit all the principal Gentlemen's Seats, Antiquities, and Objects of Interest',[65] but also to delineate all other aspects of the town and its hinterland. However, as the century progressed, town maps became steadily more practicable and less unctuous as they were designed for a less exclusive, utilitarian market.

COMMERCIAL MAPS

Urban growth was, obviously, partly a response to increased commercial activity and this, too, was reflected in specifically commercial maps and by the production of commercial directories, which frequently contained maps and plans, to serve the needs of a rapidly expanding business community. The Victorian age is peppered with examples of maps illustrating various features of economic activity, issued not only

in the increasingly lengthy thematic sections of atlases but also in other works and as one-off productions responding to a perceived mercantile demand. Augustus Petermann, for example, 'Designed and executed' a map of the chief occupations and manufacturing regions for the 1851 Census Report which represented occupational distribution by 'colours, shading and symbols', manufacturing districts by stipple shading, and 'the individual branches of manufacture' by 'coloured or shaded spots and symbols'.[66] A more sophisticated map on this theme designed by Samuel Clark and compiled and drawn by Petermann appeared in the National Society's Atlas. Alternatively, maps were designed for office use, often for wall display as a source of ready reference, satisfying wide commercial requirements through general national maps, and specific local needs with large-scale town plans usually based on those of the Ordnance Survey. George Philip, for instance, not only produced such a large-scale plan of Liverpool but also catered for wider needs with 'Philips' Industrial Map of the British Islands,' 'by WILLIAM HUGHES, F.R.G.S. Exhibiting the Chief Localities of Manufacturing and Commercial Industry, with the ratio of Population in the different Counties and the Towns classified according to their respective Populations'.[67]

The growing publication of commercial directories dated from the early years of the Industrial Revolution when improved communications began to open up wider markets, necessitating better contact between seller and consumer. Extending trade relations required a quick and easy means of reference to names, occupations, and addresses. The further commercial advances of Victoria's reign—the rail-

45: *John Bartholomew's 'really perfect Plan of the City of Edinburgh, engraved in minute and exact detail'. Detail: 'BARTHOLOMEW'S PLAN OF THE CITY OF EDINBURGH WITH LEITH & SUBURBS REDUCED FROM THE ORDNANCE SURVEY AND REVISED TO THE PRESENT DATE. BY JOHN BARTHOLOMEW, F.R.G.S. 1891'. By courtesy of John Bartholomew & Son Ltd.*

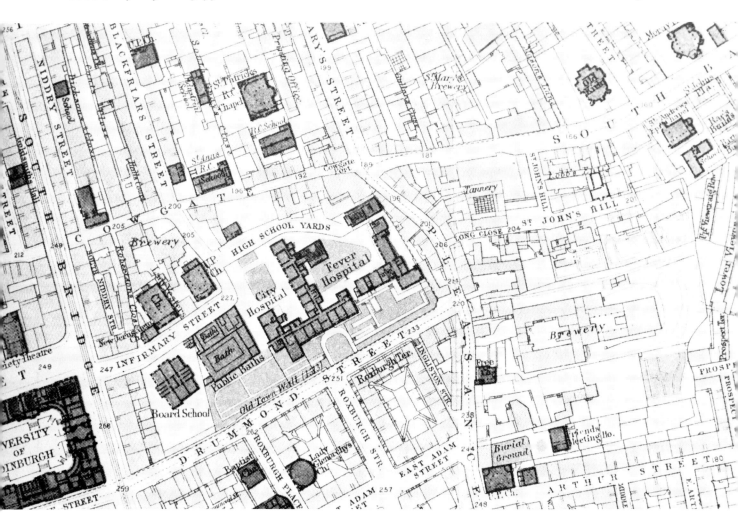

ways, the telegraph, the penny post—demanded more comprehensive provision with publishers competing vigorously to offer annual directories of ever-wider coverage both in terms of individuals and firms, and in the inclusion of such peripheral information as the area's history, institutions, transport facilities, and so on. Professional directory publishers, such as James Pigot and Frederic Kelly, produced works containing general topographical maps, town plans, and specifically commercial thematic maps. From the 1820s Pigot's great directory surveys covered the whole country at reasonably frequent intervals, but this was the exception rather than the rule, for rival national schemes (except Kelly's) tended to be short-lived, and the majority of directories were produced by local publishers to serve only their home area (as R. Todd did with *The Straw Hat and Bonnet Dealers Guide* illustrated with 'A Pictorial Map of Luton'). Some did build on local success by extending coverage to surrounding and even relatively distant areas—typical examples were: *Lascelles and Co.'s Directory & Gazetteer of the City of Coventry and Neighbourhood* (1850—'PRICE OF THE VOL.—TO SUBSCRIBERS, 4s.6d.; OR WITH MAP OF THE COUNTY, 6s.') containing 'Lascelles &

C⁰'s Map of Warwickshire'; *Craven & Co.'s Commercial Directory of Bedfordshire & Hertfordshire* (1854) with its 'Craven & C⁰'s .. Directory Map of Hertfordshire'; the directories of William Robson, Edward Cassey, and Percy Butcher with their respective re-issues of the county maps of T.L. Murray, Robert Rowe, and George Philip; and Edward Baines's directories of Yorkshire and Lancashire with their fine plans of towns in those counties. Other publishers contented themselves with more general economic guides, as George Bradshaw did with *Bradshaw's Hand-Book to the Manufacturing Districts of Great Britain; furnishing a very instructive detail of the various branches of trade carried on in the counties of Lancashire, Cheshire, Staffordshire, and Warwickshire* which was 'illustrated with well executed county maps',[68] a general map, and town plans engraved by, amongst others, John Dower.

Entrepreneurs themselves saw commercial opportunities in the use of maps as an advertising medium. Cycling advertisements accompanying cycling maps are well-known, but other business fields were equally exploitable: Waltham Brothers, for example, issued their 'Pocket Map of London' as a means of advertising their beers in 1877; British Insulated Cables presented *From Brighton to Inverness 48 Town Maps with Useful Information for Tourists* to their customers, with compliments, in 1900; and transfers from *Cary's Improved Map of England & Wales* of 1832 had advertisements added c.1895 to create 'SAVORY'S 'ECLIPSE' SERIES OF COUNTY MAPS'.

46: *Maps of a town's environs might be aimed at the day-tripper who explored the beauty-spots of his surrounding area by post-chaise, by coach, or later by horse-bus, railway or bicycle.*
Detail: 'ILLUSTRATED MAP OF THE ENVIRONS OF LONDON', by John Dower, 1862. By permission of the British Library (Maps 3479 (143)).

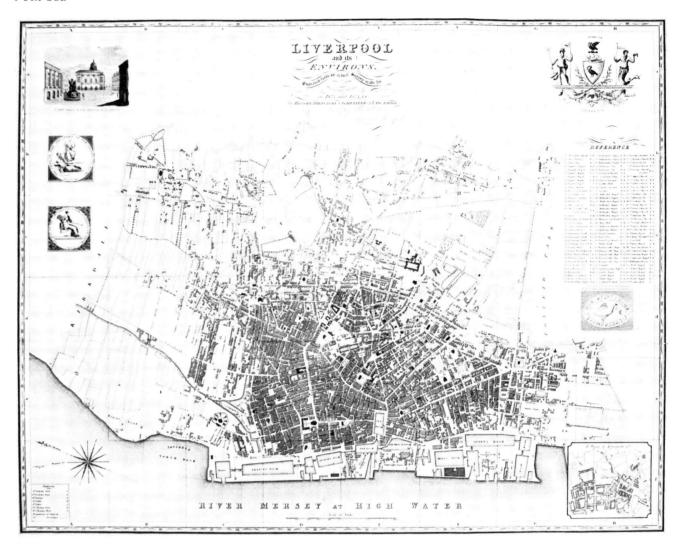

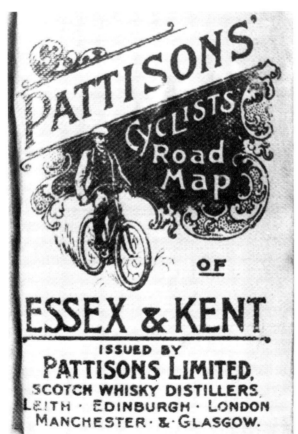

47: *'LIVERPOOL and its ENVIRONS', surveyed by William Swire for Edward Baines's* History, Directory & Gazetteer of Lancaster, *1824-5. By courtesy of Ivan Deverall.*

48: *'PATTISONS' CYCLISTS' Road Map OF ESSEX & KENT', folding into a cover measuring only 64 mm × 89 mm designed to fit into a cyclist's pocket, was merely a means of advertising Pattisons' Scotch Whisky by offering a route map, at an unhelpfully small scale, by John Bartholomew & Co., undated, but c.1897.*
i *Cover.*
ii *The map was surrounded by appropriate vignettes: 'Leith Offices', 'Gordon Duty-Paid Warehouses', 'Pattisons' Customs Warehouses', 'Yard adjoining Gordon Warehouse', 'Duddingston', 'Section of Excise Warehouse', and, of course, bottles of 'Pattisons Royal Gordon Scotch Whisky' and their liqueur whisky 'The Morning Dew'. Detail.*
iii *The reverse of the map was covered with advertisements for their whisky 'invaluable to all TRAVELLERS & SPORTSMEN ABROAD', recommending 'PATTISONS WHEN CYCLING'. Detail.*

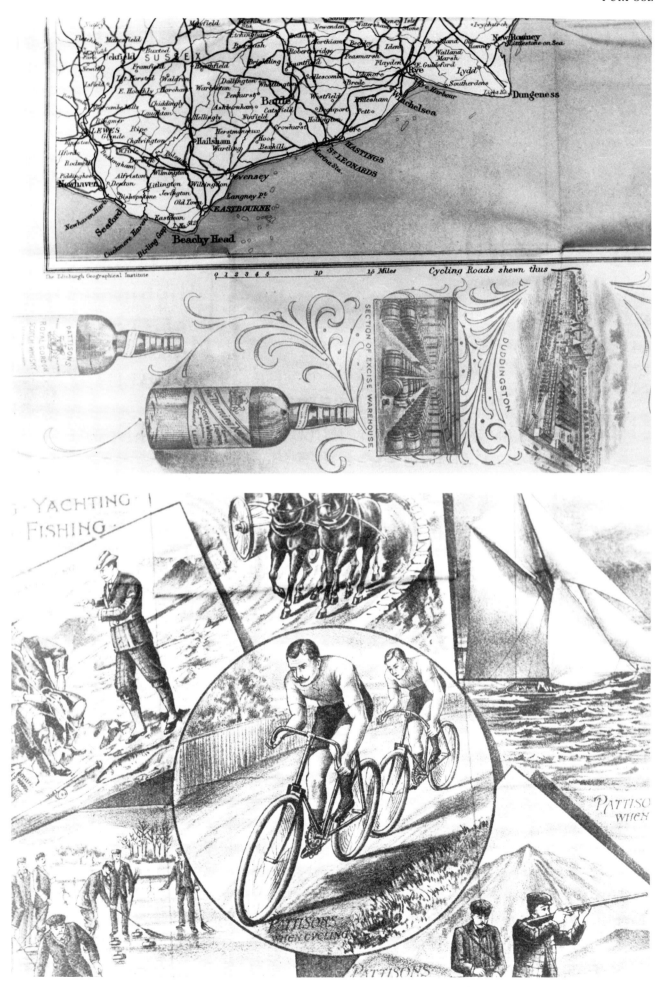

TRANSPORT MAPS

Accelerated economic development was made possible only by fundamental advances in transport and communications. The Industrial Revolution created a complex transport infrastructure of roads, bridges, canals, docks, and railroads (although several decades were to elapse before the appearance of the locomotive), and the accompanying new profession of civil engineering. This evolutionary process was accompanied at every stage by cartographic activity at both national and local level, and some map-makers specialized in mapping only transport developments. Each transport scheme was preceded by propaganda designed to win Parliamentary approval and raise finance. Promoters commissioned prospectus plans to entice a public hungry to invest and to mollify shareholders who had committed their funds. In order to obtain the private Act of Parliament necessary for a scheme to go ahead, detailed plans had to be submitted to Parliament, from 1792, providing an exact delineation of the land traversed, together with a book of reference specifying land ownership *en route*. From 1807, these plans had to be on a scale of at least 4″ to the mile and duplicates had to be deposited with the Clerk of the Peace. Such large-scale plans, usually limited to the area along the line of the proposed project, might additionally offer information on land use, tenure, and so on. Each affected landowner might receive a copy of the whole map or simply a plan of that part of his estate which the scheme crossed. Once a proposal had received parliamentary approval, detailed surveys were required to facilitate the engineering work.

In addition to the maps which were essential to bring a transport development into being, once the project was operational existing maps required revision, and special formats had to be devised to satisfy the specific needs of the transport user. The immense interest in transport development caused commercial map-makers to race to be first with the delineation of a newly opened scheme, often to the extent that some 'jumped the gun' and marked in developments as opened when they were, in fact, only proposed. Therefore, the use of transport information to date maps should be used with extreme caution, for schemes were often marked as being in operation well in advance of their completion. Furthermore, since map-makers often failed to distinguish schemes which were merely 'proposed', canals and railways were frequently anticipated on maps as fact when, in the event, they were aborted and never actually built.

Keeping maps up-to-date in respect of transport development was a commercial headache, for the public demanded the inclusion of the latest expansion; and whilst the addition of a new scheme to an existing plate or stone was comparatively easy, it nevertheless increased costs in a highly competitive situation rendering existing stock obsolete and necessitating a new printing. Some map-makers up-dated their maps only periodically, and others simply revised transport information and nothing else. J. & C. Walker resorted to drawing in new railways in red by hand on existing stock, and Henry Fisher suggested that customers should actually keep their maps up-to-date themselves: 'In one point, and one only, will these Maps be found imperfect, and even for that defect a remedy is always within the owner's power. It is the expression on the Map, of every Railroad constructed or likely to be so. As these great works are in daily progress, and as it is uncertain how many, and which particularly, will be sanctioned by the Legislature, it would have been highly injudicious to have more on each Map than had been determined on with certainty. As soon,

however, as any new Line shall have obtained its protecting Act, the Line may be laid down with any chosen colour on the various Maps it is intended to traverse, and in this way the Maps presented in this Volume can scarcely ever become obsolete.'[69]

Many cartographers produced maps of the country concentrating only on transport information. Tallis, for instance, published a fine, decorative 'Railway Map of Great Britain showing the railways up to the present time, with the steam boat tracks from the principal British and Continental Sea ports'; James Reynolds's 'Railway Map of England' showed 'The railways completed and in progress; with the proposed new lines, the turnpike roads and principal steam communications from port to port'; and A. & C. Black produced a series of 'Travelling Maps' of the nations 'Carefully compiled from the Maps of the Ordnance Survey, and beautifully engraved ... with all the Roads, Railroads, and other Topographical Information required by the Tourist or Traveller on Business'.[70] Many guidebooks contained travelling maps, such as, for example, the fine map of North Wales in the Rev. W. Bingley's *North Wales* of 1804, or Sidney Hall's map of Wales in *Leigh's Guide to Wales & Monmouthshire*. Especial note must be made of the contribution of George Bradshaw, who, having failed as an engraver in Belfast, moved to Manchester and began engraving maps which concentrated on transport information. Such was his eventual reputation and the quality of his work for members of the Institution of Civil Engineers that he was made an Associate of that body in 1842— a considerable recognition of his standing by an organization which had withheld membership from George Stephenson!

Some visionary publishers explored the possibilities of transport integration by emphasizing transfer opportunities, 'through' facilities, and the connection of the different transportation services, mirroring the diversification of such railway companies as the Great Central into ship ownership and the establishment of connecting services by train and boat to the Continent. Others tapped the profitable market presented by the mapping of urban and suburban communications, for there was a huge demand for easily readable summaries of services from all but the poor who remained largely pedestrian for most of the century, 'chained to the spot. He has not leisure to walk and he has not money to ride to a distance from his work'.[71]

Maps were devised to illustrate the provisions resulting from each new technical breakthrough. The successive introduction to suburban transport of the horse-bus, the tram (horse, cable, steam, and electric), and finally the petrol-driven bus, demanded plans of routes and stopping points. Jarrold & Sons, for instance, produced a Norwich street plan with tram routes numbered and marked in red to accompany the 'official time table of the Norwich Electric Tramways'.[72] For personalized urban carriage, by the mid-1820s a fleet of about 1,500 hackney coaches plied for hire on the London streets, calling forth maps and guides concentrating on the location of cab stands and the detailing of fares; for example, 'Reynolds's Map of London' was 'the Clearest and Best Map for Visitors, with Guide, Cab Fares, &c.'.[73] Although the cab business was most highly developed in London (particularly after 1830 when statutory regulation of their numbers was abolished) and the other national capitals, lesser towns obviously also had their taxi services which were considerably extended from 1823 with the introduction of the one-horse chaise or cabriolet which gradually superseded the hackney coach, particularly after Joseph Aloysius Hansom patented his safety cab in 1834.

Antagonism against excessive cab fares and dishonest charging brought forth passenger maps such as 'The Arbitrator or Metropolitan Distance Map' and 'The Circuiteer' to facilitate the easy calculation of distances and detail fares and regulations, and pocket-books such as *Mogg's Omnibus Guide and Metropolitan Carriage Time Table*, 'illustrated with Maps of the Metropolis and of the Environs, carefully and accurately engraved'—'The book should make cabmen honest'.[74] From the late 1880s the bicycle too came into use, extending interest in suburban maps as a means of route-finding in unfamiliar locales. Although the omnibus and the tram ruled supreme in the Victorian age and even steamships were sometimes preferred to railways, map-makers seized upon the railways as the most significant suburban transport improvement to date, despite the fact that the railway companies did nothing to encourage commuter travel by keeping fares high and station location inconvenient. Railways dominated town maps, emphasizing the close duplication of lines and rival stations, as, for instance, on Bacon's 'Railway and Station Map of London and Environs constructed to show each Company's line in a separate character—with an Alphabetical Index to nearly 300 Railway Stations—will prove of great service to those who would understand the labyrinth of the Railway Systems of the Metropolis.'[75] The final suburban-transport development of the century, creating in turn its own variety of specialist map, was the birth of the London 'Tube' system

49: *Plans accompanying turnpike proposals were often simply a bare sketch of the projected route. The broken lines on the plan of a projected London-Tilbury turnpike are the proposed new stretches, linking up the existing roads represented by the black lines. c.1809. Anonymous. Deposited with the papers of Sir Thomas Barret Lennard, Treasurer to the Tilbury Fort Trustees. Detail. By courtesy of the Essex Record Office.*

with the City and South London Railway being opened in 1890, operated with electric traction, and the Waterloo and City line—the 'twopenny' Tube—coming into operation in 1900.

Catering for a new market of commuters, commercial travellers, trippers, and holiday-makers demanded new formats of map presentation, for the traditional marbled, elaborately titled, popular slip-case, containing its folded map, was hardly suitable for consultation on a balmy day, let alone on the typically British windy, wet street corner. Experiments in conformation produced the small, bound book of sectional maps with its 'decided advantages over all other methods, by avoiding the unpleasant necessity of unfolding the whole in the street', benefiting particularly the publisher of town plans by enabling him to add references to street names—W. & A.K. Johnston advertised that their 'Atlas-Map of Scotland', for example, had been prepared because 'All who have travelled, either by Rail, Steamer, or Coach, have found the inconvenience of consulting a large folding map. To obviate this inconvenience ...' the map was sectioned so that 'the Tourist can have before him the part of the country to which he wishes to refer, without finding the other portion of the Map in his way'.[77] However, generally publishers settled for maps, often mounted on linen, folded into attractive, often flamboyant stiff covers, or for small guide-books which fitted conveniently into a coat pocket, often even into a tiny waistcoat pocket—'as small as a pocket-book, and can be carried in the recesses of a fashionable coat, without disfiguring the symmetry, or encumbering the person of the most fastidious',[78] and similarly, 'nearly as light and twice as portable as a fairly filled cigar case'.[79] Alternatively, as the century progressed, more and more publishers offered 'tourist' or 'pocket' editions of their small-scale atlases adapted for convenient handling with 'limp' covers and 'rounded' corners.

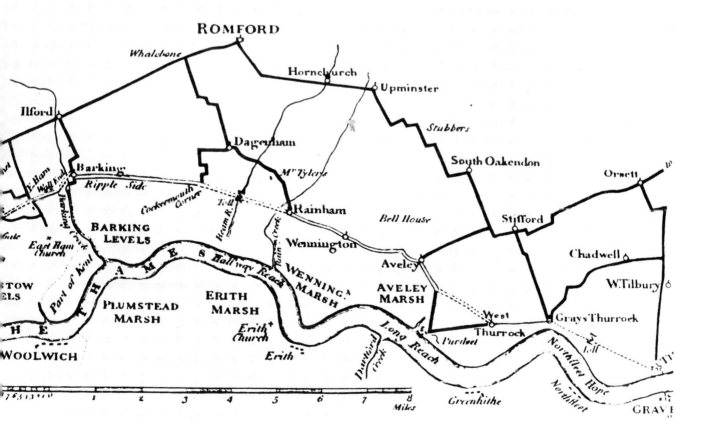

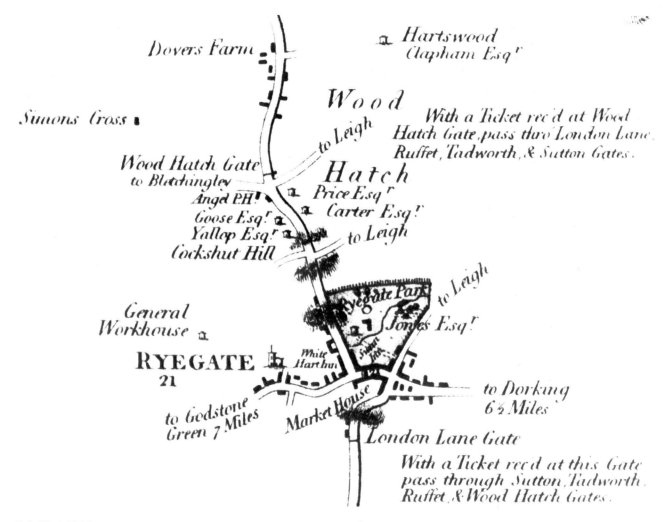

Dovers Farm

Simons Cross

Wood Hatch Gate
to Bletchingley
Angel P.H.
Goose Esq.
Yallop Esq.
Cockshut Hill

to Leigh

Hartswood
Clapham Esq.

Wood

Hatch

Price Esq.

Carter Esq.

to Leigh

With a Ticket rec'd at Wood
Hatch Gate, pass thro' London Lane,
Ruffet, Tadworth, & Sutton Gates.

Reigate Park
Jones Esq.

to Leigh

General
Workhouse

RYEGATE
21

White
Hart Inn

to Godstone
Green 7 Miles

Market House

to Dorking
6½ Miles

London Lane Gate

With a Ticket rec'd at this Gate
pass through Sutton, Tadworth,
Ruffet, & Wood Hatch Gates.

ROAD MAPS

During the early decades of the nineteenth century, urgently needed road improvement was at last being achieved by the extension of the turnpike system—creating 'an ever-increasing mileage of good highway throughout the country'.[80] The first toll-gates in England had been set-up at Wadesmill in Hertfordshire in 1663, but it was only from the second half of the eighteenth century that the turnpike trusts, created by innumerable separate Acts of Parliament, became widespread, eventually numbering over 1,100 administering 23,000 miles of road; turnpikes were being built in the farthest parts of Britain, controlled by toll-bars at which 'all carriages, droves of cattle, and travellers on horseback, are obliged to pay an easy toll'.[81] Proposals to turnpike a section of road had to be accompanied by plans which were deposited with the authorities; often these plans were simply a bare sketch of the route, but, at best, they could be highly detailed, showing buildings, field names, and ownership in areas adjacent to the proposed route. Similarly, plans necessarily accompanied the improvement of existing turnpikes and sometimes, too, the disturnpiking of roads. Turnpiking also stimulated a demand for the production of new road-books, by such commercial map-makers as John Cary, Charles Smith, and Edward Mogg, concentrating on turnpike and toll information. Cary's map of the road from London to St Albans, for example, informed the traveller that the Holloway Gate could be passed 'with S[t]. Johns or Islington Gate ticket'.[82] In his *Survey of the High Roads from London* Cary concentrated on 'The turnpike Gates'—'a subject so often complained of from the incivility as well as imposition of the Toll-gatherers, …

50: *Commercially produced pocket road-books concentrated on practical information for the traveller on turnpike arrangements and tolls.*
i *Detail: The road 'through Ryegate' engraved by Jones & Smith, published by Charles Smith, 1800, in* Smith's Actual Survey of the Roads from London to Brighthelmstone. *By permission of the British Library (Maps C.27.e.16).*
ii *Detail: London to St Albans by John Cary, 1801, from* Cary's Survey of the High Roads from London. *By courtesy of Ivan Deverall.*

distinctly marking the connection of the trust which one Gate has with another, whereby the traveller is informed of those which are separate, and those which are connected and in receipt of another's ticket, which it is presumed will be the means of preventing unpleasant altercation'.[83] Other map-makers, particularly large-scale cartographers such as the Greenwoods, conscientiously kept turnpike information up-to-date by regular revision, and emphasized the importance of these roads by special colouring.

Improvements in management and construction speeded the spread of turnpikes, and advances in vehicle technology and the demise of the highwayman, in the face of fast horses and armed guards, popularized coach travel making it a regular feature of everyday life—blossoming, from the 1780s to the 1830s, into the golden age of the stage-coach and creating a demand for maps aimed at the coach traveller. By the early 1800s upwards of 400 coaches a day were leaving London, including 18 to Brighton alone; and by 1836 the London firm of William Chaplin operated 3,000

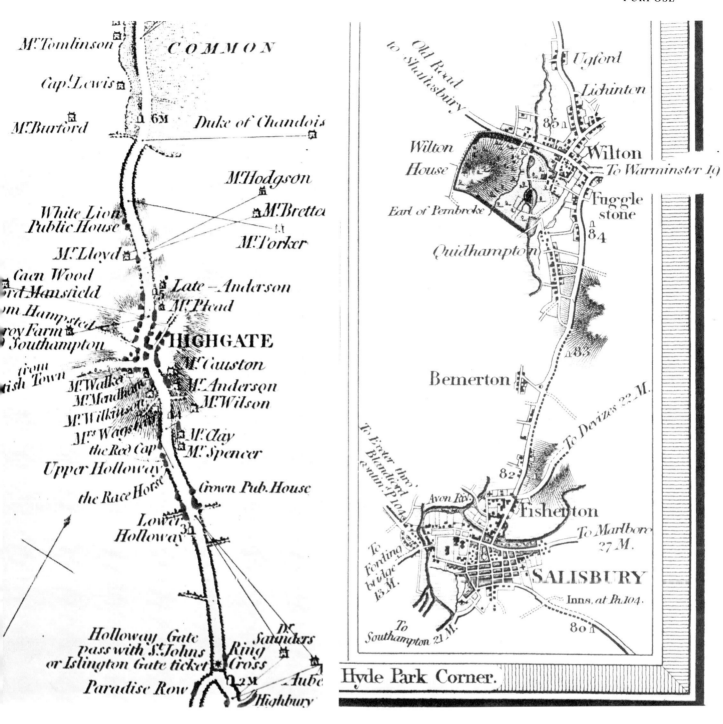

coaches using 150,000 horses and 30,000 drivers, guards, and ostlers. This massive industry created a large and steady demand for the Victorian map-maker. Coaching conferred a particular importance on the inn for it became the place where the coach and its passengers were 'furnished ... with relays of horses, and meals ... at a limited price'[84]—the 'Three Tuns' and the 'Golden Fleece' in Thirsk, for example, at one time stabled 200 horses between them. Thus, the marking and naming of inns on road maps became an increasingly pronounced and useful feature and some map-makers even went as far as recommending specific hostelries. Charles Smith, in particular, paid special attention to public houses in his *Actual Survey of the Roads from London to Brighthelmstone* of 1800: 'Where the letters P.H. Occur, it implies Public House, & when an Asterisk is annexed to the word Inn, the traveller may depend on being well accomodated, tho' not with Post Horses & Car-

riages, those Inns, in the Towns & on the Road, which supply Post Horses & Carriages are given at the bottom of each page.'[85] Likewise John Cary's *Survey of the High Roads from London*, first published in 1790, placed special emphasis on the inns: 'The public Inns on each route are ... noticed with a view to utility, as it enables a party to form a meeting with certainty, and gives them a choice of pursuing their pleasures to a greater extent than they otherwise would do.'[86] All in all, coach travel created an immense market for the map-maker to tap by the provision of great numbers of road-books aimed at the passengers af-

By J.Cary

NORTHAMPTONSHIRE

Engraver

London.to Daventry 73 M. Brackley 64 Towcester 61 Northampton 66 Rothwell 78 Rockingham 84
Kettering 74 Wellinghoro 68 Higham Ferrers 65 Thrapston 75 Oundle 77 Peterborough 77 Weldon 84
Kings Cliffe 85

London. Published July 1.1806 by J.Cary Engraver N°181 Strand.

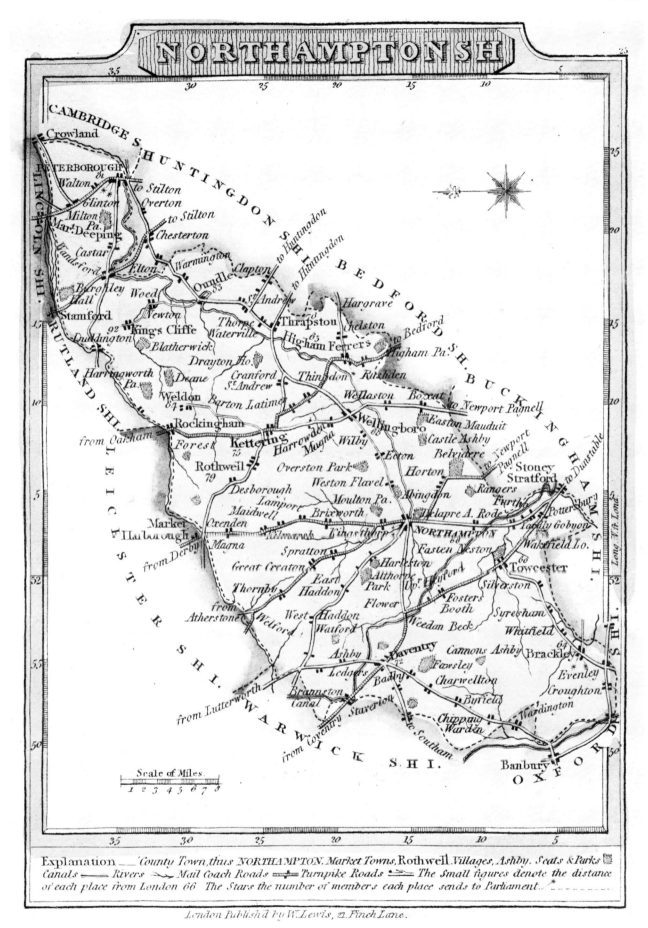

NORTHAMPTON SH

London Publish'd by W. Lewis, 21. Finch Lane.

52: *Road-books of county maps were published in vast numbers, usually following the same basic style.*

i *Northamptonshire, by John Cary, 1806, from* Cary's Traveller's Companion.
ii *Northamptonshire, engraved by James Wallis, published by William Lewis in* Lewis's New Traveller's Guide, *1836.*

fluent enough to pay the high 'inside' fare of fourpence or fivepence a mile for a fast coach or even to hire or own a post-chaise. Publishers, such as John Cary, Charles Smith, Edward Mogg, Laurie & Whittle, Charles Cooke, James Wallis, Samuel Leigh, and George Carrington Gray, produced not only the traditional strip road maps for this wide market, but also small-scale county atlases, which contained essentially only road maps concentrating on road classification and distances between places. The ever-inventive map-maker also sometimes searched for a novel approach to give his route guides a commercial edge, as, for instance, James Baker did in his *Imperial Guide* by representing the route as a single line wandering between vignettes of country houses and towns. All had the common features of being pocket-sized and easily handled, of concentrating on road and distance information, of emphasizing objects of interest close to the road, of indicating inns offering facilities for passenger and horse and offering carriage hire, and of an obsequious approach to the affluent landowners, who were the main market for such works, by the delineation of their estates and the naming of them and their country houses.

The spread of the postal service which resulted from the improvement in roads and the flowering of coach travel was doubly significant for map production. Towards the end of the eighteenth century the service had deteriorated badly due to the inefficiency of the inn-keepers who hired out horses to the post-boys, but by the early 1790s the country was covered by a highly efficient system of 'strong and well-guarded'[87] mail-coaches run with draconian zeal by Thomas Hasker, 'Surveyor and Superintendent of the Mail Coaches'. On the one hand, the spread of the postal service led, in time, to a demand for specifically postal maps, and, on the other, Hasker's appointment of John Cary to measure some 9,000 miles of road for the Post Office resulted in the publication of *Cary's New Itinerary* which ensured that early nineteenth-century map-makers were furnished with the first really accurate road measurements since Ogilby.

Obviously those areas with the heaviest traffic density were most frequently mapped and, consequently, such districts as the Home Counties were more comprehensively covered than less populated regions. Generally, Scotland and Ireland seemed content to continue using the late eighteenth-century road-books of George Taylor and Andrew Skinner, with Thomas Brown producing a reduced version of their Scottish strip maps in 1805. In Ireland, William Curry published a small road-strip atlas in 1844 which was, despite its insubstantial nature a distinct improvement on John Cumming's desultory *Traveller's New Guide through Ireland*, published in 1815, with its few road maps engraved by Burke.

Alternatively, less ambitious works were produced to cover a single route as, for example, in *The Dover Road Sketch Book; or, Traveller's Pocket Guide between London and Dover*, by J.H. Brady, published in 1837, with its quarto county map of Kent by Sidney Hall and eight tiny, delicate road maps printed back-to-back lithographically by Madeley of '3, Wellington S!. Strand'. Another form of cartographic response to this growing road-travel market was the provision of guide-books, usually containing maps and plans, to accompany road tours in particular areas. Examples include *The Scotch Itinerary*, by James Duncan, which was illustrated by maps of Scotland, Islay, and Jura, and, in later editions, Queensferry and the Central Lowlands; *The Post Chaise Companion: or Traveller's Directory through Ireland*, published by J. & J. H. Fleming in 1803,

containing a map of the Killarney lakes and the large decorative 'Wilson's Modern Pocket Travelling Map of the Roads of Ireland', engraved by Benjamin Baker; *The Route Book of Devon: A guide for the stranger and tourist*; *The Cambrian Traveller's Guide, in every direction* of 1813 with its splendid map of Wales by Samuel Neele; and *Black's Picturesque Tourist of Scotland*, 'With an accurate travelling map; engraved charts and views of the scenery; plans of Edinburgh and Glasgow', and in later editions 'ROAD CHARTS of the FIRST, SEVENTH, EIGHTH, and THIRTEENTH TOURS, and of the TOUR TO DEE-SIDE'.[88] Some publishers, such as Darton & Clark with their 'Miniature Road-Books', intended to build their guides into a series covering the whole country, but lack of demand in outlying areas caused most of such schemes to collapse after a promising start.

The coming of the railways brought an abrupt end to the great age of the turnpike trust and the stage coach, although public coaches continued to run until almost the end of the century, particularly in remote areas not penetrated by railways—a coach ran from London to Wendover as late as 1892. Similarly, private carriages remained popular for local transport and excursioning, and, consequently, map-makers continued to cater for the needs of coach and carriage travellers. Generally, however, by 1850 passengers had abandoned stage coaches in favour of the faster, cheaper railways and from 1870 the turnpike trusts were gradually wound-up by the Committee on Turnpike Trust Bills, the last surviving trust being disturnpiked in 1895 in Anglesey.

CYCLING MAPS

Towards the end of the century another fertile market for specialized road maps appeared through the spread of the bicycle. 'Of late years ... BICYCLING has become such a favourite pursuit ... that it seems more than probable that our main roads and country lanes will soon become as much frequented as in days of yore.'[89] The introduction of the Rover Safety Bicycle, the first practical production machine, in 1885, heralded the era of popular cycling and the invention of Dunlop's comfortable pneumatic tyre in 1888 extended its mass appeal. By 1893 bicycle design had reached its modern form with the diamond-shaped frame, roller-chain drive, and pneumatic-tyred wheels.

Almost as soon as practicable bicycles appeared, so too did cycling clubs to cater for the cycling excursionist and tourist, and to organize the increasing use of the new craze for rural recreation. The bicycle offered individual mobility, flexibility, and freedom, which were enthusiastically seized by a population with ever-increasing leisure time and a growing desire for active relaxation. The oldest cycling club in the world, the Pickwick Bicycle Club, was founded in London in 1870, but such small organizations were largely superseded by the formation in 1878 of the much larger Bicycle Touring Club, later to become the Cyclists' Touring Club (C.T.C.).

Here was a marvellous new commercial opportunity which map-publishers such as George Philip, George Washington Bacon, Jarrold & Sons, and Gall & Inglis embraced greedily by producing maps and series offering information 'specially suitable for tourists, cyclists, etc.'[90] Bacon, for example, produced his 'Cycling Map 150 Miles Around London with the Main Roads Specially Coloured', 'Folded in Case 1s., On Cloth in Case 2s.6d., On Cloth, Cut to Fold 3s.6d.'. In truth these were rarely newly prepared works, for the cycling data were generally simply overprinted onto existing maps, often of alarming age, with

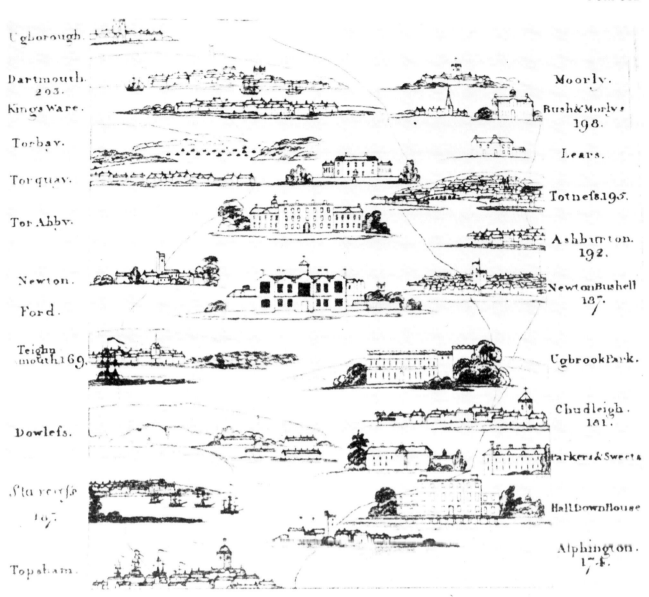

53: *Some map-makers adopted inventive alternatives to the standard approach to route delineation in an effort to capture a share of the travelling market dominated by the major publishers.*
Detail: Topsham—Plymouth, by James Baker, from The Imperial Guide, *1802.*

new titles substituted. Roads were classified 'Coloured ... very bold and distinct'[90] according to surface quality; hills which ought to be ridden down with brakes on 'with caution' and those where the cyclist should dismount were marked boldly; workshops where bicycles could be repaired, sometimes at a discount, appeared, as did refreshment places with special terms for cyclists; a variety of cycling routes were suggested; distances between towns were noted or the map face was covered with a graticule 'for readily calculating distances';[91] and towns with cycling-club representatives and public houses and hotels catering specially for cyclists were noted. The C.T.C. issued tickets for certain hotels which were marked, but cyclists soon realized that some map-makers charged hotels and workshops for inclusion irrespective of the facilities provided and, therefore, appearance on a map was no guarantee of satisfactory service. As Bacon explained to the Committee on Sale of Ordnance Survey Maps in 1896, 'Private map publishers take

special pains ... and are often paid for doing it. Places are marked on the maps where people can have their bicycles repaired, or refreshment places where bicyclists get special terms, and dangerous hills are shown ... many of the map publishers take a small fee from hotels or others for showing where cyclists can be received or where they can have their machines repaired.' In the same evidence, Bacon seriously questioned the worth of these additions, which were, he reported, '... not of much value to the cyclist, so I am generally informed, but they are valuable to the publishers who get a fee for displaying them. Cyclists tell me these features are not of much practical value to them—they say they already know the districts they frequent, and that with the brakes on the machines the marking of the hills is not of much importance. These novel features are not worth 5 per cent. of the value attributed to them when the idea was started. They are pretty well a thing of the past.'[92] Even remarkably out-dated maps were resurrected to meet this notable demand, as, for example, when Daniel Paterson's strip maps, which had first appeared in 1785 in *Paterson's British Itinerary* (subsequently re-issued for the coaching market in 1796, 1803, and 1807), suddenly reappeared lithographically in 1877 in the unfinished *British High Roads.*

Fierce competition for this new market forced publishers

54: *The emergence of the bicycle as a major mode of leisure transport brought forth a mass of maps aimed specifically at the cyclist.*
Cover: 'BACON'S COUNTY MAP GUIDE SURREY FOR CYCLISTS AND TOURISTS FROM THE ORDNANCE SURVEY', published by G.W. Bacon & Co., c.1898. By courtesy of Richard Miller.

to package their maps in attractive, colourful, pictorial covers which, along with the map itself, offered opportunities for advertisements aimed specifically at cyclists. Although many products, including Hovis bread, Dunlop tyres, and Pattisons' whisky were advertised on cycling maps, the best-known exploitation was by E. Harrison & Co., 'The West End Bicycle and Athletic Outfitters, Bicycle Costume Makers and Club Contractors', who adapted Cary's large county maps for their '"FINGER POST" BICYCLE ROAD GUIDES'—'of a size and shape compatible for carrying in the pocket of the Cyclist'. Harrison's maps were really nothing more than vehicles for the peddling of his very extensive list of cycling products which included 'Bicycle Shirts, Collars attached, with breast pocket, in all the newest patterns, very absorbent', 'Bicycle Anklets for strengthening the Ankle, especially for racing and long journeys', 'Drawers for Racing, in all Colours', 'Bicycle Helmets, in all materials', and a novel scheme of hire purchase for buying '... your Bicycle or Tricycle ... on Monthly payments at Manufacturers' Prices'.[93]

In 1893 there were an estimated half-a-million bicycles in Britain, by 1896 over one-and-a-half million. The enormous potential of the market—Bartholomew's, for example, printed 60,000 cycling maps in a single run at about the turn of the century—posed something of a dilemma for the Ordnance Survey which looked enviously on the profits made by the private sector in superimposing cycling information onto maps derived by reduction or 'improvement' from Ordnance publications: 'The whole of that business—a large and growing one—is passing out of the hands of the Department, into the hands of private publishers, who do it often somewhat unsatisfactorily.'[94] However, the Survey continued its policy of leaving small-scale production in private hands because it felt that the market was already saturated 'by the publications of particular private publishers'[94] and that there was no opportunity to break into it 'because there are so many people bringing-out maps on a reduced scale, such as Messrs. Gall and Inglis supply'.[95]

The final road-transport development of the nineteenth century opened up yet another enormous market for exploitation by the map-maker (including, this time, a more commercially-minded Ordnance Survey) with a new type of specialized map. In the early twentieth century the motorcar 'began seriously to displace the horsed vehicle, becoming the private carriage of the wealthier classes to be used on all occasions',[96] thus diverting map-makers' attention to motoring maps at the expense of other road transport cartography.

WATERWAY MAPS
By the beginning of the Victorian age, inland water communication was approaching its maximum extent with river improvement largely completed and a canal network, of some 2000 miles by 1830 and 2500 miles at its fullest extent, slowing its pace of expansion. Despite the lack of Victorian river improvement, map-publishers continued to produce navigation charts of the major rivers, as Richard Laurie did in 1831 and 1839 with his fine detailed chart of the navigable reaches of the Thames and Medway and the coast of the Thames estuary, engraved by Alexander Findlay. Similarly, maps of islands, such as Wyld's of Alderney, frequently concentrated on coastal navigation information, creating a popular hybrid of topographical map and hydrographical chart. Less ambitious producers simply concentrated on the scenic beauties and bank-side sights for 'every Oarsman, Tourist, and Angler, on the River';[97] Henry

Taunt, 'Photographer (by appointment) to the Oxford Architectural Society', for example, promoted the sale of his river photographs with his map of the Thames from Oxford to London which started the excursion with the exhortation to 'drop in on Taunt'! Others illustrated notably interesting features of a river as in the plan of the River Mole, 'Engraved at the Expence of the Editor', which illustrated the controversy amongst antiquarian commentators concerning the reasons for the river's poor flow in dry periods. In contrast, at its simplest, river mapping consisted merely of the delineation of the rivers on an otherwise virtually bare outline map sometimes designed as an educational or practical aid to illustrate the geography of river systems or the interconnection of river and canal.

Like other transport schemes, canals required both finance and parliamentary sanction before a project could go ahead. Large-scale plans were prepared for submission with project proposals to Parliament showing the strip of land adjacent to the anticipated route—narrow canals took a strip 14-16 yards wide, or five acres per mile run, and broad canals took a 30-yard strip, or 10 acres per mile. Obviously the plans delineated land beyond the required strip, showing, therefore, not only the courses of the rivers and canals, with details of bridges, fords, ferries, weirs, locks, wharves, water-mills, inns, and navigation obstructions, but also roads, footpaths, buildings, field names, ownership, land-use, occupation, industrial sites, and so on, in the surrounding area. Some plans added larger-scale insets of towns or estates, sections showing the elevation of the proposed route, distance tables, and plans of tunnels and bridges. Such detailed plans might also be drawn up when a branch was to be added, a route to be altered, or on the occasion of a take-over by a railway company. The canal builders themselves also, of course, had often to prepare large-scale accurate plans for their own engineering purposes.

After obtaining Parliamentary permission, it was necessary for the canal companies to attract investors through the issue of prospectuses which were frequently accompanied by maps and plans of the proposals. Additionally, the canals had a tremendous commercial impact, calling forth a popular demand both for general maps of the canal and navigable-river system and for maps of specific canals and routes. The fact that canals were regarded as a highway open to all comers willing to pay the toll, with the canal companies denied a monopoly of use, created a widespread demand from potential users for maps which would clarify a complex system. Many commercial map-publishers, such as Cary, John Stockdale, John Walker, and William Faden, produced general maps of a whole national or regional network, but the most reliable and popular were those published by George Bradshaw of either 'Canals and Navigable Rivers' alone or 'Canals, Navigable Rivers, Railways, etc.' for 'the Legislator, as well as the Professional and Commercial Man'.[98] Bradshaw's plans were particularly noted for their precision, having been 'carefully examined by some of the ablest engineers in the Kingdom, and compared with plans of their own; and they have declared their unqualified approbation of the accuracy ...'.[99] His maps were generally considered to be the most practically useful for the engineer because of their care in showing, for example, 'The HEIGHTS of the POOLS on the LINES of NAVIGATION also the PLANES on the Railways from a LEVEL of 6ft. 10in. under the OLD DOCK Sill at LIVERPOOL.'[100] Similarly, they were a ready source of reliable data for the plagiarizing map-maker; Augustus Petermann, for example,

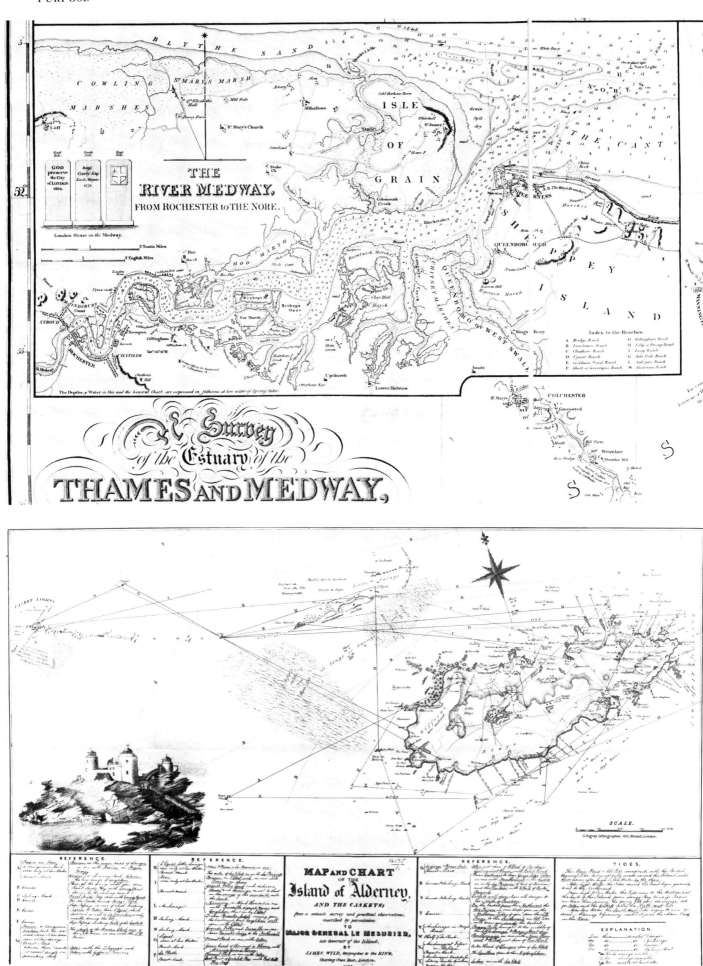

55: *Detail: 'A Survey of the Estuary of the THAMES AND MEDWAY, with the Coast FROM THORPNESS TO DOVER, and the Rivers to LONDON AND ROCHESTER. Published by RICHᴰ. H. LAURIE, 53 Fleet Stʳ. London, 12ᵗʰ of July, 1831. Improved Edition 1839', engraved by Alexander Findlay. By permission of the British Library (Maps 1240(91)).*

56: *'MAP AND CHART OF THE Island of Alderney, AND THE CASKETS; from a minute survey and practical observations; inscribed by permission TO MAJOR GENERAL LE MESURIER, late Governor of the Island, BY JAMES WYLD, Geographer to the KING, Charing Cross East, London. 1833. C. Ingrey, Lithographer, 310, Strand, London.' By permission of the British Library (Maps 14135(1)).*

57: *During the Victorian age rivers became important sources of relaxation, interest, and sport for 'every Oarsman, Tourist, and Angler'. Detail: 'TAUNT'S MAP OF THE RIVER THAMES FROM OXFORD TO LONDON', by Henry W. Taunt, c.1875. By permission of the British Library (Maps 5a68).*

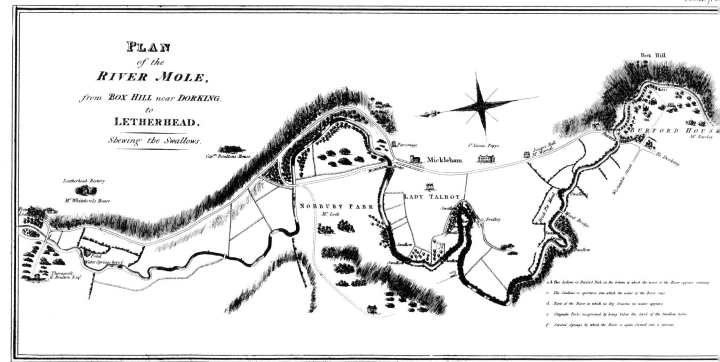

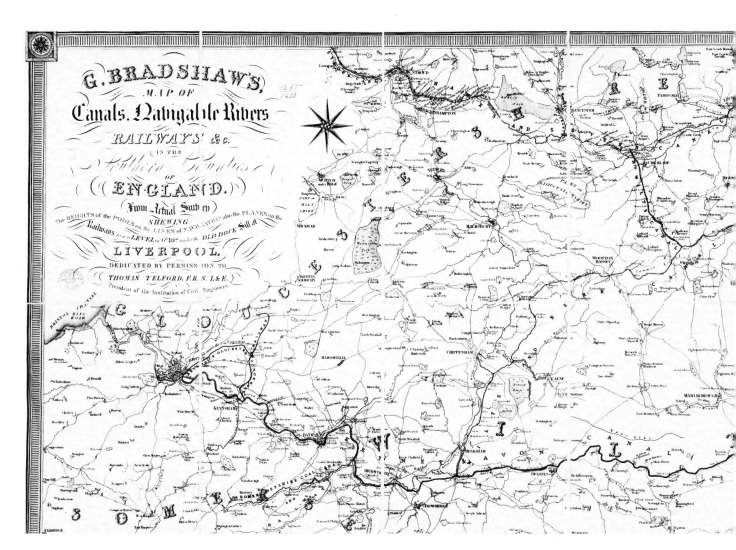

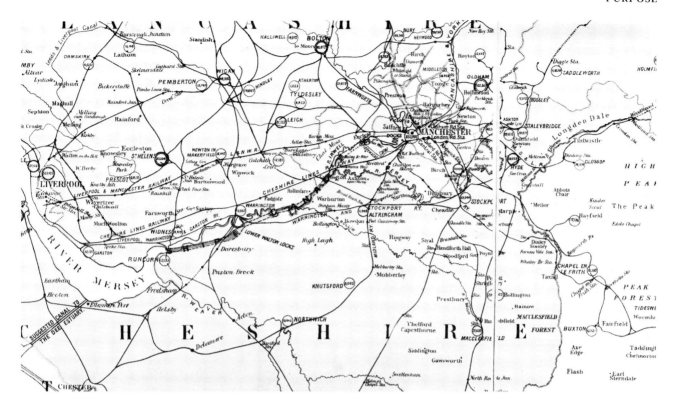

60: *The sparkling exception to the decline of canals during the Victorian age was the Manchester Ship Canal.*
Detail: 'THE PROPOSED MANCHESTER SHIP CANAL, SHEWING:—MAP OF THE DISTRICT, MAP OF THE BRITISH ISLES, SECTIONS AND PLAN OF THE SHIP CANAL, with Map of Manchester, Salford, and the Out-Townships forming GREATER MANCHESTER, AND EXPLANATORY NOTES. PRINTED FOR HENRY BODDINGTON, Junr., Strangeways Brewery, MANCHESTER. BY GRANT & CO., LONDON. NOVEMBER, 1882'. By permission of the British Library (Maps 3165(13)).

freely admitted in the notes to his 'Hydrographical Map of the British Isles' that much of it had been 'Constructed' from Bradshaw's plans. Such was the interest that plans of individual canals were published in a variety of periodicals and newspapers, and John Cary even issued an atlas of these plans, published in parts around the turn of the century—*Inland Navigation; or Select Plans of the Several Navigable Canals throughout Great Britain*, 'Plans of the different NAVIGABLE CANALS, on a Scale of Half an Inch to a Mile, accompanied with Letter-Press, containing Abstracts of the Acts of Parliament relative to them; also the length, width, number of Locks, Falls, &c. &c.'.[101]

With the sparkling exception of the Manchester Ship Canal, which was given enthusiastic cartographic support by Henry Boddington, the Manchester brewer, the age of the canal and its plans was, to all intents and purposes, abruptly halted by the coming of the railways in the 1830s. Although well established, commercially successful canals continued to function happily, new projects were shelved, existing canals were taken-over and often closed-down by railway companies, and others simply fell into disrepair, causing a dramatic diversion of cartographic interest to railway transport as canal-plan production suddenly ended.

STEAMSHIP MAPS
It was not only the railways that spelt doom for the canals because, to a lesser extent, the emergence of steamships diverted trade from inland to coastal water transport.

58: *'PLAN of the RIVER MOLE, from BOX HILL near DORKING to LETHERHEAD, Shewing the Swallows'*, engraved by James Basire, published by White & Co., 1810.

59: *Detail: 'G. BRADSHAW'S MAP OF Canals, Navigable Rivers RAILWAYS &c. IN THE Southern Counties OF ENGLAND. From Actual Survey SHEWING ... the PLANES on the Railways ...'*, c.1830. By permission of the British Library (Maps 1b22).

Although inter-continental steamship travel was to be bedevilled by high fuel consumption which raised costs and limited space until the development of the compound steam engine in the 1860s, steamships did become rapidly popular and effective over short routes for high-value traffic, particularly passengers—to such an extent that by 1825 so many steamers were competing for passengers on the Belfast-Glasgow route that deck passage was free and the first-class fare only 2s.! By the 1840s, 'steam-packets' from London ran 'daily to Ramsgate, Margate, Gravesend, Southend, Herne Bay, and Sheerness, and at stated periods, to all the ports and principal places on the coast of Great Britain and Ireland, as well as to the Continent, India, and America'.[102] Some publishers such as Edward Mogg with 'Mogg's Map of Steam Navigation' catered for the *bona fide* traveller by 'Exhibiting the Tracks pursued by the Steam Packets in their Passage to the several Outports and the Continent'[103] ('the whole is accompanied by printed observations, and forms altogether a steam-boat companion of peculiar interest'),[104] but others aimed at 'the pleasure-taking portion of Nautical Tourists'[105] who excursioned by steamboat through scenic areas. *The Scottish Tourists' Steam-Boat Pocket Guide*, for example, was 'Embellished with Plates, and illustrated with Maps of the Western Coast, including the Hebride Islands';[106] *Sylvan's Pictorial Hand-Book to the Clyde*, by Thomas & Edward Gilks, offered 'a pleasant steam-boat panorama of the exquisite country skirting the great commercial river of Scotland';[107] and *The steam boat companion and stranger's guide to the Western Islands and Highlands of Scotland* contained a 'Chart of the Clyde and its environs', engraved by W. H. Lizars, 'and ... other accompanying *Maps*, ... taken from *actual survey*'.[108] Steamship facilities even made their impact on maps concentrating on suburban transport services: 'Collins's Standard Map of London', for example, 'Enlarged and Corrected from a recent survey, and delineating the Postal Districts, the Railways, with their latest extensions, the Omnibus and Tramway routes', laid special emphasis on the location of 'Steam-boat Piers'.

The overwhelming commercial importance of sea transport, whether sail or steam and international or coastal, gave cartographic prominence not only to such great ports as Liverpool and Bristol but also to a host of small havens like Port Patrick, Whitehaven, and Silloth which served a tiny hinterland until the rapid decline occasioned by the railways eventual usurping of their coastal trade. Simple port plans delineated channels, depths, sand bars, lights, and all the developments of a period of extensive navigational improvement for small craft which did not require the minutiae of large-scale hydrographic charts for safe passage. This interest in improved coastal navigation was further fed by maps of lighthouse location—Bartholomews' *Gazetteer of the British Isles*, for example, boasted 'a special map ... showing all the lighthouses on the coasts, according to the latest Admiralty handbook'.[109] There were also maps locating wrecks such as the 'Wreck Chart of the British Isles for 1868 Compiled from the Board of Trade Register showing also the present Life-boat Stations', compiled and engraved by John Dower, published in *The Illustrated London News* of 30 October 1869.

RAILWAY MAPS

The modern railway dates from the opening of George Stephenson's line from Stockton to Darlington in 1825, for this was the first successful combination of mechanical traction and iron rails—an event destined to affect almost every person, place, and institution, not least the Victorian mapmaker. The two 'railway manias', from 1836 to 1837 and from 1845 to 1847, created a network of some 500 miles in 1838 and about 4600 by 1848. In a staggeringly short time the railway network of the British Isles was constructed and created the most fruitful field yet for cartographic exploitation in various forms.

A survey and plan had to accompany each new railway bill put before Parliament, whether this was for the construction of a new line or merely the alteration or extension of an existing one, and parliamentary Standing Orders required that bills and plans for consideration in the ensuing session had to be deposited in the railway-bill office of Parliament by 30 November. This requirement had a most unfortunate effect on the quality of the deposited plans, for it created an artificially short railway-surveying season because survey work could not start until after harvest. Surveyors reported that although it was possible to start work as early as July in some hay producing areas, it was more likely that they would be delayed until September.[110] Complaint was particularly vehement in Ireland where harvest was especially late; in the case of the Irish Great Western 'we were only able to commence the survey after the crops were off in October'.[110] Thus, in the main bursts of speculative activity there was such a frantic demand for surveys in the three autumn months that the supply of competent land surveyors was insufficient and the railway

promoters recruited from every available source. Skilled practitioners were poached from the Tithe Commission and the Ordnance Survey by the offer of far more attractive rates of pay—Brunel offered £4 a week to 'anyone who could handle a level and a theodolite',[111] and, in the peak years, rates went as high as 'two, three, and four guineas a day, and expenses'.[112] Unfortunately, demand for plans, that 'we must have within four weeks of this time',[112] was so high that it was necessary to cast the net wider, recruiting 'youngsters hardly able to tell the right end of a theodolite from the wrong'.[112] One surveyor received £10 per mile and claimed that he could level seven to eight miles a day. It is no surprise, therefore, that survey work was frequently highly inaccurate and the resultant plans almost worthless. Some railway surveyors simply obtained copies of the 6″ Ordnance Survey where it existed and brought detail up-to-date from field observation, charging the railway companies £30 to £80 per mile for maps which had cost them 10s. per mile. Where 6″ maps did not exist, surveyors used the larger-scale Tithe Commission maps, but since so few of these were 'first class',[113] the results were generally unsatisfactory, particularly as the tithe maps recorded no levels. In contrast, it was a widely admitted and accepted fact in Ireland that railways were planned on the 6″ Ordnance Survey sheets and that the parliamentary maps were prepared from them. Eminent engineers such as Charles Vignoles and James Walker went on record that this was perfectly satisfactory and for this reason specially prepared railway surveys are virtually unknown in Ireland.

It was not only rapid survey work by incompetent and unqualified surveyors that was responsible for the poor quality of so many deposited plans, but also the rush in which they had to be prepared to meet the midnight deadline. The *Annual Register*'s account of the 'extraordinary scene' at the 'office of the Railway Department at the Board of Trade' on 30 November 1845, 'the great railway year', dramatically exposes this hasty preparation. '... The projections of the Scotch lines were mostly in advance and had their plans duly lodged on Saturday. The Irish projectors, too, and the old established companies, seeking powers to construct branches, were among the more punctual. But upwards of 600 plans remained to be deposited. Towards the last the utmost exertions were made to forward them. The efforts of the lithographic draughtsmen and printers in London were excessive; people remained at work night after night, snatching a hasty repose for a couple of hours on lockers, benches, or the floor. Some found it impossible to execute their contracts; others did their work imperfectly. One of the most eminent was compelled to bring over 400 lithographers from Belgium, and failed, nevertheless, with this reinforcement, in completing some of his plans. Post-horses and express-trains, to bring to town plans prepared in the country, were sought in all parts. Horses were engaged days before, and kept, by persons specially appointed, under lock and key. Some railway companies exercised that power of refusing express-trains for rival projects, and clerks were obliged to make sudden and embarrassing changes of route in order to travel by less hostile ways.'[114]

61: *'PORTS & HARBOURS ON THE NORTH WEST COAST OF ENGLAND', drawn and engraved by John Bartholomew, published c.1865 by Archibald Fullarton in* The Royal Illustrated Atlas.

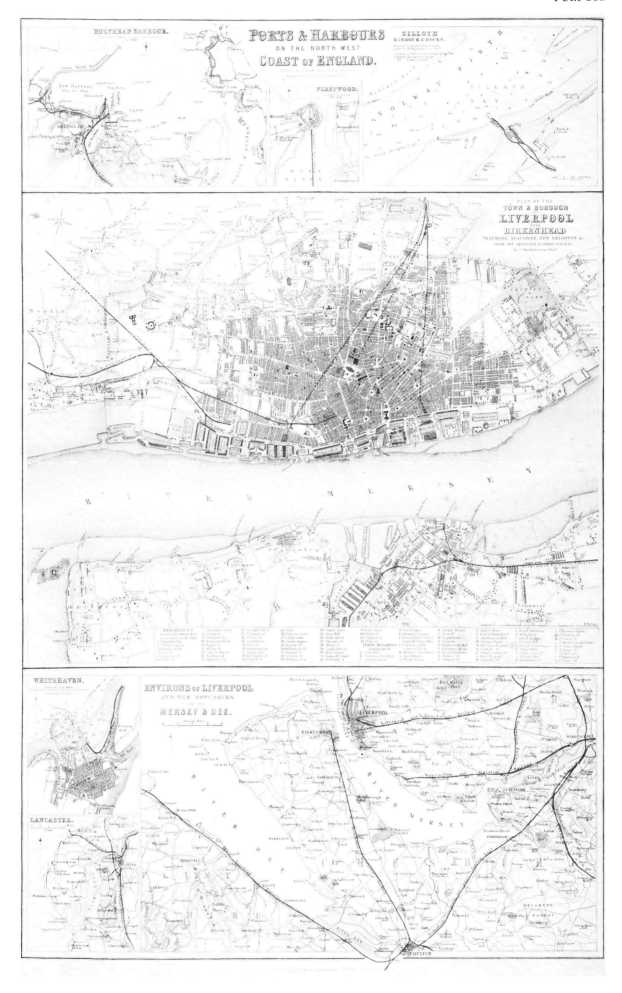

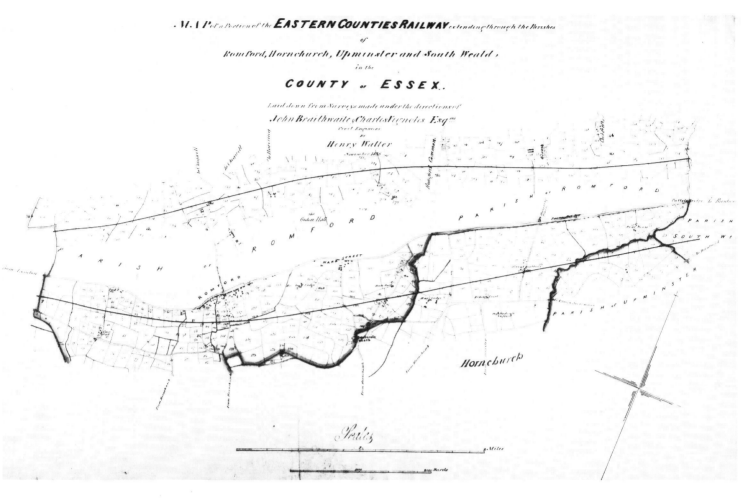

MAP of a Portion of the EASTERN COUNTIES RAILWAY extending through the Parishes of Romford, Hornchurch, Upminster and South Weald, in the COUNTY of ESSEX.

Deposition of hastily-prepared plans continued until the very last minute, 'considerable anxiety being expressed lest 12 o'clock should arrive ere the requisite formalities should have been gone through', with late submissions refused acceptance: '... just before the expiration of the first quarter of an hour a post-chaise, with reeking horses, drove up in hot haste to the entrance. In a moment its occupants (3 gentlemen) alighted and rushed down the passage towards the office door, each bearing a plan of Brobdignagian dimensions. On reaching the door, and finding it closed, the countenances of all dropped; but one of them more valorous than the rest, and prompted by the bystanders, gave a loud pull at the bell. It was answered by Inspector Ottway, who informed the ringer it was now too late, and that his plans could not be received. The agents did not wait for the conclusion of the unpleasant communication, but took advantage of the doors being opened and threw in their papers, which broke the passage-lamp in their fall. They were thrown back into the street. When the door was again opened, again went in the plans, only to meet a similar fate.'[114]

Despite poor survey and hasty preparation, a vast number of plans were prepared (for example, 248 were lodged with the Board of Trade in 1844, and 815 in 1845), particularly by Stanfords, many of which were, of course, of high quality giving a detailed delineation of the landscape for about a quarter-of-a-mile from the projected line. Where railways were to pass through built-up areas or a terminus was to be constructed, it was often necessary to prepare larger-scale plans. Additionally, all plans had to be accompanied by books of reference detailing individual fields and, from 1838, by longitudinal sections derived from precise levelling.

62: *In order to obtain parliamentary sanction of a railway proposal, it was necessary to deposit a large-scale plan of the projected route with the authorities. This detailed survey was deposited with the Clerk of the Peace showing alternative routes for a line from London to Norwich—the southerly route was in fact adopted. 'MAP of a Portion of the EASTERN COUNTIES RAILWAY extending through the Parishes Romford, Hornchurch, Upminster and South Weald; in the COUNTY OF ESSEX. Laid down from Surveys made under the directions of John Braithwaite & Charles Vignoles Esq.es Civil Engineers By Henry Walter November 1835'. By permission of the Essex Record Office.*

63: *'TALLIS'S RAILWAY MAP OF GREAT BRITAIN SHOWING THE RAILWAYS COMPLETED, AND THE STATIONS ON EACH LINE UP TO THE PRESENT TIME, WITH THE STEAMBOAT TRACKS FROM THE PRINCIPAL BRITISH AND CONTINENTAL SEA-PORTS. Compiled from Government Documents and the most recent Railway Information. By JOHN RAPKIN', published by John Tallis & Co., c.1855.*

Once parliamentary sanction was granted, it was necessary to prepare engineering plans for the actual building of the lines and prospectus plans to attract potential shareholders to the scheme. Detailed engineering plans were generally produced by the railway engineers themselves, often simply superimposing their engineering details onto existing Ordnance and Tithe Survey maps. Fortunately, the recent spectacular industrial and commercial progress ensured that most worthwhile railway projects could find the capital they needed from private sources, but these funds still had to be mobilized by 'illustrated prospectuses'[115] explaining a provisional railway route and designed to

attract shareholders. Since accuracy was unimportant, the majority of these promotional maps were simply copied from existing small-scale maps by fairly careless engraving or lithography by 'cartographers and geographical engravers'—'none were better equipped for drawing them up and reproducing them in quantity'.[115] Frequently such extra facts as the populations and industries of towns served, or the comparative mileages by rival routes, were added to the maps as further proof of the commercial viability of the project and of the favourable factors likely to induce profitable operation. Many railways, although projected, promoted, and mapped, were, of course, never built. Despite the failure of promotional maps to bolster many specious schemes, their success is amply attested by the awesome amounts of capital raised for railway construction—by 1850, total paid-up capital of railway companies was over £240 million, by 1860 £348 million, by 1870 almost £530 million, by 1880 over £728 million, by 1890 over £897 million, and by 1900 £1,176 million.

Once a railway came into operation, even greater opportunities presented themselves to the enterprising mapmaker. The most reliable and accurate maps were prepared by several employees of the Railway Clearing House (the organization, established in 1842, to apportion revenue among railway companies allowing through-running of passengers and freight along routes involving the lines of more than one company) on a semi-official basis, and, later, by the Clearing House itself. Clearing House data and these semi-official maps proved indispensable sources of accurate railway information for commercial map-makers when updating the rail network on their topographical maps and when producing general maps of the rail system such as John Tallis's 'Railway Map of Great Britain'—'Compiled from Government Documents and the most recent Railway Information'.[116] In 1851, Zachary Macaulay published a reliable railway map, drawn by James Murray and engraved by James Welland, showing every station in Great Britain, its ownership, and the ownership of the various routes. Although privately published because his request for official sponsorship had been rejected, it seems clear that Macaulay must have been allowed to use his position in the Clearing House to gather the data for the map.

The less commercially minded John Airey concentrated on producing working maps for railwaymen in general, particularly for his own 'Distances' section of the Clearing House. With the encouragement and help of Henry Oliver, the eventual head of the mileage department and his partner in the production of station handbooks, Airey published in 1867 his first *Book of Railway Junction Diagrams*. 'These maps have been drawn from the Ordnance Survey, and compiled with great care from details supplied by the Railway Companies, all of which have been duly certified. They show clearly the different systems of Railways in colours, DISTANCES in miles and chains, Stations, Junctions, Sidings, Collieries, Tunnels, Levels where lines cross, Private Lines and Works, also the Counties, Canals, Rivers, Docks, &c., and a complete list of the Running Powers and Working Arrangements in EACH district.'[117] These fine maps, prepared and regularly revised by John Emslie and, from 1876, by his sons John and William, covered railway regions, showing company ownership in distinctive colours, often with complex junctions inset at larger scales and with details of inland navigation. The junction diagrams were specifically designed to allow the calculation of rates to be charged for the 'running powers' of one railway over the lines of another and for settling disagreements between

companies. Airey's business, including his partnership with Oliver, was taken over by the Clearing House itself in 1895, including all the plates and stock, and, henceforth, the maps appeared as the 'Official Railway Maps', 'Published by H. Smart, Secretary of the Railway Clearing House, 123, Seymour Street, Euston Square, London'.[118]

The aspect of railway development which most surprised both railway promoters and stage-coach proprietors was the totally unexpected enthusiasm with which the populace adopted rail as its principal means of long-distance travel. 'It is a singular fact, that of all the railways constructed and contemplated up to the opening of the Liverpool and Manchester line, not one was undertaken with a view to the conveyance of passengers.'[119]

Year	Length of line open for traffic (miles)	Total number of passengers carried (excluding season-ticket holders) (millions)
1850	6,621	72·9
1860	10,433	163·4
1870	15,537 (line constructed)	336·5
1880	17,933	603·9
1890	20,073	817·7
1900	21,855	1,142·3

Predictably, both railway companies and commercial map-publishers responded energetically to capitalize on this unforeseen windfall. There was a huge popular demand for maps of individual railways, regional systems, and the whole network, and 'booksellers up and down the country reported that customers for maps asked one question only: "Has it got the level crossings on it?"'[121] Private-sector publishers benefited from the laggardly production of Ordnance maps resulting from meagre finance and the loss of skilled surveyors to better-paid railway work, for it left an uncontested opportunity to satisfy this new market with varying degrees of competence, creating, in passing, a specialized style of steam decoration on their maps. In contrast, the Irish Survey was responsible for the production of 'perhaps the most successful single map of Ireland that they were ever to produce'[122] on six sheets, at 4m. : 1″, to demonstrate the findings of the 1836 commission established to consider the possibility of providing Ireland with a general system of railways. Although constructed from older surveys of varying accuracy because the Survey was still at the stage of primary triangulation, this 'railway map' proved immensely popular and rather outflanked commercial rivals.

The rapid spread of the railway network was certainly depressing in one sense for commercial map-makers because it quickly rendered their maps obsolete; largely destroying, incidentally, the habit of dating maps which proved to be a growing commercial drawback since even yesteryear's date immediately branded the map as archaic. At worst, opportunist publishers, such as Cruchley and Collins, presented railway information simply by overprinting, often inaccurately, onto existing sheets depicting out-dated topographical features. Mere alteration of the map title suggested the preparation of a special railway map. Even the railway information itself was deficient, for stations, when shown at all, were seldom named and, frequently, inexactly located. At best, specialist producers issued accurate railway maps, often for wall display, such as the 'Map of England and Wales showing the Railways, Canals, and Inland Navigations' (1852) prepared for the use of the Committee of the Privy Council for Trade, and George Bradshaw's highly

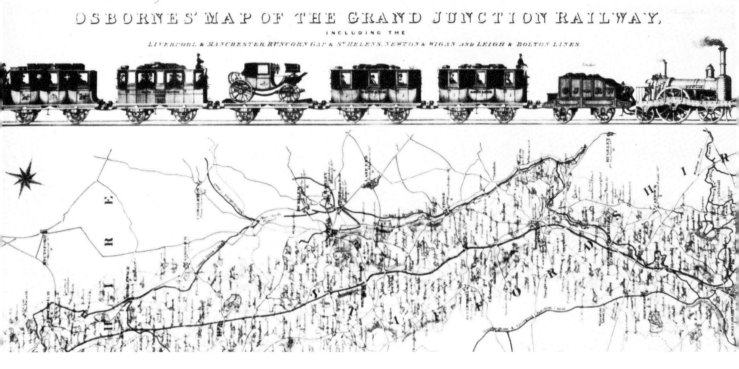

64: *The emergence of the specialized railway map created its own special brand of steam decoration with locomotives, trains and the infrastructure of the railway being widely featured in vignettes. Detail: 'OSBORNE'S MAP OF THE GRAND JUNCTION RAILWAY', c.1837. By permission of the British Library (Maps 1223(15)).*

reputed productions (including his three important regional canal maps of 1829–32), '... unmatched in England for boldness of conception, accuracy of delineation and richness of colouring. Taken from the Ordnance Survey ... the fullest and most accurate geographical information extant ... a ready school for instruction, or authority for reference, to all interested in the progress and construction of railways'.[123] Bradshaw's maps were largely corrections and enlargements of his first railway map, engraved by John Dower, published in 1839—'a marvel of ingenuity and the fruit of a really admirable enterprise. It constitutes a visible epitome of the mighty Conquests made by the Anglo-Saxon race in their memorable march—a march not of decades, but of centuries—along the broad and holy track of civilisation.'![124] Similarly, some publishers issued what were, in effect, regional railway maps, as, for example, in the case of Mogg's maps of the country 'Forty-five miles round London: a very beautiful Work, ... SHOWING ALL THE RAILWAYS' (which 'whether proceeding by road or railway, will be found a very delightful travelling companion')[125] and 'Twenty-four Miles round London, WITH ALL THE RAILWAYS.' Other publishers met the new demand with the production of whole railway atlases, as Cassell did with *Cassell's Railway Atlas*, 'Consisting of 20 Folio Maps (four being Double) of the principal English Railway Routes'.[126]

The popularity of rail travel created a market for a variety of rail guides and periodicals. The railway companies themselves realized the value of producing maps of their net-

works, both to improve administration and operation, and to advertise their services. Dependable maps concentrating almost entirely on railway information were constructed, particularly to distinguish line ownership and to show by colour the running powers of companies on each other's lines. The companies also recognized the commercial value of clear maps produced for passengers. Companies, such as the District Railway, which published small guides to coincide with international exhibitions being held in London and with such national events as the Jubilee of 1887, produced maps not only for sale but also for free distribution to the publishers of independent guides who might include them in their works (this was not as philanthropic as first sight suggests, for it not only secured free advertising for the company but saved it the expense of compiling its own guide-book!). Such was the demand for railway maps that one version alone of the Metropolitan '"District Railway" Map' allegedly sold over 465,000 copies.

Commercial publishers, particularly Bradshaw with his *Journal* 'embellished with Maps and Engravings in Steel and Wood',[127] his *Railway Gazette*, and his *Railway Companion* 'containing numerous Railway Maps and Plans of Towns',[128] produced railway periodicals designed to keep the public informed of the latest developments.

Edward Mogg was also active in this type of provision with his *Hand-Book for Railway Travellers*—'Being an entirely original and accurate Description of ALL THE TRAVELLABLE RAILWAYS hitherto completed ... THE DETAILS DEDUCED FROM OFFICIAL DOCUMENTS. Illustrated by Maps.'[129] Similarly, railway maps were included in the convenient, portable timetable-books which replaced the advertising of train times in the newspapers. Once again, Bradshaw was to the fore with his *Railway Time Tables*; 'The necessity of such a work is so obvious as to need no apology; and the merits of it can be best ascertained by a reference to the execution both as regards the style and correctness of the Maps and

65: *Remarkably ancient maps were pressed into service to satisfy the demand for maps delineating railways and communications.* 'CRUCHLEY'S RAILWAY & TELEGRAPHIC MAP OF SUSSEX', *was taken from an engraved plate which originally printed John Cary's map first published in 1801. Simple alteration of a map's title could create the impression that an entirely new map had been constructed. George Frederick Cruchley created the title* 'CRUCHLEY'S RAILWAY AND STATION MAP OF WARWICK Showing all the RAILWAYS & NAMES OF STATIONS, . . .' *for John Cary's* 'A NEW MAP OF WARWICKSHIRE' *first published in 1806.*
i 'CRUCHLEY'S RAILWAY & TELEGRAPHIC MAP OF SUSSEX, Showing all the RAILWAYS & NAMES OF STATIONS, ALSO THE TELEGRAPH LINES & STATIONS . . .', *c.1856. By permission of the British Library (Maps 5395(18)).*
ii *Titlepiece of Warwickshire, published by G. F. Cruchley, c.1875.*

Plans with which it is illustrated.'[130] Bradshaw even published separate sheets of amended times which could simply be pasted over obsolete tables, thus keeping the books up-to-date. More specifically, publishers offered guides to particular lines, usually in the form of a 'continuous chart' on which 'the Tourist has pointed out to him, without any troublesome reference, the objects of interest in his vicinity, the rivers and canals he is crossing, the remarkable places he is passing, and the distance he is travelling'.[131] Examples are legion, but the following illustrate the form: Edward Mogg's 'RAILWAY POCKET MAPS', intended eventually to offer 'Separate Maps of all the principal Lines', 'drawn from Authentic Documents, Engraved in the best Style, and neatly Coloured, folded in a Form, and fitted in case convenient for the Pocket';[132] A hand-book for travellers along the London and Birmingham Railway, 'Embellished with Twenty-five fine engravings on wood, and a map of the line of unequalled correctness and beauty';[133] James Wyld's London and Southampton Railway Guide with its maps and plans; Osborne's Guide to the Grand Junction or Birmingham, Liverpool, and Manchester Railway, with its delightfully decorated map 'Drawn & Engraved by D. Smith'—'The Map of the Line, with its neighbouring districts, is engraved as well as delineated in a very superior manner to any thing which has hitherto appeared';[134] Andrew Reid's lavishly 'Illustrated Map of the York, Newcastle & Berwick Railway'; 'Bacon's Railway Guide Map of London & Suburbs'; and Cassell's series of 'Official Guides' to railway routes. Such guides were widely available and served an extensive popular market—Mayhew's survey of London labour reported that at both street- and shop-bookstalls were 'boxes, containing works marked, "All 1d.," or 2d., 3d., or 4d.' offering 'old Court-Guides, Parliamentary Companions, Railway Plans, and a variety of sermons, and theological, as well as educational and political pamphlets.'[135]

Finally, commercial publishers responded by offering guides to areas of interest and natural beauty made newly accessible by railway penetration at a time of growing middle-class interest in the splendours of scenery and such energetic out-door activities as fell-walking and rock-climbing. M.A. Leigh, for instance, published a Guide to the Lakes, Mountains, and Waterfalls of Cumberland, Westmorland, and Lancashire which was 'Illustrated with a map of the country' and charming small maps, engraved by Josiah Neele, 'of Windermere, Derwent Water, Borrowdale, Ullswater, Grasmere, Rydal Water, and Langdale',—'now that the mighty steam-engine has gained its sway, every person may be conveyed in a few hours from the metropolis to a scene of almost unrivalled sublimity and grandeur, exhibiting in Nature's most beautiful colouring the varied prospect of rock, wood, and water; which it is impossible for any who are the least alive to Nature's work to view without being struck by the gorgeousness of the scene.'[136]

This dramatic intensification in the production of railway guides of all types was made possible only by improved retail opportunities at the stations themselves. As railways expanded, so the station bookstall, often leased by the railway company to disabled ex-railwaymen or railwaymen's widows as a convenient means of providing for them, became an increasingly familiar feature. From 1848 William Henry Smith began to acquire bookstall contracts with railway companies, so successfully that 'by 1862 the name "Smith's" had come practically to mean the same thing as "bookstalls" on nearly every railway of any importance in the country.'[137] It is no surprise that such a visionary en-

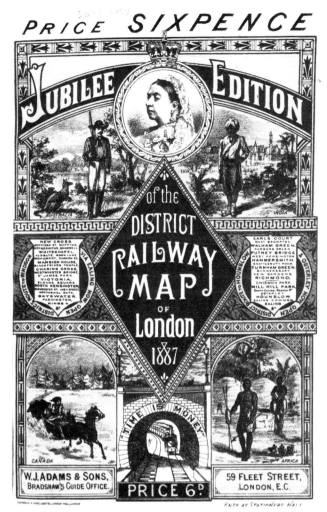

66: Cover: 'JUBILEE EDITION OF THE DISTRICT RAILWAY MAP OF LONDON 1887. PRICE 6[D].' By permission of the British Library (Maps 3480(262)).

trepreneur rapidly realized that he was not exploiting his opportunities fully by offering only the railway maps and guides of rival publishers. Consequently in the early 1850s 'Smith's' branched-out into the production of its own maps, initially for railway passengers but later for all types of travellers, with such publications as 'W.H. SMITH & SON'S SERIES OF REDUCED ORDNANCE MAPS FOR TOURISTS BY J. BARTHOLOMEW', which proudly advertised a reference to itself in J.J. Hissey's A Tour in a Phaeton: 'We always take with us Smith & Son's Shilling "Reduced Ordnance Maps". They are very clear and correct.'

EXCURSION MAPS

The concurrent development of so many new and different forms of transport which could be combined to create day-trips, sightseeing tours, and even holidays, provided yet another opportunity for the map-maker to satisfy a growing demand for multi-purpose guides which gave blanket coverage to the various modes of travel likely to be encountered on a particular trip or in a certain area. Fortunately, favourable social evolution was to make this an ever-growing market for map-makers in the second half of the century, providing many of the firms with a solid, prosperous foundation from which to develop other aspects of their cartographic output.

In the second half of the century, the larger proportion of the population was enjoying a higher standard of living as numbers moved to better-paid occupations and wages rose slightly in some industries, enabling many to take advantage of the Saturday half-holiday, first imposed on the textile industries in 1850 but quickly spreading to other industries, for local travel even if it was only to the town centre. Sundays, too, offered the opportunity for leisure trips, as did the four statutory annual bank holidays introduced from 1871. All but the poor eagerly grasped these new opportunities, offered by increased leisure and income, to travel by omnibus, railway or steamer, whether simply for a day-trip from the dismal town to the surrounding countryside or nearby coastal resort, or for the much grander annual holiday taken by the affluent minority. Between 1850 and 1855 alone passenger traffic increased tenfold as the travel habit spread, creating a potentially immense demand for the excursion map. Additionally, the emergence of excursioning and vacationing, allied with developments in the postal system, particularly the introduction of the postcard and halfpenny stamps in 1870, offered an opportunity for the production of maps on postcards such as those of English towns published by John Walker & Co., each map-card being decorated with a vignette of a local building or scene. The lure of postal communication even persuaded publishers such as 'R.W. Hume' of Leith to convert the cartographic and scenic images of an area into a 'Tourist's Envelope' with vignettes of the local attractions adorning the outside of the envelope and a touring map with details of 'routs' embellishing the interior surfaces.

It was, perhaps, individual events, more than travel for its own sake, that created and reinforced the travel habit, thus opening up the market for the map-maker. The popularity of national events was boundless, underlining the number and social spectrum of potential customers for pocket guides containing maps and plans. Sporting events, in particular, were great attractions, highlighting the surprising distances which relatively primitive transport could achieve— *The Times*, for instance, recorded that the return journey from the 1870 Derby at Epsom 'from Kennington to the Elephant and Castle, about a mile of road, occupied upwards of an hour, so crowded was the road with vehicles of every description including a large number of bicycles which had been ridden by their owners to Epsom and back'.[138] Most, if not all, of this 'inextricable mass' were potential customers for small, cheap guides and maps which would not only inform them of 'all the principal Gentlemen's Seats, Antiquities, Objects of Interest to the Tourist, &c.'[139] but also provide more practical and convivial guidance to tolls, gates, conditions, hazards, mileage, landmarks, refreshment places, and public houses. Such interest created, also, a demand for plans of the arena itself—Henry Taunt, for example, mapped the Henley Regatta course in 1886; Leeds race course, cricket and football ground were surveyed by Walter Parkinson and lithographed by McCorquodale & Co. in 1883; and Mogg's 'Plan of Ascot Race Course', 'Exhibiting all the improvements lately executed by Command of HIS MAJESTY ... will be found to contain all the information requisite for Gentlemen of the Turf, and visitors in general to this unrivalled scene of national sport'.[140]

Undoubtedly the most influential national event to nurture the excursion habit was the Great Exhibition of 1851, the first of a series of national and international exhibitions held in London firstly in Hyde Park and from 1886 at Earls Court. (These exhibitions became important showcases for

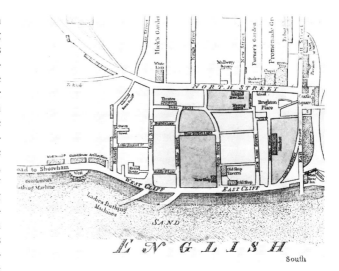

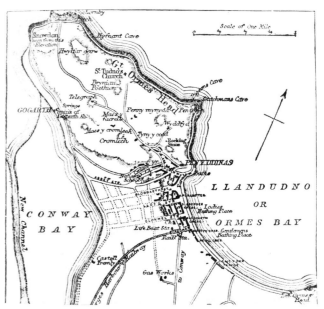

67: *Excursion maps recorded places of interest and other locations useful to the tripper. The public houses, for example, were marked in Brighton, the 'Elevation' for viewing Snowdon in Llandudno, and in both the baths and the sections of beach for single-sex bathing, with Brighton specifying the location of bathing machines.*
i *Detail: 'BRIGHTHELMSTON', by Edward Cobby, undated, but taken from the original of c.1799 for use in a Victorian guidebook.*
ii *Detail: 'PLAN OF LLANDUDNO', engraved by John Bartholomew for* Black's Picturesque Guide to North Wales, *1881.*

cartographic work; at the International Exhibition of 1862, for example, Edward Stanford was awarded a medal 'for the merit of his geographical publications'—'in the English department no maps exceed for beauty and accuracy those contributed by Mr Stanford'.)[141] Despite the high price of entrance (the *Illustrated London News* pleaded for a sixpenny entrance fee because 'an immense proportion of the population' could not afford a shilling, arguing that 'even 6d perhaps is too much'[142]), visitors flocked to the Exhibition. With an eye to the expected flood of foreign visitors, the Eastern Counties Railway was advertising its excursion trips by the beginning of 1851 not only in English but also in French and German. Including foreign visitors, six million people saw the Great Exhibition by taking advantage of the relatively cheap trips offered from the provinces; the excursion fare from Leeds for visitors to the Exhibition, for example, was only five shillings return on the Midland line and 4s. 6d. on the Great Northern (compared with a normal single fare of 35s. which was well beyond average means), and during the months when the Exhibition was open, Euston Station handled three-quarters-of-a-million passengers. Thomas Cook offered excursions to the Exhibition including board and lodging and sold 165,000 tickets. Obviously, the Exhibition offered an opportunity to sample, usually for the first time, the wider delights of the metropolis including James Wyld's 'Monster Globe' which was erected in Leicester Square as his contribution to the Exhibition. 'The globe, sixty feet high, lighted with gas and approached by galleries, was about forty feet in diameter, and far the largest hitherto constructed. Upon its interior side were delineated the physical features of the earth, the horizontal surface being on the scale of an inch to ten miles, and mountains, shown by mechanical devices, on thrice that scale. The concave surface was made of some six thousand casts taken in plaster of Paris, three feet square and an inch thick, screwed to beams and joined together, and afterwards painted over. The top of the globe outside was painted with stars.'[143] It would appear that most visitors bought maps to accompany their excursion, for an abnormally large number of London plans appeared at very cheap prices in the year of the Exhibition; for instance, 'Tallis's Illustrated Plan of London and its Environs' was produced 'IN COMMEMORATION

OF THE GREAT EXHIBITION OF INDUSTRY OF ALL NATIONS'. Similarly, later for the 'Great International Exhibition' of 1862 '... with No. 233 of CASSELL'S ILLUSTRATED FAMILY PAPER, to be published on 5th of May, will be issued a large and well-engraved MAP OF LONDON ... which has been produced upon the latest and best authorities for special issue with CASSELL'S PAPER. By the use of this MAP visitors to the GREAT INTERNATIONAL EXHIBITION, even though entire strangers, will be able to find their way in every part of London.... Notwithstanding the great expense attending the production of such a Map, we propose to issue it at the nominal price of One Penny to all purchasers of CASSELL'S FAMILY PAPER from Nos. 231 to 233, inclusive.'[144] Street-sellers of guides and catalogues (which frequently contained maps and plans) to exhibitions and the like reported that their best customers were working-class sightseers who bought them not only for their guidance but also as a memento of their visit, with the greatest number sold recorded on a fine Whit-Monday.

Thus, for the greater part of the population, horizons were extended beyond the trip to the nearest market town, and these expanded geographic limits created a demand for cheap maps and guides explaining the range of alternative transport methods available to the traveller and the interconnection of the different services. No longer did most people have to be content with acquiring their geographical knowledge of localities they could never visit second-hand from maps, plans, and topographical prints; now, guidebook or folding map in hand, they could go and see for themselves. 'Railways have accomplished what the far-famed SOCIETY FOR THE DIFFUSION OF USEFUL KNOWLEDGE, with its long train of noble and ignoble patrons and its penny magazines and penny encyclopaedias ... could never have effected; they have taught the thorough bred Londoner ALMOST to discriminate between a plough and a harrow, and to recognise a potato by its stem.'[145]

68: *Popular interest in sporting events was immense and major occasions produced a mass exodus from the towns to the venue of the event. Map-makers responded by producing small cheap plans of the arena itself.*
'PLAN of ASCOT RACE COURSE, Surveyed in 1829 by EDWARD MOGG', published 8 June 1829. By permission of the British Library (Maps 1510(1)).

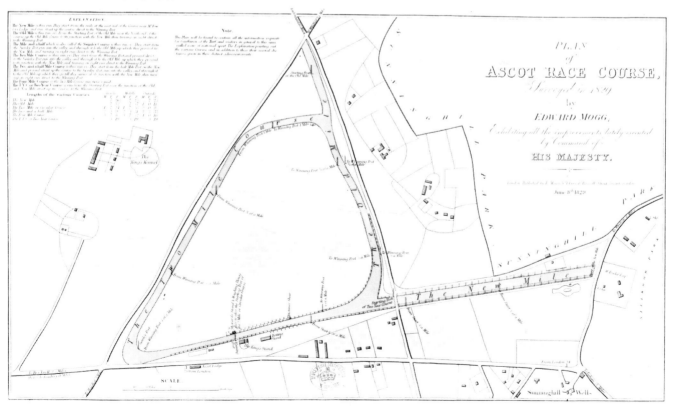

The Society for the Diffusion of Useful Knowledge had been established in 1826 by Lord Henry Brougham and 'the leading statesmen, lawyers and philanthropists of the day'[146] with the object 'by the periodical publication of treatises ... to impart useful information to all classes of the community, particularly to such as are unable to avail themselves of experienced teachers'.[146] It was not only this Society that found that the demand for its altruistic educational maps of the British Isles had withered as a result of the majority's greater mobility. Although such other philanthropic bodies as the National Society for Promoting the Education of the Poor and the Society for Promoting Christian Knowledge continued to produce their maps after the excursion habit became well established, and even after the advent of popular education, they were of declining importance to the newly mobile population—'in these days when "cheap trips" afford opportunities "to see for themselves" to persons whose eyes have been opened by previous instruction.'[147]

Guides were produced in startling numbers to cater *en masse* for walkers, ramblers, horse-carriage drivers, steamer and railway passengers, omnibus, tram, and cab riders, and, indeed, all tourists whatever their mode of transport. Town guides offered not only street plans and outline maps marking the public buildings and places of entertainment, but also plans showing canal, river, omnibus, and railway routes, stations, bus stops, cab stands, and all other useful transport data. They also provided letter-press street indexes, directions for calculating cab, coach, and watermen's fares, descriptions of transport facilities, advice on music halls, dioramas, and other entertainments, and additional useful information such as how to deal with dishonest cabmen, pickpockets, and troublesome beggars. Cassell's 'Map of London', for example, although 'published at the nominal price of One Penny', was produced with no expense 'spared in making it as complete and useful as possible. All the recent Metropolitan improvements, many of which are not to be found in Maps still on sale, are distinctly noted. The new roads and walks through the public Parks are clearly shown—the correct delineation of which is of importance to those of our country readers who may visit London, and wish to pass *en route* through any of them. The New Railway Extensions are denoted by a black line (uniform with the older lines) as far as the works at present extended; while the proposed routes, in an early stage or not yet commenced, are shown by dotted lines only'.[148]

Excursionists' maps of surrounding rural areas stressed distances between towns and places of interest, concentrating on country estates, antiquities, and interesting sights. *Black's Guide through Edinburgh and Leith*, for instance, contained 'a Description of the Pleasure Tours in the Environs. Illustrated by a Plan of the City; a Map of the Country Ten Miles round; and numerous Views of the Public Buildings and of the Neighbouring Scenery', ('This little book should be in the hands of every stranger who desires to be familiar with all that is remarkable in the Antiquities, Institutions, and Public Buildings of Edinburgh'),[149] and their *Guide through Glasgow, with Pleasure Excursions in the Neighbourhood* was, similarly, 'most tastefully got up' with a 'Plan of the City, a Map of Lanarkshire, Railway Charts, and Views of the Streets and Public Buildings'.[150]

The most commercially attractive branch of this market, however, was the provision of tourist guides to areas of notable natural beauty and tourist appeal. 'The increasing demand for Illustrated Guide Books to aid the tourist on his rambles, together with the increased facilities of railway and steam-boat communication, have suggested a want ....'[151] The greater the beauty, the greater the tourist attraction, and, hence, the greater the number of guides on offer, with scenic and coastal areas and the popular spas particularly rich in guides published both by local booksellers and as parts of handbook series by such as Abel Heywood with his 'Penny-Guides' and Thomas & Edward Gilks who specialized in this type of production. The Gilks created their 'Sylvan's Pictorial Hand-Books' 'to give a pleasant gossiping account of all the objects worthy attention on the routes',[152] frequently illuminating their text with explanatory maps; the guide to the English Lakes being, for example, illustrated 'with maps by Wyld'.[153] The outstanding scenery of Scotland stimulated an extensive output, not least due to the chauvinism of the increasingly dominant Scottish publishers mainly concentrated in Edinburgh; typical examples were *Wilson's Guide to Rothesay and the Island of Bute* 'Illustrated with Maps and Views' ('Every one visiting Bute ought to provide himself with a copy of this book. He will find it of essential use in exploring the scenery and antiquities of that lovely island')[154] and *Anderson's Guide to the Highlands & Islands of Scotland*, with its 'Maps, Views, Tables of Distances, Notices of Inns, and other information for the use of Tourists' ('Most copiously and praiseworthily minute').[155]

So enticing and prospectively profitable was this growing market that many map-publishers, whose forte was more mainstream cartographic output, dabbled in guide-book production as a remunerative sideline, particularly as it became so simple and cheap to take lithographic transfers of portions from existing general maps. As early as the late 1820s John Thomson doubled the productivity of the field-staff preparing his *Atlas of Scotland* by using them to prepare at the same time his popular *Traveller's Guide through Scotland*. 'The ITINERARY has been drawn up by the Surveyors who contributed to the compilation and correction of the Maps for the Atlas of Scotland, between thirty and forty in number, residing in various parts of the kingdom, whose local knowledge ensured the greatest accuracy.'[156] By its ninth edition, published in 1829, Thomson's *Guide* had sold 15,000 copies due to 'Public favour, time and circumstances'.[157] Later in the century, Edward Stanford issued a series of 'Tourists' Guides', illustrated by lithographically transferred portions of his 'Library Map of England & Wales' and his 'Map of England & Wales ... Projected from the Triangulation for the Survey'; and, similarly, John Murray used sections from both W. & A.K. Johnston's and John Bartholomew's general maps, in addition, possibly, to J. & C. Walker's county maps, for his 'Handbooks'. The ever-imaginative Edward Mogg combined the strip railway map with guides to the various interesting destinations, giving also details of railway times and fares, and 'hackney coach & cab fares'.[158] His *South Eastern Railway* was combined with a guide to Tunbridge Wells, and the *Great Western Railway* with guides to Windsor, Bath, and Bristol. The latter guide contained an exquisite map of the railway 'drawn from the Ordnance Survey (on which the line was originally laid down for the purpose of this work by Mr. Brunel), including a considerable portion of the surrounding country'.[159]

Despite this multiplicity, one firm dominated the guide-book market through its publication of an immense and varied range of very popular works which appeared in an avalanche of editions invariably containing maps and plans usually lithographically transferred from the creations of

John Bartholomew. During the second half of the century the firm of Adam & Charles Black poured forth a torrent of 'Guide Books & Travelling Maps'—'Without the pretension of a tutor, dictating what he shall admire, the traveller will find these books very pleasing, intelligent, and instructive companions, giving him the exact knowledge he requires at the exact time that he needs it; and very useful, not only to the professed tourist, but to any person who has at any time occasion to journey from his residence in any direction and who desires to know something more than the mere names of the places he visits.'[160]

Thus, the disparate development of the different modes of transport in the nineteenth century had come together to create a profusion of attractively packaged folding maps and guide-books designed for the tourist's pocket. A highly competitive situation forced publishers to concentrate their efforts on retaining and expanding market share through a procession of innovations and 'novelties', generally at the expense of cartographic accuracy and up-dating. The ornamenting of maps, covers, and guides was, inevitably, counter-balanced by production of the actual map at the lowest possible cost, with map-makers content to copy from out-dated sources, transfer from existing material, and revise little but the transport facilities.

COMMUNICATION MAPS

The evolution of the modern transport system was paralelled by a development of communications, which was accompanied in turn by its quota of specific maps. The adoption of Hill's uniform penny post in 1840 kindled an immediate and continuous increase in the volume of correspondence. The number of letters posted in 1840 was double that of the previous year; by 1850, letters posted had almost quadrupled; by 1870 had increased tenfold; and by 1900 had achieved a grand total of 2300 million. Significantly for the demand for commercial directories, by 1864 94 per cent of all letters were being delivered. This extraordinary growth of postal communication produced a cartographic demand for 'Post Office' maps showing, particularly, postal districts and the location of post offices and money-order facilities. Although publishers such as Edward Mogg produced individual 'postal-district' maps, generally postal maps accompanied the 'Post Office' directories, designed to ensure the correct addressing and delivery of letters, usually produced by ex-Post Office employees or, indeed, by 'moonlighting' current employees. (Kelly's use of Post Office employees was ended by public outcry in 1847.) Postal directories date from 1800, but it was only with the appearance of those produced by Frederick Kelly, from 1836, that they became widely available.

Kelly expanded aggressively from his London base ('the increased and rapidly increasing facilities of communication seemed to indicate a necessity for more extended and elaborate works ... than had before been attempted')[161] and successfully drove out established competitors from areas into which he extended his activities. James Pigot, for example, was forced from the Home Counties' market after 1840; his successor, Isaac Slater, retreated to his stronghold in the north and north-west but his firm was, nevertheless, taken over after his death by Kelly's Directories Ltd; and Bowtell & Co. abandoned the publication of William Robson's directory because they said they could no longer compete with Kelly. Kelly's *Post Office Directory*, with its apparently official red cover bearing the Royal Arms, dominated the market and brought wide circulation to his 'POST OFFICE' maps. However, there were other prod-

ucers who enjoyed limited success; the Steven's Postal Directories and Publishing Co., for example, adapted George Philip's county maps for commercial purposes, sometimes by the addition of advertisements.

Other quicker means of communication followed, particularly the adoption of the electric telegraph, which proved infinitely more satisfactory than rapid semaphores or flashing signal mirrors. The Electric Telegraph Company was formed in 1846; within a few years a network of lines connected the main cities; the service was taken-over by the Post Office in 1870 and within two years 5000 post offices were telegraph stations. There was a demand from business for maps which defined the extent of the telegraph system and, consequently, general maps of the network were produced; such as, for example, the Electric Telegraph Company's 'Chart of the Company's Telegraphic System in Great Britain, 1853'. The building of the telegraph system alongside the railways and the establishment of early telegraph offices at the stations created a natural association between the two in the map-maker's mind, and it was logical to combine railway and telegraph information on the same map; thus, for instance, Cruchley, in adapting Cary's large county series, turned them into 'Railway & Telegraphic' maps giving not only railway information but also details of telegraph lines and stations. Similarly, Henry Collins adapted William Ebden's county maps to emphasize telegraph lines and telegraph offices 'open daily only' and 'open day & night'.

EDUCATION MAPS

The growing use of transport and communications was, in part, a reflection of wider and more advanced education. At the start of the nineteenth century, remarkably, in Scotland virtually all males were literate. In England and Wales probably only one-third were illiterate, although literacy rates were not spread evenly since rural lowland areas tended to have higher rates of illiteracy, whilst London and

69: *Prior to the educational boom of the Victorian age, children were usually catered for with only the simplest of outline maps. Buckinghamshire, by John Luffman, 1803, from* A New Pocket Atlas and Geography of England and Wales. *By courtesy of Ivan Deverall.*

the rural north had lower rates. The literacy rate was of considerable significance to the map-maker for it bore a direct relationship to popular demand for cheap maps. As the rate improved during the century (by the last quarter of the century Britain had become almost wholly literate with 80 per cent of adults literate by 1870 and near-universal literacy by 1900) publishers increasingly turned their attention to the provision of maps and atlases specifically for popular educational purposes. These contrasted with the simple outline or amusingly decorated maps traditionally produced for the governesses, tutors and private schools of the wealthier classes by John Luffman, John Aikin, 'Reuben Ramble', and the like.

Despite the inadequacy of an educational system in which many children never even entered school, everywhere attendance was erratic, and the total school-life of most working-class children was months rather than years, in the early Victorian period opportunities did exist for the enterprising map-maker. Although geography was rarely taught as a subject in its own right, classrooms were nevertheless still adorned with attractive wall maps. 'There were no geography readers, and, excepting what could be gleaned from the descriptions of different parts of the world in the ordinary readers, no geography was taught. But, for some reason or other, on the walls of the schoolroom were hung splendid maps: The World, Europe, North America, South America, England, Ireland, and Scotland. During long waits in class for her turn to read, or to have her copy or her sewing examined, Laura would gaze on these maps until the shapes of the countries with their islands and inlets became photographed on her brain.'[162] Until the end of the century large wall maps were produced for use in schools by the major map-making firms through series such as 'Darton and Clark's School Room Maps' (Samuel Clark also apparently collaborated in the production of educational wall maps with Edward Stanford—as did Trelawney Saunders—and the National Society for Promoting the Education of the Poor); 'Collins' New Series of School-Room Maps; Edited by W. Lawson, F.R.G.S.'; 'Blackie's Standard Class Maps'; and 'Johnston's National School Board Series of Large Wall Maps (Adopted by nearly every School Board in Great Britain)'. 'This well-known Series [Johnston's] possesses the following advantages: From the great demand, they are constantly at press, and no Map is ever printed without being thoroughly revised. The Maps are carefully printed in permanent Oil Colours. The Series is the most extensive published, consisting of nearly 80 Maps and Illustrations, to which additions are constantly being made. They are Mounted on Cloth and Rollers, Plain or Varnished, the best materials only being used. The whole Series is of one uniform size, namely 50 by 42 inches. It is the cheapest ever published, the price being, Rollers Varnished, 12s. each: Unvarnished, 10s. It is the *only Series* accompanied by Handbooks written expressly for each Map. These are given *gratis* to purchasers. It will be found INDISPENSABLE TO TEACHERS and MANAGERS who require the GOVERNMENT GRANT.'[163]

Map-makers geared themselves specifically to meet the requirements of the Government's 'Standards' which had to be achieved by pupils of appropriate age if the school was to qualify for the Government grant. This 'Payment by Results' system—'If it is not cheap it shall be efficient; if it is not efficient, it shall be cheap'[164]—remained in force until 1897, compelling schools to concentrate on reading, writing, and arithmetic at the expense of other subjects, although there was an additional grant for efficiency in not

more than two specific subjects—in practice usually geography, history, algebra, or geometry. Although from 1870 Forster attempted to raise the level of expected achievement in the schools by raising the level of the Standards he did little to liberalize the curriculum, and only in 1882 were an extended syllabus, known as 'Standard VII', and more-advanced classes introduced; this helped to broaden the range of subjects taken, making geography an accepted subject at least for upper commercial classes. Opportunist map-makers met the requirements of the educational codes with works such as Gibson's *Test Map Book for Standard III* and his *"Up-to-date" Test Map Book for Standard IV*; W. & A.K. Johnstons' 3rd *Standard Atlas & Geography*; and Ruddiman Johnston's '"UNCROWDED" STANDARD ATLASES' ('... printed from ENTIRELY NEW PLATES specially constructed to meet the requirements of the New Code.... In addition to the ordinary Political Maps usually given in Atlases, Maps have been introduced ... in accordance with the spirit of the New Code').[165] Similarly, John Heywood's *New Maps of the Counties of England and Wales, from the Ordnance Survey* was 'Specially prepared for Standard V. of Geography under the New Code, which requires "some special knowledge of the County in which the School is situated, and a map drawing of it"'.[166] Ruddiman Johnston also catered specifically for examination preparation with his 'New Series of Examination Memory Sketch Maps,' which were kept deliberately simple by having 'No Curved Degree Lines',[167] as did G.W. Bacon with his 'Excelsior Memory Maps,' 'With a Geography Lesson facing each; specially adapted for the use of pupil teachers, candidates for the King's scholarship, certificate; and civil service examinations; also for use in secondary schools'.[168] These latter maps were available both in an atlas and 'separately on cards ½d. each' and could be used in conjunction with a matching set of 'halfpenny' 'County Maps for Standard III', 'Bacon's Memory-Map Slates. Consisting of Cardboard Slates on which Map Projections ... are drawn', and 'Bacon's Excelsior Memory-Map Sketch Books'.[169]

However, the major commercial breakthrough began only in 1870 with the passing of Forster's Elementary Education Act, designed to provide a school within the reach of every child in England and Wales through the establishment of School Boards to oversee elementary education independent of religious bodies and maintained by public money. The Act not only created many more pupil places but also opened the way for an expansion of geography teaching in the curriculum, for now the teaching of religion was to be left to ministers and parents, and school instruction was to concentrate on 'the truths of arithmetic and geography, ... spelling and writing'.[170] The study of geography was stimulated by exploration, by the 'scramble' of the European powers for African territory, and by the advances in the subject itself. Despite the formation of many new geographical societies (which created another group of largely 'lost' maps printed for distribution to accompany papers presented at their meetings and for publication in their journals) and pressure for more teaching and examination of the subject by bodies such as the Royal Geographical Society which encouraged geographical study with its gold medal award scheme and essay prizes, geography teaching in Britain lagged behind other advanced European nations. The subject was admitted to the universities of Oxford and Cambridge only in 1892, and still later to other universities. Nevertheless, there was expansion both in the amount of geography taught (not least due to the 1888 Cross Commis-

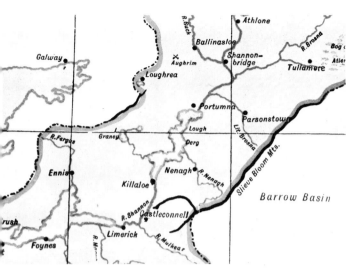

70: *Detail: 'BASIN OF THE SHANNON', from G. W. Bacon's 'Excelsior Memory Maps' series, published c.1902.*

sion's recommendation that 'The following subjects of elementary instruction are to be regarded as essential ... Geography, especially of the British Empire ...')[171] and in the number of pupils in schools; and map-publishers responded to this opportunity to equip the new schools with an increased production of textbooks, maps, and atlases, as well as more general school stationery and geographical appliances, such as globes, planctaria, relief models, and Bacon's 'Iron Map-easel'.

In addition to the wall maps and specific 'Standard' exercises, provision of geographical information came broadly in two forms. There were, on the one hand, geographical readers and textbooks, as, for example, Charlotte Mason's 'Readers' which contained Edward Stanford's rather roughly lithographed maps. Such readers often concentrated on the presentation of historical data—for instance, both Samuel Rawson Gardiner's *School Atlas of English History* (1891) and Charles Pearson's *Historical Maps of England, during the First Thirteen Centuries* (1869) offered maps illustrating the state of the country at different past dates. On the other hand, map-makers tried to undermine the common practice of map-copying ('As an exercise of memory and as a lesson in neat writing it is always useful; but as a practical aid to the study of geography its value is doubtful')[172] by boycotting rote learning in favour of structured exercises in which pupils added data to outline maps. It was still, however, necessary for pupils to memorize maps in order to meet the requirements of the 'Instructions to H.M. Inspectors' which specified that 'To obtain the mark "Good" for Geography, the scholars in Standard V. and upwards should be required to "have prepared THREE MAPS, one of which, selected by the Inspector, should be drawn from memory, on the day of the "inspection"'.[173] Examples of such educational cartographic exercises include those by Weller for 'Cassell's Map Building Series' for pupils 'to insert in their proper position upon the Map such of the places named upon the back as the teacher may select';[174] by William Murphy in *The Progressive Drawing-Book of Outline Maps, Projections. & Squares*, 'In 3 Stages, viz. Map 1—Red Lines, & Squares for Drawing on. Map 2—Latitude, Longitude, Capes, Promontories, &c. Map 3—Latitude and Longitude Lines alone'[175]; by M.T. Yates in *Heywood's Map-Drawing Made Easy* with 'Maps to be Co-

pied', 'Exercises in Lettering for Maps',[176] and so on; and Heywood's *Pupil's Blank Mapping-Book*, 'the entire construction of the map is left to the pupil's skill'.[177] Alternatively, outline maps were designed to be traced, as in J.H. Overton's well-received *Practical Method of Teaching Geography* in which 'the pupil traces the outline of the map, and again and again he inserts from memory the facts which he has learned in previous lessons', so developing 'an intimate and lasting knowledge of the outline'.[178]

A number of map-publishers, particularly those based in Scotland, specialized in educational production and enjoyed the fruits of a blossoming market—A. & C. Black, W. & R. Chambers, Cassell, and Nelson, and especially Bartholomew, Collins, Johnston, and Philip. John Heywood concentrated on publishing educational works, particularly on geography; his 'Excelsior Printing Works' in Manchester maintained a staff of '355 people ... constantly employed in the manufacture of books'[179]—and Thomas Ruddiman Johnston eventually sold his whole map-making business to the Educational Supply Association in 1889, managing the Association until 1895. Already by the 1840s John Bartholomew was producing schoolroom maps for the Scottish School Book Association. In a short time the 'demand for maps and atlases exceeded the most extravagant forecasts, building up to more than a million times five';[180] and towards the end of the century education demanded 'an immense tide of school maps and atlases, on the crests of which the house of Bartholomew will triumphantly ride'.[180] Johnstons produced their 'Pupil Teacher's Geographical Year Books,' and Collins boasted sales of 42,000 copies of 'The College Atlas' and 20,000 of 'The Junior Atlas', both 'largely adopted by the leading Schools and Colleges in the United Kingdom, America, and the Colonies'.[181] George Philip in particular enveloped the market with over 30 'School Atlases'[182] ranging in price from threepence to 21 shillings, in addition to his assignment books such as the 'Series of Map-Drawing Books'. *Philips' Systematic Physical and Political Atlas for Higher Schools and Private Students*, published in 1894, was thought to be the first British school atlas to compare with the best foreign products. As always, less scrupulous map-makers eagerly leapt onto the bandwagon. G.F. Cruchley, one never slow to exploit any commercial opening, even had the temerity to boast that his *'ATLASES AND PROGRESSIVE SERIES OF MAPS*, Have been honored by being selected for the Instruction of HIS ROYAL HIGHNESS THE PRINCE OF WALES, And the Junior Branches of the Royal Family'.[183]

Both the number of pupils and the teaching of geography expanded continually between 1870 and the end of the century as a truly national system of education emerged in which at last all children were likely to acquire a modicum of education. Despite Edward Stanford's assessment that before 1901 'Geography ... has ... been rather a Cinderella among the Sciences',[184] study of the subject increased dramatically, making the period one of momentous growth for the leading educational map- and atlas-publishing firms.

Spreading literacy combined with railway development, free newspaper postage, punctual delivery, the telegraph, and reduced taxation popularized and cheapened newspapers and periodicals to the extent that the *Daily Telegraph* became the first penny newspaper in 1855. Articles were frequently accompanied by maps, creating an ephemeral and largely lost genre of topical mapping. Publishers also used the map as a form of sales promotion to attract purchasers to both newspapers and serial publications by the tempting offer of free or cheaply priced maps. Both the

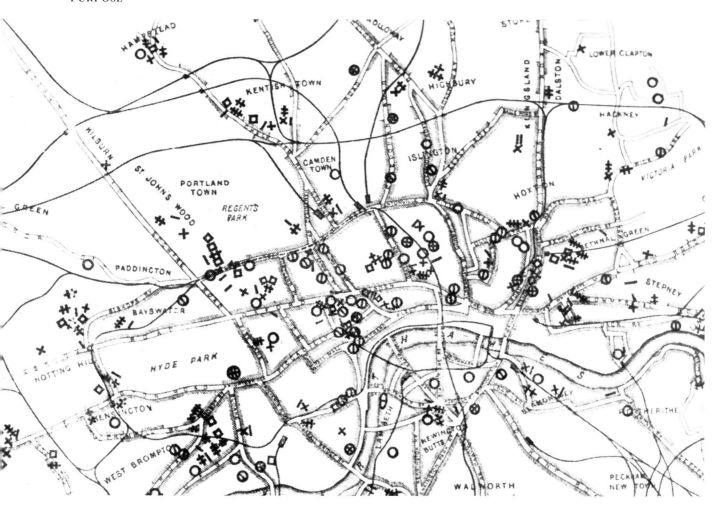

Weekly Dispatch and Cassell's Illustrated Family Paper did so with the maps of Edward Weller, John Dower, and Benjamin Rees Davies; John Tallis offered his 'Illustrated Plan of London and its Environs' free with Tallis's Illustrated London; John Dower's 'Illustrated Map of the Environs of London' was 'PRESENTED (GRATIS) WITH THE PENNY ILLUSTRATED PAPER, JUNE 7, 1862'; and John Shury's fine plan of London was 'PRESENTED GRATIS TO THE READERS OF THE United Kingdom Newspaper, BY THEIR OBLIGED & HUMBLE SERVANTS The Proprietors'.

OTHER THEMATIC MAPS

The inventive Victorians realized that thematic cartography offered them a tool of almost limitless potential which could be used to support any argument or cause, or translate any thesis. Thus, maps were adapted by a new breed of social commentators to express prejudices, obsessions, and pastimes, in addition to the representation of straightforward sociological data, to satisfy the demands of a better educated, more widely read, more inquisitive (and potentially more credulous) market. The location of 'Masonic Lodges and R.A. Chapters,' for instance, was recorded 'under the Jurisdiction of the Grand Lodge of England' for those concerned with the diffusion of freemasonry; and various ethnographic theories were illustrated by maps of racial origins, such as those published in 1843 by J.C. Pritchard to accompany The Natural History of Man, by those mainly anxious to establish any correlation between lineage and superiority.

Religion was a major obsession in an age when the church was a dominant institutional influence, even in the face of the 'pernicious' challenge to the literal interpretation of Ge-

71: Detail: 'MAP SHOWING THE ROMISH ESTABLISHMENTS IN LONDON, AND THE PUBLIC INSTITUTIONS TO WHICH ROMISH PRIESTS HAVE OBTAINED ACCESS', published in The Royal Standard, No. 4, April 1871. By permission of the British Library (Maps 3485(176)).

nesis from such as Charles Lyell in his Principles of Geology and Charles Darwin in On the Origin of Species. Hence, maps were produced to clarify diocesan organization and to emphasize, denigrate, or stress the praiseworthy or insidious and dangerous growth of particular faiths. The Rev. Edwin H. Tindall produced The Wesleyan Methodist Atlas marking those 'Townships, Parishes and Places of 250 Inhabitants and upwards WITHOUT A WESLEYAN METHODIST CHAPEL OR PREACHING HOUSE'; the British Reformation Society published in 1833 'A Map Showing the Situation of Each Roman Catholic Chapel, College, or Seminary throughout England, Scotland, and Wales' following the Catholic emancipation of 1829; and the Royal Standard, in April 1871, mapped the spread of 'Romish establishments' in London and the infiltration of public institutions by Catholic priests. Abraham Hume mapped the origins and spread of different beliefs in Liverpool and also the relative strengths of the Church of England, Roman Catholic, and 'Dissenting' religions in each parish. The Church Commission produced 28 outline maps divided into deaneries, lithographed by Samuel Arrowsmith, in 1836; and Joshua Archer engraved 17 ecclesiastical maps between 1841 and 1843 marking archdeaconries, deaneries, rectories, vicarages, 'perpetual curacies,' and 'chapels of ease', decorated

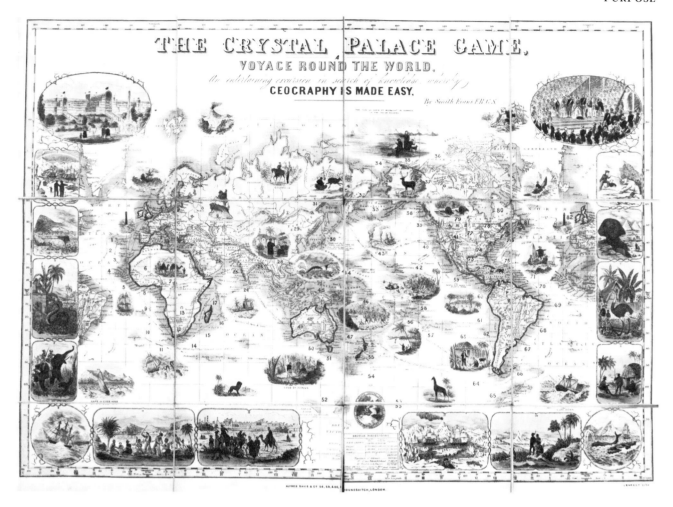

72: 'THE CRYSTAL PALACE GAME, A VOYAGE
ROUND THE WORLD, An entertaining excursion in search of
knowledge, whereby GEOGRAPHY IS MADE EASY. By Smith
Evans, F.R.G.S.', published by Alfred Davis & Co., c.1854. By
permission of the British Library (Maps 08bb7).

by the 'Arms of the Bishop', for the *British Magazine, and
Monthly Register of Religious and Ecclesiastical information.*
Various other well-known map-makers fabricated religious
maps; for example, Aaron Arrowsmith drew a map of the
Gloucester and Oxford diocese in 1814. However, the best
known were the diocesan maps published by James Thomas
Law, who constructed a set to accompany his *Lectures on
the First and Subsequent Divisions of the Kingdom into Provinces and Dioceses* delivered to the students of Lichfield
Theological College, and the atlas of diocesan maps produced by him in 1864 in collaboration with William Francis,
who continued the project after it had halted due to Law's
failing eyesight. This latter *New Set of Diocesan Maps* contained maps coloured in archdeaconries, usually decorated
with the arms of the bishopric, lithographed by W.J. Sack-
ett, showing '... the alterations which had occurred in almost every Diocese in the Kingdom, through the working
of the Ecclesiastical Commissioners' Reports'.[185]

The dilettante intellectual pretensions of a classically educated gentry were catered for by maps of their leisure
interests, such as the copies of bygone plans or those showing the location of ancient camps and roads, Roman villas,
long barrows, and so on, which accompanied archaeological
tracts and guides. Their offspring were educated as well as
amused by a selection of geographical games—'... a contin-
ual source of amusement to young people of both sexes, and
... a fund of geographical knowledge, as may prove bene-
ficial in reading and conversation'[186]—as, for example, the
jigsaw puzzle 'Eslick's Patent Dissected Map of England
& Wales, engraved by W. Hughes, designed expressly to
impress upon the minds of children the exact shape & position of each county', the railway race 'Wallis's New Railway

Game, or Tour through England and Wales', or the town
tour 'Wallis's Tour through the United Kingdom of England, Scotland and Ireland, a new Geographical Game,
comprehending all the Cities, Principal Towns, Rivers, &c.
in the British Empire'. Such instructive games ventured
further afield than just the British Isles; European geography was taught by such as 'Betts's Tour through Europe,
an Amusing and Instructive Game for Children' which
raced from Calais round the Continent to London, and
Jarrold & Sons' 'The Young Traveller's New Tour through
the various Countries of Europe, an Amusing and Instructive Game' which sprinted round Europe from Iceland to
London. Similarly, many games covered the whole world,
such as Abbé Gaultier's *A Course of Geography, by Means of
Instructive Games,* 'Betts's Voyage round the World, an
Amusing and Instructive Game for Children', and 'The
Crystal Palace Game, a voyage round the world, An entertaining excursion in search of knowledge, whereby geography is made easy' which started its 'entertaining excursion'
at the Crystal Palace and ended with the victor being received by Queen Victoria and Prince Albert!

Rich children of all ages were also entertained but not
educated by the 'curiosities' created by the representation
of countries as amusing characters; for example, Hugh

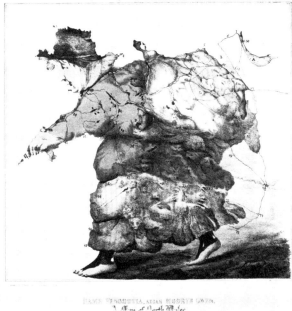

73: *'DAME VENODOTIA, ALIAS MODRYN GWEN'*,
designed by H. Hughes, drawn on stone by J. J. Dodd, published by
H. Humphreys, c.1845.
North Wales is depicted as Auntie Gwen scurrying barefoot across
the country carrying a sack which is in fact a lady in a ball-gown.
Goats, dogs and rabbits appear in the shadows of both the sack and
her clothing. By courtesy of Ivan Deverall.

Hughes, c.1845, depicted North Wales as 'aunty Gwen', an old woman carrying a sack; England and Wales appeared riding on a dolphin and similarly as John Bull on a whale; and 'Aleph' (supposedly a 15-year-old girl but in reality the London journalist William Harvey) amused her sick younger brother with *Geographical Fun: being Humerous Outlines from Various Countries* in 1869. In similar fashion, their parents were diverted, infuriated, or worried, in the later years of the century and the period of international tension heralding the First World War, by political cartoon maps, particularly representing the troubled events in Europe, by Frederick Rose and other cartographic satirists. Rose, for instance, under the pseudonym 'Nemesis' mapped the political situation in 1880 in 'The Overthrow of His Imperial Majesty King Jingo I' in which 'Public Opinion', 'Truth', and 'Revenge for broken promises' tried to unseat Disraeli, 'King Jingo', from his throne, assisted by a harassed female Ireland wearing the cloak of 'famine' and 'evictions'.

Their rumbustious sporting compatriots also presented a potentially rewarding market for the ingenious map-maker. Sport was not only 'an all-embracing enthusiasm for many landowners',[189] but was also the principal interest of professional and business men from the towns and even of the wealthier tenant farmers. Hunting was not simply a matter of a few neighbours riding over their own lands; rather, by the early years of the century, the great hunts—the Badminton, the Quorn, and others—were well established, run-

ning hounds over whole districts. Map-makers, such as A.H. Swiss of Devonport and Sidney Hall (whose 'little pocket maps ... no man going into a strange country should be without'),[188] responded by producing hunting maps, often enlivened with lusty scenes of the chase, marking the meeting places of the hounds and the areas covered by the hunts; Aaron Arrowsmith even offered his 'LARGE SCALE RAILWAY MAP OF ENGLAND AND WALES, in twenty-four sheets ... coloured to show the FOX HUNTS. Each sheet folded, 2s. 6d.; mounted, in case, 5s.; complete, mounted, in case, £6 ...'[189] Others went further with the publication of full hunting atlases— J. & C. Walker's county maps were overprinted to show the hunts for *Hobson's Fox-Hunting Atlas* and John Dower engraved attractive maps for *The Fox-Hunter's Atlas* which also offered information on 'the principal inns at which proper accommodation for hunters and race horses can be obtained'.[190]

With condemnation rather than condescension, the pastimes of the poor were also mapped. Joseph Fletcher's *Moral and Educational Statistics* delineated not only population distribution but also crime, bastardy, pauperism, 'improvident marriages', ignorance, and other social features; Henry Mayhew published 'maps and tables illustrating the criminal statistics of each of the counties of England and Wales in 1851' in his *London Labour and the London Poor* of 1862, including committals for bigamy, rape, abduction, and keeping disorderly houses, attempts to procure miscarriage, and 'Assaults, with intent to ravish and carnally abuse'; and Guerry cartographically compared France with England and Wales in terms of crimes against the person, crimes against property, murder, rape, larceny by servants, instruction, and arson—all reflecting a widespread concern for the connection between crime rates and education, or rather the lack of it, and a developing interest in *statistique morale*.[191] The morbid fascination with crime was further fuelled with maps and plans of prisons such as Laurie & Whittle's 'New Plan of the Rules of the Fleet'. However, the principal 'crime' of the working class was drink.

Increased prosperity in a period of scant recreation led to more obtrusive working-class drunkenness which was identified as the cause of poverty: 'Drink is a ceaseless cause of physical and moral degradation, poverty, and irremediable ruin.'[192] The reforming crusaders of the temperance movement, championing total abstinence in the name of social respectability, generally simply railed against the demon drink, moral failure, and the turpitude of the imbi-

74: *'The overthrow of HIS IMPERIAL MAJESTY KING JINGO I. A Map of the POLITICAL SITUATION IN 1880'*,
by F. W. Rose. Published by G. W. Bacon.
  '*The arch Jingo having been raised to power by the unholy alliance of Beer and Bible, arrogates to himself the powers of a Despot. His Cabinet, entirely subservient to him, pay their homage. The beneficent(?) results of his "great and glorious" attempts at Despotic rule are inscribed upon his banner. His throne is, however, resting upon a rotten basis.*
  '*The People's Champion, bearing aloft a truly glorious banner, is assailing him from the North with a mighty weapon, while Ireland, having met with Neglect and Ridicule, instead of Justice, is summoning all her strength to assist in his overthrow.*
  '*The powerful lever of Public Opinion being brought to bear against the foundation of the Despot's power, little remains to be done. The Tenant Farmer feels he must take his part in completing the long wished-for downfall of KING JINGO I.*'
By permission of the British Library (Maps 1078(46)).

The overthrow of
His Imperial Majesty
KING·JINGO·I
—A MAP OF THE—
POLITICAL SITUATION
·IN·
1880.
BY
NEMESIS.

EXPLANATION.

The arch Jingo having been raised to power by the unholy alliance of Beer and Bible, arrogates to himself the powers of a Despot. His Cabinet, entirely subservient to him, pay their homage. The beneficent (?) results of his "great and glorious" attempts at Despotic rule are inscribed upon his banner. His throne is, however, resting upon a rotten basis.

The People's Champion, bearing aloft a truly glorious banner, is assailing him from the North with a mighty weapon, while Ireland, having met with Neglect and Ridicule, instead of Justice, is summoning all her strength to assist in his overthrow.

The powerful lever of Public Opinion being brought to bear against the foundation of the Despot's power, little remains to be done. The Tenant Farmer feels he must take his part in completing the long wished-for downfall of

KING JINGO I.

PEACE
RETRENCHMENT
AND
REFORM
JUSTICE TO IRELAND
HONEST STATESMANSHIP

ENLIGHTENED PUBLIC OPINION

1078.(44.)

CRIMES CONTRE LES PERSONNES.
CRIMES AGAINST THE PERSON

bers; but, occasionally, in a more scientific mood, they turned to thematic cartography to provide their cause with an accurate analysis of public-house density and distribution, concluding an erroneous correlation between drink, public-house density and low income for, as was pointed out, 'a public-house in a square in which the rich live would not pay'.[193] 'The Modern Plague of London', published by the National Temperance League in the 1890s, for instance, clearly showed the lack of public houses in affluent Kensington and abundance in the seamy West End. Drink maps not only analysed distribution in the obvious industrial targets of the non-conformists, but also in such apparently tamer centres as Oxford, Norwich, York and Great Yarmouth. The editions of Ratcliff's 'Drink Map of Norwich', which distinguished beer houses, fully licensed houses, and breweries, suggest some small success for the temperance propagandists, for in 1878 it records 655 licensed houses in the town, in 1892 631, and in 1903 a mere 615!

Temperance zeal had two unforseen side-effects of long-term importance for the Victorian map-maker. John Cassell established a temperance publishing office and bookshop which eventually turned its attention to cartographic work, and Thomas Cook organized the first railway excursion, from Leicester to a temperance meeting at Loughborough— '... about 500 passengers filled some twenty or twenty-five open carriages ... and the party rode the enormous distance of eleven miles and back for a shilling, children half price ... thus was struck the keynote of my excursions, and the social idea grew upon me'.[194]

Thus, before the middle of the nineteenth century, the thematic map had become an indispensable form of expression for scientists in many fields for the demonstration of quantitative and statistical data and the recording of geographical relationships and distributions. Increasingly map-makers sought to produce atlases that not only delineated the topography of a country, but also defined its physical and human features in cartographic terms. No longer did the surveyor and cartographer work as an isolated and insulated couple, for map-making had been opened up to the influence of the geologist, the meteorologist, the natural historian, the economist, the agriculturalist, the sociologist, the demographer, the criminologist, the reformer, and, indeed, all the other disciples of the multiplying sciences.

SELECT BIBLIOGRAPHY

BAGLEY, J.J. 'County maps and town plans'. (*Historical Interpretation No. 2: Sources of English History 1540 to the Present Day; 1971*)
HARLEY, J.B. *Maps for the Local Historian. A Guide to the British Sources.* (1972)
LAMBERT, A. 'Early maps and local studies'. (*Geography, 61; 1956*)

Estate Plans
ADAMS, I. H. 'Estate plans'. (*The Local Historian, 12; 1976*)
BAKER, A.R.H. 'Local history and early estate maps'. (*Amateur Historian, 5; 1962*)
DAVIES, R. *Estate Maps of Wales 1600-1836.* (Nat. Lib. of Wales; 1982)
EMMISON, F.G. 'Estate maps and surveys'. (*History, 48; 1963*)
THIRD, B.M.W. 'The significance of Scottish estate plans and associated documents'. (*Scottish Studies, I; 1959*)

75: *'CRIMES CONTRE LES PERSONNES', from* Statistique Morale de l'Angleterre comparée avec la Statistique Morale de la France ...', *by A.-M. Guerry, 1864. By permission of the British Library (Maps 32e34).*

THOMAS, C. 'Estate surveys as sources in historical geography'. (*National Library of Wales Journ.*, 14; 1966)

Tithe Plans
CARPENTER, A.M. 'The value of the tithe surveys to the study of land ownership and occupancy in the mid-nineteenth century, with special reference to South Hertfordshire'. (*Hertfordshire Past and Present*, 7; 1967)
KAIN, R.J.P. 'The tithe commutation surveys'. (*Archaeologia Cantiana*, 89; 1974)
KAIN, R.J.P. 'Tithe surveys and landownership'. (*Hist. Geog.*, I; 1975)
KAIN, R.J.P. 'R.K. Dawson's proposals in 1836 for a cadastral survey of England and Wales'. (*Cart. Journ.*, 12; 1975)
KAIN, R.J.P. & PRINCE, H.C. *The Tithe Surveys of England and Wales.* (1985)
MUNBY, L.M. 'Tithe apportionments and maps'. (*History*, 54; 1969)
PRINCE, H.C. 'The tithe surveys of the mid-nineteenth century'. (*Agric. Hist. Review*, 7; 1959)

Parish Plans
HYDE, R. '*The Act to regulate parochial assessments 1836* and its contribution to the mapping of London'. (*Guildhall studies in London history*, II; 1976)

Ward Plans
HYDE, R. *Ward Maps of the City of London.* (Map Collectors' Circle, 38; 1967)

Scientific Maps
BAILEY, SIR E. *Geological Survey of Great Britain.* (1952)
BASSETT, D.A. *A Source-Book of Geological, Geomorphological and Soil Maps for Wales and the Welsh Borders (1800-1966).* (National Museum of Wales; 1967)
BASSETT, D.A. 'Wales and the geological map' (*National Museum of Wales Bull.*, 3; 1969)
BOUD, R.C. 'Aaron Arrowsmith's topographical map of Scotland and John MacCulloch's geological survey.' (*Canadian Cartographer*, 2; 1974)
BOUD, R.C. 'The early geological maps of the Isle of Arran 1807-1858'. (*Canadian Cartographer*, 12; 1975)
BOUD, R.C. 'The early development of British geological maps'. (*Imago Mundi*, 27; 1975)
BOUD, R.C. 'Samuel Hibbert and the early geological mapping of the Shetland Islands'. (*Cart. Journ.*, 14; 1977)
BULL, G.B.G. 'Thomas Milne's land utilization map of the London area in 1800'. (*Geog. Journ.*, 122; 1966)
CAMPBELL, E.M.J. 'An English philosophico-chorographical chart'. (*Imago Mundi*, 6; 1949)
DAVIES, G.H. 'Sheets in many colours—the mapping of Ireland's rocks, 1750-1890.' (*Studies in the History of Irish Science and Technology Series*, 4; forthcoming).
DAVIES, G.L. 'The oldest surviving geological map of Ireland'. (*Irish Naturalist's Journal*, 17; 1973)
DAVIES, G.L. 'Notes on the various issues of Sir Richard Griffith's quarter-inch geological map of Ireland, 1839-1855'. (*Imago Mundi*, 29; 1977)
DAVIS, A.G. 'Notes on Griffith's geological map of Ireland'. (*Journ. of the Soc. for the Bibliography of Nat. Hist.*, 2; 1943-52)
DAVIS, A.G. 'William Smith's geological atlas'. (*Journ. of the Soc. for the Bibliography of Nat. Hist.*; 1952)
EYLES, J.M. 'William Smith (1769-1839): a bibliography of his published writings, maps and geological sections, printed and lithographed'. (*Journ. of the Soc. for the Bibliography of Nat. Hist.*; 1969)
EYLES, V.A. 'John Macculloch, F.R.S., and his geological map: an account of the first geological survey of Scotland'. (*Annals of Science*, 2; 1937)
EYLES, V.A. 'On the different issues of the first geological map of England and Wales'. (*Annals of Science*, 3; 1938)
EYLES, V.A. 'Macculloch's geological map of Scotland: an additional note'. (*Annals of Science*, 4; 1939-40)
FENTON, C.L. and M.A. *Giants of Geology.* (rev. ed.; 1952)

FLETT, SIR J. SMITH. *The First Hundred Years of the Geological Survey of Great Britain.* (1937)

HARLEY, J.B. 'The Ordnance Survey and the origins of official geological mapping in Devon and Cornwall'. (In *Exeter Essays in Geography*, ed. by K.J. Gregory and W.L.D. Ravenhill; 1971)

HARLEY, J.B. 'The Ordnance Survey and land-use mapping: parish books of reference and the county series 1 : 2500 maps, 1855-1918'. (*Historical Geography Research Series*, 2; 1979)

JUDD, J.W. 'The earliest geological maps of Scotland and Ireland'. (*Geol. Mag.*, New Series, IV, 5, 4; 1898)

NORTH, F.J. *Geological maps, their history and development, with special reference to Wales.* (1928)

NORTH, F.J. 'From the geological map to the Geological Survey'. (*Cardiff Naturalist's Soc. Trans.*, 65; 1934)

PICKFORD, R.F. *William Smith. Father of English Geology.* (Bath Municipal Libraries; 1969)

READING UNIVERSITY *The History and Development of Geological Cartography: Catalogue of the Exhibition of Geological Maps in the University Library* ... (1967)

SHEPPARD, T. *William Smith, his Maps and Memoirs.* (1920)

SHEPPARD, T. *The Evolution of Topographical and Geological Maps.* (1920)

WALLIS, H. 'The history of land use mapping'. (*Cart. Journ.*, 18; 1981)

Statistical Maps

GILBERT, E.W. 'Pioneer maps of health and disease in England'. (*Geog. Journ.*, 124; 1958)

KOSINSKI, L.A. 'Exhibit of early distribution maps in the British Museum'. (*Geog. Rev.*, 60; 1970)

ROBINSON, A.H. 'The 1837 maps of Henry Drury Harness'. (*Geog. Journ.*, 121; 1955)

Town Plans

ASPINALL, P.J. 'The use of nineteenth-century fire insurance plans for the urban historian'. (*The Local Historian*, ii; 1975)

DARLINGTON, I. 'Edwin Chadwick and the first large-scale Ordnance Survey of London'. (*Trans. of the London and Middlesex Arch. Soc.*, 22; 1969)

DARLINGTON, I. and HOWGEGO, J. *The Printed Maps of London, c.1553-1850.* (1964; reprinted 1978 with revisions)

FORDHAM, A. 'Town Plans of the British Isles. (Map Collector's Circle, 22; 1965)

GLANVILLE, P. *London in Maps.* (1972)

HARLEY, J.B. and MANTERFIELD, J.B. 'The Ordnance Survey 1:500 plans of Exeter, 1874-1877'. (*Devon and Cornwall Notes and Queries*, 34; 1978)

HARLEY, J.B. 'The Ordnance Survey 1:528 Board of Health Town Plans in Warwickshire 1848-1854'. (In: Slater, T.R. and Jarvis, P.J. (eds.): *Field and Forest: An Historical Geography of Warwickshire and Worcestershire*; 1981)

HYDE, R. 'Notes on a collection of London insurance surveys, 1794-1807'. (*Journ. of the Soc. of Archivists*, 4; 1971)

HYDE, R. *Printed Maps of Victorian London, 1851-1900.* (1975)

HYDE, R. 'Reform Bill plans'. (*Bull. of the Soc. of Univ. Cartographers*, 9; 1975)

ROWLEY, G. *British Fire Insurance Plans.* (1984)

ROWLEY, G. 'An introduction to fire insurance plans'. (*Map Collector*, 29; 1984)

Commercial Maps

NORTON, J.E. *Guide to the National & Provincial Directories of England & Wales, excluding London, published before 1856.* (1950)

Transport Maps

HYDE, R. 'Maps that made cabmen honest'. (*Map Collector*, 38; 1967)

SMITH, G. ROYDE *The History of Bradshaw.* (1939)

Road Maps

ANDREWS, J.H. Introduction to *Taylor and Skinner's Maps of the Roads of Ireland, 1778.* (1969)

FAIRCLOUGH, R.H. ' "Sketches of the Roads in Scotland"; the manuscript roadbook of George Taylor'. (*Imago Mundi*, 27; 1975)

FORDHAM, SIR H.G. *Notes on British and Irish Itineraries and Road Books.* (1912; reprinted in *Studies in Carto-Bibliography*, 1914 and 1969)

FORDHAM, SIR H.G. *Road-Books and Itineraries of Ireland 1647-1850.* (1923)

FORDHAM, SIR H.G. *Road-Books and Itineraries of Great Britain 1570-1850.* (1924)

FORDHAM, SIR H.G. 'The road books of Wales with a catalogue 1775-1850'. (*Archaeologia Cambrensis*, 82; 1927)

NICHOLSON, T. 'Seventy years of cycling and motoring maps'. (*Int. Map Collectors' Soc. Journ.*, 2, I; 1982)

NICHOLSON, T. *Wheels on the Road. Road Maps of Britain 1870-1940.* (1984)

PIGGOTT, C.A. 'When the cycle was King of the Road'. (*Map Collector*, 13; 1980)

POWELL, R.F.P. 'The printed road maps of Breconshire 1675-1870'. (*Brycheiniog*, 18; 1978-79)

Waterway Maps

EYLES, J.M. 'A further study of the early maps of the Somersetshire Coal Canal'. (*Cart. Journ.*, 12; 1975)

TORRENS, H.S. 'Early maps of the Somersetshire Coal Canal'. (*Cart. Journ.*, II; 1974)

TORRENS, H.S. 'Further comments on the maps of the Somersetshire Coal Canal'. (*Cart. Journ.*, 12; 1975)

Railway Maps

GARNETT, D. 'The railway maps of Zachary Macauley and John Airey'. (*Railway and Canal Hist. Soc. Journ.*; 1959-71)

GARNETT, D. 'John Airey's undated maps'. (*Railway and Canal Hist. Soc. Journ.*, 17; 1971)

GARNETT, D. 'Macaulay's *Metropolitan Railway Map*'. (*Railway and Canal Hist. Soc. Journ.*, 21; 1975)

GARNETT, D. 'Airey's railway map of the East of England'. (*Railway and Canal Hist. Soc. Journ.*, 21; 1975)

GARNETT, D. 'Metropolitan District Railway maps: a tentative checklist'. (*Railway and Canal Hist. Soc. Journ.*, 23; 1977)

GARNETT, D. 'John Airey's undated early railway maps'. (*Map Collector*, 26; 1984)

OXFORDSHIRE COUNTY COUNCIL *A Handlist of Plans, Sections and Books of Reference for the Proposed Railways in Oxfordshire 1825-1936.* (1964)

Excursions

HYDE, R. 'Mr. Wyld's monster globe.' (*History Today*, 20; 1970)

W.H. Smith

CHILSTON, VISCOUNT. *W.H. Smith.* (1965)

MAXWELL, SIR H. *Life and Times of the Right Honourable William Smith M.P.* (1893)

POCKLINGTON, G.R. *The Story of W.H. Smith & Son.* (1921)

Gall & Inglis

INGLIS, R.G. *Gall & Inglis, Publishers, 1810-1960; A History.* (1960)

Other Thematic Maps

CLUTTON, E. 'On the nature of thematic maps and their history'. (*Map Collector*, 12; 1983)

HANNAS, L. *The English Jigsaw Puzzle, 1760-1890. With a descriptive check-list of puzzles in the Museums of Great Britain and the author's collection.* (1972)

HANNAS, L. 'When maps were cut into pieces'. (*Map Collector*, 12; 1980)

HILL, G. *Cartographical Curiosities.* (British Library; 1978)

HYDE, R. 'Cartographers versus the demon drink'. (*Map Collector*, 9; 1978)

ROBINSON, A.H. *Early Thematic Mapping in the History of Cartography.* (1982)

SMITH, D.A. 'The social maps of Henry Mayhew'. (*Map Collector*, 30; 1985)

WHITEHOUSE, F.R.B. *Table Games of Georgian and Victorian Days.* (1951)

Victorian Topographical Atlases 1837-1900

Introduction to Catalogue

It would be an impossible task to catalogue the vast array of maps published during Victoria's reign, for maps and plans not only appeared in atlases and other publications which can be defined satisfactorily, but also in newspapers, magazines, journals, government reports, topographical tomes, guide-books, commercial directories, scientific studies, and many other works. Similarly, this work dare not attempt any analysis of the issues of Ordnance Survey maps; however, intensive studies are gradually appearing in the on-going series of *The Old Series Ordnance Survey Maps of England and Wales* and a select bibliography of the many detailed works dealing with the Ordnance Survey is offered as a guide to useful sources. A complicating factor in any carto-bibliography is that many series were started but abandoned before completion—Daniel and Samuel Lysons, for example, managed to cover only the first nine counties of their *Magna Britannia* before Samuel's death in 1819 caused the collapse of the project; and Groombridge and Shepherd & Sutton scrapped their projected *Descriptive County Atlas of England & Wales* of c.1844 after only five parts had been published. Sometimes atlases which apparently 'existed' must be dismissed as 'ghosts'—*The London Catalogue of Books published in Great Britain from 1814-1846*, for example, recorded an atlas of 1842 entitled *Wyld's Atlas of English Counties* but this seems to have been merely hopeful anticipation of a complete reissue of James Wallis's quarto county maps by James Wyld who almost certainly did not complete the project as only a few individual maps are known bearing his imprint. Furthermore, active research sometimes reveals unknown issues, as, for example, in the startling recent discovery that Thomson's small county maps of 1823 had, in fact, appeared on a set of cards dated 1811, published by 'J. ALLEN, 3 Hampden Str. Sommers Town', 'Also by R. ROWE, Nº. 19 Bedford Str. Bedford Row London.' In addition, there were innumerable one-off issues of individual sheets connected with legislation, property sales, transport developments, improvement proposals, and so on. Fortunately, the majority of Victorian maps available were published in known atlases and topographical works, and, therefore, a catalogue of these publications covers the bulk of attainable material, thus enabling the collector to identify most of his likely 'finds'.

It is not only works actually first published during the reign of Victoria that can be called 'Victorian', for, without doubt, most of the material issued from about the turn of the century was still on sale in some form during her years on the throne. John Cary's *New and Correct English Atlas*, for instance, first published in 1787, last appeared as *Cruchley's New Pocket Companion* in 1876; his *Traveller's Companion*, first appearing in 1790, was last published as *Cruchley's Railroad Companion* about 1862; and the maps from his *New English Atlas*, which appeared in parts from 1801,

were still being issued individually at the end of the century. Similarly, Robert Rowe's county maps of 1816 were still being sold in commercial directories by Edward Cassey in the early 1870s. Even remarkably old material could suddenly reappear; Sir William Petty's Irish maps of 1685, for example, surfaced again some time between 1850 and 1875, probably printed privately by the fourth Marquess of Lansdowne. Such atlases and works have been analysed in detail elsewhere and, whilst they are very much 'collectables' of the Victorian period, it would be pointless to cover the same ground here.

'Victorian' atlases are, therefore, defined for the purposes of this commentary as those which first appeared in 1837 or later, but it must be remembered that most of the material from the four or five preceding decades was very much part of the Victorian cartographic scene.

Map production in the Victorian age usually originated with an engraved plate which was used for intaglio and/or lithographic printing, with alterations to plate or lithographic stone occurring at various stages. The history of such changes can become enormously complex as plate and stone were revised concurrently, and tedious and painstaking detective work is required to unravel the convoluted history of even a single map. Since this history is a series of steps along the same path for any particular set of maps, it is sensible to view their development as a continuum, and logical to catalogue the evolving alterations as they progressed from the original state. Inevitably, generalizations must be made, for it is impossible in a limited work to note every change to every map in every set—rather, the purpose is to provide guidance to the major stages of alteration, detailing those main changes which allow identification. Map alteration was an expensive, time-consuming activity which took place sometimes over an extended period, and, thus, atlases would be issued in the interim containing mixtures of revised and un-revised maps. Add to this the map-maker's penchant for incorporating old stock, unused in earlier issues (usually 'puffing', at the same time, that it was the most up-to-date material on the market!), and it is clear how it is possible that no two known copies of some atlases are exactly alike. Broad correspondence is the best that can be hoped for between a generalized description and any particular map.

The two most startling changes affecting Victorian maps were the advent of lithography and the demise of the county format. At the end of the eighteenth century, county maps were printed directly from engraved copper plates for a narrow wealthy market; by the end of the nineteenth, a myriad of maps, few of them concentrating on a single county, were produced lithographically for a mass market. Lithography cheapened the process of map alteration and adaptation, allowing maps to be revised more frequently to keep pace with accelerating economic and social change, and presenting new opportunities to use existing maps as sources for regional extracts or as a framework for super-imposed information. The decline of regionalism and local loyalty, brought about by such advances as the penny post, a national press, a growing railway system, and suburban transport, combined with the Ordnance Survey's early abandonment of county confines, killed off the county map as the main vehicle of presentation. The case for change was summed-up in Fullarton's *Imperial Gazetteer* (*c*.1868-71): '... The county maps hitherto issued ... are very un-satisfactory. They commonly amount to about sixty,—one for each of most of the counties, and two or three for each of the larger ones; they are usually all of one size and shape, so as to give for their territories a uniform extent of space; and they, therefore, are drawn on widely different scales. The larger counties which are also the richest in local features, are shown on a scale unduly small; and the smaller ones which are also the poorest in striking features, are engraved on a scale unduly large. Devon, for example, which has an area of 1,657,180 acres, and abounds in features of local interest, is shown on the same space as Rutland, which has an area of only 95,805 acres, and pos-sesses very little salient feature. The maps, as taken to-gether, are no fair atlas; they do not exhibit the face of the country continuously; they convey, on a rough view, a vastly contorted notion of the proportions of its parts; and they fail, even with the aid of full observation of their several scales, to give a ready view of the connexions among the multitudes of places on opposite sides of county boundary lines. Their very margins are confusing; and their differ-ences of execution, suited to their differences of scale, make wrong impressions.'[1]

This verbose justification was probably a less potent in-fluence than the fact that the advancing technology of lith-ography made it a simpler and cheaper process to take transfers from complete maps of the country. Increasingly atlases and series were constructed using sections of a com-mon map. This development creates serious problems for the carto-bibliographer since it is often very difficult to recognize the source of a particular transfer. A so-far-un-identified general map of the country was, for example, the source of transfers for at least some of *Bartholomew's New Reduced Ordnance Survey* series, *Bacon's New Library* maps, Black's guides, and W.H. Smith's *New Reduced Ordnance Survey* series. Much fine work has been done in recent years by a few notable carto-bibliographers in marrying later is-sues to their source maps, but there is still scope for further illumination; undoubtedly there remain some relationships which go unrecognized at this stage. As further research is completed, so such new information will come to light in ever-decreasing quantities. Therefore, this work can only be a reflection of the state of knowledge at this time.

The analysis of each set of maps follows a standard for-mat designed to facilitate easy identification of map and issue. Each map set appears under the heading of the cartographer, draughtsman, engraver, lithographer, or pub-lisher customarily named by map dealers in identifying the maps or under the heading most sensibly adopted for the commonest states. The dates preceded by '*fl*.' represent the map-maker's main period of cartographic activity.

All major atlases issued from the year of Victoria's accession to 1900 are fully described from their first issue. All quotations describing map issues originate from the works cited, prospectuses to them, or contemporary advertisements, and are as originally printed without the

correction or noting of spelling or grammatical errors, no matter how outrageous. The following features apply to the typical map in a set—however, remember that maps in a set frequently display varying traits and, therefore, the descrip-tions are only guidelines and the noted features are not necessarily found on all maps in all states.

a the average dimensions, given in millimetres (mm) and inches (in), of the engraved or lithographed surface, includ-ing the frame and any decoration, but excluding imprints, signatures, inscriptions, numbers, and notes appearing out-side the frame. The shortest dimension is noted first. Since paper was dampened to increase ink absorbency and then subjected to great pressure in printing, contraction and dis-tortion of the sheet was caused by both processes. It must, therefore, be remembered that since paper can shrink or expand, the dimensions of a particular map can vary be-tween impressions. Photolithographic transfer often intro-duced size changes, but only significant enlargements or reductions are noted since small changes might be the result of printing distortion rather than the transfer process itself. Maps in a set were frequently constructed at very different sizes—only those which differ greatly from the average are noted. Measurements quoted from advertisements need not correspond with stated dimensions since they may refer to sheet size or, indeed, any other chosen limits.

b the scale is expressed as 1 inch to so many miles. Scales are uniform unless stated as average (av.) in which case they vary from map to map in the set. Quoted figures do not take account of the scales of any index, thematic or general maps in the work.

c the commonest wording of the map title unless it is simply a county, region, or town name.

d the principal features of a typical map in the set are noted to allow identification. This is not a full description of the map but merely a selection of salient features.

'Issues' are noted in order of appearance. Where relevant, details of publication are noted. It is only in recent years that the complexities of publishing history have been ap-preciated, for it became increasingly common during the century to publish maps in serial form in order to spread costs, encourage sales, and feed back revenue into the further finance of the project. Although this form of pub-lication dates back to John Seller's issue of his *Anglia Con-tracta* (*c*.1694), it became an increasingly popular method as maps were aimed at a less affluent, wider market. Parts' publication in 'numbers'—sometimes sold 'by house to house visitation'[2] by canvassers, but more often by adver-tising for subscriptions—was an important means of ex-tending sales for publishers such as Tallis and Virtue. Cas-sell, for example, after purchasing the stock and plates of the *Weekly Dispatch* maps in 1863 in order to issue them as supplements to his *Family Paper*, so enlarged the market for them by door-to-door selling using colporteurs to peddle the cheap parts' publication that the individual maps could be sold at only one-third of their earlier price.

Publishers attempted to attract as wide a market as pos-sible by offering variations of serial publication to suit dif-ferent requirements; Archibald Fullarton, for example, of-fered his *Parliamentary Gazetteer of England and Wales*, which appeared between 1840 and 1843, '... in Parts, price 2s. each, containing Six sheets of Letter-press and One Map', 'alternately with Five sheets of Letter-press and Two Maps, or other Illustrations', or 'For the accomodation of persons desirous of having the Work in larger portions, ... in twelve 5s. Divisions, neatly done up in a stiff cover; and in twelve 6s. Divisions, cloth boards, lettered, according to

A CONTINUUM OF MAP EVOLUTION

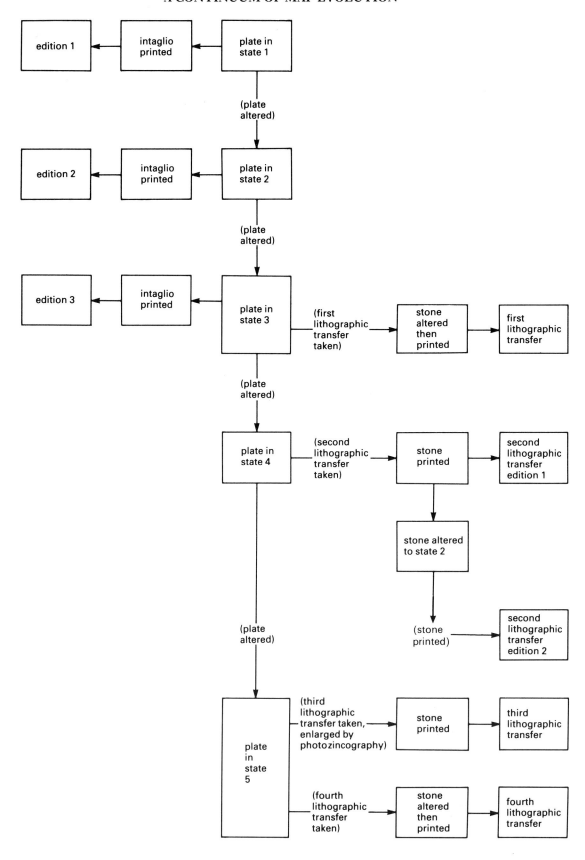

Adapted by kind permission of Donald Hodson from his *The Printed Maps of Hertfordshire* (1974)

specimens.' The dangers of the publisher extending the series beyond the promised length, of deteriorating quality, of delayed publication or even of premature cancellation were very real, as was the possibility of the customer defaulting on subscriptions. Whilst Fullarton promised that any 'overplus will be given gratis; and the quality of type, paper, and printing, will be carefully kept up to the specimen presented in the first 2s. Part', he held 'each Subscriber pledged on his part to take and pay for the whole Work as it appears'.[3] He could not, however, in the event, avoid 'the unexpected delay which has taken place in the publication of the details of the Government Census of 1841',[4] and reluctantly decided to publish the *Gazetteer* without the promised 'results of the Census of 1841',[4] apologizing that 'its issue has only been suspended in the hope of being able to comply with the wishes of many Subscribers by attaching ... an Alphabetical Digest of the Census'.[5] Similarly, for his *Imperial Gazetteer of Scotland*, he undertook 'that the work will not exceed the number of parts stated', but expected 'every Subscriber ... to take and pay for each Part as published'.[6] It was even sometimes specified that maps should be sold only by serial publication, presumably in an attempt to avoid competition with existing atlases—when John Bartholomew contracted to engrave maps for Fullarton in 1865 he stipulated that 'you are to sell the work in parts and only by canvassing and not to the regular bookselling trade'.[7]

Unless otherwise stated, production was by intaglio printing direct from the engraved plate. Major changes in the features are noted to aid identification, but no indication is given of whether these changes were made to the engraved plate or to the lithographic transfer—such detailed analysis is more properly the province of the town or county carto-bibliographer. Since the states of a map are essentially stages in a process of evolution from the original form, only changes are noted and all other features are identical with an earlier specified issue.

Particular problems occur when dating the appearance of the various atlases and map states because the date of issue does not necessarily correspond with the date given on the map or title-page. It was common practice when producing an atlas to print extra quantities of text and letterpress title-page so that the moveable type could be broken-up and re-used. It was not necessary to print extra quantities of maps since these could be produced from their engraved plates at any time, often after they had been amended and up-dated. Thus, maps frequently appeared in an atlas with a title-page originating some years earlier. J. & C. Walker even resorted to leaving the title-page date incomplete to be filled-in by the buyer on purchase! The issue date given is that of actual issue, not necessarily that given on the atlas title-page. A question mark (?) given after a date (or, indeed, any other information) indicates that some doubt exists about that information and that it is assumed on the basis of available evidence and informed opinion. Where two or more dates are given, the atlas was issued without change in each of those years. Such complicating factors as the time taken to alter all the maps in a set and the use of old stock cloud any analysis of atlas issues and map states, and it must not be assumed that the details given are definitive, for variant copies almost certainly exist and may come to light.

e the atlas title, as given on the title-page, with capital letters eliminated for clarity excepting proper nouns, titles, and the beginnings of sentences (engraved or lithographed titles frequently differed in their use of capital letters from the letterpress title. The situation is further confused by the fact that one or other of the title-pages has frequently been omitted from the atlas or is missing). Dots indicate omissions; later issues note only alterations; and minor variations are usually not noted. The elimination of capitals is adopted throughout all issue analysis not only for atlas titles but also for folding-map cover titles since these could vary between covers in a series.

f the contents of the atlas divided into related groups—e.g. general, thematic and index maps, islands (referred to by name alone), towns (usually listed except where the number involved is too great for individual specification), etc. Anglesey is included under Welsh counties, Monmouth under English counties, and Yorkshire is treated separately since its large size frequently caused it to be divided into its Ridings or regions. A plus sign (+) indicates that the areas concerned are combined on one map.

g imprints, titles, signatures, inscriptions, numbers, and notes appearing outside the map frame. Position is usually not indicated. A square bracket [ ] indicates alternative wording or material which is included in only some imprints, etc.

h Publisher. Since the place of publication is rarely other than London or Edinburgh, this is not generally specified. An ampersand joining names indicates a business association.

SELECT BIBLIOGRAPHY

ADAMS, I.H. *Scottish Record Office: Descriptive List of Plans.* 2 vols. (1966 and 1970)

ADAMS, I.H. 'The Scottish Record Office plan collection'. (*Cart. Journ.*, 4; 1967)

BRITISH MUSEUM. *The British Museum Catalogue of Printed Maps, Charts and Plans.* 15 vols. (1967)

BRITISH LIBRARY. *The British Library Catalogue of Printed Maps, Charts and Plans. Ten-Year Supplement 1965-1974.* (1978)

CHUBB, T. *The Printed Maps in the Atlases of Great Britain and Ireland. A Bibliography, 1579-1850.* (1927; reprinted 1966, 1979)

EDEN, P. (ed.) *Dictionary of Land Surveyors and Local Cartographers of Great Britain and Ireland 1550-1850.* (1975-9)

FORDHAM, SIR H.G. *Notes on the Cartography of the Counties of England and Wales.* (1908; reprinted in *Studies in Carto-Bibliography*; 1914 and 1969)

FORDHAM, SIR H.G. *Studies in Carto-Bibliography British and French and in the Bibliography of Itineraries and Road-Books.* (1914; reprinted 1969)

FORDHAM, SIR H.G. 'Road-books and itineraries bibliographically considered. (With a catalogue of the road-books and itineraries of Great Britain and Ireland to the year 1850.)' (*The Library*, 13; 1916)

FORDHAM, SIR H.G. *Hand-List of Catalogues and Works of Reference relating to Carto-Bibliography and Kindred Subjects for Great Britain and Ireland 1720 to 1927.* (1927)

FREEMAN, M.J. and LONGBOTHAM, J. *The Fordham Collection: A Catalogue.* (Historical Geography Research Series; 1981).

HODSON, D. 'Dating county maps through mapsellers' advertisements'. (*Map Collector*, 26; 1984)

HYDE, R. 'What future for cartobibliography?' (*New Library World*; May 1972)

PHILLIPS, P.L. and LE GEAR, C.E. *A List of Geographical Atlases in the Library of Congress.* (8 vols.; 1909-74)

PUBLIC RECORD OFFICE. *Maps and Plans in the Public Record Office, I. British Isles c.1410-1860.* (1967)

ROGERS, E.M. *The Large-Scale County Maps of the British Isles, 1596-1850: A Union List.* (2nd ed.; 1972)

SMITH, D.A. *Antique Maps of the British Isles.* (1982) (Contains a full listing of county and town carto-bibliographies)

TOOLEY, R.V. *A Dictionary of Mapmakers.* (1979)

TOOLEY, R.V. 'Large scale English county maps and plans of cities not printed in atlases.' (*Map Collector*; in parts from 1978)

WALTERS, B. 'Engraved maps from the English topographies *c*.1660–1825'. (*Cart. Journ.*, 7; 1970)

WHITAKER, H. *The Harold Whitaker Collection of County Atlases, Road Books and Maps presented to the University of Leeds. A catalogue.* (1947)

Ordnance Survey

ANDREWS, J.H. 'Medium and message in early six-inch Irish Ordnance maps: the case of Dublin city'. (*Irish Geography*, 6; 1973)

ANDREWS, J.H. *History in the Ordnance Maps. An Introduction for Irish Readers.* (1974)

ANDREWS, J.H. *A Paper Landscape: The Ordnance Survey in Nineteenth-Century Ireland.* (1975)

CLOSE, SIR C. *The Early Years of the Ordnance Survey.* (1926. New edition, 1969, with an introduction by J.B. Harley)

HARLEY, J.B. 'Error and revision in early Ordnance Survey maps.' (*Cart. Journ.*, 5; 1968)

HARLEY, J.B. (ed.) *Reprint of the First Edition of the One-Inch Ordnance Survey of England and Wales.* (97 sheets with accompanying notes; 1969–71)

HARLEY, J.B. and O'DONOGHUE, Y. *The Old Series Ordnance Survey Maps of England and Wales.* (1976—to be published in 10 volumes)

HARLEY, J.B. and PHILLIPS, C.W. *The Historian's Guide to Ordnance Survey Maps.* (The National Council of Social Service; 1964)

JOHNSTON, D.A. *Ordnance Survey Maps of the United Kingdom—a description of their scales, characteristics etc.* (1902)

MADDEN, P.G. 'The Ordnance Survey of Ireland'. (*Irish Sword*, 5; 1962)

SEYMOUR, W.A. (ed.) *A History of the Ordnance Survey.* (1981)

WINTERBOTHAM, H.ST.J.L. 'The small scale maps of the Ordnance Survey.' (*Geog. Journ.*, 79; 1932)

Dating of Ordnance Survey Sheets

ANDREWS, J.H. Appendix F: 'A note on the dating of Irish Ordnance Survey maps', in *A Paper Landscape: The Ordnance Survey in Nineteenth-Century Ireland.* (1975)

CLARKE, R.V. 'The use of watermarks in dating old series one-inch Ordnance Survey maps'. (*Cart. Journ.*, 6; 1969)

MUMFORD, I. 'Engraved Ordnance Survey one-inch maps—the problem of dating'. (*Cart.Journ.*, 5; 1968)

MUMFORD, I. and CLARK, P.K. 'Engraved Ordnance Survey one-inch maps—the methodology of dating'. (*Cart.Journ.*, 5; 1968)

Catalogue

ADLARD, Alfred
Engraver *fl. c.* **1840-50**

I

    a 136 x 202mm (5.4 × 8in).
    b 1:12.5m.
    c County name.
    d Note of county populations and acreages. The most striking feature of the grouped maps is the combination of non-contiguous counties and counties from different provinces, presumably to fit the chapter arrangement of the work, although even this is not consistent.

Issues:

Created by Samuel and Anna Maria Hall 'to promote the welfare of Ireland—but not by a sacrifice of truth'.

1 1841–43. 'It will be issued in Monthly Parts; each Part to contain Two Engravings of Scenery, upon Steel, an engraved Map of a County or District—carefully revised, according to the latest surveys, and, as far as possible, collated with the maps issued by the Ordnance,—with about Fifteen Engravings on Wood. ... A Number will appear on the 1st day of the month; and it is designed to complete the Work in Twenty Parts. The Price of each Part will be Half-a-crown.'

    e *Ireland. its scenery, character, &c.* by *Mr. & Mrs. S.C. Hall.*
    f Ireland. 16 county maps (six maps combine two counties each; five combine three each). Lakes of Killarney.
    g 'A. Adlard, Doctors Commons.' 'London: Published by How & Parsons, 132 Fleet Street.' Six imprints omit the Fleet Street address; Ireland, Donegal, Mayo and Galway give the publisher as 'Jeremiah How'. Cork is dated 'Nov. 1840' and Armagh '1842'.
    h How & Parsons.

2 1842–43? As (1). 'We are justified in assuming that it has not disappointed public expectation: for its sale has far exceeded our most sanguine hopes, having more than doubled the calculation of the Publishers. By the Press of England and Scotland—we believe universally—we have been greatly encouraged; and also by that of Ireland, with very few exceptions.'

    g Publisher's imprint erased.
    h Hall, Virtue, & Co.

3 1850?: by lithographic transfer. As (2).

    f Cork is a new map, with vignette, engraved by W. Hughes. Evidence suggests that other maps were later re-engraved by Hughes.
    g Adlard's signature erased from some maps. Killarney lakes engraved by F.P. Becker & C°.
    h Hall, Virtue & Co., and Virtue & Co.

ARCHER, Joshua
Engraver *fl.* **1841-65**

II

    a 180 × 230mm (7.2 × 9.2in).
    b av: 1:6m.
    c County name.
    d Numbered reference key to administrative divisions.

Issues:

Most issues up-dated railway information, and those before *c.*1843 often mixed Archer's maps with those by Cole & Roper, the latter being mainly replaced by Archer's from about 1842 in most cases.

1 1835–41?

    e *Curiosities of Great Britain. England & Wales delineated historical, entertaining & commercial. Alphabetically arranged by Thomas Dugdale, antiquarian. Assisted by William Burnett, civil engineer ....*
    f Two maps of England + Wales. 39 English counties. North; Part of the North; West; Part of the East + West Ridings. Wight. 12 Welsh counties.
    g Plate-number. 'Drawn & Engraved, by J. Archer, Pentonville, London.' 'Engraved for Dugdales England and Wales Delineated.' The reference to Dugdale's work seems to have been progressively erased from the series *c.*1843-46.
    h Tallis & Co.; John Tallis; L. Tallis. The work was issued in varying numbers of volumes *c.*1842-3 by John Tallis (who also issued it in weekly parts) and by L. Tallis.

2 1846? As (1).

    e *The universal English dictionary ... By the Rev. James Barclay.*
    f One index map only.
    h J. & F. Tallis.

3 1846? As (1).

    g The reference to Dugdale's work had been erased from all maps by about this date.
    h J. & F. Tallis.

4 1846?; 1847? As (3) with minor alterations, particularly the addition of railways.

5 1848? As (4) with minor alterations, particularly the addition of railways.

    h L. Tallis.

6 1848? As (2) with the plate states of (5).

    h John Tallis & Co.

7 1858–60? As (6) with minor alterations, issued in weekly parts and bound together *c.*1860.

    e *Dugdale's England and Wales delineated. Edited by E. L. Blanchard.*
    h L. Tallis.

8 1860? As (7) with minor alterations, particularly to railways.

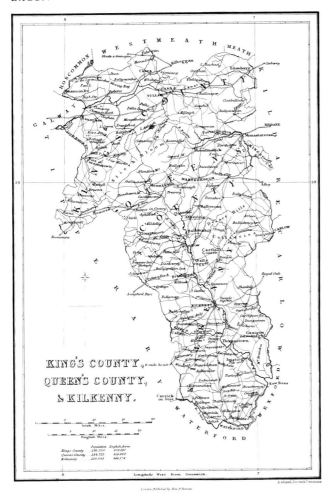

76: 'KING'S COUNTY, QUEEN'S COUNTY & KILKENNY', engraved by Alfred Adlard, published by How & Parsons in Ireland: its scenery, character ..., c.1842.

e *The topographical dictionary of England and Wales.*
9 1860? As (8).
e *The topographical dictionary of England and Wales. Edited by E.L. Blanchard.* It appears that Blanchard's work was also issued in six parts at 7s. 6d. each by L. Tallis, under the letterpress title *Tallis's topographical dictionary of England and Wales* and the spine title *Tallis's topographical dictionary of England & Wales with maps*, with binding instructions and title-pages for conversion to Blanchard's dictionary.
10 1860? As (9).
e *Tallis's topographical dictionary of England & Wales. With a road & railway county atlas.* (spine title).

BACON, George Washington
Publisher *fl.* 1862–98

III
Details given generally refer only to British county and regional maps.
  a 287 × 412mm (11.5 × 16.5in).
  b av: 1:3m.
  c 'THE DISPATCH ATLAS ...' by Edward Weller, B. R. Davies, John Dower, or J. W. Lowry. Sometimes 'FROM THE ORDNANCE SURVEY'. The title is surmounted by Mercury flying above a hemisphere, with a scroll bearing the attribution to the *Dispatch Atlas*.

d Based on the Old Series 1″ Ordnance Survey. Reference notes on parliamentary representation and county acreage. 'The British Isles are so fully given in the County Maps and Supplementary Maps of Environs, that scarcely a hamlet, in many instances scarcely a farm, is omitted. No other Atlas pretends to compete with this minute and laborious fulness. The Railway Series is a perfectly unique one. Every Station is accurately laid down to the day of publication, and every object of importance or interest in the neighbourhood of the Lines is indicated for the gratification of the traveller.'

Issues:
The following lithographic transfers were taken from plates which were apparently never used for direct intaglio printing. They continued in use until the early 1930s.
  1 1856–62: by lithographic transfer. Issued with the *Weekly Dispatch* newspaper. 'The idea of the work originated in the Editor's experience of the fact that by no Atlas existent at the commencement of this Publication could he pursue the narrative of events, as presented to him in his daily reading, in their geographical or topographical bearings. To supplement the most costly volumes, it was necessary to purchase larger Maps of the countries in which events of interest were occurring, and though this might be no heavy tax upon those whose duty it is to study the topics of the day, it is clear that no ordinary newspaper reader would incur the expense requisite to give him the means of satisfactorily understanding the accounts he might peruse. The Proprietors were determined to afford this facility to the purchasers of the WEEKLY DISPATCH, and, presenting every week for more than five years some portion of a delineation, the fullest, the most complete and accurate which the geographical science at their command could furnish ... .' Minor differences sometimes appear between copies issued with the newspaper. The maps were probably also sold separately from this time.
  g Draughtsman's and/or engraver's signature of Edward Weller, B. R. Davies, or John Dower. Imprint of the *Weekly Dispatch*. Lithographer's signature of Weller or 'Day & Son Lith.ʳˢ to The Queen.' These were sometimes interchanged *c.*1863.
  2 1863: by lithographic transfer. The atlas was made up using the variants issued under (1). 'The Subscribers to the WEEKLY DISPATCH have in this Collection the most full and accurate survey of the World's surface that has yet been presented to the Public in any single series.'
  e *The Dispatch atlas.*
  f British Isles; England + Wales (four sheets); Wales (4); Scotland (4); Ireland (4). 36 maps of English counties (Cumberland + Westmorland (2); Devon (2); Hampshire (2); Leicester + Rutland; Northampton (2); Shropshire (2); Worcester + Gloucester (2); Monmouth + River Wye). Yorkshire (4). Eight maps of railways. Kent watering places; Killarney lakes; Thames. Man; Channel Islands; Orkneys + Shetlands (two maps on one sheet). 20 maps of London, its suburbs + environs. Birmingham; Leeds; Liverpool; Manchester + Salford; Cambridge + Oxford; Edinburgh; Glasgow. Environs of: Glasgow; Dublin; Cork; Belfast. Edinburghshire.
    In all, the atlas contained 234 maps covering the whole world.

g Some copies have a plate-number, printed from type, varying according to copy.

h 'PUBLISHED AT THE "WEEKLY DISPATCH" OFFICE.'

3 1863–7?: by lithographic transfer. As (2). Cassell, Petter & Galpin purchased the plates and stock of the *Dispatch* maps about August 1863 and advertised their atlas at this time. It is likely that the taken-over stock was issued by them without alteration until the appearance of the second state of the maps, issued initially in 19 monthly parts, of six maps each, from February 1864 to August 1865 with five supplementary parts published September 1866 to January 1867. 'In Monthly Parts, price one shilling each, Cassell's Universal Atlas: A series of about 260 beautifully engraved folio maps, corrected to the present time, and including all the most recent Geographical Discoveries. ... Each monthly part will contain six coloured sheets.'

Maps were also issued weekly as loose sheets to the readers of *Cassell's illustrated family paper* beginning on 12 September 1863 with the nine-sheet map of London. 'Messrs. CASSELL, PETTER, and GALPIN beg to announce that they have made arrangements by which an opportunity will be afforded to the readers of CASSELL'S ILLUSTRATED FAMILY PAPER who may desire it, to become possessed of the complete and very valuable SERIES OF MAPS known as the "Dispatch Atlas." These Maps will be published by Messrs. Cassell, Petter, and Galpin at One Penny each for single, and Twopence for double sheets. The plates have been drawn and engraved by the first draughtsmen and engravers of the day, and are justly regarded as the most comprehensive and accurate delineation of the Surface of the Globe ever produced. ...' Maps were issued separately folding in 1863; probably under the title *Cassell's folio county atlas* also in 1863; and as *Cassell's complete atlas containing two hundred and sixty folio maps* again c.1863. It also appears that Cassell intended to issue these maps, sometimes altered, as 'Cassell's Topographical Guides,' c.1865, but it seems that only a very few were published.

The designs of Mercury, scroll and hemisphere have been erased. Railway information was added throughout the issue period, and the statistical and parliamentary notes were replaced from c.1864 by comprehensive topographical and statistical notes, taken from the Census returns of 1861 and other sources, transferred to the stone from type, sometimes involving the erasure of some topographical detail. All references to the *Dispatch* have been omitted; names of stations are printed on the map, with round dots as signs for the stations; other minor revisions.

Sussex only has the added note 'CASSELL'S COUNTY MAPS'. The maps (except: British Isles; England + Wales; Railways; London, its suburbs + environs), were also sold loose, sometimes altered, as 'Cassell's County and Home Maps. In Sheets, 3d. each; folded in a neat Wrapper, for the Pocket, 4d. each; or mounted on cloth, and folded in a cloth case, 1s. each.'

e *Cassell's British atlas: consisting of the counties of England, with large divisional maps of Scotland, Ireland, and Wales; copious maps of all the principal routes of railway throughout the country, with indications of every object of importance and interest to the traveller along the lines; separate maps of cities, towns, and places of importance; great map of London, (on a scale of nine inches to the mile,) with the suburbs and environs, and also a fac-simile of Ralph Aggas's map of old London, as it was in the time of Queen Elizabeth.*

f '122 Maps, consisting of the Counties of England and Wales; Divisional Maps of Scotland and Ireland; copious Maps of all the prominent Routes of Railway throughout the Country, with indications of every object of importance and interest to the Traveller along the Lines; separate Maps of Cities, Towns, and Places of Importance, &c. &c. &c. Price, in Paper Boards, *One Guinea*. Strongley Half-bound, price *Twenty-eight Shillings*.'

g The attribution to the *Weekly Dispatch* has been deleted; this is sometimes simply struck out by hand in early issues. Maps now bear the publisher's imprint: 'LONDON, PUBLISHED BY CASSELL, PETTER, & GALPIN, LA BELLE SAUVAGE YARD, LUDGATE HILL, E.C.' New plate-number. Lithographer's and draughtsman's/engraver's signatures usually deleted, but the latter are now sometimes placed under the title. A few maps have the new lithographer's signature of 'MACLURE, MACDONALD & MACGREGOR'S, STEAM LITHO: MACHINES, LONDON.'

h Cassell, Petter & Galpin.

4 1869: by lithographic transfer, enlarging the maps. As (3) with signs for railways, stations, canals, and roads added. Railways added, parliamentary representation altered, and stations marked by large black dots, the original small dots having been erased. Some titles have 'BACON'S MAP OF' added from a separate engraved plate in ornamental lettering; and the outline letters of the county name have been filled with an ornamental pattern. Topographical and statistical notes usually removed.

e *Bacon's county atlas: comprising forty-two beautifully engraved and coloured maps of the counties of England and Wales. Also including maps of Liverpool, Manchester, and Birmingham.*

f England + Wales; Wales: (both large folding). 36 English county maps (Cumberland + Westmorland (two sheets); Leicester + Rutland; Worcester + Gloucester (two sheets joined and folding); Shropshire (2); Devon, Hampshire, Lancashire, Northampton are all large folding). Yorkshire (two sheets joined and folding). Liverpool; Manchester; Birmingham.

g 'LONDON, G. W. BACON & Cº, 337, STRAND, [OPPOSITE SOMERSET HOUSE.']' All other imprints deleted.

h G. W. Bacon & Co.

Remaining stocks of maps in this state were probably sold loose about 1891. The long time-lag between preparation and issue necessitated much alteration including probably a new imprint 'LONDON, G. W. BACON & Cº LTD. STRAND', the removal of the cartographer's name and the reference to the Ordnance Survey in the title, the addition of a graticule with reference letters and numbers, the shortening of the parliamentary note, the addition of the 1885 parliamentary divisions and a related colour key, the addition of a new key denoting railways and stations, and an up-dating of railway information.

5 The maps were issued folding in covers from c.1868 as 'Bacon's new series of county maps'—'In Cloth Case, 6d.; Mounted on Cloth, 1s.'. The series comprised 38 English county maps (Leicester + Rutland,) plus York-

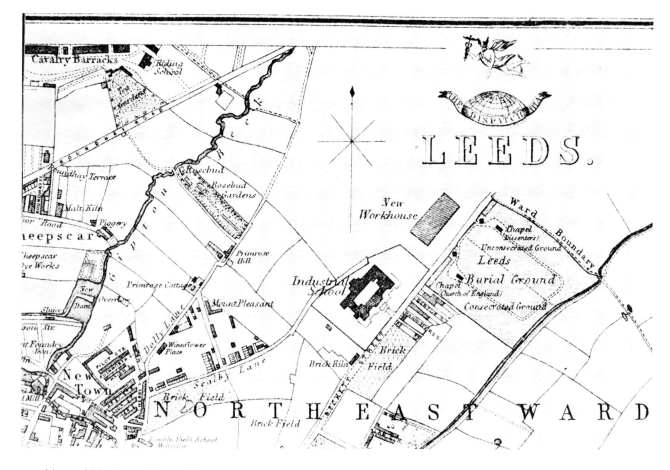

shire and North and South Wales. Cumberland, Devon, Hampshire, Lancashire, Northampton, Shropshire, and North and South Wales were '20 by 20 inches; the others 14 by 20 inches. YORKSHIRE being a Double Map (22 by 28) the price is 1s. and 2s.'. Cover titles varied: e.g. 'Bacon's new pocket map of ... from the Ordnance Survey. With the name of every railway station', 'Bacon's new tourist's map of ... from the Ordnance Survey, with the name of every railway station', 'Bacon's tourist's map of ...'. The maps were altered appropriately with revisions of key, notes, title, and railway and parliamentary information. Early issues retained the 337, Strand address in the imprint but this was later changed to 127, Strand, and later c.1876 to 'Bacon's Map Establishment, 127 Strand'. Also issued c.1870, probably as loose sheets, titled 'BACON'S IL-LUSTRATED MAP OF ...'. (Bacon also used transfers from other plates for some of the maps in this series; for example, from *Cary's improved map of England & Wales*.)

6 1876? : by lithographic transfer. As (4) with a note on the style of lettering used for station names added from a separate engraved plate. Parliamentary county divisions and boroughs are coloured. Some maps refer to Bacon in the title but others simply give the county name; similarly some titles quote the map-maker. Representation information revised.

e *Bacon's new quarto county atlas: comprising 55 beautifully engraved and coloured maps of the counties of England and Wales.*

f England; Wales (four sheets each). 43 English county maps (Cumberland + Westmorland (two sheets); Devon, Hampshire, Lancashire, Northampton, Shropshire (two sheets each); Leicester + Rutland; Worcester + Gloucester (2))/Yorkshire (4).

77: i *Detail: 'LEEDS', drawn & engraved by Benjamin Rees Davies, lithographed by Day & Son, published in* The Dispatch Atlas, *1863.*
ii *'DERBYSHIRE REDUCED FROM THE ORDNANCE SURVEY. Divided into 5 mile squares', drawn and engraved by John Dower, published by G. W. Bacon in the* New Large Scale Ordnance Atlas of the British Isles, *1884.*

g Plate-number printed from type. Some maps still bear an engraver's signature. 'Bacons Map Establishment, 127 Strand London.'

7 1883?; 1884; 1885?: by lithographic transfer slightly enlarged. As (6) with the cartographer's name in the title sometimes erased, any existing reference to the Ordnance Survey erased, and the statistical and parliamentary notes removed. Railway information, place-names, title wording, key, and other information were revised for and during these issues. New title: '... REDUCED FROM THE ORDNANCE SURVEY ... Divided into 5 mile squares.' The title and information below are now usually enclosed in a rectangle, and a graticule of fine lines dividing the map into 5 mile squares has been drawn on the map with reference letters and figures. The colouring indicates the parliamentary county divisions and the boroughs. 'In the forty English County Maps (which are on the largest scale published) the names of Railway Stations are engraved in a bold and distinctive character, thus greatly facilitating ready reference, ensuring clearness, and bringing out the Railway Systems in a special manner.' Variants of this state were issued in other works at about this time.

e *New large scale Ordnance atlas of the British Isles with plans of towns, copious letterpress descriptions, alphabetical indexes and census tables.*

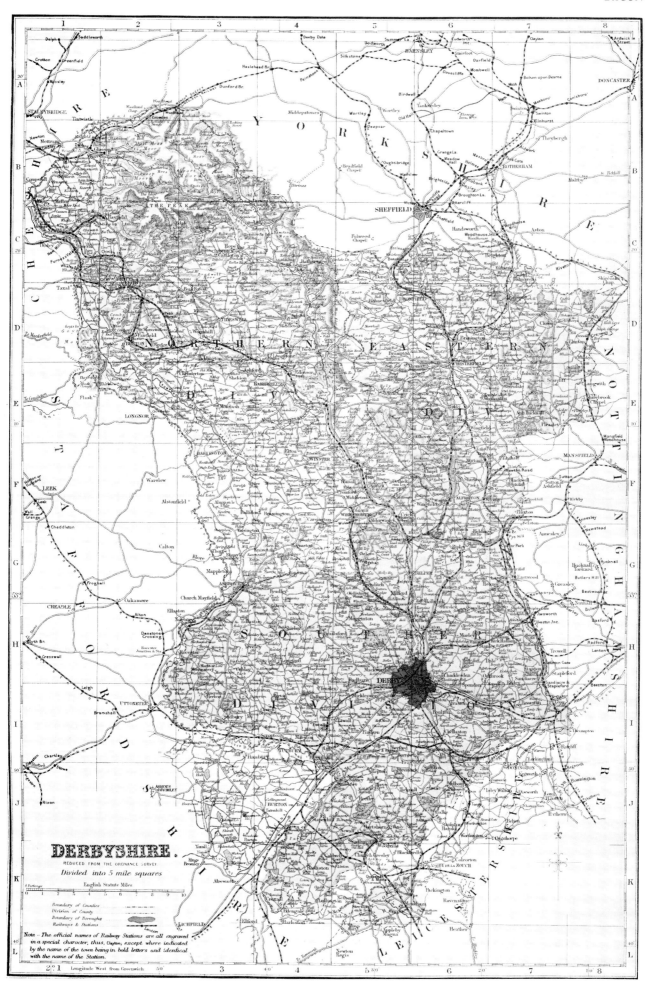

DERBYSHIRE.
REDUCED FROM THE ORDNANCE SURVEY
Divided into 5 mile squares

English Statute Miles

Boundary of Counties
Division of County
Boundary of Boroughs
Railways & Stations

Note.— The official names of Railway Stations are all engraved in a special character, thus, Clayton, except where indicated by the name of the town being in bold letters and identical with the name of the Station.

f England + Wales; Scotland; Ireland; Wales (four sheets); Scotland (4); Ireland (4); England geological (2). English counties as before. Birmingham; Bradford; Brighton; Bristol; Chatham; Cheltenham; Edinburgh; Glasgow; Hastings; Hull; Leeds; London (4); Liverpool (2); Manchester; Newcastle; Plymouth; Portsmouth; Sheffield; Southampton; Tunbridge Wells. Environs of: Belfast; Cork; Dublin; Edinburgh; Glasgow; London; Liverpool; Manchester. Man; Wight; Channel Islands; Orkneys + Shetlands (two maps on one sheet); Killarney lakes. Most of the town plans, plus a few others, became available, until the early twentieth century, separately for the pocket 'In Cloth Case, Coloured, 6d. On Cloth in Case, Coloured, 1s.'

g Publisher's imprint deleted. New plate-number printed from type.

8 1886?: by lithographic transfer. As (7) with the boundaries of the new (1885) parliamentary divisions added, the key altered, and a colour key to the parliamentary divisions hand-coloured on the map.

e *New large scale atlas of the British Isles . . . .*

Berkshire, Essex, Hampshire, Hertford, Kent, Middlesex, Surrey, and Sussex, plus 34 maps of Central London, 25 of Greater London, a railway map, and four of London's environs, in appropriate states, appeared without plate-number c.1885 and with plate-number in 1886 in the *New large-scale Ordnance atlas of London & suburbs with supplementary maps.* The same counties plus other maps of London were issued in 1891 in *Bacon's new large-scale atlas of London and suburbs reduced from the Ordnance Survey with supplementary maps* (the 1895 edition of this atlas contained maps of London only).

County maps also appeared from about this time, without plate-number, folding under various cover titles, e.g. 'A guide to the county of . . .', 'Bacon's county guide and map of . . . from the Ordnance Survey'. 'The Guides contain much valuable information condensed within a small compass, conveniently classified under distinct headings. . . .' States issued correspond roughly to atlas states.

9 1887?: by lithographic transfer. As (8).

e *New large scale Ordnance map of the British Isles . . . by George W. Bacon, F.R.G.S.*

10 1888?: by lithographic transfer. As (9) with some titles altered and shortened, and other minor revisions to some maps.

11 1889?; 1890: by lithographic transfer. As (10) with the addition of railway information and the cartographer's name in the title erased from some more maps.

e *New large scale atlas of the British Isles from the Ordnance Survey . . . . (1889?). New large-scale . . . . (1890).*

f World; British Isles; England + Wales; Scotland; Ireland; England geological (two sheets). Counties as before and 22 towns. Man; Channel Islands; Killarney lakes. Environs of: Aberdeen; Belfast; Cork; Dublin; Dundee; Edinburgh; Glasgow; Liverpool; Manchester. Some plans are reduced to half-sheet; some are added, and some are omitted.

g Plate-number deleted. Plate reference, comprising the county name and the plate-number, added.

12 1891: by lithographic transfer. As (11) with the addition of railway information and the revision of station names.

e *New large-scale atlas of the British Isles . . . .*

13 1891; 1893: by lithographic transfer. As (12) but in 1893

some titles were further shortened and a new key to signs, a new colour key, new statistical information, and new railway information were added.

f Wight added.

g Some maps have the added imprint: 'London: G. W. Bacon & Co. Ltd. 127 Strand.'

14 1895: by lithographic transfer. As (13) with the revision of railway information and the addition of stations, place-names, and parks. Some maps have a new key to signs, a new colour key, a new key to the county area and population statistics based on the 1881 and 1891 Census returns. '. . . REVISED THROUGHOUT BY THE NEW ORDNANCE SURVEY Divided into 5 mile squares'.

e *Commercial and library atlas of the British Isles from the Ordnance Survey . . . . Plans of towns . . . . Edited by G. W. Bacon, F.R.G.S.*

f World; British Isles; England + Wales; Scotland; Ireland; England (three sheets); Wales (3); Scotland (3); Ireland (3); England geological (2). Counties as before and 24 towns. Islands and environs as before plus London. London railways.

g Some double-sheet maps have a reference to adjoining sheets. Most maps have 'Bacon's Geographical Establishment'. County name and reference to adjoining counties. Plate-number printed from type.

15 1895; 1896; 1897: by lithographic transfer. As (14) with railways revised during the course of the issues.

e *Commercial and library atlas of the British Isles from the Ordnance Survey . . . Edited by G. W. Bacon, F.R.G.S.*

f England geological, Wight, Man, Channel Islands, Killarney lakes, town plans (except London), and environs (except London) omitted.

g Plate-number lithographed, not printed from type. Some correction of references.

16 c.1896–1902: by lithographic transfer. Bacon published a series of enlarged county maps folding into covers bearing variant titles: e.g. 'Bacon's county guide map of . . .'; 'Bacon's county guide map of . . . for cyclists & tourists'; 'County guide map of . . .'; 'Bacon's county map & guide for cyclists & tourists from the Ordnance Survey'; 'Bacon's county map & guide from the Ordnance Survey'; and with maps printed back-to-back 'Bacon's reversible maps . . . with guides'. Maps originally printed on two sheets were simply joined, but single-sheet county maps were enlarged to a corresponding size. Map titles vary: e.g. '. . . REDUCED FROM THE ORDNANCE SURVEY, DIVIDED INTO 5 MILE SQUARES'; 'NEW MAP OF . . . AND SURROUNDING COUNTIES'; 'BACON'S MAP OF . . . REDUCED FROM . . .'; 'BACON'S MAP OF . . . REVISED THROUGHOUT BY THE NEW ORDNANCE SURVEY DIVIDED INTO 5 MILE SQUARES'; '. . . REVISED ACCORDING TO THE LATEST ORDNANCE SURVEY, DIVIDED INTO FIVE MILE SQUARES'; 'BACON'S MAP OF . . . REVISED ACCORDING TO THE LATEST ORDNANCE SURVEY. Divided into 5 mile squares.'

The maps bear Bacon's imprint and the main roads have been overprinted in colour. By the turn of the century, both map and cover titles had been altered in some cases and there was an increased concentration on cycling information with, for example, the marking of 'Hills to be ridden with caution' and 'Hills dangerous'. By the late years of the nineteenth century, Bacon had developed an extensive list of touring maps including 76 'Environs and District Maps' available in 'Cloth Case', 'On Cloth in Case' and on 'Flexible Linen', plus, as described above, 'BACON'S Cycling County Maps ... Specially suitable for Tourists, Cyclists, etc. These County Maps are on large scales, very clear and distinct ... Coloured. Roads very bold and distinct. MAIN ROADS SPECIALLY COLOURED. Price in Case, 6d. net. Mounted on Cloth in Case, 1s. net' (comprising maps of each English county, with Leicester combined with Rutland). The latter were replaced from c.1898 (although they were still on sale in the early twentieth century) by 'Bacon's New Series of CYCLING ROAD-MAPS Scale 2½ Miles to the Inch. An entirely New Series of Maps, specially prepared from the Ordnance Survey and carefully brought up to date. Main roads very distinctly coloured, parks coloured Green, coloured lines showing Five Mile Circles from principal towns. The best and clearest Cycle Maps ever issued. 22 by 30 inches. On Cloth in Case, 2s., in Case, 1s.'

17 1898: by lithographic transfer. As (15) with some railway revision.

g Printer's reference, '... M10', added, often faintly.

18 1899: by lithographic transfer. As (17).

e *Commercial and library atlas of the British Isles from the new Ordnance Survey* ....

19 1899; 1900; 1901: by lithographic transfer. As (18).

g Printer's reference sometimes altered or erased.

20 1907: by lithographic transfer. As (19) without the population statistics.

e *Bacon's popular atlas of the British Isles* ....

IV

a 133 × 180mm (5.3 × 7.2in).

b 1:14m.

d Overprinted outline colour. Most sections have 'Main Cycling Routes coloured Red.' Red circled reference numbers appear outside the frame.

Issues:

1 1898: by lithographic transfer from a complete map of the British Isles.

e *Bacon's cycling and touring pocket atlas of the British Isles.*

f England + Wales; Scotland; Ireland. 15 sectional maps of England + Wales. Six sections of Ireland. Seven sections of Scotland. London environs.

g Page number.

h G. W. Bacon.

BARTHOLOMEW, John, & Sons
Publishers, engravers, and cartographers *fl.* c. 1840-

SELECT BIBLIOGRAPHY
ALLAN, D.A. 'John George Bartholomew: a centenary'. (*Scottish Geog. Mag.*, 76, 2; 1960)
GARDINER, L. *Bartholomew 150 years.* (1976)

V

a 162 × 230mm (6.5 × 9.2in). Some maps and plans are double-size.

b av: 1:7m.

c County name, outside the frame.

d Overprinted colour to county area and water only. For maps appearing in volumes issued after 1885: numbered parliamentary divisions, in accordance with the Redistribution of Seats Act, 1885, are shown by red boundary lines; maps have a numbered refer-

ence listing of parliamentary divisions. Details of parliamentary divisions were added to other maps for the 1892 issue.

Issues:
The engraved plates from which the following lithographic transfers were taken were apparently never used for direct intaglio printing. They do not appear to have been used after c.1899.

1 1875-88: by lithographic transfer.

e *The encyclopaedia Britannica. A dictionary of arts, sciences, and general literature. Ninth edition.*

f England; three thematic maps of England; Ireland; Scotland; Scotland historical. 32 English county maps (Leicester + Rutland; Oxford, Buckingham, + Berkshire; Huntingdon + Cambridge; Northampton + Bedford; Shropshire, Stafford, + Cheshire). Yorkshire. Central London; London. Lanark. 106 maps of various parts of the world (by W. & A.K. Johnston).

g 'VOL. ...'. 'PLATE ...'. 'ENCYCLOPÆDIA BRITANNICA, NINTH EDITION.' 'J. Bartholomew, Edin!' The maps of the nations are by W. & A.K. Johnston.

h Adam & Charles Black.

2 *The encyclopaedia* was re-issued in 1890, 1892, 1895, and 1896. It probably contained the maps as above, or, in later issues, as (4) printed by W. & A.K. Johnston.

3 1892: by lithographic transfer. As (1) but maps previously without the parliamentary information relating to the 1885 Act have parliamentary divisions marked, numbered, and usually keyed. Railway information has been revised and added, and railways are now marked by thick black lines. Some county maps have been slightly enlarged by the substitution of a new, similar frame and the extension of the topographical detail. Some titles have been altered.

e *Black's handy atlas of England & Wales. A series of county maps and plans with descriptive index and statistical notes. Edited by John Bartholomew, F.R.G.S. &c.*

f Ten physical and thematic maps of England + Wales; Wales (two sheets). 34 English county maps (as before with Shropshire, Stafford, and Cheshire on separate sheets). Yorkshire (now separated on two sheets). Man + Channel Islands. Lake District. Bath + Bristol; Birmingham; Brighton; Hull; Liverpool + Birkenhead; Central London; London parliamentary divisions; London county; Manchester; Newcastle; Oxford + Cambridge; Plymouth + Devonport; Portsmouth + Southampton; York.

g 'Plate ...'. 'Published by A. & C. Black, London.' 'John Bartholomew & Co.' 'The Edinburgh Geographical Institute'. 'Black's Handy Atlas of England & Wales'.

4 1898; 1899: by lithographic transfer. As (1) with railway information added. Some maps have had the reference numbers and key to the parliamentary divisions removed. Maps were also issued in Black's guides at about this time.

g 'Page ...'. 'W. & A.K. Johnston, Limited.' 'PLATE ...'. 'ENCYCLOPAEDIA BRITANNICA, NINTH EDITION.' 'VOL. ...'

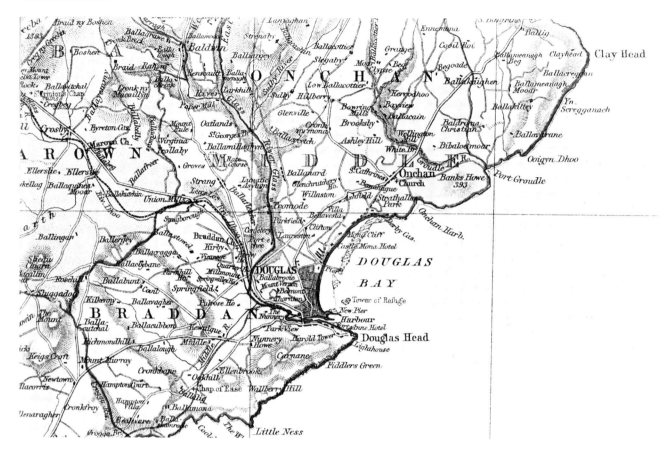

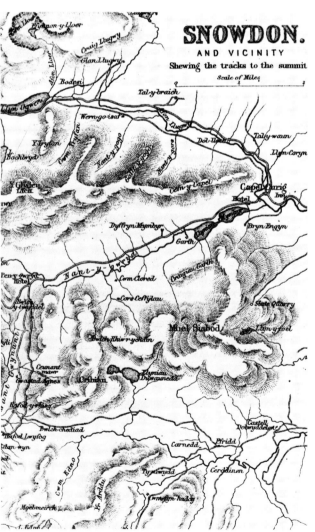

78: *The firm of John Bartholomew became a prolific engraver of maps as the century progressed not only for its own publications but also for many other important cartographic firms such as George Philip & Son and A. & C. Black.*
i *Detail: Isle of Man, from* Philips' Atlas of the Counties of England, *1875. By courtesy of Richard Miller.*
ii *Detail: 'SNOWDON. AND VICINITY. Shewing the tracks to the summit' from* Black's Picturesque Guide to North Wales, *1881.*
iii *Detail: 'COUNTY OF GALWAY', published by George Philip & Son, 1883, in* Philips' Atlas and Geography of Ireland.

VI

   a Page size: 166 × 245mm (6·5 × 9·6in). Maps are single- or double-page.

   d 'A series of specially prepared maps, intended to illustrate some of the most interesting features of the physical, political, and commercial geography of the country.... The statistical maps may be regarded as graphic summaries ... the parliamentary maps have been carefully prepared, with the object of showing at a glance the borough and the county representation of each country; and in the railway maps, which ought to be used along with the list of railways in the appendix, the chief object has been to distinguish by colours the different systems with their subsidiary lines. Among the physical and general maps, a special map is given showing all the lighthouses on the coasts, according to the latest Admiralty handbook.'

Issues:

   1 1887: by lithographic transfer. The atlas continued to be issued with revisions until 1943.

   e *Gazetteer of the British Isles statistical and topographical. Edited by John Bartholomew, F.R.G.S. With appendices and special maps and charts.*

f 23 plates of physical, 'vital and industrial', parliamentary, railway, and general maps.

g 'Bartholomew's Gazetteer of the British Isles'. 'Plate …'. 'J. Bartholomew, Edinʳ'.

h A. & C. Black.

VII

a 125 × 188mm (5 × 7·5in). Some maps are printed several to a sheet.

b av: 1 : 27m.

c County name.

d Most regional maps have a key to signs for railways and county towns, and have a graticule based on latitude and longitude. Overprinted colour. Some maps have a colour-keyed reference table.

Issues:

1 1887; 1888: by lithographic transfer.

e *Pocket atlas of England & Wales by J. Bartholomew, F.R.G.S. With index and geographical statistical notes.*

f Four thematic maps of England + Wales on three sheets. Wales. Seven regional maps of England. 11 maps of urban areas on five sheets.

g. 'Plate …'. Each sheet bears the draughtsman's signature of J. Bartholomew, and 'Pocket Atlas' or 'Pocket Atlas of England & Wales'.

h John Walker & Co.

VIII

a 125 × 193mm (5 × 7·7in).

b Regional maps: 1 : 10·5m.

c Area or subject title.

Issues:

1 1887; 1893: by lithographic transfer. The 'Second Edition' was issued also in 1887.

e *Pocket atlas of Scotland by J. Bartholomew, F.R.G.S. With index and geographical statistical notes.*

f 25 thematic and regional maps on 16 sheets.

g 'Pocket atlas of Scotland'. 'Plate …'. 'J. Bartholomew, Edinʳ' It is usually the whole sheet which bears the inscription, etc. rather than each individual map.

h John Walker & Co.

IX

a 124 × 189mm (5 × 7·5in).

b av: 1 : 10m.

c Area or subject title.

Issues:

1 1887: by lithographic transfer.

e *Pocket atlas of Ireland by J. Bartholomew, F.R.G.S. With index and geographical statistical notes.*

f 20 thematic and regional maps on 12 sheets.

g 'Pocket Atlas of Ireland'. 'Plate …'. 'J. Bartholomew, Edinʳ' It is usually the whole sheet which bears the inscription, etc., rather than each individual map.

h John Walker & Co.

X

'The Council of the Royal Scottish Geographical Society, conscious of the absence of any standard Atlas of Scotland, cordially adopted a proposal to support the publication of such an Atlas, considering it a national

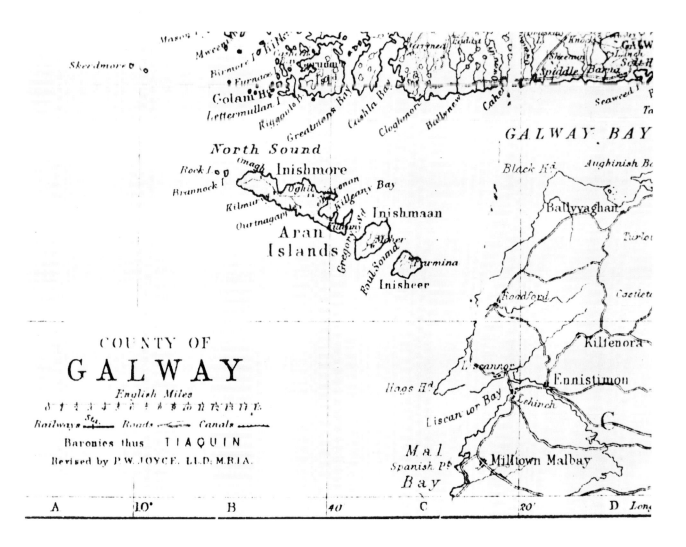

enterprise worthy of the Society's support, and a work which would commend itself to the appreciation of its Members.'

a 412 × 530mm (16·5 × 21·2in).

b Sectional maps: 1 : 2m.

c Area title.

d Regional maps have an 'EXPLANATORY NOTE' and an 'Index to adjoining sections'. The maps are decorated with the arms of the Royal Scottish Geographical Society and its name upon a ribbon. A 'scale of colours' denotes 'orographical colouring and bathygraphical colouring'.

Issues:

The first series of Bartholomew's 'Half-Inch' maps appeared in 30 'District' sheets as the 'Reduced Ordnance Survey Maps of Scotland', between 1875 and 1886, published by A. & C. Black. 'Size of each sheet, 28 by 20 inches. Colored in cloth case, 2s. 6d. each; mounted on cloth and in case, 3s. 6d. each.' Publication of the series was at first very slow with only 10 sheets published by 1885. The maps were replaced in 1890 by a new series in 29 sheets, 'In Case—Paper, 1/6, on Cloth, 2/-, on Cloth, dissected, 2/6 per Sheet net.' The complete series was available 'Dissected, Mounted on Cloth and in Solid Leather Case, suitable for Motorists £4, 17s. 6d. net. Mounted on Cloth, in Four Special Cloth Cases ... 62s. net' being 'specially constructed for tourists and cyclists. Clearly Engraved, showing all Roads, Footpaths, and Places of Interest.' The 1 : 2m. map of Scotland was then resectioned into a larger number of smaller sheets and brought together in the 1895 atlas.

1 1895: by lithographic transfer. 'The basis of the Atlas is a reduction of the Ordnance Survey, in forty-five sectional maps, on the uniform scale of half-an-inch to the mile. On these Section Maps every part of Scotland is given in Topographical detail, including all physical and political features of any importance. On this scale each map is coloured in contour lines, to show the height of land and the depth of seas and lakes so far as surveyed. The Ordnance Survey being in many respects out of date, the half-inch-scale maps have been submitted to a thorough and systematic revision by official and other local authorities, which, it is hoped, has insured the insertion of all new roads, hamlets, mansion houses, hotels, inns, etc., and the deletion of such as no longer exist. The new County and Parish boundaries, as determined by the recent Boundary Commission, are here shown complete for the first time. Railway and steamer routes have been subjected to revision by the various Companies. The series of town plans has also been thoroughly revised to present date by local officials.'

e *The Royal Scottish Geographical Society's atlas of Scotland. A series of sixty-two plates of maps and plans illustrating the topography, physiography, geology, natural history, and climate of the country. Designed by and prepared under the direction of J.G. Bartholomew, F.R.S.E., F.R.G.S. Hon. Secy. Royal Scottish Geographical Society ...*

f 10 sheets of thematic maps. 45 'Reduced Ordnance Survey in sections'. Edinburgh environs. Edinburgh + Leith; Glasgow; Greenock; Paisley; Dundee; Aberdeen, Stirling, Perth, Oban, Inverness, Peebles, St Andrews.

g 'John Bartholomew & Co.' 'Copyright'. John Bartholomew's trade-mark and 'THE EDINBURGH GEOGRAPHICAL INSTITUTE'. 'PLATE ...'.

Most maps also have 'ATLAS OF SCOTLAND'.

h Edinburgh Geographical Institute.

2 1912: by lithographic transfer. As (1).

e *The survey atlas of Scotland. A series of sixty-eight plates of maps and plans. ...*

f 'Eight of the most representative maps from Blaeu's Atlas of 1654 have been reproduced in facsimile; they are of special value to the historian and form an interesting comparison with the present-day topography.'

BLACK, Adam & Charles
Publishers *fl.* 1829-

XI

a Sheet size: 462 × 481mm (18·5 × 19·25in).

b 1 : 4m.

d Printed outline colour with hatching in brown.

Issues:

Published initially in 1862 as 'BLACK'S NEW LARGE MAP OF SCOTLAND', 'TWELVE SHEETS Each Sheet mounted on Cloth. Price Eighteen Shillings'; later as 'BLACK'S LARGE TOURIST MAP OF SCOTLAND COMPILED FROM THE ORDNANCE, ADMIRALTY & OTHER SURVEYS', 'Each District 6d. in Paper Covers folded. Each District 1s. in Cloth Case Mounted on Cloth'; by the 1880s as 'BLACK'S LARGE MAP OF SCOTLAND', 'Separate Sheets, in Cases, 2s. 6d.'; and by the turn of the century as 'BLACK'S TOURISTS' & CYCLISTS' MAP OF SCOTLAND', 'As a Wall Map on rollers, varnished, ... £1:10s.; or in separate sheets, mounted on linen and folded in cloth case, 18s.'. '... everything notable in the country is set down in a most distinct and satisfactory manner.'

1 1862: by lithographic transfer.

e *Black's new atlas of Scotland. A series of twelve maps, compiled from the best sources, on the scale of four miles to the inch.*

f 12 sectional maps of Scotland.

g Most sheets have: 'SHEET ...'. 'BLACK'S LARGE MAP OF SCOTLAND'. 'Drawn & Engraved by J. Bartholomew, Edin[r]. F.R.G.S.'. 'SCALE ¼ INCH TO A MILE'. 'PUBLISHED BY A. & C. BLACK, EDINBURGH.' Sheets 5 and 11 bear the lithographer's signature of W.H. M[c]Farlane.

h A. & C. Black.

BLACKWOOD, William
Bookseller and publisher *fl.* 1839-53

XII

a 189 × 240mm (7·5 × 9.6in).

b av: 1 : 5m.

c County name.

Issues:

1 1838.

e *Blackwood's atlas of Scotland: containing thirty-three separate maps of the counties, together with the Orkney, the Shetland, and the Western Islands. Constructed and engraved by W.H. Lizars expressly for the New Statistical Account of Scotland, now publishing for the benefit of the sons of the clergy.*

f 27 Scottish county maps (Elgin + Nairn; Fife + Kinross; Perth + Clackmannan). Bute; Orkneys; Shetlands; Western Islands.

g 'Eng[d] on steel by W.H. Lizars'.

h William Blackwood & Sons.

2 1839. As (1) with the addition of some roads.

   e *Blackwood's atlas of Scotland: containing thirty-one separate maps....*

   f Scotland added ('Drawn & Eng^d. by W.H. Lizars').

3 Berwick (1837), Elgin + Nairn (1837), Perth + Clackmannan (1841), Peebles (1843) were issued geologically coloured in *Prize-essays and transactions of the Highland and Agricultural Society of Scotland*, published by William Blackwood between 1837 and 1847.

4 1845. As (2) but issued separately folding and in parts completed in 1845. The work was still being advertised in 1852.

   e *The new statistical account of Scotland....* '... 15 large vols. 8vo. Price l.16, 16s. The Counties are sold separately.' The county maps also probably appeared as the 'Travelling Atlas of Scotland, 31 Maps of the Several Counties, neatly bound in Leather. Price 16s.' at about this time.

5 1847; 1848; 1853: by lithographic transfer in 1853. As (4) with railways added to some maps and other minor revisions. Some maps have a key to the railway sign added: 'N.B. The Railways are marked thus'. The maps were folded into a travelling case in these smaller volumes.

   e *Blackwood's atlas of Scotland: containing twenty-eight separate maps....*

6 1884–5: by lithographic transfer. As (5).

   e *Ordnance gazetteer of Scotland: a survey of Scottish topography, statistical, biographical, and historical. Edited by Francis H. Groome....*

   f 31 maps of the counties and islands (the full complement of 31 maps was not always bound into the work). Clyde estuary; Firths of Beauly, Cromarty, and Moray; Greenock; Aberdeen; Glasgow; Forth estuary; Firth of Tay; mineral districts of Lanarkshire + Linlithgow, and Ayrshire; tweed manufacturing districts; Edinburgh.

   g Lizars' signature erased from Aberdeenshire, Argyll, Ayr, and Banff. The new maps have: 'JOHN BARTHOLOMEW EDINBURGH' and 'ORDNANCE GAZETTEER MAPS OF SCOTLAND'.

   h Thomas C. Jack (Jack purchased the stock and copyrights of Archibald Fullarton c.1880).

BOUNDARY COMMISSION, 1867

XIII

   a Approximately 240 × 330mm (9·6 × 13·2in) but some plans were larger, folding and laid on linen.

   b Variously 1 : 1m., : 0·5m., : 0·3m., : 0·16m.

   c Town name.

   d 'REFERENCE'. Overprinted colour represents the parliamentary boundary 1832, the proposed parliamentary boundary 1868, the municipal boundary, and the parish and township boundaries.

Issues:

1 1868: by lithographic transfer. 'A map of each Borough and County taken from the Ordnance Survey plans is appended to the Reports for the purpose of illustrating the existing and proposed Boundaries. These maps, however, many of which are of old date, are far from conveying an adequate idea of the extension of building which has taken place in recent years, and must not be considered as indicating the character of the Districts within the proposed new Boundaries. In order to avoid confusion, the maps have been coloured so as to indicate the line of high-water mark.'

   e *The Representation of the People Act, 1867.... Report of the Boundary Commissioners for England and Wales.*

   f 196 plans of English boroughs (Newport, Isle of Wight, is represented by two different plans) and 51 plans of Welsh boroughs.

   g 'Henry James. Colonel Royal Engineers.' 'Zincographed at the Ordnance Survey Office Southampton under the superintendence of Captn. R.M. Parsons F.R.A.S. Col. Sir H. James RE. F.R.S. &c Director.'

   h Her Majesty's Stationery Office.

Although the Report purported to include 'a map of each Borough and County', very few county or part-county maps were actually included. Those that were, were reproduced from the Ordnance Survey 4″ : 1m. with the above imprint and signature, and were designated in the title as 'NEW DIVISIONS OF COUNTY'.

BOUNDARY COMMISSION, 1885
ENGLAND AND WALES: COUNTIES

XIV

   a Sizes vary very considerably. The standard sheet size is 260 × 365mm (10·5 × 14·5in) but some maps are much larger, being folded into the work.

   b Standard scales between 1″ and 4″ to the mile.

   c County name, 'NEW DIVISIONS OF COUNTY', within a lozenge-shaped panel.

   d The following lithographic transfers were taken from the plates of a larger map, which probably covered the whole of England and Wales, apparently variously unrevised since between c.1858 and c.1871. A frame has been added to the stone and all projecting detail erased, projecting place-names having been cut short rather than fully erased. Boundaries of proposed parliamentary divisions, and boundaries and names of existing petty-sessional divisions, have been marked, and the names of the proposed parliamentary divisions are overprinted in red. A 'REFERENCE' notes boundaries of proposed parliamentary divisions, boundaries of petty-sessional divisions, and parliamentary boroughs, usually coloured red, blue, and slate respectively. The title, scale, key, and signature appear in panels either situated outside the frame or formed by removing map detail.

Issues:

The Commission was appointed as a result of the passing of the Representation of the People Act, 1884, which extended the household and lodger franchise to counties, and in preparation for the Redistribution of Seats Act, 1885. The maps were initially issued as loose sheets in an early state without the overprinted colouring of the boundaries and with other minor variations.

1 1885: by lithographic transfer. 'We have ... appended maps of all the counties ... divided by us....'

   e *Boundary Commission (England and Wales). Report of the Boundary Commissioners for England and Wales. 1885.... Presented to both Houses of Parliament by command of Her Majesty.*

   Individual sections of the Report were also published separately at this time.

   f 37 English counties (no Rutland). Lancashire on four sheets. Yorkshire on five sheets. Carmarthen; Carnarvon; Denbigh; Glamorgan.

   g 'Zincographed at the Ordnance Survey Office, Southampton .. 1885.' 'R. Owen Jones Lt Colonel R.E.'

2 1885: by lithographic transfer. As (1) with all details outside the county boundary erased except for a few projecting place-names. The new divisions have been named and the petty-sessional divisions are now outlined by heavy black lines. The panels have usually been removed; the county boundary is no longer outlined in red; and the names of the divisions are now overprinted in large black letters. A blank label usually obscures the word 'proposed' in the key entry for 'Boundaries of proposed Parliamentary Divisions'; alternatively it is simply erased. Other minor alterations.

e *Redistribution of Seats Act, 1885 (contents of county divisions). Return to an address of the Honourable the House of Commons, dated 7 July 1885;—for, "Return showing with respect to each of the several counties ... divided by 'The Redistribution of Seats Act, 1885', the contents of each division as constituted by that Act ..." "The return to be published separately for each county, and to be accompanied by a map showing the boundaries of each division"....*

g The position of the printing imprint has sometimes been altered.

3 Transfers from some of the same plates, with the addition of railway information and other alterations, were sold as loose sheets and used in other publications in subsequent years.

ENGLAND AND WALES: BOROUGHS

b Standard scales between 1″ and 6″ to the mile.
c Borough name: 'EXTENDED BOROUGH'. 'DIVISIONS OF EXTENDED BOROUGH'. 'DIVISIONS OF NEW BOROUGH'.
d 'EXPLANATIONS' of various entries relating the names and boundaries of existing and proposed boroughs and wards.

Issues:
1 1885: by lithographic transfer. 'We have ... appended maps of all the ... boroughs divided by us, and also of the boroughs where an extension of boundary has been either made by the Bill or recommended by us, except in those cases where the extension is merely that of the parliamentary to the municipal boundary. In some instances the borough maps will not show the extent of buildings down to the present date, as no recent surveys were available.'
e *Boundary Commission (England and Wales)* ...
f 38 borough plans, including 15 in London.

SCOTLAND: COUNTIES

a Sizes vary considerably between 330 × 393mm (13·2 × 15·7in) and 460 × 647mm (18·4 × 25·9in).
b Vary between 1 : 1·5m. and 1 : 5·25m.
c County name, 'NEW DIVISIONS OF COUNTY'.
d Divisions named in large black letters. A 'REFERENCE' notes 'Boundaries of proposed Parliamentary Divisions' (pink) and 'Parliamentary Burghs' (slate).

Issues:
1 1885: by lithographic transfer.
e *Boundary Commission (Scotland). Report of the Boundary Commissioners for Scotland. 1885.*
f Fife; Lanark; Perth; Renfrew.
g Script signature of John Bayly, 'General R.E.' 'Zincographed at the Ordnance Survey Office, Southampton. 1885.'
2 1885: by lithographic transfer. As (1) but with the word

'proposed' removed from the 'REFERENCE.'
e *Redistribution of Seats Act, 1885....*

SCOTLAND: BURGHS

b 2 : 1m.
d Key to names and boundaries of wards, borough divisions, polling districts, and proposed extensions.

Issues:
1 1885: by lithographic transfer.
e *Boundary Commission (Scotland)....*
f Aberdeen; Edinburgh; Glasgow.

IRELAND: COUNTIES

a Sizes vary considerably between approximately 230 × 340mm (9·2 × 13·6in) and 450 × 680mm (18 × 27·2in).
b 1 : 4m.
c County name.
d Divisions named in large overprinted red letters. A 'REFERENCE' usually notes 'Boundaries of Proposed Parliamentary Divisions' (red), 'Barony Boundaries' (black), and 'Parliamentary Boroughs' (shaded).

Issues:
1 1885: by lithographic transfer.
e *Boundary Commission (Ireland). Report of the Boundary Commissioners for Ireland, 1885. Presented to both Houses of Parliament by command of Her Majesty.*
f 31 Irish counties (no Carlow).
g 'J.C. Macpherson Major R E'. 'Ordnance Survey Office, Dublin. January, 1885.'
2 1885: by lithographic transfer. As (1) but with the word 'Proposed' in the 'REFERENCE' deleted in red on appropriate maps.
e *Redistribution of Seats Act, 1885 ....*

IRELAND: BOROUGHS

b 3 : 1m.
Issues:
1 1885: by lithographic transfer.
e *Boundary Commission (Ireland). ....*
f Belfast; Dublin.

BOUNDARY COMMISSION, 1888

XV
a Maps: approximately 400 × 400mm (16 × 16in). Plans: approximately 240 × 330mm (9·6 × 13·2in) but some are larger, folding, and laid on linen.
b Maps: 1 : 4m. Plans: varying between 1 : 1m. and 1 : 6m.
c Maps: 'LOCAL GOVERNMENT BOUNDARIES COMMISSION. DIAGRAM of the ALTERATIONS PROPOSED BY THE BOUNDARIES COMMISSION, In the COUNTY OF....'
Plans: Town name.
d The Commissioners' proposals have been superimposed on the base map in colours.
Maps: 'References'. Civil parishes added to the county—hatched red; civil parishes transferred from the county—hatched green; urban sanitary districts—coloured grey. Many maps have 'Enlarged sketches', town plans, or maps of 'detached parts'.

Plans: 'REFERENCE'. The plans feature sanitary-district boundaries, present and proposed county boundaries, and municipal boundaries.

Issues:

The transfers were derived from a drawing reproduced by photozincography, rather than engraved plates, which appears to have temporarily been the basis of 1/4″ maps of the country. Earlier transfers in 1888 were used as the index maps to the Ordnance Survey of the counties 'Shewing CIVIL PARISHES', and as the basis of other 'official' maps.

1 1888: by lithographic transfer.

  e *Local Government Boundaries Commission. Report of the Boundary Commissioners of England and Wales. 1888.*

  f 39 English counties. East; North; West Ridings. 12 Welsh counties. 47 town plans.

  g Lithographer's signature of Dangerfield of Bedford Street, Covent Garden. Signature of 'Rob. Owen Jones'.

CASSELL, John
Publisher *fl.* 1864–98

SELECT BIBLIOGRAPHY

NOWELL-SMITH, S. *The House of Cassell 1848–1958.* (1958)

XVI

  a Usually 191 × 267mm (7·6 × 10·7in), but some maps are half-sheet.

  b 1 : 7m.

  c Regional maps have 'ENGLAND [SCOTLAND/IRELAND], MAP ...'

  d Outside the frame, 'Map ... Page ...', and usually 'Vol ...', to indicate connecting maps. Printed outline colour with the county names overprinted in red.

Issues:

1 1893–98: by lithographic transfer. Issued in parts. 'A special series of Maps has been prepared, one of which will be presented with each part, so that the purchaser will always have at hand a ready means of reference to the geography of Great Britain and Ireland.'

  e *Cassell's gazetteer of Great Britain and Ireland being a complete topographical dictionary of the United Kingdom with numerous illustrations and sixty maps.*

  f British Isles. 25 regional maps of England + Wales. Man. 16 regional maps of Scotland. Four maps of the Shetlands, Orkneys, and Hebrides. Eight regional maps of Ireland. Liverpool; Manchester. Environs of: Birmingham; Leeds; London; Glasgow.

  g Most maps bear the imprints of W. & A.K. Johnston and Cassell & Co. The British Isles has 'Stanford's Geographical Establishment'. London environs is signed by F.S. Weller.

  h Cassell & Co.

XVII

Cassells also began publishing a series with county maps *c.*1872 which was apparently never completed—'Cassell's County Geographies. By Professor D.T. ANSTED, M.A., F.R.S. Price 1d. each, or containing Map of County, 2d. each'. The few maps published show only county divisions, main roads, railways, and rivers; bear the signature 'Vincent Brooks, Day & Son, Lith.' and the attribution 'CASSELL'S COUNTY GEOGRAPHIES'; are titled 'THE COUNTY OF ...'; measure 135 × 185mm (5·3 × 7·1in); and have a

numbered reference listing of administrative divisions and a key to signs for county boundary, county divisions, railways, unfinished railways, and roads.

COLLINS, Henry George
Publisher *fl.* 1850–8

XVIII

  a 53 × 77mm (2·1 × 3in).

  b Approximately: 1 : 35m.

  c County name(s).

  d Detail of adjoining counties extends to the frame.

Issues:

1 1852?: by lithographic transfer. The sectional maps, printed on cards with plain backs, were transferred, with revisions, from a plate engraved with a single map and this appears to be the first use of this method of transfer to produce regional British maps. Lithographed transfers of the whole map were issued in *Collins' indestructable atlas of the earth* and *Collins' one shilling atlas of the world*, both probably published in 1858. The full map, which was probably issued also in other works, was 'Drawn & Engraved by J. Archer, Pentonville, London.'

  e *Collins' pocket ordnance railway atlas of Great Britain.*

  f 29 sectional maps of England. Three sectional maps of Wales. 14 sectional maps of Scotland.

  g Plate-number.

  h Henry George Collins.

COLLINS, William, & Sons
Publishers *fl. c.*1860–

XIX

  a 150 × 200mm (6 × 8in).

  b av: 1 : 10m.

  c County name(s).

  d Key to signs for railways and on some maps canals and roads. Some maps have a key to parliamentary divisions. Overprinted colour designates parliamentary divisions.

Issues:

1 *c.*1872–75: by lithographic transfer. The plates from which the following lithographic transfers were taken appear never to have been printed from directly.

  e *Collins' county geographies. Edited by W. Lawson, F.R.G.S. Geography of .... Adapted to the new code. By .... With full coloured map and illustrations.*

  f 36 English county maps (Cumberland + Westmorland; Cambridge + Huntingdon; Leicester + Rutland; Bedford + Hertford). Yorkshire (larger folding map). Six Welsh county maps (Denbigh + Flint; Carnarvon + Anglesey; Merioneth + Montgomery; Cardigan + Radnor; Pembroke + Carmarthen; Brecon + Glamorgan).

  g Most maps bear the engraver's signature of either Edward Weller or John Bartholomew, and the publisher's imprint of William Collins.

  h William Collins, Sons & Co.

2 1877; 1877?: by lithographic transfer. As (1). 'The following Maps, with one exception, were designed in the first instance for a series of County Geographies, which have had an extended sale; and it occurred to the publishers that the Maps alone, published in a convenient form and at a reasonable price, might be acceptable to the public at large. As the principal Roads and Chief Lines of Railway are distinctly marked, it is believed that this little Atlas will be found a useful companion to

travellers and tourists whether journeying by road or rail.'

e *Collins' series of atlases. Atlas of England and Wales, containing maps of all the counties, coloured into the parliamentary divisions, and showing railways, roads, and canals; together with a railway map of England.*

f 'A Map of England is prefixed to the series, so that the tourist may plan out his journey as a whole before turning to the separate Maps of the various counties for fuller details.'

g Most maps now bear Collins' publisher's imprint and a plate-number, but the engraver's signature has been deleted.

3 Maps from this series were altered for use as the regional cover illustrations of the atlas series of world maps: 'The ... counties atlas consisting of sixteen maps, full colored constructed & engraved by John Bartholomew, F.R.G.S. ...' published, by lithographic transfer, at sixpence each, c.1878, by William Collins, Sons, & Co. Map sizes varied considerably, and the maps lacked the plate-number, the publisher's imprint, and other features.

DAWSON, Robert Kearsley
Surveyor *fl. 1832-7*

XX

a 230 × 330mm (9·2 × 12.2in).

b 1 : 0·25m. The index plans are at a scale of 1 : 1m.

c Borough name, 'Enlarged from the Ordnance Survey'.

d Wards are labelled and identified in a colour-coded reference key. Large boroughs are covered by more than one plan and 95 have an index plan(s) of the entire borough. 'We wish to acknowledge our obligation to Lieut. Colonel Colby for the assistance we have derived from the documents of the Ordnance Survey, from which the accompanying Plans have been, for the most part, prepared; and a very considerable expense has thus been avoided. It may be proper at the same time to mention, that as the Plans are given merely as Illustrations for the Reports, a great portion of the detail of the original Surveys has been purposely omitted.'

Issues:

1 1837. 'We consider ourselves very fortunate in the co-operation of Lieutenant Dawson ... in the preparation of the Plans ... the preparation of the Maps to illustrate the Reports has been entirely conducted under his superintendence.'

e *Plans of the municipal boroughs of England and Wales; showing their boundaries and divisions into wards.*

f 178 town plans of England and Wales. 'We thought it would be convenient if Plans could be inserted into our Reports of such places as, not having been specified to us, are to retain their ancient Boundaries, so as to form a complete collection of Plans of all the Boroughs enumerated in the Schedules of the Statute; and as we found that such Plans could be obtained from the Ordnance Survey at a very trifling additional expense, we have inserted them in their order, but of course without any Report.'

g Script signature 'R:K: Dawson Lt.R.E.'

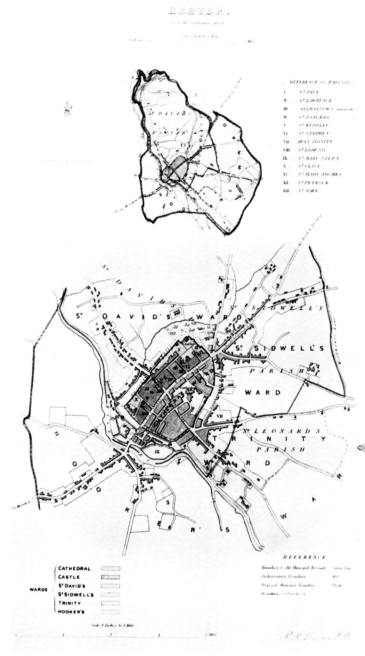

79: *Exeter, by Robert K. Dawson, published in the* Plans of the Municipal Boroughs of England and Wales, *1837. By courtesy of Ivan Deverall.*

FISHER, Henry
Publisher *fl. 1816-37*d.

XXI

a 262 × 335mm (10·5 × 13·4in). Lincoln is a double-sheet.

b av: 1 : 4m.

c County name.

d Notes on parliamentary representation. Key to ecclesiastical signs. 'The form, extent, and superficial delineation of each are inevitably faithful, being deduced from the Ordnance Survey, a most perfect Geographic record; and the scale on which these Maps are constructed is as large as portability would admit. By the enactments of the Reform Bill, ancient borough boundaries were altered, and many new boroughs created; these changes have been carefully observed ... in the construction of each Map. ...'

Issues:

1 1845? 'The statement of the means employed, sources drawn from, and labour expended, in the compilation of this Volume, must necessarily obtain public confidence in its accuracy and value. The progress of England in population, agriculture, commerce, manufactures, and mechanical science, has been so rapid and so extensive within the last half-century, that former Geographies or Gazetteers are altogether obsolete—former County-Maps absolutely untrue.... An Atlas to be useful should be complete to the day of publication, both as regards superficial delineation and descriptive matter. That accuracy and completeness have been secured in this instance is scarcely questionable, when the authority from which these Maps have been deduced is remembered ... Having drawn from the best modern authorities, employed the best artistic and literary talent, regardless totally of expenditure, and having published their Atlas at a price which has placed it within the reach of the great bulk of educated society, they look with perfect confidence for remuneration to patrons—the Public—who uniformly reward where the conduct of the labour has been meritorious.'

c *Fisher's county atlas of England and Wales. Compiled from authentic surveys, and corrected to the present time. With a topographical and statistical description of each county.*

f England + Wales. 38 English county maps (Leicester + Rutland). West; North; East Ridings. Wales (six sheets).

g The preparation of the atlas was apparently started by James Gilbert and the earliest seven maps bear both his name and imprint: i.e. 'London, Published April 1. 1842 for the Proprietor M. Alleis, by James Gilbert, 49 Paternoster Row.' (five maps) or 'Published for the proprietors by Gratton & Gilbert, Map agents by appointment to the Hon. Board of Ordnance 49, (removed from 51) Paternoster Row.' These maps were 'Drawn & Engraved by J. Archer, Pentonville, London.' for 'GILBERTS COUNTY ATLAS'.

The project then appears to have been taken-over by Fisher & Co. and the new imprint 'FISHER, SON & Cº. LONDON & PARIS.' was substituted on Gloucester and Oxford although retaining the reference to Gilbert's atlas. The remainder of the maps all bore Fisher's imprint and usually the draughtsman's and engraver's signatures of F.P. Becker & Co.

h Fisher, Son & Co.

2 1845? As (1).

g Gilbert's imprint has been replaced by 'Fisher, Son & Cº. London & Paris.' on the first nine maps, although they retain Archer's signature and the reference to Gilbert's atlas.

FULLARTON, Archibald
Cartographer and publisher *fl.* 1833–70

XXII

a 115 × 170mm (4·6 × 6·75in).

b av: 1 : 8m.

c County or town name.

d 'INDEX TO PARISHES'. The county maps have a decorative foliated frame. 'The Imperial Gazetteer will be illustrated with a beautifully-coloured Map of the country; various chorographical maps of its more important sections, plans of its principal Cities, Ports, Harbours, and Havens, and an Atlas of County Maps, all similarly coloured .... In this department of the work, as in the printing, no exertions will be spared to make it a work as beautiful as it is interesting and useful.'

Issues:

1 1854–56?: by lithographic transfer. 'The Imperial Gazetteer will be published in Monthly Parts at Two Shillings.... It will also be issued in Parts at One Shilling and Four Shillings each, and in Half Volumes at Eleven Shillings and Sixpence in elegant Boards.... It will be completed in Twenty such Parts at Two Shillings, and will form when complete Two handsome Volumes....'

e *The imperial gazetteer of Scotland or dictionary of Scottish topography compiled from the most recent authorities and forming a complete body of Scottish geography physical, statistical and historical. Edited by the Rev. John Marius Wilson....*

f Scotland. 27 Scottish county maps (Elgin + Nairn; Fife + Kinross; Perth + Clackmannan; Ross + Cromarty). Orkneys; Shetlands; Bute; Western Islands. Four maps of ports and harbours. Edinburgh + Leith; Glasgow. Clyde estuary.

g 'A. Fullarton & Cº. London & Edinburgh.' A few plans bear the engraver's signature of G.H. Swanston.

h Archibald Fullarton.

2 1857?: by lithographic transfer. As (1) but some frame patterns have been altered.

e *The county atlas of Scotland, in a series of thirty-two maps, accurately engraved on steel, from recent surveys, and exhibiting all the lines of road, rail and canal communication.*

f 'Highland Clans' substituted for Scotland. The plans of ports, harbours, Edinburgh, Glasgow, and the Clyde have been omitted.

3 1859; 1861?: by lithographic transfer. As (1) but issued both in parts between these dates and as an atlas in about each year, with railway information revised and some frame patterns altered.

4 1865? (in parts); 1868?: by lithographic transfer. '... published in Twenty Parts price Two Shillings each, containing 80 and 96 Pages of Letterpress alternately, and Three Illustrations, of which two will be coloured; and will form, when complete, Two handsome volumes, Imperial 8vo, with Sixty Illustrations. It will also be issued in Forty Parts at One Shilling each.' As (3) with the frame patterns simplified, bearing a heraldic lion at each corner.

g 'THE NEW IMPERIAL GAZETTEER will be illustrated with a beautifully-coloured Map of the country; various chorographical maps of its more important sections, plans of its principal Cities, Ports, Harbours, and Havens, and an Atlas of County Maps, all similarly coloured ...'

h A. Fullarton & Co. Later issues added 'Fullarton, Macnab & Co., New York'.

XXIII

a Maps and plans are printed on single (161 × 268mm—6·4 × 10·7in) or double (268 × 322mm—

10·7 × 12·9in) sheets. The sectional sheets of the atlas are mostly: 470 × 690mm (18·5 × 27·2in).

b Sectional maps: 1 : 4m.

c Regional title, sometimes 'BY J. BARTHOLO-MEW, F.R.G.S.' Sectional sheets are untitled.

d Some plans have a numbered reference key to important buildings.

Issues:

1 c.1868-71: by lithographic transfer. Produced as a replacement for *The parliamentary gazetteer*. 'The IMPERIAL GAZETTEER AND ATLAS is published in Thirty Parts, price Two Shillings and Sixpence each; Twenty-two Parts comprising the Gazetteer and Eight Parts the Atlas portion of the work.... The Parts of the Atlas portion contain each two Maps, plain, folded, with wrapper, large folio.... It is expected that the publication will proceed on an average at the rate of one part monthly until completion.—If preferred by Subscribers, they can be furnished with the Atlas portion of the work, beautifully Coloured, at the price of Three Shillings and Sixpence per Part.'

e *The imperial gazetteer of England and Wales; embracing recent changes in counties, dioceses, parishes, and boroughs: general statistics: postal arrangements: railway systems, &c.; and forming a complete description of the country. By John Marius Wilson.*

f 'Besides plates of scenery and architecture ... a series of interesting and beautifully-executed-and-coloured maps and plans of estuaries, harbours, havens, cities, and towns.... The Imperial Gazetteer is accompanied with a Sheet Atlas, or large map, of England and Wales.... It is a reduction from the Ordnance and other actual surveys, on a scale so large, and in such a manner, as to give a complete and correct picture of the country. It is engraved on the uniform scale of 4 miles to an inch; it comprises 16 sheets, each having an engraved portion of 26 inches by 18; it measures, when put together, 8 feet 3 inches by 6 feet 6 inches; and it can either be retained in its sheet form or pieced up as one large wall-map. It is executed in the best style, and has been produced by immense labour and at great cost. It shows the lines of railways as corrected, and brought up to the time of publication, by the engineers of the respective companies. It distinctly exhibits every hill, valley, stream, canal, railway, railway branch, railway station, road, cross-road, and important tourists' foot-path; every town, village, parish church, gentleman's seat, castle, important ruin and site of battle; every object of historical, antiquarian and tourist interest; and all lights, beacons, banks, shoals, and other objects of marine interest on or near the coast. It is divided by engraved lines into equal rectangular spaces, with reference-letters for indicating positions.'

England + Wales on 16 sectional sheets. Nine maps of urban areas. Nine maps of estuaries and harbours on eight sheets. Channel Islands; Scilly Islands. The sections of the *Imperial map* were apparently available c.1866 as 'BLACK'S NEW LARGE MAP OF ENGLAND & WALES ON THE SCALE OF FOUR MILES TO AN INCH'—'Price two shillings and sixpence, colored. Mounted on rollers and varnished £4 4s. Mounted on Cloth and folded in a case for the Library £2 15s. Separate sheets in cloth cases colored 2s 6d each.' As well as being available

with *The imperial gazetteer*, the sectional map was sold separately c.1869-91 (possibly longer) as 'Bartholomew's large map of England and Wales' or the 'NEW LARGE MAP OF ENGLAND & WALES' 'mounted on cloth and rollers, and varnished.... Price £3. 8s.; or, folded in case, price £2. 10s. Sectional Divisions ... size, 27 in. by 20 in. Price 2s. 6d. each folded in case for the pocket. Also a portion ... (Sheets 5 and 8) Bartholomew's Map of the Environs of Manchester, on cloth and rollers, varnished. Size, 54 in. by 20 in. Price 10s. 6d. And (Sheets 1 to 9), Bartholomew's Map of the North of England. Size, 52 in. by 42 in. On cloth and rollers, varnished. Price £1. 1s. Suited for the Counting House, Hall, or Library. Price 15/6, mounted on cloth and folded in case ...' By c.1894 it had become the 'TOURISTS' AND CYCLISTS' MAP OF ENGLAND & WALES'. The sectional map, in various guises, was presumably available separately over a long period.

g Most sheets have the engraver's signature of J. Bartholomew. Most sheets have the publisher's imprint of A. Fullarton & Co. The sectional maps also have 'SHEET ...' and usually 'IMPERIAL MAP OF ENGLAND & WALES'. When issued as individual maps, folding in covers, Fullarton's imprint was usually erased and Bartholomew's signature was sometimes obscured by the seller's label.

h A. Fullarton & Co.

2 Throughout the life of these plates, transfers at different sizes, in similar style but newly titled and with appropriate revisions particularly of railway and parliamentary information, were taken to produce a variety of county and excursion maps and local guides by publishers such as Houlston & Son (c.1868: 'HOULSTON & SONS' NEW SERIES OF DISTRICT HANDY MAPS FROM THE ORDNANCE SURVEY'), Houlston & Wright (c.1868: 'TOURISTS' HANDY MAPS FROM THE ORDNANCE SURVEY'), W.H. Smith (c.1875-96: 'W.H. SMITH & SON'S SERIES OF REDUCED ORDNANCE MAPS FOR TOURISTS'—'These splendid Maps, unquestionably the most perfect ever published, have been compiled from the Ordnance and Admiralty Surveys, with railways up to the latest date. Their particulars are most minute and accurate; every possible information that a Map can give is afforded'), A. & C. Black (c.1879-96: Black's guides), John Bartholomew & Co., John Murray ('MR. MURRAY'S ENGLISH HANDBOOKS With Maps and Plans' of which there were 23 by 1890 including handbooks to Scotland, Ireland, and North and South Wales), Simpkin, Marshall & Co., Ward, Lock & Co., Darlington & Co., Methuen & Co., Dulau & Co., Abel Heywood & Sons, and probably others. The latter two publishers produced guide-book series typical of the genre. Dulau & Co. published the 'Thorough Guide Series' with these maps from c.1883 until the early twentieth century with the guides often evolving through several editions. By the turn of the century the series consisted of 19 guide-books each of which contained numerous maps and plans—'Mr. Baddeley's guide-books are well known to every tourist in the British Isles, whether he travels by coach, cycle, or rail, or prefers the laborious delights of tramping afoot. They are as accurate as human fallibility can make them, they are bountifully supplied with excellent coloured maps which show every road, and the

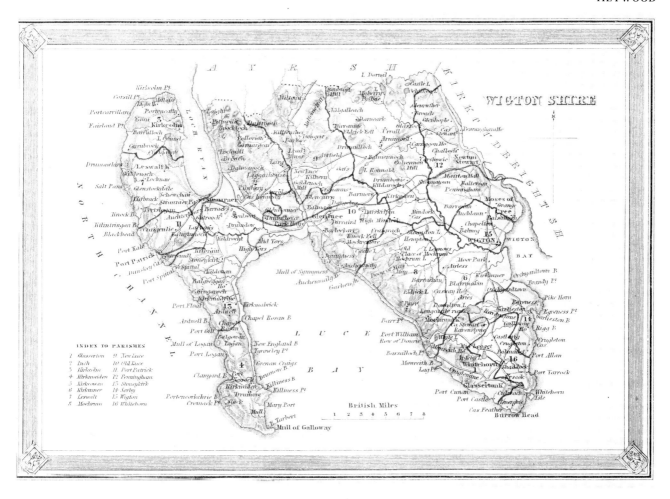

*80: 'WIGTON SHIRE', published by A. Fullarton & Co.,
c.1856, in The Imperial Gazetteer of Scotland.*

descriptions of scenery are written with good literary taste—a happy medium between the baldness of some guide-books and the stilted jargon of others'. Abel Heywood's 'PENNY GUIDE BOOKS' were extremely popular being published containing these transfers for about 30 years from *c.*1868—'The matter is as good as the books are cheap, and the Guides only require to be known to secure a large demand'. Heywood's guide list grew rapidly—by 1870, 65 guides were listed which were mainly available either without map at 1d. each or at 2d. 'with an elaborate Map of 2000 square miles around the locality' or with 'a correctly engraved Plan'. These guides were also available at 3d., 'with both the Plan and the Map of the locality', and a small selection 'from the PENNY GUIDES are published, bound in stiff covers, with Maps and Plans complete'. Plans were also available separately 'printed in colours, on thick paper, and folded in neat case' or 'mounted on cloth and rollers, and varnished'. The plates, much revised, continued in service until at least 1938. A frame was usually drawn round the map and projecting place-names erased. Where the names of surrounding counties projected, the whole name was removed.

3 March 1899—May 1900: by lithographic transfer. Sections of the *Imperial map* were used by Bartholomew for *The royal atlas* published in 20 parts, each 'Price 6d. net', for 'cyclists, tourists, businessmen, and general reference'.

e *The royal atlas of England and Wales reduced from the Ordnance Survey. A complete series of topographical maps, physical and statistical charts, town plans, and index of 35,000 names. Edited by J.G. Bartholomew, F.R.G.S.*

f 16 sheets of index and thematic maps of England + Wales. 31 sheets of regional maps. Birmingham; Blackpool + Sheffield; Bournemouth + Solent; Brighton; Buxton, Cheltenham, + Warwick; Eastbourne; Harrogate + Scarborough; Hastings + St Leonards; Liverpool; London; Manchester + Salford; Newcastle + Hull; Nottingham; Oxford + Cambridge; Plymouth + Devonport; York + Durham.

g 'ROYAL ATLAS OF ENGLAND'. 'PLATE ...'. 'John Bartholomew & Co., Edinʳ.'

h George Newnes Ltd.

HEYWOOD, John
Publisher *fl.c.* 1842-64d.

XXIV
a 153 × 201mm (6.1 × 8in).
b av: 1:7m.
c County name.
d Maps printed back-to-back.

Issues:

1 1879?: by lithographic transfer. 'It is not only a marvel of cheapness, but supplies a deficiency which has long been felt.' 'Well printed on good paper, and are published at a price which places them within the reach of everybody. Such maps could not have been obtained a generation ago for twenty times the money ...'

e *John Heywood's county atlas of Wales. With all the railways & roads.*

f 12 Welsh counties.

g 'JOHN HEYWOOD, PUBLISHER & EDUCATIONAL BOOKSELLER, EXCELSIOR BUILDINGS, RIDGEFIELD, MANCHESTER, AND 11, PATERNOSTER BUILDINGS, LONDON, E.C.'

h John Heywood.

HUGHES, William
Geographer and engraver *fl.* 1840-68

XXV

a 233 × 306mm (9.3 × 12.3 in).

b av: 1:5m.

c County or area title.

d Key to sign for railways and sometimes boundaries. Some maps give a key to parliamentary divisions. The area within the county boundary is overprinted in full colour; this was one of the first series of county maps to be coloured mechanically.

Issues:
The plates from which the following lithographic transfers were taken were apparently never used for direct intaglio printing.

1 1863-8; 1875?: by lithographic transfer. 'The NATIONAL GAZETTEER will be completed in about Thirty-five Parts of 80 pages each, imperial octavo, or in about 12 Divisions at 7s. 6d. It will comprise a series of upwards of Sixty Coloured Quarto Maps, especially prepared for the illustration of the work.'

e *The national gazetteer: a topographical dictionary of the British islands. Compiled from the latest and best sources, and illustrated with a complete county atlas, and numerous maps.*

f 'To render the work more useful, a series has been added of seventy maps of the counties, drawn from the best authorities, on such a scale as to insure both efficiency and convenience, the railways and railway stations being indicated, and the whole verified on the Ordnance Survey'. England + Wales; Inland navigation; British Isles; British population distribution; Scotland; Ireland; North Atlantic. 39 English counties. East; West; North Ridings. North; South Wales. Man; Wight; Channel Islands. 10 maps of Scottish counties on nine sheets (Argyle + Bute; Edinburgh, Linlithgow, + Haddington; Inverness, Ross, + Cromarty; Outer Hebrides + 'Southerland and Caithness' (two maps on one sheet); Roxburgh, Berwick, Selkirk, + Peebles; Aberdeen, Banff, Elgin, Nairn, + Kincardine; Dumfries, Kircudbright, Wigtown, + parts of Lanark and Ayr; Perth, Forfar, Fife, Kinross, + Clackmannan; Stirling, Dumbarton, Renfrew, + parts of Lanark and Ayr). Connaught; Leinster; Munster; Ulster.

g Engraver's signature of W. Hughes. Publisher's imprint of James Virtue or Virtue & Co.

h Virtue & Co.

2 1868: by lithographic transfer. Issued in 12 divisions. As (1) with added railway information.

e *The national gazetteer of Great Britain and Ireland* . . . .

g Some copies of some maps appeared without the publisher's imprint, presumably erased in preparation for its later alteration, and/or without the engraver's signature.

3 1868; 1870?: by lithographic transfer. As (2) with added railway information. Some maps have altitudes added to some hills and the note 'Heights in Feet'.

g Some imprints have been altered to that of Virtue & Co. and some maps are without a publisher's imprint. Engraver's signature sometimes restored.

4 1873?: by lithographic transfer. As (3) with the addition and revision of railway information. Many additional stations have been marked and the sign used has been added to that for railways. Where necessary place-names have been added to identify the stations.

e *A new county atlas of Great Britain and Ireland containing sixty-eight coloured maps by W. Hughes, Esq., F.R.G.S.*

g The publisher's imprints are still a mixture of those of either James S. Virtue or Virtue & Co., or no imprint at all.

5 1875?: by lithographic transfer. As (4).

e *The national gazetteer* . . . .

6 1886?: by lithographic transfer. As (4) with added railway information and red overprinting to show the boundaries and names of the county divisions.

e *A new parliamentary and county atlas of Great Britain and Ireland containing seventy-two coloured maps by W. Hughes, Esq., F.R.G.S. and others edited by Professor A. H. Keane, B.A. . . .*

f 18 small maps of boroughs, usually printed six to a sheet of 270 × 362mm (10.8 × 14.5 in), with borough divisions marked and named by red overprinting, have been added.

g The imprint of J. S. Virtue & Co. Ltd now appears on all maps.

h J. S. Virtue & Co.

JOHNSTON, W. & A. K.
Engravers, printers, cartographers and publishers *fl.* 1826-80

SELECT BIBLIOGRAPHY
Johnston, W. & A. K. *One Hundred Years of Map-Making.* (1925)

XXVI

a 112 × 164mm (4.5 × 6.6 in).

b av: 1:15m.

c County names printed on the map face in black.

d Printed colour to relevant area. Printed back-to-back.

Issues:

1 1878?: by lithographic transfer from a complete map of England and Wales.

e *Johnston's 3rd. standard atlas & geography. England & Wales.*

f England + Wales. Nine maps of grouped English counties. Two maps of grouped Welsh counties.

g Plate-number at top outer corner of page.

h W. & A. K. Johnston.

XXVII

a 198 × 200mm (7.9 × 8in).

b 1:7.5m.

d 'Within the border of each division of the large Map are the degree figures showing the longitude and latitude, also the letters of the alphabet used in connection with the Index of Places at the end of the volume. Outside the border, on the four sides, are figures, printed in red, which indicate the numbers of the adjoining Maps.'

Issues:
'All who have travelled, either by Rail, Steamer, or Coach, have found the inconvenience of consulting a large folding map. To obviate this inconvenience "The Atlas-Map of Scotland" has been prepared, by which the Tourist can have before him the part of the country to which he wishes to refer, without finding the other portion of the Map in his way.'

1 1881: by lithographic transfer.
  e *The tourists' atlas-map of Scotland with an easy reference index to the 12,000 names of places shown on the map.*
  f Key map. 24 sectional maps.
  g 'MAP ...'
  h W. & A. K. Johnston.

XXVIII
  a The maps vary considerably in size since they have a fairly uniform scale, and some small counties are printed two-to-a-sheet. All maps are printed on sheets of 282 × 374mm (11.3 × 15in).
  b av: 1:7m.
  c County name.
  d Printed outline colour. Graticule with reference capital letters at top and bottom, and reference lower-case letters at the sides.

Issues:
The following lithographic transfers were taken from the plates of a map of the whole country entitled 'MODERN MAP OF ENGLAND AND WALES CONSTRUCTED BY W. & A. K. JOHNSTON, Geographers to the Queen' which seems to have been first published in 1889 (although transfers from various parts of the plates had been used to prepare maps for use in guide-books from as early as 1856). The plates continued to be used for transfer certainly until 1914.

1 1889: by lithographic transfer.
  e *The modern county atlas of England & Wales comprised in fifty seven maps, all on one scale arranged alphabetically with complete index.*
  f England + Wales. 39 English counties. East; North; West Ridings. London. Man; Channel Islands. 12 Welsh counties.
  g 'W. & A. K. Johnston, Edinburgh & London.'
  h W. & A. K. Johnston.

JOYCE, Arthur
Surveyor *fl. c.*1898

XXIX
  a 356 × 456mm (14.25 × 18.25in).
  b Scales vary between about 1:2m. and 1:4m.
  c 'COUNTY COUNCIL MAP OF ... .'
  d 'REFERENCE'. Reference lists of urban districts, county electoral divisions with space for the insertion of councillors' names, and rural districts with space for the insertion of the chairman's name. Printed colour with county electoral divisions 'coloured separately with names in Red' and 'Urban Districts Are Coloured Red'.

Issues:
1 1898?: by lithographic transfer.
  f 32 Irish counties.
  g The maps bear the signatures of Arthur E. Joyce 'COUNTY SURVEYOR, WESTMEATH' and the printers Cherry & Smalldridge, Ltd of Dublin. Some maps note that they are 'COPYRIGHT'.

KELLY, Frederic, & Co.
Publishers *fl.* 1845-99

XXX
  a 219 × 275mm (8.75 × 11in). Some transfers were enlarged to approximately 300 × 375mm (12 × 15in).
  b av: 1:5m.
  c 'POST OFFICE MAP OF .... 18...' with the date of first issue. This date was periodically revised throughout the issue period, but Kelly seems to have post-dated his maps as a matter of habit. The maps were undated in the *c.*1861 atlas issue. The title was sometimes later reduced to 'KELLY's MAP OF ...' or 'MAP OF ...', or later still, from the early 1870s, simply to the county name either with or without the date.
  d Statistical notes give details of the county area, population, and parliamentary representation. 'Reference to the Hundreds'. 'Places of Election'. Key to signs for polling places and Post Office money-order towns. Polling places and money-order towns were erased *c.*1870-80. Railways and a key to signs for complete and projected railways appeared *c.*1850. Projected railways were erased *c.*1874-6 and the key was entirely erased *c.*1878. Throughout the issue period, map detail, particularly railway information, was revised and up-dated periodically, as was the hundred, statistical and parliamentary information.

Issues:
The following lithographic transfers were taken from plates which were apparently never used for direct intaglio printing.

1 Issued, by lithographic transfer, by Kelly & Co. in their regional commercial 'Post Office' directories from 1845; the 'maps engraved expressly for the work' and later 'corrected to the time of publication'. Publication began with directories of the six Home Counties and of Birmingham, Warwickshire and part of Staffordshire in 1845. It rapidly covered other counties in an expanding circle with London at its centre, but only reached the extreme west and the north in the late 1850s and the last English county covered was Monmouth in 1871. New editions of the county directories were issued irregularly and continued to appear in the twentieth century, and the individual county sections of the regional directories were also sold separately. Maps from other series were also sometimes issued in the directories particularly towards the end of the issue period. Maps were also available separately as loose sheets, on rollers or 'in case'.
  g Publisher's imprint of Kelly & C? at the Post Office Directory Offices. Early imprints give the address as '19 & 20 Old Boswell Court, Temple Bar', or S! Clements, Strand; but from *c.*1855, Kelly took-over the premises at No. 21 and progressively added this to the imprints. After about 1868, the address altered to 51, Great Queen Street, Lincolns Inn Field, and in the mid-1890s Kelly moved to 182-4, High Holborn. Draughtsman's and/or engraver's signature of B. R. Davies or F. P. Becker. This signature was temporarily erased from some maps *c.*1851; and *c.*1874-78 it was erased or temporarily replaced by the signature of F. Bryer. A further printer's imprint was added temporarily *c.*1868-74, sometimes replacing the engraver's signature: e.g. 'J. M. JOHNSON

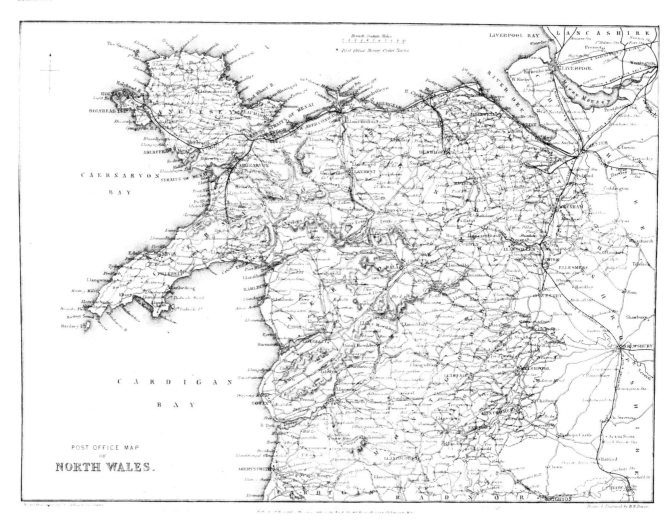

81: 'POST OFFICE MAP OF NORTH WALES', drawn and
engraved by B. R. Davies, from The Post Office Directory Atlas of
England and Wales., c.1861. By permission of the British Library
(Maps 3d4).

& SONS, PRINTERS, 3, CASTLE STREET,
HOLBORN & 56, HATTON GARDEN, LON-
DON.'

h Kelly & Co.

2 Between c.1874 and c.1884 the first series of maps was
replaced by a second set at an enlarged scale with some
'large maps engraved expressly for the work' being as
large as 2′ × 3′. The plates from which these lithographic transfers were taken were apparently never used
for direct intaglio printing. Based on the Old Series 1″
Ordnance Survey sheets, these larger maps were also
sold separately from the directories 'Plain Sheet ... 2s
od/On Roller ... 4s od/In Case ... 5s od' and there was
an overlap between the issue periods of the two sets.
The maps show similar details to the earlier smaller sets.
Key (sometimes erased c.1888); statistics of area, population, and parliamentary information; hundreds. 'Reference to the Hundreds'. 'Places of Election'. Minor revisions throughout the issue period, particularly of
railway information, statistics, parliamentary information, place-names and hundreds.

g Publisher's imprint of Kelly & Co. at the Post Office
   Directory Office initially at Great Queen Street, but
   from c.1894 at 182, 183, 184, High Holborn. W.C.

This imprint was sometimes altered c.1898 to 'London—Kelly's Directories Limited, 182 to 184 High
Holborn, W.C.'. Draughtsman's and/or engraver's
signature of F. Bryer or Kelly & Co. This was sometimes erased c.1886. Some early copies carried an
additional printer's signature: e.g. 'J. M. Johnson &
Sons, Steam & Chromo Printers, 56 Hatton Garden.'
or 'C. R. Cheffins, Steam Litho. 6, Castle S! Holborn.' This was erased for later issues but sometimes
was replaced temporarily by other printers' signatures, e.g. 'Lithog. Kelly & C? London & Kingston.'
or 'Charles Hooper & Co., Ld. White Hart Court,
and Alderman's Walk, London, E.C.'

h Kelly & Co.

3 1861?: by lithographic transfer. As (1) with the title date
deleted and other minor revisions. Coloured in parliamentary divisions. 'These maps were originally published with the directories for the respective counties,
and have been corrected to the present time. December,
1860.'

e The Post Office directory atlas of England and Wales.

f England + Wales. 40 English county maps (including both North and South Divisions of Lancashire).
   East; West; North Ridings.

g Publisher's imprint of Kelly & Co. Draughtsman's
   and/or engraver's signature of B. R. Davies or F. P.
   Becker. 'Printed from Stone by C. F. Cheffins & Son
   London.' (except Cheshire).

KIRKWOOD, John
Engraver *fl.* 1839-49

XXXI

a 163 × 208mm (6.4 × 8.25in).
b av: 1:6m.
c County name.
d Boundaries between adjoining counties are marked by a decorative cruciform at their meeting point with the county border. The style of the maps appears to follow the county series of Bernard Scalé.

Issues:

1 1848. Apparently Kirkwood intended to produce an up-dated version of Scalé's atlas of 1776 since not only are the maps very similar in style but also the only ones produced correspond to the first four counties of the earlier atlas. The series was to be produced in parts at 2s. 6d. each, but apparently failed after the issue of the first instalment.
    e *The county atlas of Ireland, drawn and engraved by John Kirkwood. With descriptive letter-press.*
    f Louth; Dublin; Meath; West Meath.
    g 'Engraved on Steel by J. Kirkwood'.
    h James McGlashan, William S. Orr & Co., and Sutherland & Knox.

LAWSON, John Parker
Topographer *fl.* 1842

XXXII

a 99 × 152mm (4 × 6.1in).
b av: 1:9m.
c County name.
d Numbered index to parishes.

Issues:

1 1842. '... THE GAZETTEER OF SCOTLAND, recently issued by the same publishers, to which this DESCRIPTIVE ATLAS is intended as a suitable companion. The MAPS of the several Counties impart to this volume a peculiar feature, rendering it equally convenient to the tourist and to the ordinary reader.'
    e *The descriptive atlas of Scotland. By John Parker Lawson ....*
    f Scotland. Scotland geological. 27 county maps (Elgin + Nairn; Fife + Kinross; Perth + Clackmannan; Ross + Cromarty). Bute; Orkneys; Shetlands.
    g 'Drawn & Engraved by J. Brown N. Bridge Edinʳ'. 'The Edinburgh Printing & Publishing Cº. Nº. 12, South Sᵗ. David Street.'
    h Edinburgh Printing & Publishing Co.; John Smith & Son; John M'Leod; Lewis Smith; James Chalmers; Smith, Elder, & Co.

LEWIS, Samuel
Cartographer and publisher *fl.* 1831-50

XXXIII

a 190 × 245mm (7.5 × 9.5in).
b av: 1:4m.
c County name.
d Scale-bars of English and Irish miles.

82: *Detail· 'MEATH', by John Kirkwood, 1848, from* The County Atlas of Ireland.

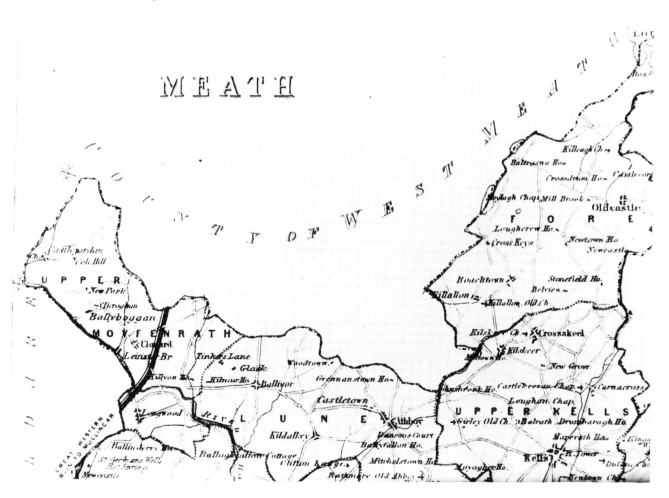

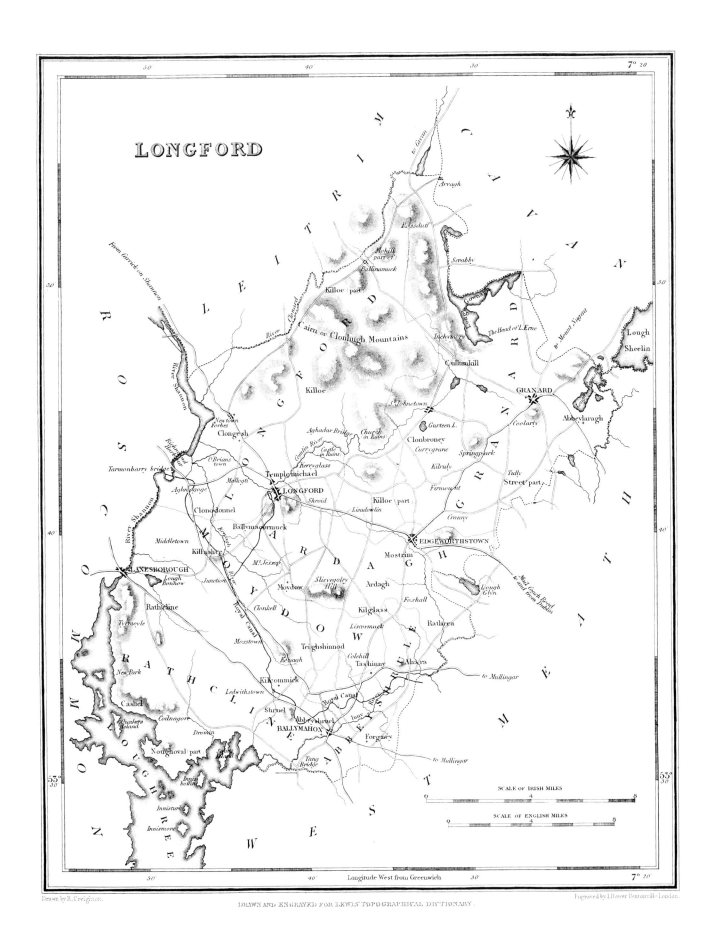

83: *'LONGFORD', drawn by R. Creighton, engraved by John Dower, published by Samuel Lewis, 1837, in* Lewis's Atlas comprising the Counties of Ireland.

Issues:

1 1837; 1840; 1842.

   e *Lewis's atlas comprising the counties of Ireland and a general map of the kingdom ....*

   f Ireland. 32 Irish counties.

   g 'DRAWN AND ENGRAVED FOR LEWIS'S TOPOGRAPHICAL DICTIONARY'. 'Drawn by R. Creighton'. 'Engraved by J. Dower, Pentonville, London.' Ireland bore Lewis's publishing imprint in 1837.

   h S. Lewis & Co.

2 1846; 1847; 1850; 1851. As (1) with railways added to some maps and other minor revisions.

3 1849. As (2).

   e *Atlas to the topographical dictionary of Ireland ...*

LIZARS, WILLIAM HOME
Engraver *fl.* 1818-59

XXXIV

   a 95 × 165mm (3.7 × 6.5in).

   c Route title and distance.

   d 14 of the road maps are divided into strips of varying width.

Issues:

1 1844. The maps may also have appeared in other works and have been sold separately.

   e *Road maps for tourists in Ireland.*

   f Ireland. 16 road-strip maps, 14 of which are printed back-to-back.

   g 'Dublin, Published by W. Curry Jr. & Co.' 'Engd by W. H. Lizars.'

   h William Curry Jnr. and Longman, Brown & Co. William Curry also published *Fraser's hand-book for Ireland*, *c.*1843, 'with Seventeen additional Maps of Routes, 16s. cloth'. The 'Seventeen Road Maps' were also 'sold separately in a case, 5s.' by Curry as were other maps and plans of Ireland.

XXXV

   a 146 × 168mm (5.4 × 6.7in).

   b av. 1.8m.

   c County name.

   d Numbered index listing of parishes usually set within a plain panel.

Issues:

1 1862: by lithographic transfer. 'In addition to the letterpress the volume contains small, but exceedingly distinct and accurate, maps of 27 counties, which, it is believed, will greatly enhance the value of the work.'

   e *The abridged statistical history of the Scottish counties: illustrative of their physical, industrial, moral, and social aspects, and civil and religious institutions, from the most authentic sources. ... and illustrated with twenty-seven county maps, by the late James Hooper Dawson ....*

   f Scotland. Population distribution. 26 county maps (Fife + Kinross; Ross + Cromarty; Stirling, Dumbarton + Clackmannan; Ayr + Bute; Elgin + Nairn). Orkney + Shetlands and the Western Isles (two maps on one sheet). Earlier issues of the *History* contained general maps only.

   g Plate-number. Most maps have 'Drawn & Engd by W. H. Lizars'.

   h John Menzies.

XXXVI

   W. H. Lizars also engraved most of the few plans and road-strip, tour, geological, and general maps which appeared from the 1834 fifth edition in *The Scottish tourist and itinerary or, a guide to the scenery and antiquities of Scotland and the Western Islands* published by Stirling & Kenney, Whittaker & Co., J. Duncan, Simpkin & Marshall, and J. Cumming.

MACKENZIE, William
Publisher *fl.* 1866-95

XXXVII

   a 206 × 262mm (8.25 × 10.5in).

   b Maps: av: 1:4.5m.

   c County name or 'Plan of ...'.

   d Maps: include large areas of adjoining counties. Overprinted colour to parliamentary divisions. Most have a key to roads, railways and canals. Plans: overprinted colour, predominantly pink for urban areas.

Issues:

The plates from which the transfers were taken appear never to have been used for direct intaglio printing.

1 1893-5?: by lithographic transfer.

   e *The comprehensive gazetteer of England and Wales. Edited by J. H. F. Brabner, F.R.G.S.*

   f England + Wales. 39 English county maps (Leicester + Rutland; Lancashire on two sheets). Yorkshire on four sheets. Man. 10 Welsh county maps (Carnarvon + Anglesey; Denbigh + Flint). Birmingham; Bristol; Bradford; Hull; Leicester; Leeds; Manchester + Salford; London; Liverpool; Portsmouth + Gosport; Plymouth, Stonehouse + Devonport; Nottingham; Newcastle-on-Tyne + Gateshead; Sheffield.

   g Publisher's imprint of William Mackenzie. Most have the draughtsman's signature of F. S. Weller. Some plans note their source.

   h W. Mackenzie.

2 Variants are known used in other publications as early as *c.*1884 and as late as 1906 exhibiting appropriate changes such as the marking of the pre-1885 parliamentary divisions and the revision of railway information.

MOULE, Thomas
Topographer, writer, bookseller and publisher *fl.* 1822-42

SELECT BIBLIOGRAPHY
Campbell, T. 'The original monthly numbers of Moule's "English Counties".' (*Map Collector*, 31; 1985)

XXXVIII

   a 210 × 270mm (8.4 × 10.75in).

   b av: 1:7m.

   c County name set within a decorative cartouche.

   d Numbered reference key to administrative divisions. Most maps are highly decorative including titled vignettes and heraldry. Maps of some counties are known without their decoration in later issues. Vignettes were occasionally altered or substituted.

Issues:

1 Issued in parts from 1830 to 1836 as *Moule's English counties.* 'Since the commencement of its publication, in May 1830, the proprietors of the work have been changed more than once; other untoward circumstances left the Editor, at one period, without even a hope of his labours being completed. He has to acknowledge with gratitude the kind and liberal attention he received from the present proprietor Mr G. Virtue, by whose

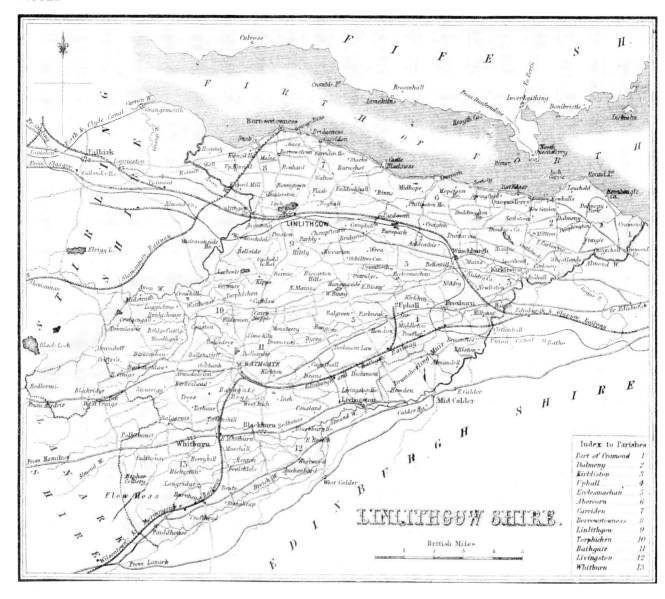

84: 'LINLITHGOWSHIRE', drawn and engraved by W. H.
Lizars, published by John Menzies, 1862, in The Abridged
Statistical History of the Scottish Counties.

spirited exertions alone the Editor was enabled to per-
form his duty, and to continue the account to the end.
Mr. Virtue's chief object has been to produce a work of
obvious utility at a reasonable price, so as to place it
within the reach of every class, not without incurring a
very great expense, and at considerable risk.' Subsequently the maps were sold individually as 'Moule's
Pocket County Maps.'

h George Virtue; Simpkin & Marshall; Jennings &
Chaplin.

2 1837; 1838. As (1) but issued as a complete topographical work.

e The English counties delineated; or, a topographical description of England. Illustrated by a map of London,
and a complete series of county maps. By Thomas
Moule . . . .

f England + Wales; Inland navigation. 39 English
counties. East; West; North Ridings. Thanet; Wight;
Man. London; Metropolitan boroughs. Cambridge;
Bath; Oxford; Boston. Environs of: Plymouth + Devonport; Portsmouth; Bath + Bristol; London.

g Most copies have 'Engraved for MOULES'

ENGLISH COUNTIES, by . . .' either James Bingley, John Dower, or W. Schmollinger. During the
period 1837-9, the plates were revised to exchange
some engravers' names. A few maps have the publisher's imprint of G. Virtue. This was sometimes
erased during 1837-9. Maps without engraver's signature and/or publisher's imprint were also sold during the issue period, and yet others lost their imprints
due to close cropping during binding.

h George Virtue.

3 1838; 1839. As (2) but from 1838 onwards the plates
appear to have been under constant revision particularly
to incorporate and up-date railway and parliamentary
information. Virtue enthusiastically issued old stock at
the same time as he issued revised maps.

f Inland navigation omitted.

4 1842? As (3).

e A complete and universal English dictionary, by the
Rev. James Barclay, illustrated by numerous engravings
& maps. Revised by Henry W. Dewhurst, Esq.
F.E.S.L. . . . .

f The various versions of Barclays dictionary were
clearly made up from whatever maps were to hand,
for the content varies considerably from copy to copy.
The commonest content was: England + Wales
('Engraved by the Omnigraph. F. P. Becker & C°.

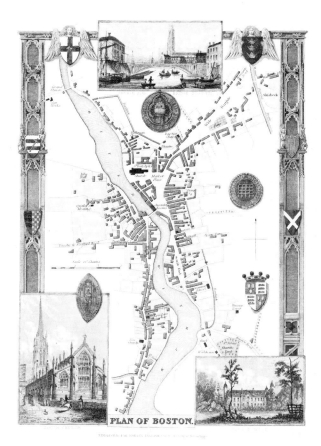

85: *'PLAN OF BOSTON'*, *engraved by W. Schmollinger, for Thomas Moule's* English Counties, *1837.*

Patentees.'). 39 English counties. North; East; West Ridings. Thanet; Wight; Man. Oxford. Environs of: London; Portsmouth. However, the following were certainly issued in some copies: Scotland; Ireland. Bath; Boston; Cambridge. Environs of: Bath + Bristol; Plymouth + Devonport.

g Most maps had the imprints erased and replaced by a plate-number. However, subsequently plate-numbers were added or erased without discernible pattern. Some maps sometimes carry George Virtue's imprint. London environs is a new map, without decoration, engraved by W. Hughes. Since the various issues of *Barclays dictionary* were slightly smaller than Moule's original topography, the maps frequently had to be trimmed during binding, producing little or no margins and the loss of imprints and plate-numbers.

5 1842? As (4) with slight revision of railway information.
  e *Barclay's universal English dictionary, newly revised by Henry W. Dewhurst, Esq: F.E.S.L. ....*

6 1844? As (4) but railways are now marked by three lines, instead of two, with cross-hatching, and stations are indicated and the sign explained. Other minor revisions.

7 1845? As (6) with minor revisions.

8 1848? 1850? As (7) with minor revisions.
  e *A complete and universal dictionary of the English language. ... By the Rev. James Barclay. A new edition ... by B. B. Woodward, B.A. ...*

9 1852? As (8) with minor revisions.
  h James S. Virtue.

10 Most of the counties (usually about 30 but numbers vary greatly between copies) are also found in some sets of *The history of England by Hume and Smollett*, which was published by George Virtue in varying numbers of volumes. Possibly maps were available separately to subscribers and were bound in by them, probably to a parts' edition of 1876-7.

MURBY, Thomas
Topographer and publisher *fl. c.*1874

XXXIX
a 95 × 134mm (3.8 × 5.3in).
b av: 1:12m.
c 'THE COUNTY OF ...'.
d Shows only railways, rivers, towns and a few hills. Maps printed on the inside cover of the booklet.

Issues:
'... Thomas Murby. ... His publications seem to have a speciality for striking out of the antiquated time-beaten track, in which previous educational publishers have been satisfied to move along.' Despite such accolades, Murby's educational series of tiny booklets covered only a few counties.

1 *c.*1874: by lithographic transfer.
  e *Murby's county geographies. ...*
  f Stafford; Norfolk; Kent; Surrey; Middlesex; Devon. Yorkshire (double-sheet).
  g 'THO^S MURBY, 32 BOUVERIE S.^{T} FLEET S^T [LONDON]'. Some maps bear the engraver's signature of W. Dickes.
  h Thomas Murby.

NELSON, Thomas
Publisher *fl.* 1859-64

XL
a Page size: 110 × 176mm (4.4 × 7in).
b av: 1:9m.
c 'MAP FOR ... DIVISION ...'.
d Most maps have: 'The Routes described in Guide coloured Red. The Tinted portion shews the extent of the Divisions.' Also: 'The Map is divided into 10 Mile Squares.' Most maps have a key to railways and roads below the lower frame.

Issues:
1 1860: by lithographic transfer.
  e *Nelsons' hand-book to Scotland: for tourists. Illustrated by maps, plans, and views. By the Rev. John M. Wilson.*
  f Scotland. 17 maps of the 'Divisions into which it cuts the country' which 'are adjusted upon the lines of travelling, and will give facility for reference.'
  g 'MAP ...'. Most have 'Page ...'.
  h T. Nelson & Sons.

PHILIP, George, & Son
Publishers *fl.* 1848-

SELECT BIBLIOGRAPHY
Philip, G. *The Story of the Last Hundred Years.* (1934)

XLI
a 325 × 406mm (13 × 16.25in).
b av: 1:3.3m.
c County name. Maps by Weller are signed 'BY EDW^D. WELLER, F.R.G.S.'.
d Parliamentary divisions are named by lettering across the face of the map. Sometimes coloured by hand but otherwise coloured in parliamentary county divisions by overprinted colour. This was one of the first series of county maps to be mechanically coloured.

Issues:

The following lithographic transfers were taken from plates which were apparently never used for direct intaglio printing.

1 *c.*1858–65: by lithographic transfer. The maps were issued when prepared and, with appropriate revisions, throughout the issue period until the early years of the twentieth century: 'In sheet and folded in cover, mounted on cloth, superior style, in case', variously titled, e.g. 'One shilling, Philips' new series. From the Ordnance Survey of county maps' and 'Philips' new series of county maps. From the Ordnance Survey, by George Philip & Son.' Some maps were used in other publications at later dates with appropriate up-dating, particularly of railway information, and other alterations. The series was possibly issued bound under the title *Philips' county atlas of England and Wales* in 1857 and 1873.

   f 38 English county maps (Leicester + Rutland). North-East; North-West; South-East; South-West Yorkshire. Wight.

   g 'GEORGE PHILIP & SON, LONDON & LIVERPOOL.' Maps by Bartholomew have 'Drawn & Engraved by J. Bartholomew & Son.'

   h George Philip & Son.

2 1865; 1866?; 1868: by lithographic transfer. As (1) but all maps now have overprinted colours. Some maps have been replaced by new ones with minor alterations including an added reference to the colouring, the addition of latitude and longitude graduations, and a graticule with reference numbers and letters placed within the framelines. The reference to colouring, e.g. 'The Colouring represents the Parliamentary Boroughs', and the other additions were added to other maps *c.*1875–81. Railway information up-dated throughout the period of issue.

   e *Philips' atlas of the counties of England, reduced from the Ordnance Survey. By Edward Weller, F.R.G.S.*

   f Lancashire now appears on two sheets.

   g Maps by Bartholomew have had his engraver's signature removed and his name inserted after the title to match those by Weller, i.e. 'BY J. BARTHOLOMEW, F.R.G.S.'.

3 1875; 1876; 1880: by lithographic transfer. As (2) with the addition and revision of railway information. Maps in variants of this state were also sold as loose sheets and folding in covers titled 'Philips new series—...—from the Ordnance Survey—of county maps' with the appropriate up-dating of railway information but without plate-number. Cartographer's name sometimes erased from the map title.

   e *Philips' atlas of the counties of England ... New edition, with a complete consulting index, by John Bartholomew, F.R.G.S.*

   f England and Man added.

   g Plate-number added.

4 April 1876–July 1881: by lithographic transfer. The maps were issued as supplements to *The Pictorial World—An illustrated weekly newspaper* with the new title above the map in large ornamental letters 'THE "PICTORIAL WORLD" MAP OF ...', 'SUPPLEMENT TO THE PICTORIAL WORLD' with the date of issue. On the back of most maps appear statistics of the county and population tables of the parishes and townships. All references to Weller and Bartholomew have been removed, as has the original title.

f It is probable that eight county maps (Cumberland, Hereford, Lancashire, Leicester + Rutland, Oxford, Shropshire, Westmorland) and two of the Yorkshire regions were never published, and that a map of the whole of Yorkshire was added.

   g Publisher's imprint and plate-number deleted.

5 1883; 1885: by lithographic transfer. As (3) with the addition and revision of railway information and the addition of some stations throughout the issue period.

6 1885: by lithographic transfer. As (5) with the revision and addition of railway information, and the addition of some stations. Main roads, lakes and reservoirs, signs for hills, Cyclists Touring Club agents, repairers and hotels have been marked with overprinted colour. The plate-number and the note on colouring have been erased from some maps. Otherwise uncoloured. Arrows indicate 'Hills to be ridden down with caution', 'Break on' (*sic*), and 'Dangerous—Dismount'. The letters H (hotels), X (places where cycles may be repaired), and C (places where there is a Consul of the Cyclists' Touring Club) are explained on a slip pasted on to the back of the map. 'Folded in neat Cloth Case, One Shilling. Mounted on Cloth and in Case, Two Shillings.' Variations of this cycling-adapted map were produced lithographically from current states, with appropriate alterations, and were issued separately as folding maps into the 1890s.

   e *Philips' cyclists' maps of the counties of England, shewing the main roads distinctly coloured reduced from the Ordnance Survey.*

   f 38 English county maps (Leicester + Rutland). North-East; North-West; South-East; South-West Yorkshire. Wight. North; South Wales.

A few of these maps (apparently only Surrey, Kent, Hertford, Essex, Sussex, Devon, and Derby), also adapted for cycling, appeared in 1897 in *Pearson's 'Athletic Record'* 'every Wednesday morning. Price 1d. Full of interest to Cyclists and all other sportsmen. One of these maps will be given each week ...'. The maps have been photographically reduced in size, have added cycling information, and bear the note 'PEARSON'S "ATHLETIC RECORD" COUNTY CYCLING MAPS. N°. ...'

7 1885: by lithographic transfer. As (5) with borough boundaries erased and the names and boundaries of the new (1885) parliamentary divisions added. The note on colouring has been altered to cover the colouring of the constituencies, e.g. 'The Colouring represents the Parliamentary Divisions of County. each returning 1 member.' Revision of railway information on some maps. References to Weller and Bartholomew have by now been removed.

   e *Philips' atlas of the counties of England including maps of North & South Wales, the Channel Islands, and the Isle of Man. Reduced from the Ordnance Survey, and coloured to shew the new political divisions, according to the Redistribution Bill, 1885. New revised edition.*

   f Index map. 39 English county maps (Leicester + Rutland; Lancashire on two sheets). North-East; North-West; South-East; South-West Yorkshire. Wight; Man; Channel Islands.

8 1889?; 1890?: by lithographic transfer. As (7) with minor revisions of railway information.

   e *Philips' atlas of the counties of England ... coloured to shew the new parliamentary divisions ....*

9 *c.*1892–9: by lithographic transfer. As (8) with the re-

vision and addition of railway information. The sign for 'Railways constructing' has been removed from the key and the plate-number has been erased. The notes on constituencies and the colouring of the map have been removed. 'EACH VOLUME CONTAINS A MAP AND NUMEROUS ILLUSTRATIONS. Price, paper covers, 1/- each; post free, 1/2. A Cloth Edition, with Map printed on linen, is published at 2/6.'

e *The way-about series of gazetteer guides.*

f Apparently only Surrey, Kent, Warwick, Derby, Norfolk, Suffolk, Sussex, and Hertford were actually produced in this series.

g 'ILIFFE & SON, MAP PRINTERS, COVENTRY & LONDON'.

h Iliffe & Sons; and of later issues c.1899, Iliffe, Sons & Sturmy Ltd.

10 1896?: by lithographic transfer. As (8) with the addition of railway information.

e *Philips' atlas of the counties of England ... new and revised edition, with a complete consulting index.*

11 1899?; 1900: by lithographic transfer. As (10) with railways now shown by solid black lines. Maps also appeared at about this time in Kelly's Post Office directories.

12 1904?: by lithographic transfer. As (11) with the addition and revision of railway information.

e *Philips' atlas of the British Isles. A series of 61 plates comprising 51 maps of England and Wales, with complete index of 45,000 names, and 10 supplementary maps of Scotland and Ireland.*

f England; England railways (two sheets); Scotland (4); Scotland railways; Ireland railways. 39 English county maps (Leicester + Rutland; Lancashire (2)). Yorkshire (4). Wight; Man; Channel Islands. North; South Wales. Ulster; Connaught; Munster; Leinster.

g Plate-number erased although traces sometimes remain. The new maps bear the imprint of George Philip & Son at 'The London Geographical Institute'. The atlas was issued slightly later, c.1904-5, under the imprint: 'LONDON: THE GEOGRAPHICAL INSTITUTE, 32, FLEET STREET. LIVERPOOL: PHILIP SON & NEPHEW, 45-51 SOUTH CASTLE ST.'

XLII

a 137 × 170mm (5.5 × 6.8in).

b av: 1:5m.

c County name(s).

d 'Index to Parishes.' Key to sign for railways. 'The Maps are clearly and distinctly engraved, and show the Roads, Railways, Villages, Parishes, Country Seats, Rivers and Lakes, Places of Interest to Tourists, &c. ...'

Issues:

Sold also individually as 'Philips' [Tourists'] Maps of the Counties of Scotland, with illustrative Letterpress, descriptive of the Scenery, Statistics, and Antiquities of the Country. In neat cloth case for the pocket, each 6d.'

1 1858: by lithographic transfer. Sold until at least 1864, initially uncoloured or with hand colouring, but later with 'The Maps beautifully printed in Colours. Small 8vo., neatly bound in Cloth, 5s.; the same Work with the Maps plain, 3s. 6d.'

e *Philips' tourist's companion to the counties of Scotland and pocket atlas for the angler, sportsman, and traveller; with the roads, railways, villages, country-seats,*

&c.; *and accompanying descriptions of the scenery, statistics, and antiquities of the counties.*

f Scotland. 26 Scottish county maps (Ayr + Bute; Stirling, Dumbarton, + Clackmannan; Fife + Kinross; Elgin + Nairn; Ross + Cromarty). Western Islands + Orkneys and Shetlands (two separate maps on one sheet).

g Plate-number. 'GEORGE PHILIP & SON, LONDON & LIVERPOOL'.

h G. Philip & Son, W. P. Nimmo, and Thomas Murray.

2 1860: by lithographic transfer. As (1).

e *Philips' atlas of the counties of Scotland; a series of twenty-seven maps, shewing the roads, railways, villages, country seats, places of interest to the tourist, &c, accompanied by a general map of Scotland.*

g Plate-number moved on some maps to appear at the top right of the page.

h George Philip & Son.

3 1870?; 1873?: by lithographic transfer. As (2) with overprinted colour and the addition of railway information.

g Since the maps were re-arranged alphabetically, the plate-numbers have been altered. Bartholomew's engraver's signature has been removed from the large folding map of Scotland.

XLIII

a 151 × 188mm (3 × 7.5in).

b av: 1:5m.

c County name.

d Uncoloured.

Issues:

1 1860-63?: by lithographic transfer. Also sold individually as 'Philips' Tourist's Maps of the Counties of Wales, showing the Roads, Railways, Villages, Country Seats, Rivers and Lakes, Places of Interest to the Tourist, &c. Constructed by JOHN BARTHOLOMEW, F.R.G.S. Full colored, and folded in neat case, 6d. each.'

e *Philips' tourist's companion to North & South Wales, a series of fourteen maps, forming a pocket atlas and guide for the angler, sportsman, and traveller.*

f Wales. 12 Welsh counties. Snowdon + vicinity.

g Plate-number. 'GEORGE PHILIP & SON, LONDON & LIVERPOOL'.

h George Philip & Son.

2 1867: by lithographic transfer. As (1) with railways added.

3 1872: by lithographic transfer. As (2) with railway information added, a key to 'Railways' added to some maps, and the title altered to 'THE COUNTY OF ...'. Printed colour.

e *Philips' atlas of Wales, comprising twelve maps, full colored. By J. Bartholomew, F.R.G.S.*

f 12 Welsh counties.

g Maps usually have an altered plate-number.

4 1876; 1880; 1881?: by lithographic transfer. As (3) with further addition of railway information. 'Crown 8vo, neatly bound in cloth, 1s.6d.' Some maps also appeared in Black's guides to Wales at about this time.

e *Philips' handy atlas to North & South Wales, a series of fourteen maps, including a general map of Wales, and a map of Snowdon and its approaches. New and revised edition.*

f Wales. 12 Welsh counties. Snowdon + vicinity.

g Plate-numbers altered.

5 1882?: by lithographic transfer. Issued until at least *c*.1894. As (4).

   e *Philips' handy atlas of North and South Wales, a series of sixteen maps, forming a useful guide for the angler, sportsman, or tourist. Pocket edition, neatly bound in limp cloth with rounded corners 2s.6d.*

   f Railway maps of North and South Wales. 12 Welsh counties. Snowdon + vicinity; Cader Idris + vicinity.

   g Plate-numbers altered.

6 1882; 1883; 1887; 1889: by lithographic transfer, slightly enlarged (158 × 198mm). As (5) with further addition of railway information. A graticule, with reference letters and numbers within the frame, has been added. 'Crown 8vo, neatly bound in cloth, 2s.6d.; French morocco, gilt edges, 4s.6d. TOURIST EDITION, limp cloth, rounded corners, 2s.6d.' The atlas was issued throughout the period.

   e *Philips' handy atlas of the counties of Wales: constructed by John Bartholomew, F.R.G.S. with consulting index.*

7 *c*.1890: by lithographic transfer. Issued until at least 1892. As (6) with railway information added.

XLIV

   a 145 × 194mm (5.8 × 7.75in).

   b av: 1:7.5m.

   c 'THE COUNTY OF ...'.

   d Reference key to names of parliamentary divisions and signs for railways, roads and canals. Sometimes uncoloured; sometimes overprinted colour marking parliamentary divisions.

Issues:

The plates from which the following lithographic transfers were taken were apparently never used for direct intaglio printing. Some certainly continued in use until the early years of the twentieth century.

1 *c*.1872-3: by lithographic transfer. Published in individual county sections.

   e *The geography of ... for use in schools. By ....*

   g 'PHILIPS' EDUCATIONAL SERIES OF COUNTY MAPS'. 'GEORGE PHILIP & SON, LONDON & LIVERPOOL'.

   h George Philip & Son.

2 1873: by lithographic transfer. As (1) with some railway information added. County area printed one colour and the surrounding area another. Some maps have parliamentary divisions coloured and numbered with a reference listing, and the area surrounding the county still coloured. Atlases were sometimes bound up containing old stock in the first state.

   e *Philips' handy atlas of the counties of England, by John Bartholomew, F.R.G.S.*

   f England railways. 35 English county maps (Cambridge + Huntingdon; Cumberland + Westmorland; Leicester + Rutland; Oxford + Buckingham). East + North; West Ridings. North; South Wales.

   g Plate-number. 'GEORGE PHILIP & SON, LONDON & LIVERPOOL.'

3 *c*.1873: by lithographic transfer. Some of the maps were sold at about this time as 'BUTCHER & CO'S SERIES OF DIRECTORY MAPS' by Percy Butcher, and later states were also published in other commercial directories.

4 1874: by lithographic transfer. As (2) with the further addition of railway information.

   g Position of the plate-number altered to correspond with the new smaller format of the atlas.

5 1876; 1877: by lithographic transfer. As (4) with the addition of railway information. Stations are now marked throughout and the sign used is added to the sign for railways in the key. A graticule based on every 10 minutes of a degree has been added usually with reference letters and numbers in the frame. The county only is now printed in uniform colour or in coloured parliamentary divisions. Maps were also published in other works from about this time.

   e *Philips' handy atlas of the counties of England: new and revised edition, with a consulting index. By John Bartholomew, F.R.G.S.*

6 1878?: by lithographic transfer. As (5).

   e *Philips' handy atlas ...?*

7 1879; 1880: by lithographic transfer. As (5).

   e *Philips' handy atlas of the counties of England: new and revised edition, with a consulting index by John Bartholomew, F.R.G.S.* (1879). *Philips' handy atlas of the counties of England: by John Bartholomew, F.R.G.S. New and enlarged edition, with consulting index.* (1880).

8 1881; 1882 (this issue of the atlas was still on sale as a 'Pocket Edition ... neatly bound in limp cloth with rounded corners' as late as 1894): by lithographic transfer. As (7) with the addition and revision of railway information.

   e *Philips' handy atlas of the counties of England, a series of forty-three maps, showing the physical features, towns, villages, railways, roads, &c.; with a railway map of England; forming a useful guide for the angler, sportsman or tourist. ...* (1881). *Philips' handy atlas of the counties of England. By John Bartholomew, F.R.G.S. New and enlarged edition, with consulting index.* (1882).

   f Wight, Man, and the Channel Islands added and Lancashire is now divided onto two sheets.

9 1885; 1886; 1887; 1891: by lithographic transfer. As (8) with the names and boundaries of the new (1885) parliamentary divisions added. 'The Colouring represents the Parliamentary Divisions each returning 1 member.' Addition and revision of railway information. Maps in this state were also used to illustrate explanations of the 1885 Act and were probably also issued in local guides and tours, etc. Railway information added in 1891.

   e *Philips' handy atlas of the counties of England including maps of North & South Wales, the Channel Islands, and the Isle of Man. Reduced from the Ordnance Survey, and coloured to shew the new parliamentary divisions, according to the Redistribution Bill, 1885 ....*

10 *c*.1881-91: by lithographic transfer. During this period some of the maps, in appropriate states but sometimes altered, were issued by the Stevens' Postal Directories and Publishing Co. of 2, Adelaide Buildings, London Bridge, to illustrate most of its (approximately) 76 postal directories. Usually the maps were adapted by the removal of George Philip's imprint and plate-number and the substitution of either a surround of advertisements or Stevens' address and the note 'STEVENS' SERIES OF DIRECTORY MAPS'.

11 1893: by lithographic transfer. As (9) with the addition and revision of railway information. Some maps have altered colouring and note: 'The Colouring represents the Parliamentary Divisions, and Boroughs.'

12 Advertised as early as 1892 and probably issued at about that date; 1895; 1896? by lithographic transfer. 'Neatly

bound in cloth, 5s.; French morocco, gilt edges, 7s.6d. TOURIST EDITION, limp cloth, rounded corners, 5s.' As (11) with the addition and revision of railway information. Stations are now more fully named. A note on station names has been added, e.g. 'Note. Railway Stations marked 'Sta.' bear the same name as their nearest town or village'. The colouring note has been altered on some more maps.

e *Philips' handy atlas of the counties of England, with maps of the County of London, North and South Wales, the Channel Islands, the Isle of Man, and plans on an enlarged scale of the environs of six important towns. A series of forty-eight maps. ... The maps are coloured to show the parliamentary divisions ... shewing every railway station in England and Wales.*

f As above, plus London; Liverpool environs; Manchester environs; Black Country; Tyne ports; Yorkshire manufacturing districts.

13 1898: by lithographic transfer. As (12) with the addition and revision of railway information.

h George Philip & Son and Philip, Son & Nephew.

14 1903?: by lithographic transfer. As (13) with the addition of railway information.

g 'London Geographical Institute'. 'George Philip & Son, L^{td}.'

15 Maps appeared later, c.1908, in *Philips' handy administrative atlas of England and Wales, adapted to display the rural districts,* published by 'George Philip & Son Ltd' from 'The London Geographical Institute'.

16 A few maps (probably only Warwick, Suffolk, Stafford, Norfolk, Middlesex, Kent, Essex, and Oxford + Buckingham) also surfaced again, c.1910, as the maps for junior and senior educational geography card series—respectively 'Philips' Model County Maps' and 'Philips' Model Duplex Maps'.

XLV

a 153 × 210mm (6.1 × 8.4in).

b av: 1:7m.

c 'COUNTY OF .... Revised by P. W. JOYCE, LL.D., M.R.I.A.'.

d Key to railways, roads, baronies, and canals. Railways were revised throughout the issue period.

Issues:

The atlas was also undoubtedly sold at intervening dates.

1 1881; 1883: by lithographic transfer. 'Crown 8vo, neatly bound in cloth, 3s.6d.'.

e *Philips' handy atlas of the counties of Ireland: constructed by John Bartholomew, F.R.G.S. Revised by P. W. Joyce, Ll.D., M.R.I.A. ...*

f Key map. 32 Irish counties.

g 'GEORGE PHILIP & SON, LONDON & LIVERPOOL'. 'J. Bartholomew, Edin?' Page number.

h George Philip & Son.

2 1885; 1886; 1894?; 1899?: by lithographic transfer. As (1) with 'Parliamentary Divisions' added to the key and to the map with overprinted names.

e *Philips' handy atlas of the counties of Ireland. Constructed by John Bartholomew, F.R.G.S. Revised by P. W. Joyce, Ll.D., M.R.I.A. Reduced from the Ordnance Survey, and coloured to shew the new parliamentary divisions, according to the Redistribution Bill, 1885.* ...

f 'A series of Thirty-three Full-Coloured Maps, showing the Roads, Railways, Country Seats, Parishes, Lakes, Rivers, &c.; ... Crown 8vo, neatly bound in cloth, 3s.6d.; French morocco, gilt edges, 6s. TOURIST EDITION, limp cloth, rounded corners, 3s.6d.'

g Engraver's signature deleted.

XLVI

a 153 × 204mm (6.1 × 8.2in).

b av: 1:7m.

b 'COUNTY OF ...'.

d 'Reference to Parishes.' Key to signs for railways, roads, and sometimes canals. Railways were up-dated throughout the issue period. Printed colour to the sea and county area only.

Issues:

The atlas was undoubtedly also sold throughout the entire issue period.

1 1881?; 1882; 1885?; 1887: by lithographic transfer.

e *Philips' handy atlas of the counties of Scotland: constructed by John Bartholomew, F.R.G.S. ...*

f Scotland. 27 Scottish county maps (Argyll + Bute; Elgin + Nairn; Fife + Kinross; Ross + Cromarty; Stirling + Clackmannan). Western Islands; Orkney + Shetland. Edinburgh environs; Glasgow environs.

g 'GEORGE PHILIP & SON, LONDON & LIVERPOOL'. 'J. Bartholomew, Edin?' Page number.

h George Philip & Son.

2 1891; 1892?; 1894?: by lithographic transfer. As (1) with a note on parliamentary representation added to most maps and the names of the parliamentary divisions overprinted in black. Minor revisions to some maps.

3 1898; 1902: by lithographic transfer. As (2) but the note on representation has been removed from some maps.

e *Philips' handy atlas of the counties of Scotland: constructed by John Bartholomew, F.R.G.S. New and revised edition. With consulting index.*

g Engraver's signature deleted.

h Philip, Son & Nephew.

4 Photographic reproductions of the maps were issued in *A genealogical atlas of Scotland* (1962).

XLVII

a 180 × 240mm (7.2 × 9.6in).

b av: 1:6m.

c 'COUNTY OF ... Revised by P. W. JOYCE, Ll.D; M.R.I.A.'

d Key to railways, roads, canals, and baronies. Maps printed back-to-back. Printed colour. The maps are enlarged copies of those in *Philips' Handy Atlas of the Counties of Ireland.*

Issues:

1 1883: by lithographic transfer.

e *Philips' atlas and geography of Ireland, a description of the country, and of the several counties. By P.W. Joyce, Ll.D., M.R.I.A. and thirty-three coloured maps. By John Bartholomew, F.R.G.S.*

f Ireland. 32 Irish counties.

g 'GEORGE PHILIP & SON, LONDON & LIVERPOOL.' 'J. Bartholomew, Edin? Plate-number.

h George Philip & Son.

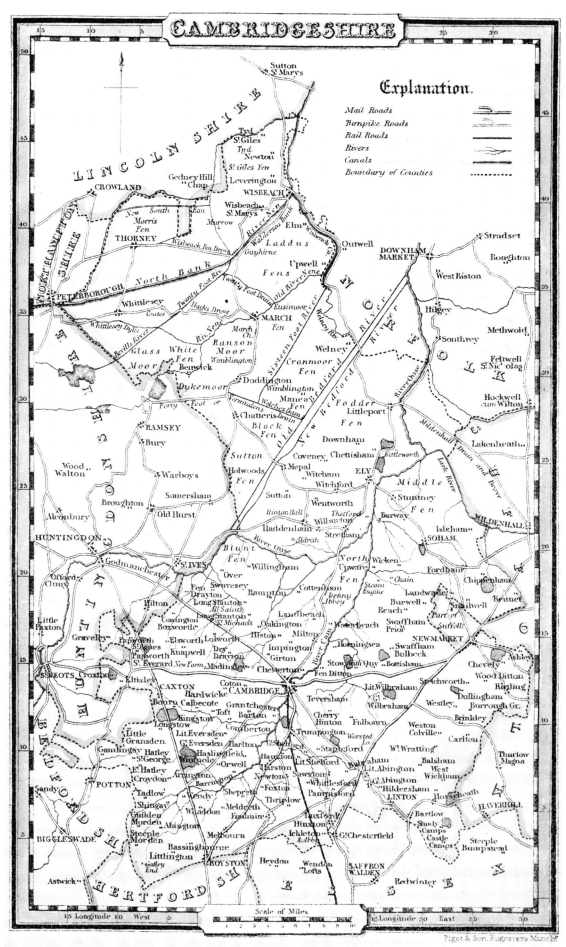

CAMBRIDGESHIRE

Explanation.

Mail Roads
Turnpike Roads
Rail Roads
Rivers
Canals
Boundary of Counties

Scale of Miles

Longitude West

Longitude East

Pigot & Son. Engravers Manch.ª

PUBLISHED BY PIGOT & Cº LONDON AND MANCHESTER.

PIGOT, James
Engraver and publisher *fl. 1811–43d.*

XLVIII

    a 105 × 160mm (4.25 × 6.4in). Yorkshire is a larger folding sheet 300 × 350mm (12 × 14in).

    b av: 1:10m.

    c County name set within a panel.

    d The scale-bar appears within a panel. 'Explanation'.

Issues:

  1 From *c.*1835 the maps were issued lithographically in individual county sections but their fortnightly appearance seems to have ended at part 25 (covering Nottingham). The first 25 parts were subsequently issued bound together. The plates from which the transfers were taken do not appear to have been used for direct intaglio printing.

  2 1841?; 1850?: by lithographic transfer.

    e *A pocket topography and gazetteer of England: with historical and statistical descriptions ... By Pigot & Co. ...*

    f England + Wales. 38 English county maps (Leicester + Rutland). Yorkshire. 'The Publishers of the POCKET TOPOGRAPHY deemed it more convenient for travellers, to prevent the necessity of taking both volumes with them on a journey, to divide the Kingdom into two nearly equal portions, & to place the Northern & Midland Counties in one Volume; & the Southern, South-eastern & South-Western in the other. The Maps are engraved from the very latest and best surveys, & exhibit, distinctly & faithfully, every Town, Travelled Road, Canal & Railway Line, that is laid down upon more costly and larger maps.'

    g Most copies of most maps bear the engraver's signature of Pigot & Slater, Pigot & Son, or Pigot & Co. Some of these were altered *c.*1850 to name Slater alone. Most copies of most maps bear the publisher's imprint of Pigot & Co. This was altered *c.*1850 to that of Isaac Slater.

    h Pigot & Co.; Longman & Co.; Sherwood & Co.; Simpkin & Marshall; Pigot & Slater.

REYNOLDS, James
Publisher *fl. 1845–70*

XLIX

    a 162 × 231mm (6·5 × 9·25in).

    b av: 1 : 8m.

    c County name(s).

    d Key to signs for railways under construction and completed.

Issues:

  1 1848: by lithographic transfer.

    e *Reynolds's travelling atlas of England: with all the railways and stations accurately laid down. Constructed from the surveys of the Board of Ordnance, railway companies, and other authorities.*

    f England + Wales. 16 maps of single counties; North

Cumberland; Oxford + Berkshire; Cambridge + Huntingdon; Gloucester + North Wiltshire; Hereford + Monmouth; West Yorkshire + Lancashire; Leicester + Rutland; Surrey + Sussex; Warwick + Worcester; Middlesex, Hertford, Bedford + Buckingham; Dorset, Somerset + South Wiltshire. East Yorkshire. Lake District. North; South Wales.

    g 'Published by J. Reynolds 174 Strand.' 'Drawn & Engraved by John Emslie.' Plate-number.

    h Simpkin, Marshall & Co. and James Reynolds.

  2 1854?; 1856?: by lithographic transfer. As (1) with railway information revised and added.

  3 1860: by lithographic transfer. As (2) with geological formations added by thin lines and reference numbers, and the revision and addition of railway information. The maps have been hand coloured to display the geology. 'In constructing THE GEOLOGICAL ATLAS OF GREAT BRITAIN, an endeavour has been made to combine convenience and portability of form, with clearness and accuracy of information. The Geographical portion of the Maps has been drawn from the most reliable sources, including the Ordnance Surveys; and the Railways have been inserted to the period of publication. The great interest now taken in Geological science, has led to the belief that the representation in such a work of the Geological features of the several Counties and Districts would prove of interest and utility, both to Geologists and the public in general. ...'

    e *Reynolds's geological atlas of Great Britain, comprising a series of maps in which the roads, railways, and geological features of England and Wales are accurately laid down with a geological map of Scotland. The whole compiled from the most authentic sources.*

        The atlas also appeared at about this date under the title: *Reynolds's geological atlas of Great Britain ... of England and Wales are clearly shown; with a geological map of Scotland. ...*

    f Scotland added.

    h James Reynolds.

  4 1864?; 1867?; 1869?: by lithographic transfer. As (3) with railway information up-dated throughout the issue period, coalfields named on the map, and the frame reduced from a triple to a single line. 'GEOLOGICAL ATLAS OF GREAT BRITAIN, from the GOVERNMENT SURVEY, &c., 33 Maps, Geologically coloured; with Description of the Geological Structure of Great Britain, its Mineral Products, &c. Cloth 10s. 6d. This Geological Atlas is unrivalled for the copiousness, clearness, and accuracy of its information.' A reduced version was also sold: 'Popular Atlas of Geology, illustrating and describing the Principles of the Science, with Coloured Sections, Views, Geological Map of England, &c., 2s.'

    e *Reynolds's geological atlas of Great Britain; comprising a series of maps geologically colored, preceded by a description of the geological structure of Great Britain, and the geological features of the several counties of England & Wales, mineral products &c; with sections & views. New edition.* (Lithographed title; the letterpress title is as 1889.)

    f Scotland replaced by a new map 'Engraved by Becker's patent process on steel' at a scale of 1 : 32m.

    g Both the engraver's signature and the publisher's imprint have been deleted. The plate-number now appears on the map face instead of outside the frame, and some numbers have been altered.

  5 1864?: by lithographic transfer, slightly smaller. As (4)

86: '*CAMBRIDGESHIRE*', '*Pigot & Son, Engravers Manch'.*', *published by Pigot & Cº, c.1841, in* A Pocket Topography and Gazetteer of England. *By courtesy of Jason Musgrave.*

without geological colouring. 'The geological features of the several counties are indicated on the maps by figures.' 'The Maps may be had Geologically Coloured, with a Geological Map of Scotland, and interesting Description, Statistics, &c., forming "THE GEOLOGICAL ATLAS OF GREAT BRITAIN", price 10s. 6d.'

   e *Portable atlas of England and Wales; with tourists' guide to the principal places of interest, fishing streams, finest views and scenery, &c. of each county. Thirty two maps.*

   f Scotland omitted.

6 1889: by lithographic transfer. As (4) with some revision of railway information and geological boundaries. A graticule showing the sheets of the 1″ Geological Survey has been added; an 'Index to Sheets of Geol Ordᶜᵉ Map' with an explanatory diagram is given; and 'interesting and instructive marginal notes' have been added outside the county border, e.g. 'Footprints of labyrinthodonts in keuper sandstone' (Cheshire) and 'Mammoth in drift at Leamington' (Warwick + Worcester). 'Advantage has been taken of the advanced state of the Geological Ordnance Survey, from which source the Geological Information given by the maps has, in the main been derived, to re-draw the Geological boundary lines; and the better to serve the convenience of those who may be seeking fuller information than it is possible to convey on the scale upon which this Atlas has been constructed, the sheet lines of the 1-inch Survey maps have, at the suggestion of an eminent Geologist been also drawn in, and indices inserted.'

   e *Reynolds's geological atlas of Great Britain, comprising a series of maps geologically coloured, from the best authorities; preceded by a description of the geological structure of Great Britain, and the geological features of the several counties of England and Wales, mineral products, &c. with sections and views. Second edition.*

   f Scotland replaced by a larger-scale map at the scale of 1 : 26·6m.

   g Publisher's imprint altered to: 'London: Published by James Reynolds & Sons, 174, Strand.' The small format of the atlas caused many imprints to be lost through cropping.

7 1904: by lithographic transfer. As (6) with printed colour and other alterations. 'Reynolds's *Geological Atlas* has long been regarded as a useful companion and guide to those, journeying on business or pleasure in Great Britain, who take interest in the geology of the country.... In the present volume the general plan of the older work has been followed ...'

   e *Stanford's geological atlas of Great Britain [Based on Reynolds's geological atlas] with plates of characteristic fossils preceded by a description of the geological structure of Great Britain and its counties; and of the features observable along the principal lines of railway by Horace B. Woodward, F.R.S., F.G.S.*

   f England + Wales replaced by Great Britain; and Scotland replaced by separate maps of North and South Scotland.

   g The maps now bear Stanford's publishing imprint.

   h Edward Stanford.

8 1907; 1913; 1914: by lithographic transfer. As (7). 'The maps in the original atlas were based to a large extent on those of the Geological Survey, and they have been revised, as far as the scale has permitted, from the later published maps of that institution, with the help also of Sir Archibald Geikie's Geological Map of Scotland....

The scope of this work has been enlarged by the addition of a sketch of the geological features of Ireland, its counties and main lines of railway; and the subject is illustrated by a geological map of the country ...'

   e *Stanford's geological atlas of Great Britain and Ireland....*

   f North and South Ireland added.

SAUNDERS, Trelawney William
Geographer *fl.* 1847-85

L

   a Sheet size: 672 × 964mm (26·9 × 38·6in).

   b Usually 1 : 2m.

   c 'INDEX to the TOWNLAND SURVEY of the COUNTY OF ...'

   d 'Key to CHARACTERS used in the Writing and CHARACTERISTICS which indicate the several BOUNDARIES with other TOPOGRAPHICAL REFERENCES ON THE SIX INCH ENGRAVINGS OF THE TOWNLAND SURVEY' set within a panel. 'SCALE OF PRICES.' set within a panel. 'TABLE OF AREAS' set within a series of panels.

Issues:

1 1847.

   e *Atlas of the counties of Ireland. Published by order of the Honourable Board of Ordnance. Coloured to indicate the extent of bog lands, for the Irish Amelioration Society.*

   f 32 Irish counties.

   g 'Engraved at the Ordnance Survey Office Phoenix Park under the direction of Lieutenant Larcom, R.E. ...' Dated between 1832 and 1846.

   h Trelawney Wm. Saunders.

STANFORD, Edward
Publisher *fl.* 1852-81

SELECT BIBLIOGRAPHY

AYLWARD, J. 'The retail distribution of Ordnance Survey maps and plans in the latter half of the nineteenth century—a map seller's view.' (*Cart. Journ.*, 8; 1971)

STANFORD, E. *The Ordnance Survey from a Business Point of View.* (Published for private circulation; 1891)

STANFORD, E. *Edward Stanford, 1902, with a note on the history of the firm from 1852.* (1902)

STANFORD, LT. COL. J.K. and GODFREY, E.G. *House of Edward Stanford Ltd. 1852-1952.* (1952)

LI

   a Variously sized maps on a page of 100 × 160mm (4 × 6·4in).

Issues:

1 1879: by lithographic transfer.

   e *A short geography of the British Islands. By John Richard Green ... and Alice Stopford Green. With maps.*

   f Europe; England; Scotland; Ireland. 23 physical and regional maps of the British Isles.

   g 'Stanford's Geogl Estabᵗ'.

   h Macmillan & Co.

LII

   a 81 × 137mm (3·25 × 5·5in). Some maps are double-page.

   b 1 : 13·3m., '... a uniform scale, to convey a just idea of the relative size of the counties.'

   c County name superimposed on topographical detail.

   d The lithographic transfers have been taken from the

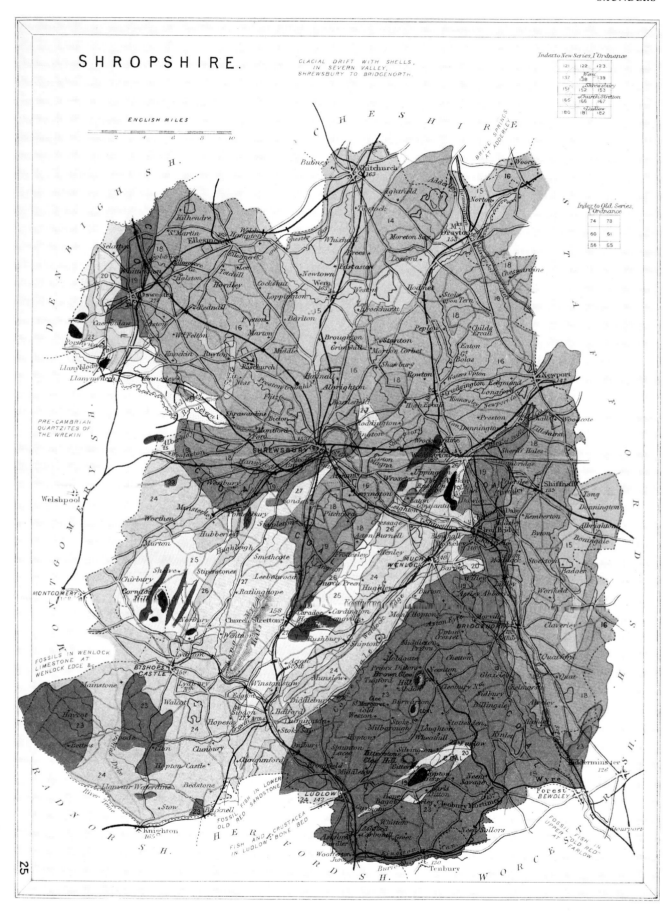

SHROPSHIRE.

GLACIAL DRIFT WITH SHELLS,
IN SEVERN VALLEY,
SHREWSBURY TO BRIDGENORTH.

ENGLISH MILES

87: 'SHROPSHIRE', 'London: Edward Stanford L.^{td.} 12, 13, &
14, Long Acre W.C.' A late issue, c.1904, by Stanford of James
Reynolds's geological county map first published as a county map in
1848 and first adapted as a geological map in 1860. Stanford added
printed colour.

plate of a map of England and Wales and a frame has been drawn round the map. Projecting place-names have been erased, and the names of adjacent counties redrawn so as to appear in full on the sections.

Issues:

1 1881: by lithographic transfer. 'English children should have such a familiar and intimate knowledge of the geography of their own country as would make a railway journey a delight; and this is especially the case in these days when "cheap trips" afford opportunities "to see for themselves" to persons whose eyes have been opened by previous instruction.'

e *The London geographical series. Geographical readers for elementary schools. By Charlotte M. Mason ... Book III for Standard IV. The counties of England. With thirty-six maps.*

f England + Wales. 34 sectional maps of England.

g 'Stanford's Geogᶦ Estabᶦ, London'. Some maps have a printer's signature printed from type.

h Edward Stanford.

The maps were still in use as 'The Ambleside Geography Books' in the early twentieth century: 'These "Geography Books" appeared originally as the "London Geographical Readers", and formed part of Mr. Stanford's "London Geographical Series".'

2 (June) 1886: by lithographic transfer. As (1) but 'The series of sixty-four maps accompanying the text, show, with considerable clearness, the divisions of the new electoral districts as fixed by the Boundary Commissioners, the Town plans being given upon an enlarged scale. Each map is coloured to show the political party with which the Members, representing the divisions, are associated, and thus affords at a glance an index to the representation of each county. Places which returned Conservatives are coloured yellow; Liberals, red; and Nationalists or Home Rulers, Green'. Overprinted colour with the names of the parliamentary divisions in red. Other colouring to show the representation of each parliamentary division is by hand. Addition of some railway information and the county title; and the revision of the number of members returned to Parliament. The town plans are titled 'THE PARLIAMENTARY DIVISIONS OF ...' and have the ward names overprinted in red. Some plans are double-page.

e *Stanford's handy atlas and poll book of the electoral divisions of Great Britain and Ireland....*

f England + Wales (two double-page maps); Scotland; Ireland. 21 single English counties on single sheets; five single English counties on two sheets each; Cambridge + Huntingdon; Hereford + Monmouth; Leicester + Rutland; Bedford, Hertford + Middlesex; Cumberland + Westmorland on two sheets; Northumberland + Durham on two sheets. Yorkshire (large folding). 10 Welsh counties grouped in pairs; Cardigan; Glamorgan. Belfast; Birmingham; Bradford; Bristol; Dublin; Edinburgh; Glasgow; Leeds; Liverpool; London; Manchester + Salford; Nottingham.

g Most sheets bear Stanford's imprint. Page number.

h Edward Stanford.

3 (October) 1886: by lithographic transfer. As (2): 'The general approval with which the first issue ... was received, proved that such a work was required, and it is believed that the present enlarged issue, combining as it does the polling returns for the last two General Elec-

tions, will form a most complete and convenient comparative record of the Parliamentary Representation of the United Kingdom.' The maps are now coloured in accordance with the new 1886 election results with Conservatives yellow, Liberals pink, Unionists slate, and Nationalists green. The map title is now dated 1886.

LIII

a Map sizes vary considerably because some maps are half-sheet and others are large folding. The standard sheet size is 176 × 238mm (7 × 9·5in).

b 1 : 7.7m. 'A scale of miles is engraved around the borders of all the County maps, by which a sufficiently accurate estimate of any distance within the county can be made readily by the eye without recourse to compasses or pencil.'

c County name.

d 'The County Maps ... show by red hard lines the parliamentary divisions of the county, and by red shading or ruled lines the limits of the parliamentary boroughs. Where a borough extends into a neighbouring county, as in the case of Bristol, the ruled lines are extended into such county, but the tint used for the county is confined to the county proper. Again where a portion of the county under inspection is included in a parliamentary borough situated in a neighbouring county, the portion so included is shown by ruled red lines, and a thin outline of red, also with ruled red lines, indicates the extent in the neighbouring county of such parliamentary borough. The names of towns and villages are engraved in various types, indicating by size and character the relative population. Railways and stations, canals and locks, and other particulars, are duly entered; all known British and Roman remains, such as camps, castles, and roads, are engraved in a special type easily recognisable, and the following particulars are given by means of script letters attached within brackets to the names of the cities and towns:—C. County Town; B. Municipal Borough; A. Assize Town; Q. Quarter Session; + Cathedral Town; M. Military Headquarters; P. Port of Entry. Other particulars are also given, as C.G.S., for Coast Guard Station; Lt.Ho., Light House; Light Vessels and Lifeboat Stations are also marked and named.' Printed colour.

Issues:

The following lithographic transfers were taken from the plates of a map of the whole country entitled 'STANFORD'S LIBRARY MAP OF ENGLAND & WALES CONSTRUCTED ON THE BASIS OF THE ORDNANCE SURVEY & THE CENSUS and adapted to the various branches of civil or religious administration. With Railways & Stations, Roads, Canals, Principal Parks, Antiquities and other Features of Interest', probably first published about 1881 and certainly still in use in 1909. Based on the Ordnance Survey maps adapted by the Boundary Commissioners for the Redistribution of Seats Act, 1885. Place-names projecting beyond the frame added on the transfer have been erased, and the names of adjacent counties have been re-drawn, sometimes by erasing place-names, so as to appear in full within the area of the map.

1 1885: by lithographic transfer.

e *Stanford's parliamentary county atlas and handbook of England and Wales containing also geological and oro-*

graphical maps of Great Britain, and physical, statistical, and administrative maps of England and Wales with lists of parishes, petty sessional divisions and unions, population tables, and other particulars relating to county statistics, local administration, and the new parliamentary constituencies.

f 23 thematic maps of England + Wales. 43 regional maps of England. Man; Jersey; Guernsey, Alderney, Sark, + Herm. Seven regional maps of Wales. 10 'Plans of all the Borough towns in England that return more than two members to Parliament, with their divisions into single membered constituencies', i.e. Bristol, Liverpool, Manchester, Nottingham, Wolverhampton, Birmingham, Hull, Leeds, Sheffield, Bradford. London—'The first shows the parliamentary boroughs and divisions of boroughs created by the Act of 1885 that be within the Metropolis Local Management Act Area; the second gives on an enlarged scale the topography of Central London, and shows also the new parliamentary boundaries; the third gives the distribution of population, showing the density of colours and degrees of colour, and is accompanied by a list of all the registration districts and subdistricts, with their population.'

g 'Stanford's Geographical Estab!..' Most maps have: 'London: Edward Stanford. 55 Charing Cross.' Plate-number at top right corner. 'The County Maps, 24 to 86 ... in accordance with usage are arranged in alphabetical order, but they are also numbered in agreement with the foregoing general Registration map, agreeing with the Census Tables and Poor Law publications.'

h Edward Stanford

2 28 maps, lithographically transferred at various scales, were also issued as 'STANFORD'S TWO SHILLING SERIES OF COUNTY GUIDES. Fcap. 8vo, Cloth, with Maps and Plans' published by Edward Stanford firstly from 55, Charing Cross and later from '26 & 27, Cockspur St., Charing Cross, S.W.' from the late 1870s to the 1890s. 'For the pedestrian, horseman, and bicyclist, a handy pocket guide is almost indispensable. Mr Stanford has estimated the situation correctly, and, as far as we can judge, has made most creditable provision. Nothing can be more convenient than the volumes of this little two shilling county series; the type, though closely printed, is clear, and they are nearly as light and twice as portable as a fairly filled cigar case.' The maps were entitled: 'MAP TO ACCOMPANY THE GUIDE TO ...', bore Stanford's imprint and signature, and were revised particularly in respect of railway information. Some transfers were taken from the 'LIBRARY MAP' and others from 'A MAP of ENGLAND & WALES Divided into Counties, Parliamentary Divisions & Dioceses SHEWING The principal Roads Railways Rivers & Canals and THE SEATS OF THE NOBILITY AND GENTRY WITH THE DISTANCE OF EACH TOWN from the GENERAL POST OFFICE, LONDON Projected from the Triangulation for the Survey made under the Direction of the Honourable The Board of Ordnance on a Scale of Five Miles to an Inch and corrected to THE PRESENT TIME Drawn by R. Creighton. Engraved by J. Dower. London Edward Stanford MAP SELLER & MAP MOUNTER TO HER MAJESTY'S STATIONERY OFFICE 6, Charing Cross. ADDITIONS TO 1860' which had been first published in 1855. The same maps

also appeared during the same period in 'STANFORD'S TWO-SHILLING SERIES OF TOURISTS' GUIDES. Fcap. 8vo, Cloth, with Maps, &c.' which contained information on 'Approaches, Means of Locomotion, Hotel and Inns, Lodgings, Outline Tours, Walking Tours'. 'The authors of these handy guides speak from adequate personal knowledge of their respective counties, and each guide is well provided with useful maps and plans. We should think these portable and carefully written County Guide-books would be welcome, not only to those who are compelled to consider the question of expense, but to those—and they are many—who object to the constant irritation of the more bulky guide-books, which are a burden in the hand, and cannot be put into any reasonable pocket.' Stanford also published in the 1880s 'JENKINSON'S PRACTICAL GUIDES. WITH MAPS AND VIEWS'—'The landmarks are pointed out as we ascend or descend, so that a wayfaring man, though a fool, cannot err in his ramble', and 'JENKINSON'S SMALLER PRACTICAL GUIDES, WITH MAPS AND VIEWS'—'His directions to the pedestrian are so minute and clear that it is hardly possible to go wrong, and his advice as to what to see and what to avoid is always worthy attention.'

TALLIS, John, & Co.
Publishers *fl. c.*1835-61

LIV

a Either single-page, 245 × 325mm (9·5 × 13in) or double-page 345 × 490mm (13·75 × 19·7in).

b av: 1 : 0·25-0·5m.

c Town name set within the frame.

d Decorative frame and several titled vignette scenes.

Issues:
Varying numbers of plans were issued, unindexed, in some copies of the atlas only.
   *c.*1850-60.

e *The illustrated atlas and modern history of the world. Geographical, political, commercial & statistical. Edited by R. Montgomery Martin. ...*

f Bath; Birmingham; Bradford; Brighton; Clifton + Bristol; Exeter; Leeds; London + environs; Liverpool; Manchester + environs; Newcastle-on-Tyne; Plymouth, Devonport + Stonehouse; Preston; Sheffield; Southampton; York. Aberdeen; Edinburgh; Glasgow; Perth. Belfast; Cork; Dublin.

g 'JOHN TALLIS & COMPANY, LONDON & NEW YORK.' The vignettes and plans bear the draughtsman's/engraver's signature of H. Bibby, D. Pound, J. Rapkin, or H. Winkles.

h J. & F. Tallis, and later 'The London Printing & Publishing Co.'

TYMMS, Samuel
Topographer *fl. c.*1831-42

LV

a 68 × 125mm (2.75 × 5in).

b av: 1 : 12·5m.

c County name.

d Note of distances from the county town and sometimes London.

Issues:

1 *c.*1831-42. The work was prepared in seven volumes covering the 'Circuits' of England. The separate 'Cir-

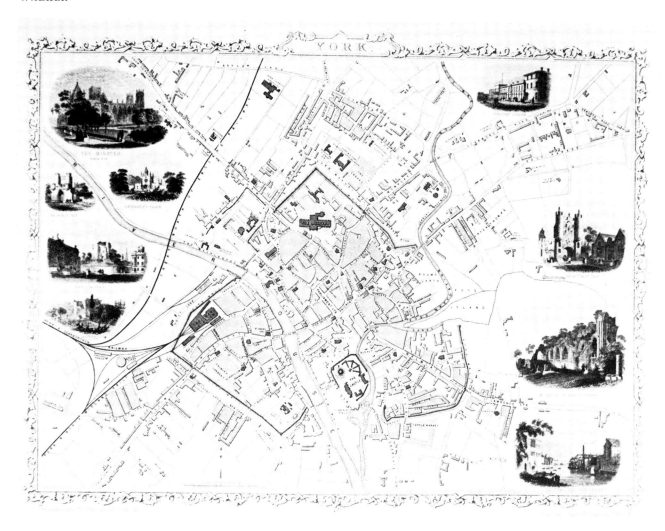

cuits' were published individually at 5s. each when prepared. Completion took an unexpectedly long time: '... some apology is due for the length of time which the work has been passing through the press. But ... it has been pursued, only as an instructive amusement, in the intervals, few and short, which could be snatched from literary labours of another kind, demanding close and continued application....' However, the long preparation was sustained by the work's good reception: 'As a directory to every thing that can be seen in the Counties on which it treats, it ought to occupy a corner in the portmanteau of every tourist ...'; 'A remarkably neat and intelligible Map is prefixed to the account of each County ...'; 'Our antiquaries are becoming a very sensible and useful generation; they have put aside their old cumbrous quartos, and left off their garrulous gossip— they now cut their coats according to the fashion, and model themselves upon the Utilitarian system of the nineteenth century.' Some slight revisions during the issue period.

e *The family topographer: being a compendious account of the antient and present state of the counties of England. By Samuel Tymms.*

f 38 English counties (no Middlesex). East; West; North Ridings. The final volume should have contained maps of Middlesex and London, but bears signs of rushed production.

g Publisher's imprint of B. Nichols & Son, dated between 1831 and 1842.

h J.B. Nichols & Son.

2 1842?: As (1), but old stock was sometimes used since

maps in an earlier state than (1) were included in some copies.

e *Camden's Britannia epitomized and continued; being a compendious account of the antient and present state of the counties of England. By Samuel Tymms.*

h Henry G. Bohn.

WALKER, John & Charles
Engravers and cartographers *fl.* 1825–*c.*1870

LVI

a 320 × 390mm (13 × 15·5in).

b av: 1 : 4m.

c County name set within a panel surmounting the signature 'BY J. & C. WALKER'.

d Numbered reference key to administrative divisions. Listings of boroughs, places of election, and polling places. Statistical information. Railways actually built were usually marked in red by hand and did not necessarily correspond with those printed on the map; this allowed the use of old stock in many atlas copies.

Issues:

The various states were probably issued individually, progressively and continuously, from 1835 to 1890 folding in covers labelled 'Walker's ... Price 2s. 6d.'. Some were also issued *c*.1842 by G.F. Cruchley under the cover title 'New map of ...'. Old stock was frequently used in later atlases, and maps also appeared in other works. The maps appear to have been progressively revised throughout, particularly in respect of railway and statistical information. Issued as boxed sets from 1837 as *Walker's county atlas*.

1 1837.
  e *To their Royal Highnesses the Duchess of Kent & the Princess Victoria, this British atlas comprising separate maps of every county in England ... compiled from the maps of the Board of Ordnance and other trigonometrical surveys, is ... dedicated by ... J. and C. Walker.*
  f England + Wales. 39 English counties. East; West; North Ridings. North; South Wales: (two sheets each).
  g Publisher's imprint of Longman, Orme, & Rees, sometimes in partnership with Brown or Hurst (despite his retirement from the partnership in 1826!), dated between 1835 and 1837. Some imprints were later redated to 1837.
  h Longman, Rees & Co. and J. & C. Walker.
2 1837. As (1) with a few minor revisions.
  e *To Her most excellent Majesty Queen Victoria, and to Her Royal Highness the Duchess of Kent, this British atlas....*
3 1839; 1840; 1841; 1842; 1843?; 1844?; 1845; 1846?; 1849?; 1851. As (2) with minor revisions, particularly of railway information, being carried out during the issue period. From *c*.1849 place-names were revised to allow transfers taken for *Hobson's fox-hunting atlas* to show the meeting places of hounds.
  f Scotland and Ireland added from *c*.1845.
  g Some imprints were altered and/or progressively redated during the course of these issues and some dates were erased from *c*.1849.
4 1852; 1854; 1856; 1860; 1861; 1862; 1864; 1865?; 1869; 1870; 1872; 1873; 1877; 1879. As (3) with minor revisions, particularly of railway information, throughout the issue period. Maps are found in John Murray's 'Handbooks' issued in the late 1870s, possibly being replacements for the original maps which were easily lost from the 'pocket at the end'.
  g The imprint was altered on some maps to accommodate the Walkers' move to 9, Castle Street, Holborn. This alteration was made progressively during the course of the issues; however, other maps bear the original imprint without date, some bear a variation of it, and some are without imprint.
5 *c*.1880–early '90s: by lithographic transfer. Copies of the atlas continued on sale until the early 1890s. As (4) with minor revisions, particularly of railway information. After 1885 atlases were issued with a printed note of the revised parliamentary representation stuck over the list of polling and election places.
  g Some maps have had the imprint deleted and some have had the address altered to 37, Castle Street.
6 1884: by lithographic transfer. As (5) with the revision of railway information, the addition of administrative and topographical information shown by coloured signs listed in the key, the deletion of the title and the cartographers' names, and added overprinted colour. The new title gives the county name and 'LETTS, SON & C? LIMITED'. The statistics, table of hundreds, note of boroughs, list of places of polling and election, and note of borough boundaries have all been deleted and replaced by a list of statistics with a note of the county

town. A new key, including a new sign for dangerous hills, a new list of hundreds, a graticule with reference letters, and notes of population, area, rental, inhabited houses, poor rates, paupers, and manufactures have all been added. Evidence suggests that loose sheets were later sold individually by James Wyld since copies are known with the publisher's signature and imprint obscured by printed labels bearing his imprint.
  e *Lett's popular county atlas. Being a complete series of maps delineating the whole surface of England and Wales, with special and original features....*
  g 'LETTS, SON & Co. LIMITED, LONDON BRIDGE, E.C.'.
  h Letts, Son & Co.
7 1887: by lithographic transfer. As (6) with minor revisions, particularly the addition of the new 1885 parliamentary divisions.
  h Mason & Payne.
Lithographic transfers were taken from the current states of the Walkers' county maps for *Hobson's fox-hunting atlas* and the folding hunting maps issued separately.

Issues:

8 1849?: by lithographic transfer. The names of the hunts with numbers referring to the maps of adjacent areas have been drawn on the stone in outline lettering and the boundaries of the hunts have been marked. Black dots, with underlining of the appropriate place-names, have been added throughout the maps and this sign is explained as 'PLACES OF THE MEETING OF FOXHOUNDS'. The outline lettering is generally hand coloured.
  e *Hobson's fox-hunting atlas; containing separate maps of every county in England ... comprising forty-two maps.... Compiled from the maps of the Board of Ordnance, and other surveys. By J. and C. Walker.*
  f 39 English counties. East; West; North Ridings.
  g 'Published by Longman, Orme, Rees & C? Paternoster Row London.' Hurst is sometimes also listed! Plate-number.
  h J. & C. Walker.
9 1850?; 1851?; 1852?; 1855?: by lithographic transfer. As (8) but the names of the hunts and reference numbers have been removed from the stone and the map has been overprinted in blue with the names of the hunts. Minor revisions.
  g A few imprints were altered *c*.1855 to take account of the Walkers' move to 9, Castle Street, Holborn.
10 1860?; 1866?; 1868?; 1869?; 1875?; 1878?: by lithographic transfer. As (9) with minor revisions, particularly the addition of railways progressively during these issues and the addition of an explanation of railway and station signs *c*.1866. Some maps had hunts revised and added *c*.1866, *c*.1868, and *c*.1869.
  g Further imprints were revised during the issue period to 9, Castle Street, Holborn, but others bear the original imprint without date, or a variation of it. From *c*.1869 maps began to appear with the address given as 37, Castle Street and the imprint sometimes dated.
11 1880?; 1882?; 1886?: by lithographic transfer. As (10) with some hunts slightly revised during these issues.
  e *Walker's fox-hunting atlas; containing separate maps of every county in England ... comprising forty-two maps ... compiled from the maps of the Board of Ordnance, and other surveys. By J. and C. Walker.*

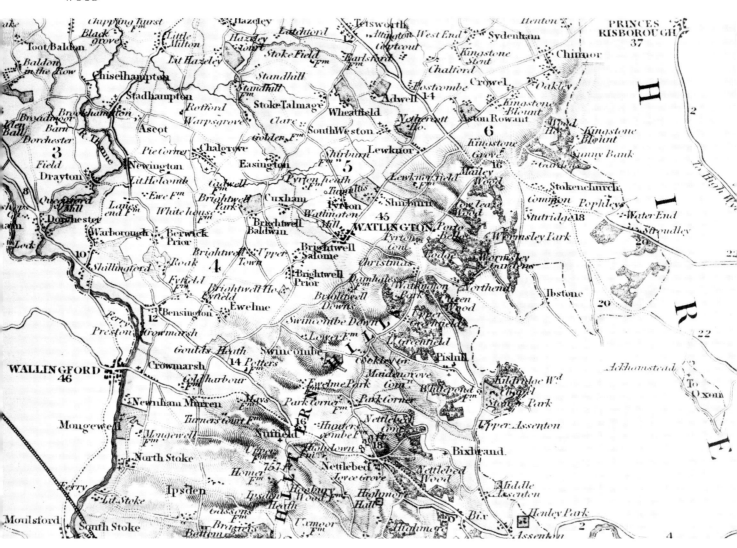

89: *John Walker Junior's experience of engraving charts for the East India Company combined with a family tradition of high-class official engraving work to create a partnership responsible for some of the finest engraving of the Victorian age both for its own publications and for such other map-makers as the Greenwood brothers.*

i *Detail: Oxfordshire, engraved by J. & C. Walker, from their* British Atlas, *c.1839. By courtesy of Jason Musgrave.*
ii *Wiltshire, engraved by J. & C. Walker, published by Longman, Rees, Orme, Brown & Co., 1836, in the* British Atlas.

12 1892; 1894; 1895: by lithographic transfer. As (11) but some maps were revised during the issues including the addition of railway information, the revision of parliamentary information, and the erasure of the polling- and election-place lists, the note of the sign for borough boundaries, and the references to the parliamentary representation of the boroughs.

  e Atlas title slightly altered in 1894/5: *Walker's foxhunting atlas; ... compiled from the maps of the Board of Ordnance. By J. and C. Walker.*

  g Some imprints have been deleted and others now give the address as 37, Furnival Street, Holborn.

WOOD, J.W.
'Lithographer & Map Publisher' of '1, Sedley Place, Oxford Street.' *fl. c.1879*

Wood embarked on the production of roughly lithographed outline county maps, bearing his imprint and the note 'WOOD'S SERIES OF COUNTY MAPS FOR SCHOOLS', 'Price One Penny', but only Essex, Kent, Middlesex, and Surrey seem to have appeared.

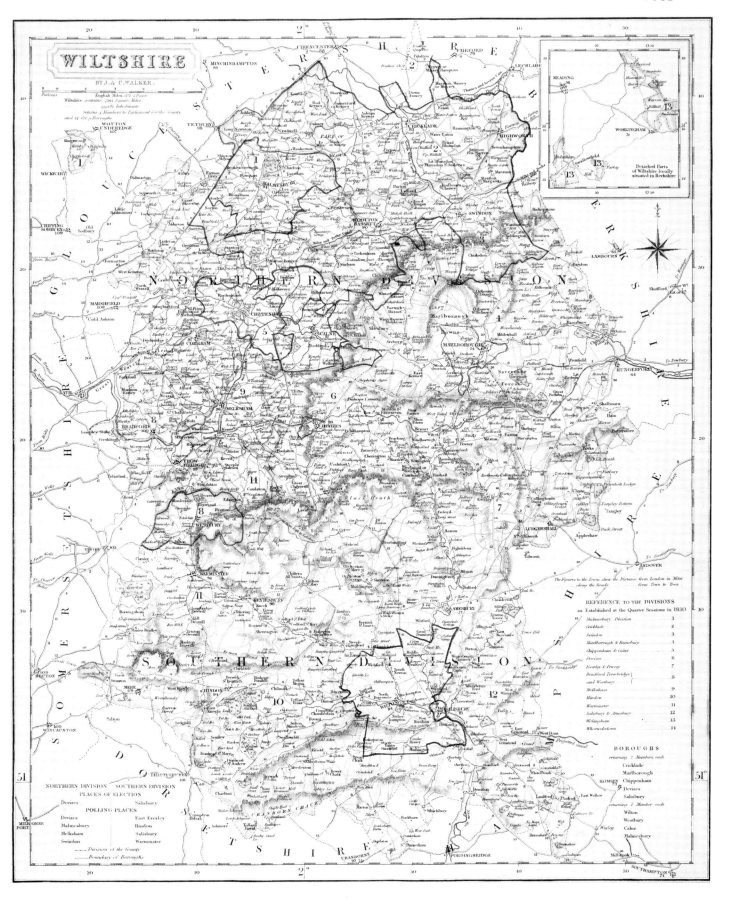

Notes

Preface

1 Rowse, A.L.: *The England of Elizabeth* (1950).
2 Advertisement for *Mogg's Improved Edition of Paterson's Roads* (1826).
3 Antony à Wood quoted by Samuel Tymms in *The Family Topographer* (1832).

Introduction

1 Harley, J.B.: 'The Society of Arts and the surveys of English counties 1759-1809' (*Journal of the Royal Society of Arts*, 112, 1963-4).
2 Andrews, J.H.: 'The French school of Dublin land surveyors' (*Irish Geography*, 5, 1967).
3 Fortescue, Sir J.: *The Correspondence of George III* (1927). Memoir from Roy to George III.
4 Close, Col. Sir C.: *The Early Years of the Ordnance Survey* (1926). Sir Joseph Banks when presenting the Copley Medal to Major James Rennell, 1791.
5 Adams, I.H.: 'The Edinburgh school of geographical engravers' (unpublished).
6 Andrews, J.H.: *History in the Ordnance Map. An Introduction for Irish Readers* (1974).

I Production

1 Farquharson, Sir J.: 'Twelve years' work of the Ordnance Survey' (*Geog. Journ.*, XV, 1900).
2 Robinson, A.H.: 'Mapmaking and map printing: the evolution of a working relationship' (in Woodward, D. (ed.): *Five Centuries of Map Printing* (1975)).
3 Farquharson, Sir J.: op. cit.
4 Advertisement (1787).
5 Stanford, E.: *The Ordnance Survey from a Business Point of View* (1891).
6 Portlock, Lt. Col. J.E.: *Memoir of the Life of Major-General Colby* (1869).
7 Andrews, J.H.: *A Paper Landscape: The Ordnance Survey in Nineteenth-Century Ireland* (1975).
8 Official Catalogue to the Exhibition (1851).
9 Ordnance Survey: *Account of the Methods and Processes Adopted for the Production of the Maps of the Ordnance Survey* (1875).
10 *Atlas to accompany the Second Report of the Commissioners ... Railways for Ireland* (1838).
11 Portlock, Lt. Col. J.E.: op. cit.
12 Ordnance Survey Office, Southampton, Letter Book, f. 340.
13 Portlock, Lt. Col. J.E.: op. cit.
14 Ordnance Survey: *Account of the Methods and Processes Adopted for the Production of the Maps of the Ordnance Survey* (2nd ed., 1902).
15 Advertisement to the 'Improved Map of England & Wales' 1819.
16 *Report of the progress of the Ordnance Survey to 31-12-1870*.
17 Leach, G.A.: Obituary notice of Larcom (*Royal Engineers Journal*, 1879).

18 Gardiner, L.: *Bartholomew 150 years* (1976).
19 Farquharson, Sir J.: op. cit.
20 *Inquiry into Present Condition of Ordnance Survey: Minutes of Evidence* (House of Commons Papers, 1893-4, LXXII). Evidence of James Wyld.
21 Senefelder, A.: *A Complete course of lithography* (1819).
22 Philip, G.: *The Story of the Last Hundred Years* (1934).
23 Senefelder, A.: op. cit.
24 Philip, G.: op. cit.
25 Senefelder, A.: op. cit.
26 Close, Sir C. & Winterbotham, Col. H. St. J.L. (eds.): *Text Book of Topographical and Geographical Surveying* (1925).
27 Gardiner, L.: op. cit.
28 Senefelder, A.: op. cit.
29 Gardiner, L.: op. cit.
30 Senefelder, A.: op. cit.
31 Burch, R.M.: *Fifty Years Recollections of an Old Bookseller* (1837).
32 Stannard, J.: *The Art Exemplar* (c.1859).
33 Close, Sir C. & Winterbotham, Col. H.St. J.L. (eds.): op. cit.
34 Stannard, J.: op. cit.
35 Patent taken out by William Siemans & Joseph Woods in June 1844 for 'Improvements in producing and multiplying copies of designs and impressions of printed or written surfaces.'
36 *Report of the progress of the Ordnance Survey to 31-12-82*.
37 'Curious specimen of polyautography, or lithography' (*Gentleman's Magazine*, 85, 1815).
38 Smith Williams, W.: 'On lithography' (*Society of Arts (London) Transactions*, May 1849?, part 2).
39 Wilme, R.P.: *A Hand Book for Plain and Ornamental Mapping* (1846).
40 Harris, E.M.: 'Miscellaneous map printing processes in the nineteenth century' (in Woodward, D. (ed.): *Five Centuries of Map Printing* (1975)).
41 *Report of the progress of the Ordnance Survey to 31-12-82*.
42 Osborne, J.W.: 'On a new photo-lithographic process' (*Transactions of the Philosophical Institute*, 1859).
43 Scott, Capt. A. de C.: *On Photozincography and Other Photographic Processes Employed at the Ordnance Survey Office, Southampton* (1862).
44 *Report of the progress of the Ordnance Survey to 31-12-82*.
45 Wakeman, G.: 'Lithography, photography and map printing' (in *Aspects of Victorian Lithography*, 1970). Quoted from the report of a committee chaired by Sir Roderick Murchison, 1858.
46 *Report of the progress of the Ordnance Survey, 1859*.
47 Ordnance Survey: *Account of the Methods and Processes Adopted for the Production of the Maps of the Ordnance Survey* (1875). Introduction by James.
48 *Report of the progress of the Ordnance Survey to 31-12-82*.
49 Seymour, W.A. (ed.): *A History of the Ordnance Survey* (1980).
50 *Report of the progress of the Ordnance Survey to 31-12-82*.
51 Close, Sir C. & Winterbotham, Col. H. St. J.L. (eds.): op. cit.

II Paper
1 Curwen, H. *A History of Booksellers*. (1873).
2 McCarthy, J.: *A History of Our Own Times*. (1892).
3 *Inquiry into Present Condition of Ordnance Survey: Minutes of Evidence* (House of Commons Papers, 1893–4, LXXII). Evidence of James Wyld.
4 Stanford, E.: *The Ordnance Survey from a Business Point of View* (1891).

III Presentation and Content
1 Advertisement for 'Bartholomew's Half-Inch to Mile Maps'.
2 Fullarton, A. (publ.): *The Parliamentary Gazetteer of England and Wales* (1842).
3 Cary J.: *Cary's British Traveller* (1803). 'Statement of the Proceedings'.
4 Paterson, D.: *A New and Accurate Description of all the Direct and Principal Cross Roads in England and Wales* (13th. ed., 1803). 'Advertisement'.
5 Williams, E. & Mudge, W.: 'An account of the trigonometrical survey carried on in 1791, 1792, 1793, and 1794' (*Philosophical Transactions of the Royal Society*, LXXXV, 1795).
6 Seymour, W.A. (ed.) *A History of the Ordnance Survey* (1980). Quoted from the Military Commission of 1811.
7 Williams, E. & Mudge, W.: op. cit.
8 *Leeds Mercury*, 27-7-1816.
9 Select Committee on Railway Bills (Ireland) (1845). Evidence of Sir J. Macneill, Q.470, and of W.S. Moorsom, Q.540.
10 Advertisement (1810).
11 Letter from Mudge to the Board of Ordnance, 28-9-1816.
12 Notice sent to the 'Offices of the Times, Morning Advertiser, Courier & London Gazette' on 28-2-1816 by the Board of Ordnance.
13 Ordnance Survey Letter Book. f142.
14 Stanford, E.: *The Ordnance Survey from a Business Point of View* (1891).
15 Treasury Minute issued in August 1887.
16 Wilson's reply to Henry Tipping Crook's criticisms of the Ordnance Survey, given firstly in a lecture to the British Association in Leeds in 1890.
17 Oliver, R.: Private communication.
18 Advertisement (1790).
19 Advertisement (1790).
20 Prospectus for 'A SERIES OF NEW MAPS OF THE COUNTIES OF ENGLAND AND WALES, From actual Survey, BY C. AND J. GREENWOOD',25-11-1822.
21 Robinson, A.H.: 'The 1837 maps of Henry Drury Harness' (*Geog. Journ.*, 121, 1955).
22 Report of the Poor Law Commission, 1834.
23 Lipman, V.D.: *Local Government Areas 1834–1945*. (1949).
24 Report of the Local Government Boundaries Commission, 1888.
25 *Philips' Handy Administrative Atlas* (*c*.1908).
26 *Parliamentary Papers, Accounts and Papers*, XXI (1825).
27 Report of the Local Government Boundaries Commission, 1888.
28 *Report of the progress of the Ordnance Survey to 31-12-82*.
29 Report of the Local Government Boundaries Commission, 1888.
30 *Parliamentary Papers. Estimates & Accounts*, XXI (1826).
31 Report of the Boundary Commissioners for England and Wales, 1868.
32 Report of the Local Government Boundaries Commission, 1888.
33 Public Record Office WO 47/2385, 26-10-1802.
34 Cary, J.: *Cary's New and Correct English Atlas* (1787). 'Advertisement'.
35 Cary sent a map-proof folded in half, with a letter written on the reverse, dated 4-3-1823, to Sir John Dashwood.
36 Greenwood, C. & J.: *Surrey Described* (1823).
37 James, Sir H.: *Account of the Field Surveying and the Preparation of the Manuscript Plans of the Ordnance Survey* (1873).
38 Seymour, W.A. (ed.): *op. cit.*

39 Close, Sir C.: *The Early Years of the Ordnance Survey* (1926).
40 Jones, Y.: 'Aspects of relief portrayal on 19th century British military maps (*Cart. Journ.*, II, 1974).
41 Shepherd, T.: *William Smith: His Maps and Memoirs* (1920). Appendix: 'A: W. Smith's Claims'.
42 Carmichael-Smyth, J.: *Memoir upon the Topographical System of Colonel Van Gorkum* (1828).
43 Letter from William Mudge dated 8-9-1803.
44 Andrews, J.H.: *A Paper Landscape: The Ordnance Survey in Nineteenth-Century Ireland* (1975).
45 Carmichael-Smyth, J.: op. cit.
46 *Committee on Sale of Ordnance Survey Maps: Minutes of Evidence* (House of Commons Papers, 1896, LXVIII). Evidence of George Washington Bacon.
47 Skelton, R.A. 'The Military Survey of Scotland' (*Royal Scottish Geographical Society Special Publication*, no. I, 1967). Description of the surviving fair-copies of William Roy's drawings.
48 *Inquiry into Present Condition of Ordnance Survey: Minutes of Evidence* (House of Commons Papers, 1893–4, LXXII). Evidence of James Wyld.
49 Review of the 'Census of the population of Ireland in 1841' (*The Athenaeum*, 13-1-1844).
50 Bacon, G.W.: *Bacon's "Excelsior" Memory-Map Atlas* (1893). 'General Directions for Drawing Memory Maps'.
51 Advertisement for 'Bradshaw's Second Edition of his New Map of the Railways of Great Britain' (1845).
52 Bacon, G.W.: *Catalogue of Bacon's Maps, Atlases, & Globes* (1912).
53 Close, Sir C. and Winterbotham, Col. H. St. J.L. (eds.): *Text Book of Topographical and Geographical Surveying* (1925).
54 Gardiner, L.: *Bartholomew 150 years* (1976).
55 Ordnance Survey: *Account of the Methods and Processes Adopted for the Production of the Maps of the Ordnance Survey* (1875).
56 *Parliamentary Debates*, 1848. Vol 97, cols. 1014–16.
57 *Parliamentary Debates*, 1868. Vol. 193, cols. 962–3.
58 *Parliamentary Debates*, 1848. Vol. 96, col. 419.
59 Johnston, A.K.: *The National Atlas* (1843). Note accompanying Gustav Kombst's 'Ethnographic Map of Europe'.
60 Smith, W.: *A Memoir to the Map and Delineation of the Strata of England and Wales, with Part of Scotland* (1815).
61 Report to the Geological Society in 1840 (*Proc. Geol. Soc.*, Vol III, 1840).
62 Phillips, J.: *Memoirs of William Smith, Ll.D.* (1844).
63 Col. Sir Charles Wilson in a paper on the methods and processes of the Ordnance Survey read to the Society of Arts, 18-2-1891.
64 *Inquiry into Present Condition of Ordnance Survey: Minutes of Evidence* (House of Commons Papers, 1893–4, LXXII). Evidence of James Wyld.
65 *Committee on Sale of Ordnance Survey Maps: Minutes of Evidence* (House of Commons Papers, 1896, LXVIII). Evidence of Col. J. Farquharson.
66 Andrews, J.H.: op cit. (1974).
67 *Committee on Sale of Ordnance Survey Maps: Minutes of Evidence* (House of Commons Papers, 1896, LXVIII). Evidence of Col. J. Farquharson.
68 Philip, G.: *The Story of the Last Hundred Years* (1934).
69 Ordnance Survey: Correspondence concerning the coloured 1″ map (1899–1903) and the removal of the steam press to Southampton (1904–5).
70 Booth, C.: *Life and Labour of the People in London* (1892–97).
71 Advertisement (1880).
72 Gardiner, L.: op cit.

IV Purpose
1 Adams, I.H.: *Descriptive List of Plans in the Scottish Record Office* (Vol. I, 1966).
2 Hull, F.: *Catalogue of Estate Maps 1590–1840 in the Kent County Archives Office* (1973).
3 Advertisement (*c*.1780).
4 Advertisement (*c*.1880).

5 Select Committee on Survey of Parishes (Tithe Commutation Act) (*Parliamentary Papers*, VI, 1837).

6 Advertisement (1896).

7 Gardiner, L.: *Bartholomew 150 years* (1976).

8 Advertisement (*c*.1912).

9 *Geographical Journal*: Obituary of Trelawney William Saunders by John Bolton (Sept. 1910).

10 M'Leod, W.: *Physical Atlas of Great Britain and Ireland* (1861). Introduction.

11 National Society for Promoting the Education of the Poor: *Maps Illustrative of the Physical and Historical Geography of the British Empire* (*c*.1852).

12 British Museum: *The British Museum Catalogue of Printed Maps, Charts and Plans* (1967).

13 Lister, M.: 'An ingenious proposal for a new sort of maps of countrys' (*Philosophical Transactions of the Royal Society*, 1684).

14 Woodward, H.B.: *The History of the Geological Society of London* (1907).

15 Maton, W.: *Observations Relative Chiefly to the Natural History, Picturesque Scenery, and Antiquities, of the Western Counties of England, Made in the Years 1794 and 1796* (1797).

16 *Report of the Select Committee on the Ordnance Survey* (*Scotland*), 1851.

17 Flett, Sir J. Smith: *The First Hundred Years of the Geological Survey of Great Britain* (1937). Quoting Sir Archibald Geikie.

18 Smith, W.: Prospectus for 'A Map of the Strata of England and Wales with Part of Scotland' (1815).

19 A note written by William Smith, dated Jan. 1796, while staying at the Swan Inn near Dunkerton.

20 Fitton, W.H.: 'Notes on the history of English geology' (*Philosophical Magazine*, I, 1832).

21 Boud, R.C.: 'The early development of British geological maps' (*Imago Mundi*, 27, 1975).

22 Prof. Adam Sedgwick when presenting the Wollaston Medal of the Geological Society in 1831.

23 Smith, W.: op. cit. (1815).

24 Advertisement (1823).

25 Presidential address of George Greenough to the Geological Society in 1834.

26 Sir Roderick Murchison in accepting the Geological Society's Wollaston Medal on behalf of De la Beche in February 1855.

27 Report by Sir Archibald Geikie in 1855.

28 Report of the Wharton Committee, 1901.

29 White, T. Pilkington: 'The romance of state mapping' (*Blackwood's Edinburgh Magazine*, 144, 1888).

30 *Second Report of the Commissioners ... Railways for Ireland* (1838). Appendix III.

31 Petermann, A.: 'Population Distribution Map of England' (1852).

32 Advertisement (1881).

33 'Lander's Electoral District Map of the City and County of Bristol', 1840.

34 'A Map of England & Wales, shewing the state of the representation before the Reform Bill of 1832. As amended by the Reform Bill of 1832 and the Government Reform Bill as proposed by Lord John Russell', 1860.

35 *Census of Ireland, 1841*. Plate 2.

36 'Explanation' of Hume's map of Liverpool accompanying his *Condition of Liverpool* (1858).

37 Lazarus, M.: *Victorian Social Conditions and Attitudes, 1837–71* (1969). Quoted from *The Times*.

38 *Report on the Sanitary Condition of the Labouring Population* (1842).

39 Shapter, Dr T.: *The History of Cholera in Exeter in 1832* (1849).

40 Petermann, A.: 'Cholera map of the British Isles showing the districts attacked in 1831, 1832 and 1833' (1852).

41 Snow, Dr J.: *On the Mode of Communication of Cholera* (2nd ed., 1855).

42 Perry, R.: *Facts and Observations on the Sanitary State of Glasgow During the Last Year; with statistical tables of the late epidemic, shewing the connection between poverty, disease, and crime* (1844).

43 Engels, F.: *The Condition of the Working Classes* (1844).

44 *The Times*, March 1861.

45 Mogg, E.: *Mogg's New Picture of London and Visitors' Guide to its Sights* (1847).

46 'Plan, presented to The House of Commons, of a Street proposed from Charing Cross to Portland Place, leading to the Crown Estate in Mary-le-Bone Park,—On a reduced scale' (1813).

47 'A Plan of the intended New Street between Pall Mall, opposite Carlton House, and Portland Place', by J. Booth (1818).

48 Reader, W.J.: *Victorian England* (1974). Quoting Joseph Chamberlain.

49 Advertisement (1862).

50 Hyde, R.: *Printed Maps of Victorian London 1851–1900* (1975).

51 Advertisement (1840).

52 Advertisement (1840).

53 Advertisement (1858).

54 Mogg, E.: op. cit. (1847).

55 Hodgson, T.: *London at a Glance* (1859). Introduction.

56 Fry, H.: *London* (1892). Title-page.

57 Hodgson, T.: op. cit.

58 Reader, W.J.: op. cit.

59 Bruce, J.: *The History of Brighton, with the latest improvements to 1835* (4th. ed., 1835).

60 Advertisement (1850).

61 Gardiner, L.: op. cit.

62 Hunter, Rev. H.: *History of London and its Environs* (1811).

63 Owen, H.: *The Staffordshire Potter* (1901).

64 Mogg, E.: op. cit. (1847).

65 Advertisement for 'Philips' Excursionist's Map of the Environs of London' (1881).

66 *Census of Great Britain, 1851*.

67 Advertisement (1873).

68 Bradshaw, G.: *Bradshaw's Hand-Book to the Manufacturing Districts of Great Britain* (1853).

69 Fisher, H. (publ.): *Fisher's County Atlas of England and Wales* (*c*.1845).

70 Advertisement (1850).

71 Charles Pearson, solicitor to the City of London, in evidence to the Commission on Metropolitan Termini, 1846.

72 *Official Time Table of the Norwich Electric Tramways* (*c*.1901).

73 Advertisement (*c*.1864).

74 Advertisement (1847).

75 Bacon, G. W.: 'Railway and Station Map of London and Environs' (1896).

76 Cruchley, G.F.: 'Cruchley's New Plan of London in Miniature' (1830).

77 Advertisement (1881).

78 Advertisement for Mogg's *Omnibus Guide and Metropolitan Carriage Time Table* (1847).

79 Advertisement (*c*.1880).

80 *Royal Commission on Transport, Final Report*. (Cmd. 3751, 1930).

81 Defoe, D.: *Tour Through the Whole Island of Great Britain* (1724–7).

82 Cary, J.: *Survey of the High Roads from London* (1808). Map of London–St Albans.

83 Ibid. 'Advertisement'.

84 Leigh, S.: *New Picture of London; or a view of the Political, Religious, and Moral State of the British Metropolis: presenting a Luminous Guide to the Stranger, on all subjects connected with General Information, Business or Amusement* (1824–5).

85 Smith, C.: *Actual Survey of the Roads from London to Brighthelmstone* (1800). 'Explanation'.

86 Cary, J.: *Survey of the High Roads from London* (1790). 'Advertisement'.

87 Savage, C.I.: *An Economic History of Transport* (1959).

88 Black, A. & C.: *Black's Picturesque Tourist of Scotland* (4th ed., 1845). Preface.

89 *North and North-Eastern Routes. British High Roads. Arranged for the Use of Tourists.* (1877).

90 Bacon, G.W.: 'Bacon's County Map of Sussex with parts of Adjoining Counties' (c.1898).

91 Bacon, G.W.: 'Bacon's Map of Buckinghamshire Revised according to the latest Ordnance Survey Divided into Five Mile Squares' (c.1898).

92 *Committee on Sale of Ordnance Survey Maps: Minutes of Evidence* (House of Commons Papers, LXVIII, 1896). Evidence of G.W. Bacon.

93 Advertisement (c.1883).

94 *Committee on Sale of Ordnance Survey Maps: Minutes of Evidence* (House of Commons Papers, LXVIII, 1896). Evidence of J.C. Rogers.

95 Ibid. Evidence of F. Hall.

96 Rolls, C.S.: Article on motor vehicles in the *Encyclopaedia Britannica* (1911).

97 Advertisement for 'Taunt's Map of the River Thames, from Oxford to London' (c.1875).

98 Bradshaw, G.: 'G. Bradshaw's Map of Canals, Navigable Rivers Railways &c. in the Southern Counties of England' (c.1830).

99 Bradshaw, G.: 'G. Bradshaw's Map of the Canals and Navigable Rivers of the Midland Counties of England' (1829). Appendix.

100 Bradshaw, G.: op. cit. (c.1830).

101 Cary, J.: Advertisement for *Inland Navigation; or Select Plans of the Several Navigable Canals* (1795–).

102 Mogg, E.: op. cit. (1847).

103 Mogg, E.: Advertisement for 'Mogg's Map of Steam Navigation'. (1840).

104 Mogg, E.: op. cit. (1847).

105 Mogg, E.: op. cit. (1840).

106 Advertisement (1839).

107 Advertisement (1850).

108 Lumsden, J. & Co. (publ.): *The Steamboat Companion and Stranger's Guide to the Western Islands and Highlands of Scotland* (1820).

109 Bartholomew, J.: *Gazetteer of the British Isles* (1887).

110 Select Committee on Railway Bills (Ireland) (*Parliamentary Papers*, X, 1845). Evidence of W.S. Moorsom.

111 Andrews, J.H.: *A Paper Landscape: The Ordnance Survey in Nineteenth-Century Ireland* (1975).

112 *The Builder*, iii, 22-11-1845.

113 Seymour, W.A. (ed.): *A History of the Ordnance Survey* (1980).

114 *Annual Register*, 30-11-1845.

115 Gardiner, L.: op. cit.

116 'Tallis's Railway Map of Great Britain' (c.1855). Titlepiece.

117 Leaflet issued by John Airey in 1894.

118 'Official Railway Map of Gloucestershire & Oxfordshire Districts. Prepared and Published at the Railway Clearing House London, 1897.' Imprint.

119 Porter, G.R.: *Progress of the Nation* (1851).

120 *Railway Returns*, 1913.

121 Gardiner, L.: op. cit.

122 Andrews, J.H.: op. cit. (1975).

123 Bradshaw, G.: *Bradshaw's Railway Gazette*, Nov. 1845.

124 Bradshaw, G.: 'Bradshaw's Map of the Railways of Great Britain' (1839).

125 Advertisement (1847).

126 Advertisement (c.1867).

127 Royde Smith, G.: *A History of Bradshaw* (1939).

128 Announcement in *Bradshaw's Railway Gazette*, 12-7-1845.

129 Mogg, E.: *Mogg's Hand-Book for Railway Travellers* (1840). Title-page.

130 Address in *Bradshaw's Railway Time Tables* (1839).

131 Black, A. & C.: *Black's Iron Highway* (1850).

132 Advertisement (1840).

133 Groombridge, R.: *A Hand-Book for Traveller's Along the London and Birmingham Railway* (c.1839).

134 Osborne, E.C. & W.: *Osborne's Guide to the Grand Junction or Birmingham, Liverpool, and Manchester Railway* (1844).

135 Mayhew, H.: *London Labour and the London Poor* (1851).

136 Leigh, M.A.: *Leigh's Guide to the Lakes, Mountains, and Waterfalls of Cumberland, Westmorland, and Lancashire* (4th ed., 1840).

137 Pocklington, G.: *The Story of W.H. Smith & Son* (1921).

138 *The Times*, 2-6-1870.

139 Advertisement for 'Philips' Excursionist's Map of the Environs of London … Constructed by Edward Weller' (c.1866).

140 Mogg, E.: 'Plan of Ascot Race Course' (1829).

141 *Report of Juries*, class XXIX (1851).

142 *Illustrated London News*, 30-8-1851.

143 *Punch* (XXI, 1851): 'A journey round the globe'.

144 Advertisement (1862).

145 *The Railway Times*, 1837.

146 Curwen, H.: *A History of Booksellers* (1873).

147 Advertisement (c.1880).

148 Advertisement (1862).

149 Advertisement (c.1850).

150 Advertisement (c.1850).

151 Advertisement (1850).

152 Advertisement (1850).

153 Advertisement (1850).

154 Advertisement (1850).

155 Advertisement (c.1851).

156 Thomson, J.: *Traveller's Guide Through Scotland* (1808). 'Advertisement'.

157 Ibid. (1829).

158 Advertisement (1842).

159 Mogg, E.: *Mogg's Great Western Railway and Windsor, Bath, and Bristol Guide* (1841).

160 Advertisement (c.1851).

161 Kelly, W. & Co.: *Post Office Directory. Birmingham, etc.* (1845). Preface.

162 Thompson, F.: *Lark Rise* (1939).

163 Advertisement (1880).

164 Robert Lowe in the House of Commons, 1861.

165 Advertisement (c.1894).

166 Advertisement (c.1879).

167 Advertisement (c.1894).

168 Bacon, G.W.: *Bacon's "Excelsior" Memory-Map Atlas* (1902).

169 Bacon, G.W.: *Bacon's "Excelsior" Memory-Map Atlas* (1893).

170 McCarthy, J.: *A History of Our Own Times* (1892).

171 *Report of the Committee of Council on Education, 1886–87* (1887).

172 Cassell & Co.: 'Cassell's Map Building Series' (c.1890). 'Instructions'.

173 Bacon, G.W.: op. cit. (1893).

174 Cassell & Co.: op. cit. (c.1890).

175 Murphy, W.: *The Progressive Drawing-Book of Outline Maps, Projections & Squares* (c.1864).

176 Advertisement (c.1879).

177 Advertisement (c.1879).

178 Overton, J.H.: *A Practical Method of Teaching Geography* (1898).

179 Curwen, H.: op. cit.

180 Gardiner, L.: op. cit.

181 Advertisement (c.1854).

182 Advertisement (c.1881).

183 Advertisement (c.1863).

184 Stanford, E.: *Edward Stanford, 1902, with a note on the history of the firm from 1852* (c.1902).

185 Law, J.T. and Francis, W.: *A New Set of Diocesan Maps* (1864). Address to the students of Lichfield Theological College.

186 Harris, J.: 'Geographical Recreations of a Voyage Round the Habitable Globe' (1809).

187 Mingay, G.E.: *Rural Life in Victorian England* (1976).

188 Surtees, R.S.: *A Chivey through Cheshire* (1835).

189 Advertisement (1882).

190 Pittman, M.A. (publ.): *The Fox-Hunter's Atlas* (1850).
191 Guerry, A.-M.: *Essai sur la statistique morale de la France* (1833). This was the first work to use the designation 'moral statistics'.
192 Rousiers, P. de: *The Labour Question in Britain* (Translated by F.L.D. Herbertson, 1896).
193 Fairfield, C.: *Some Account of George William Wilshere, Baron Bramwell* (1898).
194 Cook, T.: *Leisure Hour* (1860).

Introduction to the Catalogue
1 Fullarton, A. & Co. (publ.): *The Imperial Gazetteer of England and Wales* (c.1868). Preface.

2 Curwen, H.: *A History of Booksellers* (1873).
3 Fullarton, A. & Co. (publ.): 'Plan of Publication' for *The Parliamentary Gazetteer of England and Wales* (1843).
4 Fullarton, A. & Co.: 'Notice to Subscribers'. Dated May 8th 1843.
5 Fullarton, A. & Co. (publ.): op. cit. (1843).
6 Fullarton, A. & Co.: Prospectus to *The Imperial Gazetteer of Scotland* (c.1865).
7 Gardiner, L.: *Bartholomew 150 years* (1976).

SELECT BIBLIOGRAPHY

The Mapping of Scotland. (IVth International Conference on the History of Cartography: 1971)
BONAR LAW, A. *Three Hundred Years of Irish Printed Maps.* (1972)
BOOTH, J. *Antique Maps of Wales* (1977).
BOOTH, J. *Looking at Old Maps.* (1979)
COPPOCK, J.T. 'Maps as sources for the study of land use in the past'. (*Imago Mundi*, 22; 1968)
EDINBURGH UNIVERSITY LIBRARY. *The Development of the Mapping of Scotland.* (1974)
FERGUSON, P. *Irish Map History. A Select Bibliography of Secondary Works, 1850-1983, on the History of Cartography in*

Ireland. (Tenth International Conference on the History of Cartography; 1983)
FORDHAM, SIR H.G. *John Cary. Engraver, Map, Chart and Print-Seller and Globe Maker 1754 to 1835.* (1925; reprinted 1976; see also: *Studies in Carto-Bibliography*, 1969 and 1974)
MOIR, D.G. *The Early Maps of Scotland.* (Vol. 1, 3rd. ed.; Royal Scottish Geographical Society; 1973; Vol. 2; 1983)
THOMPSON, F.M.L. *Chartered Surveyors: the Growth of a Profession.* (1968)

Index

The Index is divided into four sections: the *General Index*, the *Index of engravers, publishers etc.*, the *Index of place names given as addresses for engravers and publishers*, and the *Index of titles*. Page references are indicated in roman type, and illustration numbers in italic.

Index of engravers, publishers etc.

Additional names indicate partnerships.

Index of place names given as addresses for engravers and publishers

Index of titles

Titles of books, atlases, covers and individual maps cited in the main text or illustrated. For atlases the date of first issue is given unless a later specific issue is illustrated or referred to in the text. Atlas and book titles are given in italics with capitals omitted apart from proper nouns. Map titles and cover titles are given in roman type.